ENVIRONMENT & BEHAVIOR:

planning and everyday urban life

ENVIRONMENT & BEHAVIOR:

planning and everyday urban life

J. Douglas Porteous
University of Victoria, British Columbia

ADDISON-WESLEY PUBLISHING COMPANY
READING, MASSACHUSETTS
MENLO PARK, CALIFORNIA • LONDON • AMSTERDAM
DON MILLS, ONTARIO • SYDNEY

ISBN 0-201-05867-7
ABCDEFGHIJ-HA-7987

For Carol,
who can, and does

PREFACE

This book has a triple purpose. It is meant, first, as a text for students who wish to obtain a fairly comprehensive overview of the burgeoning multidisciplinary field of urban man-environment relations (MER). Second, because it derives data and concepts from several social science and design disciplines, it may serve as an interdisciplinary sourcebook for professionals in those fields which concern themselves with the interrelationships between environment and behavior. Further, if the book promotes contextual rethinking among the *cognoscenti* of specific subfields of particular disciplines, it will have fulfilled its third purpose. Because of this interdisciplinary, generalist point of view, and the emphasis on everyday human behavior in cities, the author will be most gratified if the book is also read by the nonprofessional.

The need for this book arises from the confusion which presently exists at the interface between the subdisciplines of

environmental psychology,
behavioral geography,
social biology,
architectural psychology,
urban anthropology,
urban sociology,

and the behavioral aspects of urban planning and architectural design.

Although all these disciplines are concerned with man's behavior in his environment, their approaches vary greatly. Variation occurs in terms of scale, ranging from the study of single individuals or of the smallest building-blocks of behavior (much of psychology, psychiatry, neuropsychology) to the investigation of behavior in large social groups or aggregates (sociology, geography). Some disciplines, such as geography, have paid great attention to environment; others, like psychology, have, until recently, ignored the environment as a behavioral variable. Research methods also vary considerably, and include rigorous experimental procedures, interview and questionnaire techniques, the collation of aggregate census-type data, intuitive phenomenological approaches, and observational techniques. Goals vary from an emphasis on the intrinsic value of knowledge generation to the very practical aims of urban designers. Further, no agreement has yet been reached on the meaning of the words *environment* and *behavior*. This book attempts to find some common ground among this disparity.

An initial element of this common ground is a general underlying concern about the quality of the fit between human behavior and the environment in which it takes place. MER is concerned with both the influence of the environment upon the organism and of the organism upon its environment. By means of a rather specialized form of behavior, the design and planning of urban environments, the human organism changes its environment which, in turn, influences the behavior of that organism. This multidisciplinary MER field, which emerged rather suddenly in the 1960s and as yet has no commonly recognized name, has spawned numerous university institutes and programs with such all-encompassing titles as "Environmental Studies," and "Man-Environment Relations," "Studies," or "Systems." It has also produced a vast amount of research which has only tentatively been collected together in:

New Journals, such as *Environment and Behavior, Man-Environment Systems,* and *Design and Environment;*

Conference Proceedings, such as Esser, *Behavior and Environment* (1971), and the annual volumes of the Environmental Design Research Association;

Bibliographies, notably Bell *et al., Urban Environments and Human Behavior* (1973);

Directories, especially the *International Directory of Behavior and Design Research;* and

Readers, including Proshansky *et al., Environmental Psychology* (1970) and Lang *et al., Designing for Human Behavior* (1974).

Several reviews of the MER field have appeared in professional journals, the work of Craik (1970) being especially important. As yet, however, there have been very few comprehensive attempts to pull the whole area together, although Michelson's sociological viewpoint in *Man and his Urban Environment* (1970) provides a brief overview of almost half of the field.

In the sociopolitical climate of the 1970s, there are at least three major prerequisites for the emergence of a new field of study. First, a valid name is required. If achieved, the integration of those subdisciplines concerned with the environment-behavior interface will require a title somewhat less vague and more interdisciplinary in nature than the multidisciplinary MER, yet less restrictive than the commonly used "environmental psychology." The author tentatively suggests *Human Ethology*, ethology being the study of animal behavior in its natural setting. Man's natural setting is increasingly an urban environment (see Chapter 1).

A second prerequisite is the necessity for the new interdiscipline to have an effective influence on the world beyond academe. This might be achieved by the integration into the interdiscipline not only of the MER-oriented social science subdisciplines but also of the behaviorally oriented sections of the urban design professions. This in turn may require new forms of communication. Despite the formation of such groups as the Environmental Design Research Association, research-oriented social scientists and production-oriented planners and designers still experience problems when attempting to communicate.

Lack of the third prerequisite, a paradigm or structure for the study of environmental behavior, has been noted frequently in the last decade. *Environment & Behavior* therefore attempts to provide, as far as possible from an interdisciplinary point of view, an initial organization of the urban MER field. It is, hopefully, something more than a text for the MER area which Boulding (1956) has referred to as:

> an "invisible college" which represents almost a new discipline, cutting across the old disciplines of geography and psychology, with a considerable dash of the other social sciences.

Rather, it is conceived as an initial step toward the formation of an interdiscipline which embraces the design professions as well as the social sciences. The suggestion of this organizational framework is not regarded as an end in itself, but rather as a means of stimulating a debate which might clarify the content, frontiers, and goals of the interdiscipline.

In terms of structure, the book is divided into three sections: behavior, environment, and planning. This sequence involves an initial account of human spatial behavior, followed by an investigation of this behavior in various environments, with a final discussion of the manipulation of both behavior and environment via urban planning and design. Reading and research aids include a large number of parenthetical in-text references which relate to a Reference section of over one thousand items. For a broader view of a particular topic, the Further Readings at the end of each chapter will provide an initial elaboration of the concepts outlined therein. Those wishing to explore a particular theme which is not treated as a unit in this book will find textual forward and backward references and a comprehensive Index. A guide to general Sources, including conference proceedings, readers, bibliographies, and compilations of techniques, appears as an appendix. Summaries appear at the ends of Chapters 2–11; besides their value as reinforcements of what was learned in the chapter, these often controversial statements may serve as bases for discussion. Chapters 12–14 are specifically meant to generate discussion; thus summaries are not appended.

No one text can hope to cover all aspects of urban MER studies. Enmeshed in the twiglets of ongoing research, we cannot see the forest for the trees. This initial attempt to organize the urban MER area does not hope to cover the whole forest, and falls somewhat short of this author's image of what that forest is. It is hoped, however, that the reader may acquire a synoptic view, if not of the whole forest, then at least of a fairly representative stand of timber.

York, England   J. D. P.
May 1976

ACKNOWLEDGMENTS

No author of a comprehensive synthesis of existing knowledge can claim to have worked in intellectual isolation. I am heavily indebted to the authors of the 1029 references listed elsewhere in this book, and in particular to those who have previously attempted reviews of the interdisciplinary area of Man-Environment Relations. Of these the most notable are Craik (1970), Michelson (1970), and Rapoport (1970), while the compilations of Proshansky *et al.* (1970) and Bell *et al.* (1973) also provided valuable assistance.

Ann Gosse, Mick Micklewright, and Alex Porteous read parts of the manuscript and made useful criticisms. Bill Hall read it all, made many suggestions, and provided welcome assistance in reference finding, bibliographic compilation, and index structuring. Mark Walmsley contributed several useful ideas. Renee Stovold typed and retyped the manuscript with her invariable good humor and tolerance. Ian Norie of the Department of Geography, University of Victoria, created a number of the diagrams and photographs, assisted by Ole Heggen and Ken Quan. John Bryant also drew several diagrams, and Chuen-Yan Lai, Roman Cybriwsky, Hugh Massey, The Victoria Press, and the University of Victoria Department of Geography kindly provided photographs. The students of my Urban Social Geography course must be thanked collectively for criticizing, commenting upon, and adding to the material during the years 1971–1975. Acknowledgment is given to the Association of American Geographers, the American Geographical Society, and the University of Victoria Geography Department for permission to use material previously published, respectively, in the *Annals* (Vol. 64, No. 3, 1974), the *Geographical Review* (Vol. 66, No. 4, 1976), and the *Western Geographical Series* (Vol. 5, 1973). Assistance for related research and travel was provided by the Canada Council, the International Development Research Centre (Ottawa), the J. F. Kennedy Trust (London), and the University of Victoria, British Columbia. The Institute of Advanced Architectural Studies, University of York, England, provided me with a pleasant environment in which to undertake final revisions. For all this help I am most grateful. None of the above-named are in any way to blame for the final product, which remains the author's awesome responsibility.

Carol Porteous, however, was in large measure responsible for stimulating my interest in ethology and environmental psychology. In addition, she has offered helpful criticism of the whole project and, despite her own career commitments, has provided sustained support in many ways. It is now impossible to decide which are her ideas and which are mine. Finally, I acknowledge the support of Tofino Porteous, cat, whose mere presence during the long hours of writing was an inestimable boon.

CONTENTS

1

BEHAVIOR,
THE URBAN ENVIRONMENT,
AND PLANNING

Most authorities in economics and sociology regard such an organization as a city an impossible structure, not only from the economic standpoint, but from the sociological and psychological as well. No creature of the highly nervous structure necessary to develop a culture, they point out, would be able to survive within such restricted limits. The result if it were tried, these authorities say, would lead to mass neuroticism which in a short time would destroy the very culture which had built the city.*

Rover et al.

Clifford Simak's novel *City* (1952) portrays a world, several thousand years hence, from which humans and cities have disappeared and in which dogs form the intelligentsia. From their lofty perspective the dog historians regard tales of their former lives in human cities as mere folklore. Dog social scientists, whose opinions are quoted above, believe that the physical environment of a city would induce aberrant behavior in its inhabitants, and would necessarily result in the collapse of the social organization of any group of sensitive beings.

The dogs' opinion of the city is becoming increasingly prevalent among humans in the highly urbanized nations of the late twentieth century (White and White, 1962). The flight to the suburbs, the abandonment of certain inner city areas or their occupation by minority groups, high rates of violence and deviance, the counterculture attempt to return to the land, and the wholesale evacuation of Cambodian cities by Khmer Rouge forces during 1975, are all symptoms of a widespread lack of faith in the city as a suitable milieu for

---

*   Rover *et al.*, in Clifford Simak (1952), *City*, New York: Anchor Books.

1

human life. Through the action of the media, particularly in North America, a generalized anti-urban feeling is becoming prevalent. Cities are considered to be restrictive, coercive, and dehumanizing. In particular, the city is said to threaten both group cohesion and personal individuality, while heightening nonconstructive individualism.

Such assertions require deeper investigation. In particular, one should consider how far the physical and social structure of the city facilitates, hinders, or supports the everyday activities of human beings. This book is therefore concerned with the spatial behavior of a biological entity, which we arrogantly term *homo sapiens,* in the human artifact we know as the city.

The Urban Environment

As many of the theoretical constructs upon which the book relies could readily be applied to human groupings outside cities, this concentration upon man's urban environment requires explanation. In brief, although the writer is willing to investigate Peterson's thesis that *Cities are Abnormal* (1946), he must agree with Davis (1973, 5) that, in statistical terms at least, "In all industrial nations it is now the rural population that is abnormal, not the cities." City life is the normal experience of most western, and many non-western, people today. In the near future the city is likely to be the everyday physical environment of the bulk of the world's population.

the recency of urbanization

The recency of this urban phenomenon is remarkable. The current "urban revolution" is the latest of several revolutionary changes in life-style and habitat which have redirected human evolution. Leaving arboreal vegetarianism for an omniverous hunting life on the African savanna was a major change for man's remote ancestors. Hunting populations were small and scattered. As mobility was a prerequisite, the trappings of culture, such as physical artifacts, remained few. Man operated in the natural environment like any other animal, and thus his numbers remained small and in approximate equilibrium with his available resource base.

But the domestication of animals and plants and the development of an agrarian life-style meant that man could, for the first time, occupy certain sites indefinitely. His growing ability to manipulate his resource base permitted not only permanence of domicile but also the creation of permanent physical artifacts, from prosaic irrigation works to major religious structures such as the funerary pyramids of Egypt. And, more ominously, man was no longer directly dependent upon fluctuating supplies of physical resources.

With the development of storage techniques, famine could be averted. Released at last from the homeostatic constraints that contain the population growth of other animals, man was at last able to obey the biblical injunction to multiply and replenish the earth and have dominion over it.

One expression of man's attempted domination of both the earth and his fellow men was the invention of the city. City development required not only an abundant food base but also the administrative capacity (1) to organize the production, storage, and exchange of food; (2) to plan and direct major construction projects; (3) and to supervise the collection, storage, and retrieval of data (Sjoberg, 1960). With the city came literacy and numeracy, an extreme division of labor, the creation of a number of sharply defined social classes, the opportunity for a variety of ethnic groups to live in close proximity to each other, and the development of a large bureaucracy engaged in planning and control functions. These are fundamental features of both ancient and modern city life. They have social consequences for the individual and have physical expression in the built environment of the city.

The transition to hunting, and then to agriculture, probably took place over a considerable period of time. Nomadic wanderings and the occupation of agricultural settlements characterize 99 percent of human evolution. In sharp contrast, cities appeared on the scene less than 10,000 years B.P., and mass urbanization began only a few generations ago. Since the late nineteenth century the mass relocation of populations from countryside to city has proceeded at an unparalleled rate. In North America, Europe, the Soviet Union, Australasia, and East Asia, many urban residents are still less than three generations removed from a rural way of life. Students of urbanism are often able to apply their firsthand experience, or that of their recent forebears, to this latest of several fundamental changes in the human condition.

The future will probably involve a continuation of this trend toward the mass urbanization of the world's population (Davis, 1973). The number of world cities of over 100,000 inhabitants rose from 962 in 1950 to 1,725 in 1970. Should present trends continue, cities of this size will quadruple in number in the fifty years 1950–2000. Large cities are also growing faster than smaller settlements. For all world cities with over 100,000 inhabitants the average size in 1950 was 422,000. By 1970 it had risen over the half-million mark, and by the year 2000 is expected to be 645,000. Whereas in the early 1970s only one continuously urbanized area exceeded 15 million inhabitants (New York–Northeast New Jersey, 16.5 million), the continuation of present trends should see several cities in the 20–30-million range within two decades. In absolute terms, less than half a billion people inhabited cities of over 100,000 inhabitants in 1950. By 1970 the figure had more than doubled to 860 million. The projection for the year 2000 is 2,500 million, three times larger. More significantly, the proportion of the world's population living in urban environments is rapidly accelerating. A mere 5 percent of the world's population occupied cities of over 100,000 inhabitants in 1900. By 1950 this proportion had risen to 16.2 percent, and by 1970 to 23.7 percent. The estimate for A.D. 2000 is approximately 40 percent. The year 2000 is less than a generation away. Within the life span of many readers of this book more than half the global population may find itself living in major urban agglomerations.

The metropolis: normal environment of the future. Sydney, Australia, downtown and endless suburbia. (Courtesy of *Western Geographical Series,* University of Victoria, B.C.)

the totality of urbanization

Reviewing the figures above, and allowing for the possibility of errors in projection, it is hardly possible to avoid the conclusion that man is in the midst of an overwhelming evolutionary change, a transition from a largely rural (1900) to a largely urban (say 2030) way of life which may be completed in as little as three or four generations. In much of the western world, the process is already completed. Though the definition of what is regarded as urban differs from nation to nation, it is generally much lower than 100,000 inhabitants. On these terms it is generally accepted that the populations of Western Europe, North America, Australia and New Zealand, and the Soviet Union are in the last stages of the urbanization process, where the latter is defined narrowly as the movement of people from the countryside to urban settlements.

Moreover, even those remaining in the countryside are themselves undergoing a process of pseudo-urbanization. In urbanized nations today, cities control and disseminate information, goods, and services which in turn shape the attitudes, preferences, and life-styles of nonurban populations. In terms of communications, we may not yet have reached the "global village" stage envisaged by McLuhan (1964), but the rural populations of North America and Britain have certainly become as finely attuned to current urban life-styles as the urban populations among which such styles originate. From the spread of supermarkets to the diffusion of streaking, urban culture has become dominant and rural culture recessive. Economically, socially, and politically, society at large is fast becoming indistinguishable from urban society. We live in a posturban world.

The example of Canada is sufficient to illustrate this point. The outsider's, and indeed, the Canadian, view of Canada may be one of vast plains, high mountains, dark forests, and icy waters. Reality is somewhat different; on the isodemographic map of Canada (Fig. 1.1), areas represent their population content rather than raw physical space. Thus low-density rural areas almost disappear, and Canada is seen, in terms of population distribution, to be a truly urban nation. Montreal and Toronto dominate the map. Occupying less than one hundredth of one percent of the area of Canada, these two city regions contain almost five million people, more than one sixth of the whole national population, and produce more than one quarter of the gross national product. Including Montreal and Toronto, about 100 cities in Canada provide the everyday physical environment for nearly 70 percent of the Canadian population. Most significantly, the children being brought up in these surroundings are becoming wholly urban in attitude and life-style.

problems of total urbanization

Society's problems are thus largely urban problems. The basic human situation today is that of a species, which evolved through millenia to occupy a predatory hunter niche in the tropical savanna, attempting to adapt to the closed spaces of the urban environment. For example, the human body is fairly well fitted to a striding or loping gait across grassy plains, but must

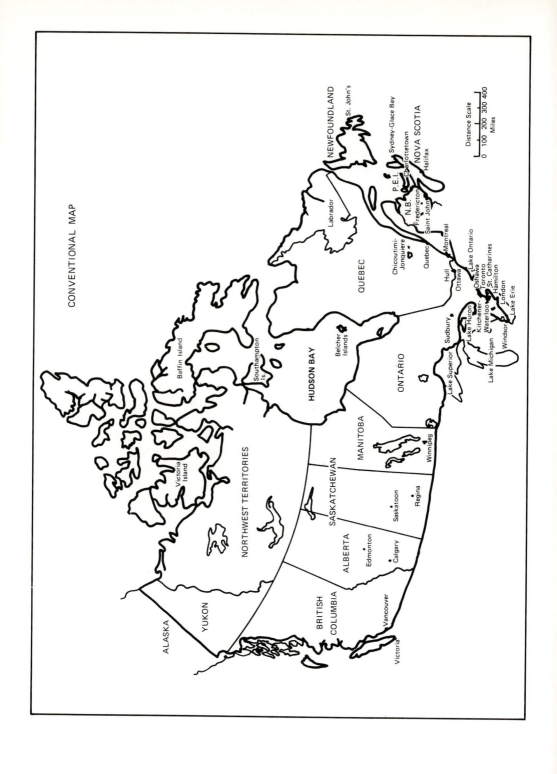

CONVENTIONAL MAP

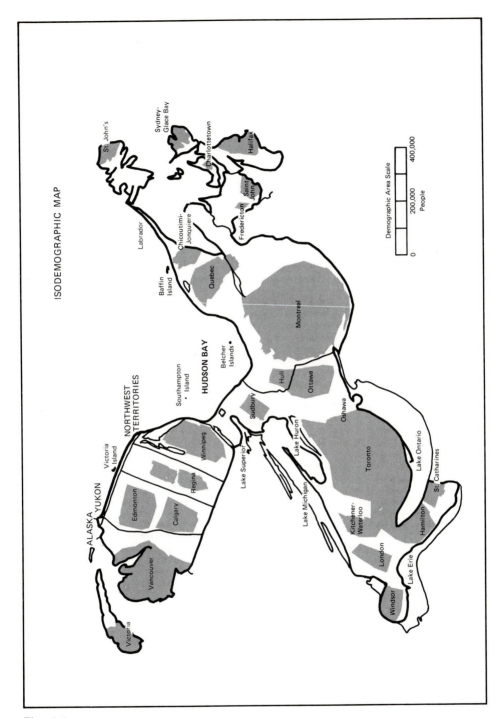

Fig. 1.1

Canada: Conventional space versus isodemographic space. (Reproduced by permission of Information Canada from Geographic Paper No. 50.)

adopt less natural standing or sitting postures for a greater part of each day. One might, therefore, postulate a general physical degeneration of urban man, only partly relieved by jogging and other measures taken to achieve a minimum degree of fitness in a physical environment conducive to the opposite.

Coping with city spaces is one of the major behaviors of modern man. It is a paradox that as man has solved the problems of long distance space, so the problems of short distance space become more acute. The speed of human travel has increased remarkably since 1800. Long distance space means much less to the city dweller of the latter half of the twentieth century than it did to his great-grandfather; a few hours are sufficient to cover the intercity distances which took months from the lives of earlier voyagers and emigrants.

But as long distance space is progressively tamed, short distance space assumes everincreasing significance as man continues to crowd into large urban areas. Thus the relatively short flight between two distant airports is immensely prolonged by the familiar lengthy crawl from airport to city center. Indeed, cities have exploded in the present century and short-space movement between points within them is becoming increasingly difficult. Until the late nineteenth century with its development of railroad and streetcar suburbs, the city could well be symbolized by the appropriate Egyptian hieroglyphic (Fig. 1.2). The city was a communications crossroads and was often contained by a wall that denoted enclosure, security, and spatial integrity. Nineteenth-century mass transit systems began the destruction of this walking city, which has been finally annihilated by the mass use of automobiles in rich nations and, to a lesser extent, by cheap bus services in the less affluent. Because of this spatial liberation through technological innovation, the crossroads within the wall has become the crossroads within the sprawl, where downtown retains many of its central functions but is increasingly difficult to reach. Future multicentered cities, to which Los Angeles perhaps points the way, may be a partial solution to the problems of traffic movement but will probably not solve other, more subtle problems which arise because of man's recent rush to conglomerate in ever larger urban units.

These short-space urban problems essentially concern the quality of life in modern urban environments. Thus, while the city is statistically the normal environment for a large part of the world population, and despite the fact that "civilization" and "city" are derived from the same Latin root, there is a growing feeling that, behaviorally, cities are abnormal. We have, perhaps, built cities too large and too fast. Our rural origins have been a poor preparation for life in a human artifact characterized by great areal extent and relatively high density. In the last decade politicians, planners, and the public alike have become increasingly aware of the shortcomings of our everyday urban environment, and it is now popular to speak of "the urban crisis." Indeed, the gross manifestations of this crisis are fast becoming part of a

developing urban folklore. Traffic and pollution problems, inadequate policing, housing, and government, mounting racialism and violence, and increasing urban sprawl are the components of a familiar litany.

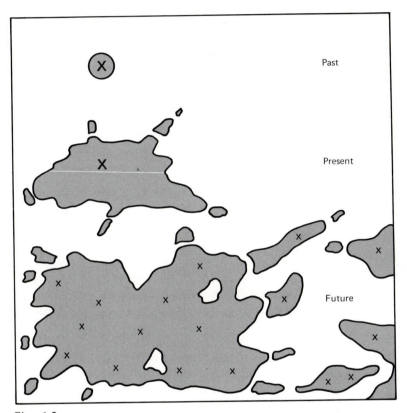

Fig. 1.2

Changes in urban form A.D. 1800–2000. Past: the crossroads within the wall.
Present: the crossroads within the sprawl. Future: no primary crossroads at all.

From the individual's point of view, problems frequently encountered in
the city include personal anonymity, crowding, the determination of one's
behavior by both the physical environment and social pressures, lack of
privacy, the difficulty of establishing personal and group identity, the lack of
flexibility in urban design, and the feeling of powerlessness in the face of the
inexorable corporate and governmental planning of change in both the social
and built environments. Particular areas where such problems most readily
emerge are ghettos, slums, apartment blocks, residential neighborhoods,

suburbia, and institutions. There are frequent mismatches between human behavior and the built enviroment which result in personal frustration and inefficiency.

Public awareness of these problems is high, and protest and discontent are rife. Action groups are formed to prevent development. Neighborhood associations compete for government funds. A large body of protest against the urban environment has appeared in the form of reports, novels, and poetry. Others vote with their feet; counterculture groups leave the city to recreate the Jeffersonian ideal, the pastoral landscape, in a countryside which today has become little more than the urban breadbasket and pleasure-ground. In a reaction against the perceived evils of the city, wilderness land is overrun by vacationing urbanites, who seek to catch a glimpse of the cleaner, purer life which is part and parcel of the modern anti-urban wilderness mythology.

Behavior in the City

Permanent escape from the city, however, is unlikely without radical changes in technology and life-style. Simak's *City* describes in science fiction terms the demise of cities as we know them, given the development of large-scale hydroponic agriculture and private helicopters. Assuming, however, that an urban life-style is likely to continue for some time as the foremost thrust of human evolution, it is imperative that we attempt to understand how man behaves in cities. Only with an understanding of this behavior can we logically make changes, whether radical, reactionary, or reformist, in the human urban situation.

The subject of human spatial behavior in the city has been approached by many disciplines. The research input into such a vague and generalized area of study is immense and diverse, and draws both concepts and data from anthropology, economics, ethology, geography, political science, psychology, and sociology. Basically, however, behavior normally occurs in response to a stimulus. The stimulus may be self-generated (motivations, needs, drives) or may be derived from the environment beyond the organism.

In seeking to understand the processes underlying human behavior in the city, basic human needs and drives, which motivate and underlie our purposive behavior, require preliminary elucidation. Maslow (1954; Lang *et al.*, 1974) has put forward a preliminary framework of needs which form a descending hierarchy from strongest to weakest.

1.   *Physiological Needs*, such as hunger and thirst. Shelter may fulfill physiological needs, and in particular the quality of shelter is of great importance (see Chapters 9, 11, 14).

2. *Safety Needs*, which include, besides protection from physical harm, the opportunity to reduce psychic threats from others, to encourage personal privacy, and to promote self-orientation within the urban environment (see Chapters 2–5, 8).

3. *Affiliation Needs*, such as love. This also includes the need for group membership, which involves the urban designer in the difficult problem of producing designs which promote comfortable interpersonal interactions, and yet preserve privacy (see Chapters 3, 4, 8, 13).

4. *Esteem Needs*, which relate to personal integrity (self-evaluation) and the perceived esteem of others for oneself. The satisfaction of esteem needs is closely related to one's ability to personalize one's environment (see Chapters 2–5, 14).

5. *Actualization Needs*, the need for self-fulfillment, according to one's capacities. This relates strongly to the individual's actual or perceived control of his environment (see Chapters 12–14).

6. *Cognitive/Aesthetic Needs*, relating to our personal concepts of beauty and our need to learn (see Chapters 5, 9).

The particular need or combination of needs which underlie any specific overt action clearly depends upon the individual and upon the context of that action. When translated into overt action, these basic motivations of human behavior are conditioned and colored by a variety of subsystems of behavior, which according to Talcott Parsons (1966) are the physiological, social, cultural, and personality subsystems.

1. *Physiological Subsystem.* Physiology clearly controls and limits human action. Our knowledge, from past experience, of these limitations strongly affects our activities. Important physiological constraints on human behavior are age, sex, and somatic imperfections (see Chapter 9).

2. *Cultural Subsystem.* This refers to the values, norms, traditions, and beliefs held by particular groups, and which again color and constrain the individual's behavior. National, ethnic, and subethnic groupings are of importance here (see Chapter 11).

3. *Social Subsystem.* The processes by which groups are held together within a particular culture clearly affect the roles which an individual plays within and without the group. In particular, one of the major determinants of a person's behavior may be the role he is expected to play within his particular learning, working, or socializing group (see Chapters 7, 10).

4. *Personality Subsystem.* This is the complex subsystem of predispositions to action, such as preferences, opinions, and attitudes, which makes each individual's covert reaction to an environmental stimulus unique, though his overt reaction may be constrained by physiology, social grouping, and culture (see Chapter 9).

Parsons' fifth subsystem was termed the *environmental subsystem*. The environment has frequently been regarded as simply the matrix encompassing the other four systems, or merely the physical setting of a particular activity. However, environment should be considered an equal of the four other subsystems in that the environment may influence and direct behavior. For the moment (but see Chapter 6), environment may be regarded as any condition or influence outside the organism, system, or whatever entity is being studied. As such, other members of one's species (and thus Parsons' cultural and social subsystems) are as much a part of one's environment as natural objects and artificial structures.

The environment, then, is a nonself entity which has generally been regarded as both an external stimulus and the scene of action. Behavior is the overt action performed by the individual in response to an environmental or self-generated stimulus, and mediated by the subsystems discussed above. Some confusion reigns here, however, for except in the case of reflex actions and fixed action patterns, the individual clearly evaluates the stimulus before selecting the appropriate response. This process of evaluation, or cognition, is rightly regarded by psychologists and physiologists as a behavior. For the context of this work, however, we are concerned with overt behavior and in particular with overt spatial behavior.

Planning

Behavior, to some degree, is influenced by the environment. Of fundamental importance, however, is the realization that certain behaviors may result in an alteration of the environment, especially if the environment itself is a human artifact such as the city. Thus we are able to modify the stimuli which affect the spatial behavior of ourselves and others. Such modifications may be planned or unplanned.

Fundamentally, *homo sapiens* is a planner. We all plan our lives to some extent. Planning becomes of vital importance when it involves other people. Before the invention of the city, hunting and agricultural groups cooperated to plan hunting strategies, field layouts, irrigation schemes, and other fundamental features of their everyday lives. On the other hand, plans were often laid down directly by king or priest, citizens being expected to concur without question. In modern societies, however, planning has increasingly become the prerogative of elite professional and bureaucratic groups which are theoretically accountable to the citizen but to which the individual citizen has little access. As such, more emphasis has been placed on design aesthetics, fashion, technological innovation, engineering solutions, and functional efficiency, than on the needs and satisfactions of the users of the planned environment. Thus emerges the major issue of *environmental control*, which lies at the heart of the environmental quality debate so actively pursued today by architects, planners, politicians, and the public at large.

The latter group is of especial importance. It comprises those people whose behavioral patterns are assessed by social scientists and who will occupy, but not commission, the built environments envisioned by urban designers and approved by politicians. If the goal of planning is not only sound technology and efficient layouts but also the satisfaction of the users of the structure, it would seem logical that the needs and values of the general public should be more closely considered in the process of urban planning.

Since the 1960s there has been increasing concern among designers to include input from the public into the planning process. These attempts are not always successful, however, and the techniques by means of which the public are able to become actively involved are as yet in their infancy. Moreover, the thrust of related research is occurring as much in the social sciences as in the design fields, and the communications links between these two areas of endeavor are as yet poorly developed. As recently as 1973 Parr could write:

> I recently searched the architectural literature but could find no evidence that the mental and emotional needs of our species has been subjected to any kind of open-minded inquiry and debate among those directly responsible for the creation of our man-made surroundings.

Synthesis

The interrelationships between environment, behavior, and planning are simplified in Fig. 1.3 (a more complex view of this interdigitating system is found in Chapter 9). The succeeding chapters of this book are laid out in a form consistent with Fig. 1.3.

Chapters 2–5 consider overt *behavior* in the urban environment. Behavior is studied at three scale levels, from microspace (ranging from the individual's body area to a room) to macrospace (extending to the city region as a whole). At each scale level one or more major constructs is considered in relation to the human needs it satisfies. Such constructs include personal space, home, neighborhood, activity pattern, and cognitive mapping. The approach emphasizes the individual or small group, rather than the aggregate, as has been the case with much traditional social science work. An egocentric view of the world, which divides all phenomena into *self* and *not-self*, is stressed. The focus, moreover, is upon the *everyday* life of human beings in cities, rather than on irregular occurrences such as responses to natural hazards.

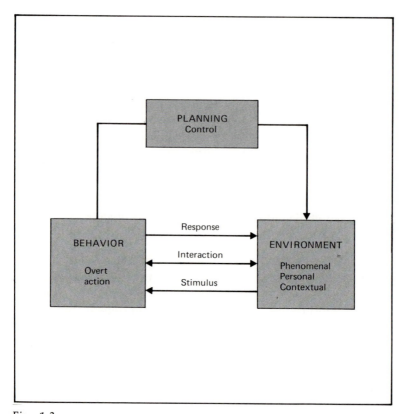

Fig. 1.3

Interaction of environment, behavior, and planning (simplified: see Chapter 9).

The various influences on behavior are collectively considered in Chapters 6–11 as *environment*. The physical and human environments of the individual and his contextual or sociocultural group environments interact with his personality in a complex manner to influence his overt behavior. Emphasis is given to environments associated with specific social groups, such as suburbia, apartments, and institutions.

Having considered the influence of environment upon behavior, it is essential to consider the influence of behavior upon environment. If this influence is purposive, it frequently involves some form of design or planning. And if the physical environment does influence our behavior to any extent, then those who control the shaping of that environment also affect our behavior therein. Chapters 12-14 therefore consider the complex problem of environmental control through the behavior known as *planning*. Whereas Chapters 2-11 are strongly research-based, the issue of environmental control is fundamentally a moral one. Designers of the built environment still rely to a large extent on personal beliefs and intuition; data on the behavior of the users of the environment should be a more important input. The problem is a moral one also in the sense that the individual should perhaps participate more fully in the planning of his urban environment, or, if this is impossible, should at least have some appreciation of the attitudes and beliefs of environmental designers and planners.

As far as possible, the concepts developed in Chapters 2-11 are applied in the studies of planned environments and planning thought contained in Chapters 12-14. Planning, however, is an enormous discipline area, and this book can only hope to serve as a generalized introduction to it. Hence, it is hoped that the reader will engage in a program of readings and discussions related to the problems of planning and the need for a behavioral input into the planning and design processes. To this end the planning section of this book has deliberately been left brief and open-ended.

The city was built for man, and not man for the city. Before we change the world we should first understand it. The study of human behavior in the urban environment may thus be of value for both the *design* of new urban environments and for the better *management* of the old. To this end the concepts gathered in Chapters 2-11, if confirmed and applied humanely, rather than in the tradition of social engineering, may eventually result in cities more attuned to the needs of the individual. To achieve this we may need more, or less, or better planning, but it is clear that such ends will never be realized unless we design with people (Porteous, 1971) and plan with man in mind (Perin, 1970).

Further Reading

CRAIK, K. (1970), "Environmental Psychology," in *New Directions in Psychology*, Vol. 4, pp. 1-121. New York: Holt, Rinehart & Winston.

JACOBS, J. (1961), *The Death and Life of Great American Cities*. New York: Vintage Books.

LANG, J., C. BURNETTE, W. MOLESKI, and D. VACHON, "Fundamental Processes of Environmental Behavior," in J. Lang *et al.* (eds.), *Designing for Human Behavior*, pp. 83-97. Stroudsburg, Pa.: Dowden, Hutchinson & Ross.

MILGRAM, S. (1970), "The Experience of Living in Cities," *Science* 167: 1461-68.

I

BEHAVIOR

2

TERRITORIALITY

Keep off,
It's mine.*

Erving Goffman

As a child in England, I noticed that robins did not flock, but each seemed to confine itself to a certain area of the garden. Other robins, approaching this area, would be driven off by the occupant. As a student, reacting to the anarchist Proudhon's dictum: "property is theft," I concluded that robins were real-estate owners of dubious character. The resolution of this absurdity emerges in the work of an English ornithologist, Eliot Howard. Based on lengthy, painstaking observation of bird behavior, Howard's *Territory in Bird Life* (1920) proposed the concept of territoriality, whereby aggression among individual animals of the same species is involved in the securing of property rights which confer upon the individual a series of valuable advantages. The occupant of a territory is not considered to be the owner of the tract in the sense of human ownership with its paraphernalia of deeds and covenants, but rather has control or jurisdiction over the territory, often for a limited time or purpose.

The Nature of Territoriality

Not all animals exhibit territorial behavior, and among those which do the variation in behavior is great, from species in which only the male defends the area to species where there is joint territorial defense by all the members of

---

*   Erving Goffman (1963), *Behavior in Public Places.* New York: Free Press.

the group. Nevertheless, territoriality is general among mammals and birds, and because of certain parallels in human behavior, demands further consideration. One of the most complete definitions is provided by Nice (1941, 442):

> The theory of territoriality in bird-life is . . . that pairs are spaced through the pugnacity of males towards each other of their own species; that song and display of plumage are a warning to other males as well as an invitation to the female; that males fight primarily over territory, and not over females; that the owner of a territory is nearly invincible on his own ground; and finally, that male birds who fail to secure a territory form a reserve from which replacements come in case of the death of territorial owners.

Territoriality, then,

1.   involves the exclusive control of a tract of land by an individual, a pair, or a group;

2.   is *intraspecific*, i.e., the use of the territory by other members of the same species (conspecifics) is restricted, whereas members of other species may often freely enter;

3.   involves aggression, displays of which are necessary to defend the territory against encroaching conspecifics;

4.   confers upon the controlling individual the will to *defense* of the tract; numerous experiments in biology have demonstrated that even a weak individual derives strength from territorial ownership and is able successfully to keep stronger conspecific intruders at bay;

5.   may confer the *right to breed,* although activity between individuals is directly related not to sex (control of females) but to the occupation and defense of land.

As territorial defense invariably involves aggression, it was inevitable that the concept of territoriality would be caught up in the debate on human aggression which culminated in the late 1960s. Briefly, Konrad Lorenz, "the father of ethology," suggested in *On Aggression* (1966) that aggression is instinctive in all animals, including man. Niko Tinbergen, an associate of Lorenz, suggested that territoriality is also instinctive (1953). These conclusions were popularized by Robert Ardrey in a best-selling book, *The Territorial Imperative* (1966), but vehemently opposed by many scientists, whose views were gathered into anthropologist Ashley Montagu's *Man and Aggression* (1968). The problem has since been taken up by biologists, ethologists, anthropologists, psychologists, geographers, and urban planners. Two basic issues emerge from this chaos of unresolved debate: Is territorial behavior instinctive or learned? (an offshoot of the hoary nature-or-nurture, heredity-or-environment debate); and, How far are conclusions drawn from animal studies applicable to man (i.e., does man display territorial behavior)?

There is little doubt that among nonhumans territorial behavior is innate. Moreover, it is important in the social process. Klopfer and Hailman (1967) suggest that the organization of animal societies rests on four major behavior patterns: leadership, parental care and mutual stimulation, dominance relationships, and territoriality. There is much controversy over whether human territoriality is genetically or culturally determined. Although Pontius (1967) suggests that human territorial behavior "may be based on physiologically old brain structures which are still functioning in man," it is clear that culture must at least be recognized as a major behavior modifier.

Recent work on human spatial behavior, much of which is reported in Chapters 3 and 4, leaves little reason to dispute the fact that man displays the behavior pattern known as territoriality. Altman (1975) has produced a wide-ranging review of human territorial behavior. Much recent work has stressed the biological foundations of the variety of ways in which humans perceive and utilize space. Rene Dubos concludes that "laying claim to a territory and maintaining a certain distance from one's fellows are probably as real biological needs in man as they are in animals, but their expressions are culturally conditioned" (1965, 108). Anthropologist E. T. Hall (1959, 1966), regards culture as a synergistic composite of interpersonal communications media. Among the ten primary message systems which he regards as vital modes of human communication, territoriality has a prominent place.

Man, then, exhibits territorial behavior to some degree, and this pattern may possibly have some instinctual base, though heavily modified by cultural conditioning. Above this guarded statement, unfortunately, rises the specter of *reductionism*. Scientists have a tendency toward the reductionist point of view, which may be epitomized in the views of the extreme behaviorist psychologist ("man's activities are nothing but a chain of conditioned responses") or biochemist ("man is nothing but a complex biochemical mechanism") or Freudian psychiatrist ("art is nothing but a substitute for inhibited sexuality"). The nothing-butism of the reductionist mistakes a part, or even the sum of the parts, for the whole (Koestler, 1968).

The sin of reductionism is common in the field of human behavior and especially in the areas of territoriality and aggression. Thus man, a *Naked Ape*, yet *So Human an Animal*, emerged from his *African Genesis* with a *Social Contract* based *On Aggression*, and now manipulates a *Silent Language* and a *Hidden Dimension* in order to survive in the *Human Zoo*, an environment which threatens his ability to obey the *Territorial Imperative*.* The obvious dangers of biological reductionism are represented by a decline of anthropomorphism, (the noble lion, cunning fox, diligent beaver) in favor of zoomorphism, involving the drawing of unwarranted conclusions about human behavior from the study of animal activities (Callan, 1970).

Nevertheless, similarities in territorial behavior between humans and nonhumans, if not *homologies* (derived from a common origin, as in the words *mother, mater, mutter, madre, matka*), may certainly be regarded as *analogies* (acquired adaptations to similar drives and stimuli, as with the bankside hole nesting of both rodents and birds).

The Functions of Territoriality

Territorial control of space has a number of functions in animal societies. The operation of this "space-associated intolerance" (Eibl-Eibesfeldt, 1970, 309) suggests that, somewhere between the chaos of Tennyson's "nature red in tooth and claw" and other poets' belief that birds sing for the mere joy of living, is a natural, logical system whose goal is *species survival*. This goal is furthered by the interrelated food and sex components of territorial functioning.

The *food* component is directly related to the control of living-space. Intraspecific competition for space effects an efficient dispersal of the group over the whole of the spatial resource base, assuring an adequate supply of food for the dependents of those animals who are able to lay claim to and defend a territory. Those who are unable to control space form a biological surplus which provides a food base for predators. The food-related function of territoriality is confirmed by studies of red grouse in Scotland (Watson, 1966). In seasons of abundant food supply, territory size contracts; however, in bad seasons territory size expands to include the necessary minimum amount of forage.

Territorial drives come to the fore most markedly in the breeding season. This *sex*-related territorial component frequently involves the control of space by males, which in turn attracts the female. In the Uganda kob (a small antelope) females prefer to mate with males possessing those territories most central to the general mating arena. Among many seals, only those able to secure a territory will attract females; territorial bankrupts must remain bachelors. Studies of the American sage grouse suggest that in any particular

---

* A collage of titles from recent writings of, respectively, Morris, Dubos, Ardrey, Ardrey, Lorenz, Hall, Hall, Morris, Ardrey (see References).

group of grouse 87 percent of all copulations are performed by three percent of the males (Allee, 1938).

Clearly, whether operating through its nutritional or reproductive components, or both, territoriality is a mechanism for group survival. It prevents immediate overpopulation and, in the long term, acts as an agent of natural selection, favoring the survival in the gene pool of the characteristics of only the fittest animals. It is notable that aggression between conspecifics is not related directly to the attainment of control over food or sex, but rather takes the form of conventionalized competition leading to the conventionalized goal of territorial control which then confers food and sex privileges (Wynne-Edwards, 1962).

Although the above description may bring to mind certain analogies between human and nonhuman behavior, other functions of territoriality appear to have more relevance for the study of human spatial behavior. Besides providing group benefits in nutritional and reproductive terms, the control of space also provides the individual, as well as the group, with security, stimulation, and identity.

Security is the most obvious feature. The animal may spend a considerable portion of its day beyond its territorial limits, but regularly returns to its nest area, within the territory, for sleep, when it is most vulnerable. The individual's right to territorial control is generally accepted by its conspecifics. Many societies are held together by a *dominance* structure, in which every individual knows its place. The pecking-order of chickens and human feudal and caste societies are well-known examples. But whereas the dominance hierarchy is essentially a social mechanism, territorial control mediates dominance by emphasizing the rights of the individual. This is most commonly expressed in the home-base effect, even a low-status animal being able to defend its territory against higher-status intruders. For example, Esser *et al.* (1965) have found that while dominant mental patients do not necessarily feel the need to possess a territory, less dominant individuals frequently retreat to defensible spaces (e.g., a favorite chair), which are recognized and respected by others, as a means of avoiding contact.

Stimulation is essential for organic existence. Most gregarious beings seek stimulation from their own kind. Absence of stimulation, whether from the physical environment or from other beings, usually results in severe psychic and behavioral disorders in both humans and nonhumans (see Chapter 7). Territorial control, while giving security at the territorial core, will also provide stimulation at the territorial boundary. Studies of birds and deer suggest that security, food, and sex are not the only motives for territorial behavior. The cuckoo, a common field and hedgerow bird in Britain, lays its eggs in the nests of other birds. These foster parents, reacting to the larger size of the cuckoo chick, frequently feed it at the expense of their own offspring, which may also be pushed out of the nest by the young cuckoo. The parent cuckoo, relieved of the problem of feeding its young, has also reduced sexual competition, as it is polyandrous (several males per female) in habit. Yet cuckoos actively defend territories against their conspecifics (Ardrey, 1966). Similarly, two deer released in a moorland area large enough to encompass many deer territories of average size, did not establish territories of above normal size; nor did they establish territories at the further edges of the moor. On the contrary, each set up its territory so that a mutual boundary was created. Again, monkeys liberated on an island divided themselves into mutually competitive troops with definite boundaries (Carpenter, 1965).

Presumably, one aim of these territorial maneuvers was stimulation, which can occur only if conspecifics recognize a mutual, though not always linear, boundary between their domains. In the case of rhesus monkeys on the island of Cayo Santiago, opposing groups line up opposite each other. Subsequently, members of each group make a foray towards the other, fight briefly, and return to their own troop. Others take their place, and the ritual proceeds until the boundary is confirmed and stimulation needs are satisfied (Wilson, 1968). Other species of monkeys, such as howlers, simply indulge in cross-boundary screeching competitions. According to Carpenter (1942) analogies to human behavior are obvious. Certainly, anthropologists have described ritualized "wars" in which spears are flung across the boundary deliberately to miss the opponent (Eibl-Eibesfeldt, 1970).

Identity, or rather the loss of it, appears to be a growing problem in urban mass society. One of the chief functions of territoriality is to confirm and support the individual's self-conception of his identity, as well as his position within the group. Identity involves place. Even among nomads, the question "Who are you?" involves "Where do you come from?" Identities may be explicitly place names, as in Oklahoma Slim, the Vicar of Wakefield, and von Neustadt. The knowledge of an individual's name, like possession of his nail parings or hair clippings, may be used magically against him. The remnants of this magical quality of name and place inhere in the children's name and place avoidance rhyme:

> What's your name? — Mary Jane
> Where do you live? — Penny Lane
> What's your number? — Cucumber

Comparative ethology and much psychological research suggest that both humans and many nonhumans feel a strong need to identify themselves as individuals within a group, and as members of a particular group in contrast to other possible groups. The control of an exclusive tract of space is a strong support for such self-identity at both the individual and group levels. Coupled with security and stimulation, the identity function of territoriality provides the individual with a strong basis for self-identification, personal integrity, and psychic survival. In short, territorial behavior is a support for the self.

territorial control mechanisms

Individuals and groups exercise territorial control by means of two mechanisms which are termed *defense* and *personalization*. Indeed, Hedigger has defined a territory as "an area which is first rendered distinctive by its owner in a particular way and, secondly, is defended by the owner."(Sommer, 1969, 14)

The *defense* mechanism consists of the large variety of ways by which an individual or group maintains its territorial integrity. Habitual howling and ritual fighting among both monkeys and men have already been mentioned. Though some animals' defense systems may involve passivity or avoidance, in many cases offensive border displays are the rule. However, actual combat with resulting death or serious injury is rare. Instead, the animal performs *displacement activities* which are substitutes for combat. Thus opposing gulls will tear up grass near their mutual border, and neighboring stags will horn bark from trees with great ferocity. The magnificent horns of the oryx antelope may be used to impale lions or other nonspecifics, but rarely to stab another oryx; to prevent excessive population loss during the spacing-out period, the animal's intraspecific aggressive tendencies are displaced, to form elaborate threat rituals and combat dances (Eibl-Eibesfeldt, 1970). Such rituals of redirected aggression are common among humans, from territorially relevant games, such as football, the Olympics, and Trobriand Islands cricket, to the U.S.A.-U.S.S.R. space race of the 1960s.

Personalization is necessary for the individual's self-identity and also to mark off the space in the eyes of other species members. Methods of delimiting an area in such a way that other members of the species recognize it as having a specific owner vary widely, but are known collectively as *marking* behaviors. The boundaries used may be apparently arbitrary, but frequently natural landmarks are incorporated, and a domestic pet may on occasion mark along its owner's property lines. The deposition of urine traces by dogs, the spray-dunging technique of the hippopotamus, the glandular secretions of numerous animals, and the secure or symbolic fences erected around houses are all species-specific boundary marking techniques. Within the territory further personalization may occur, ranging from the elaborate nests of the New Guinea bower bird to the plastic gnomes on the lawns of New Jersey.

Territorial Organization

The ethological literature presents a bewildering array of territoriality studies, which describe the *stationary* territories of nesting gulls and the *moving* territories of wolves, the *permanent* or semipermanent territories of many monkeys and the *temporary* territories of breeding seals, the *individual* territory of the Uganda kob and the *collective* territory of baboon troops. Temporary forms are themselves of great variety, as in the contrast between the heavily marked terrestrial territories of the nocturnally feeding hippopotamus and its collective splashing in the river by day. Among domestic cats, many male cats may use the same area, but are careful to observe a strict time-scheduling pattern of temporary use (Leyhausen, 1965a).

In Altman's recent extensive review of the territorial behavior of the human animal, he distinguishes three major types of territorial space. *Primary* territories are owned exclusively by individuals or groups, are relatively permanent, and are central to our everyday lives. They include homes, rooms, and other private spaces which can be rendered "off-limits" to other people. *Secondary* territories are "less central, pervasive, and exclusive" (Altman, 1975, 114). Yet there is usually some sense of in-group exclusivity, as in private clubs, gang turfs, and neighborhood bars. *Public* territories, in contrast, are areas only temporarily occupied, and over which an individual or group has no long-term jurisdiction. Public territories, such as parks and transportation systems, cover all spaces not occupied by primary or secondary territories.

Although this is a useful distinction, the definition of secondary territories, neither public nor private but having qualities of both, is somewhat difficult. In reality there is a continuum, with several subtle levels of gradation, between exclusively private territories and public spaces wholly open to everyone. Moreover, Altman excluded the individual's body-space from his definition of human territoriality. Yet the bubble of space surrounding one's body is precisely the space about which we feel the greatest sense of territoriality. An important part of our identity, we personalize it with clothes and other adornments and defend it with vigor.

Several other organizing models of human territorial behavior have been attempted (Fig. 2.1). Roos (1968) suggested that territorial behavior could be broken down into four components: *range* is the total area traversed by the animal; *territory* is the area defended; *core area* is the area preponderantly occupied; and *home* is the area slept in. Lyman and Scott (1967) did not consider the spatial relationships of their four types of territories, which they termed *public, home, interactional,* and *body* territories. Body territories refer to a private, inviolate bubble of space around the individual's body. Interactional territories permit social gatherings on a formal basis, with rules of entry and exit and clearly marked boundaries. Home territories are public areas, such as a park bench, a gang turf, or a gay bar, which are taken over by groups or individuals. Public territories, such as parks, provide freedom of access but not freedom of action. In a somewhat different system, Stea (1965) also identified four territories, including the mobile *personal space* bubble. His three other territories are: the *territorial unit* (a fixed space around one's desk, for example), the *territorial cluster,* which encloses the people and territorial units

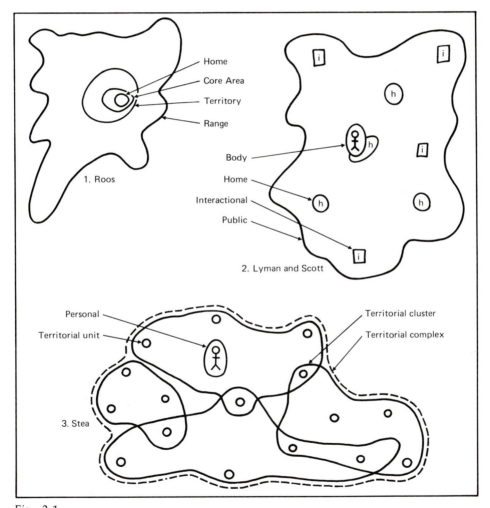

Fig. 2.1

Three organizing models of territoriality (after Lyman and Scott, Roos, and Stea).

visited by the individual, and the *territorial complex,* a loose aggregation of clusters.

From Fig. 2.1 and Table 2.1 it is clear that any organizing model proposed must clear up the terminological confusion, complete areas of omission, and confirm areas of agreement. It must also recognize that territories may be individual or group (collective), and apply equally well to both human and nonhuman animals.

TABLE 2.1

A COMPARISON OF TERRITORIAL MODELS

Author	Microspace (the body area, always occupied)	Mesospace (private area most frequently used)	Macrospace (private areas in public areas, maximum range of wanderings)
Roos	—	Territory Core area Home	Range
Lyman and Scott	Body	Home	Interactional Home Public
Stea	Personal	Territorial unit Territorial cluster	Territorial cluster Territorial complex

There is considerable agreement that for many animals, including man, territorial behavior occurs at three distinct spatial levels nesting one within the other (Fig. 2.2). It is, therefore, possible to put forward the following organizing model as a framework within which to study such behavior.

1. *Microspace. Personal space* is the minimum space necessary for the organism to exist free of physical or psychic pain. It is our inviolate personal bubble of privacy, which we actively defend against unwarranted intrusion. Personal space may be expanded to cover a wider territorial unit than the immediate body zone, such as an office or a park bench. Personal space may even have collective manifestations, as when a small group occupying a restricted space will collectively discourage the invasion of intruders. When not expanded to cover fixed features of the environment, personal space is mobile, carried along with the body as the individual moves through space.

2. *Mesospace.* Beyond personal space, mesospace refers to larger areas, usually semipermanent, which are actively defended by their occupants.

Mesospace units may be static. but can be moved. They may be individual or relate to a small primary group (nest, house, and yard) or collective (the neighborhood). In either case the area operates as the *home base* for the individual or group, the area in which much time is spent in feeding, grooming, resting, reproducing, and sleeping behaviors.

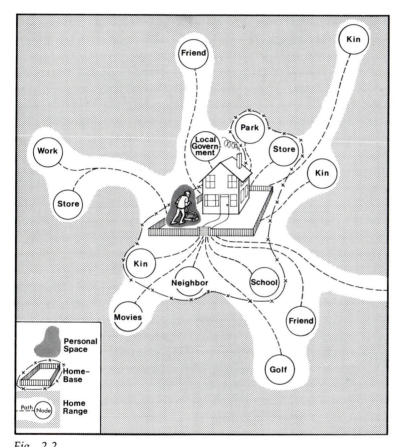

Fig. 2.2

An organizing model of urban territoriality. (Reprinted by permission from *B.C. Geographical Series* 12, 1971.)

3. *Macrospace.* The organism may venture beyond its home base for the purpose of acquiring food or satisfying other drives. The total area traversed is termed the *home range.* Unlike personal-space and home-base territories, home range is not a discrete unit of space completely occupied and defended

by one animal or group. Rather, it is an undefended public area within which various individuals wander, coalescing into groups and disaggregating once more according to need. The individual's occupance of the area is thus restricted to a series of paths and nodes. Nodal areas, temporarily occupied, may be defended, as when the executive exerts jurisdiction over his desk and office between the hours of nine and five, but abandons them to the janitor after the latter hour.

This territorial model differs from earlier classifications in being based on ethological principles, and in being relatively simple, thus having great generality in application. Using it as a conceptual framework, the everyday behavior of *homo sapiens* in the urban environment is outlined in the three following chapters. In each case territorial behavior at the particular scale level is discussed, and implications for urban design are then explored.

Summary

1. Territoriality, involving the exclusive control of space by an individual or group, is intraspecific, involves aggression, and confers valuable privileges.
2. For the individual, territorial control provides security, stimulation, and identity. Control mechanisms include personalization and defense.
3. An organizing model of territory, based on ethological principles, comprises a nested series of spaces:
    a) microspace — personal space;
    b) mesospace — home base;
    c) macrospace — home range.

Further Reading

ALTMAN, I. (1975), *The Environment and Social Behavior*. Monterey, Calif.: Brooks/Cole, Chapters 7,8.

ARDREY, R. (1966), *The Territorial Imperative*. New York: Atheneum.

LYMAN, S. M. and M. B. SCOTT (1967), "Territoriality: A Neglected Sociological Dimension," *Social Problems* 15: 236–49.

STEA, D. (1965), "Space, Territoriality, and Human Movements," *Landscape* 15: 13–16.

3

MICROSPACE BEHAVIOR: PERSONAL SPACE

Some thirty inches from my nose
The frontier of my Person goes
And all the untilled air between
Is private pagus *or demesne.*
Stranger, unless with bedroom eyes
I beckon you to fraternize,
Beware of rudely crossing it:
I have no gun but I can spit. *

W.H. Auden

Personal-space, or microterritorial, behavior refers to the maintenance, around the individual's body, of a bubble of privacy into which intruders may not come. It has been suggested that personal-space behavior, if not instinctive in humans, is strongly rooted in our biological past (Hall, 1966). Its basic function, that of spreading out the individuals of a group so that the personal integrity of each is maintained, corresponds with the ethologist's *individual distance.* Personal space normally operates on an individual basis, but examples of collective personal-space behavior include the joint defense of a park bench by the group occupying it. Detailed studies of the development of personal space in the individual have yet to be made, but it is suggested that children use more space as they grow older, and that personal-space norms are fully operational among children by age twelve (Evans and Howard, 1973).

---

* W. H. Auden (1965), Postscript, "Prologue: The Birth of Architecture," *About the House.* New York: Random House, and London: Faber and Faber, Ltd. Reprinted by permission.

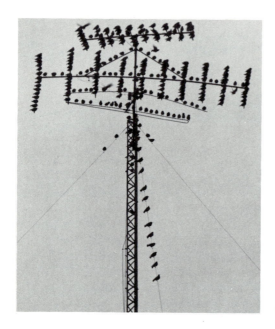

Personal space among starlings.
(Courtesy of Victoria Press.)

Personal space among *homo sapiens*. Note collective and individual personal
space territories. Centennial Square, Victoria, B.C. (Courtesy of Victoria Press.)

Defining Personal Space

Behavior associated with personal space is within every reader's experience. Many flocking birds are so spaced within the flock that no bird is within pecking distance of another; this is most easily seen when the birds perch on telephone wires (Fig. 3.1). Persons entering a bus seek out unoccupied seats; the enforced intimacy of two-person bus seats may be a factor in the preference of North American commuters for the automobile. In bars, solitary individuals are frequently found in the pattern suggested by Fig. 3.1.

Other conspecifics are allowed into the personal-space zone only by invitation. We repel intrusions and establish rituals for the selective invasion of strangers. One of the most common of these rituals is the handshake. Nonstrangers may indulge in closer spatial relationships during the meeting ritual, such as the embrace. In crowded situations individuals may draw themselves in to avoid contact with others, as on the subway. Should one's personal space be unintentionally invaded, as when the subway train jerks and fellow passengers collide, the hapless aggressor must resort to appeasement gestures. These are usually accompanied by ritual appeasement phrases such as "Sorry" or "Excuse me."

The above description suggests that personal space is actively defended by the individual against violation. As suggested in the last chapter, defense and personalization are the two behavioral criteria for territoriality. Personal space is clearly the most personalized of the three territorial levels, if only because it contains the individual's person. Within the bubble of privacy, individuality may most readily be displayed in terms of clothing or other decoration, or by idiosyncratic behavior. Invitations to enter one's personal space, or alternatively, gestures of repulsion, may be transmitted via eye, mouth, or hand signals. Both personalization and defense components are supported by our use of body language.

The value of personal-space behavior relates to its basic function, that of achieving an optimal spatial distribution of individuals such that each possesses a minimum stress-free area of operating space. The maintenance of the personal-space bubble is probably necessary for the individual's feeling of self-identity, and prevents excessive interpersonal threats to one's psychic health (Horowitz *et al.*, 1970).

Argyle (1968) and his associates suggest that personal-space behavior is also a mechanism for the maintenance of an optimum level of interaction between individuals. In maintaining this equilibrium of interaction between persons, interpersonal distance and eye-contact appear to act as compensating variables. For example, experimental subjects approached closer to a portrait with closed eyes than to the identical picture with its eyes open (Argyle and Dean, 1965). The same authors note that as distance between

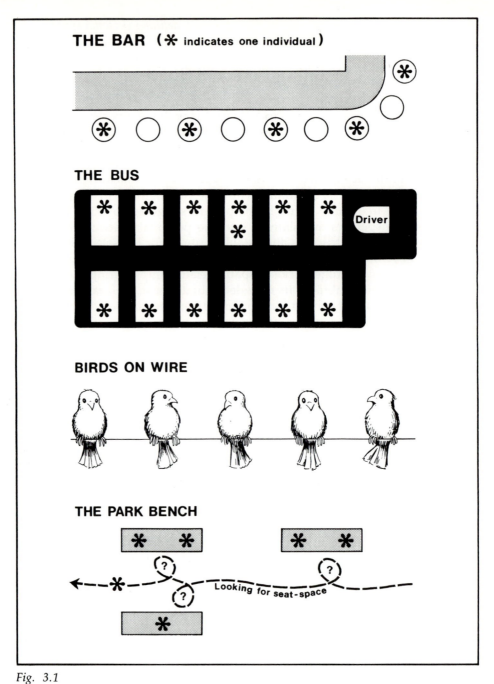

Fig. 3.1

Personal space patterns of strangers in a variety of public situations. (Reprinted by permission from *B.C. Geographical Series* 12, 1971.)

individuals decreases, so does frequency of eye contact, for eye contact, especially the behavior we term staring, is regarded as an aggressive violation of personal space.

An experiment by Albert and Dabbs supports these conclusions. A speaker delivered his persuasive message with his face either 1–2 feet, 5–6 feet, or 14–15 feet away from each of the ninety subjects. Analysis of the subjects' experiences showed that attention to the message was greatest at the medium distance, suggesting that this is close to an optimal distance for persuading behavior. At both the closer and farther distances, subjects paid more attention to the physical appearance of the speaker than to his message. At the closer distance, attitude changes on the part of the subjects suggest that the speaker aroused resistance to a perceived pressure on the subject's personal-space freedom. Moreover, "As distance decreases, the speaker appears to focus his attention more intently on the listener and gives the impression of trying to influence him. As a consequence it is difficult for the listener to relax . . . one way of resisting the pressure was to resist what the speaker had to say" (Albert and Dabbs, 1970, 269).

Measuring and Classifying Personal Space

Experiments such as the above suggest that personal space can be measured. Much measurement, however, depends on subjective interpretation. For example, the work of Argyle on eye contact has been questioned because of the difficulty of determining the point at which eye contact is made (Aiello, 1972).

A more objective attempt at measurement was performed by Horowitz *et al.* (1970). Experimental subjects were asked to walk over to three different objects, a male, a female, and a hatrack of semihuman proportions. They approached the objects from the front, behind, the two sides, and the four diagonal approaches. When the subject stopped moving toward the object, the distance between the subject's feet and those of the test object were recorded. Several slightly different experiments were performed. Figure 3.2 shows that the resulting personal-space zone is larger toward the front of the individual, somewhat reduced behind, and even smaller to the sides.

A wide variety of other techniques has been used in eliciting personal-space data (Evans and Howard, 1973). Data on voice loudness, hand tremors, and eye contact have been collected. People have been observed going about their normal routines, with conflicting results. In experimental situations, subjects have been asked to approach other persons or inanimate objects. Data collected here range from the distance from the object at which the subject stopped and the number of times the invaded subject moved away, to subjective ratings by experimental subjects of how they felt during the intrusion of their personal space. In other cases, subjects have been asked to visualize an interpersonal interaction and record their movement configurations on diagrams or by using miniature representations of people (Leibman, 1970). It is very probable that these varied techniques may not be measuring the same phenomenon.

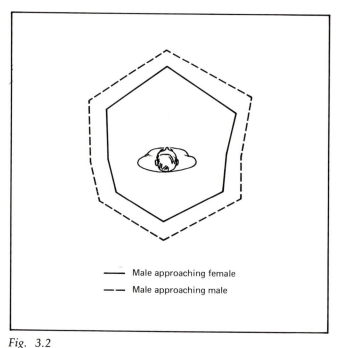

Fig. 3.2

The shape of personal space. (Redrawn by permission from *Archives of General Psychiatry*, December 1964, Volume 11. Copyright 1964, American Medical Association.)

Several measures of personal space were found by Dosey and Meisels (1969) to be poorly correlated. Because of the questionable validity of many such experimental studies, naturalistic observations and personal intuition may still make important contributions.

Indeed, the most complete measurement-classification system of interpersonal relationships is based on observation and intuition, rather than experiment. In *The Hidden Dimension* (1966) Hall delineates a set of spatial distances which he regards as norms for certain sectors of white middle-class American society. This classification is a revised and simplified version of a set of eight significant distances proposed in *The Silent Language* (1959). Hall terms the study of interpersonal distances *proxemics,* and defines it in terms of the transactions which normally take place only at certain distances from the subject. This work is important because while it confirms the importance of eye-contact in interpersonal relationships, it also notes that personal space may be violated by auditory, olfactory, kinesthetic, or other means.

Intimate distance   The close phase of this distance is one of wrestling, making love, and comforting. There is maximum physical contact, visual detail is blurred, olfactory sensations increase, and both muscles and skin participate in the act of communication. In the far phase (6–18 inches) vision is still distorted, voices are kept to a whisper, hands may touch extremities, and the heat and odor of breath can be detected.

This area of interaction lies well within the personal-space boundaries of the individual. Invitations, often involving ritual gestures, are required before an individual's intimate space may be entered. Violations of these norms are met with such phrases as "get off my back," "he was breathing down my neck," "he gets under my skin," "stop treading on my toes," "she shook her fist in my face," in all of which the words indicating position suggest unwarranted penetration.

Personal distance   The close phase of personal distance (1.5–2.5 feet) is the best distance for appreciating the three-dimensional quality of objects, notably the human face. Fine details of the face are readily apparent, and holding or grasping the other person is quite possible. At the far phase (2.5–4 feet), the periphery of personal space is being reached. Other persons are now at arms length, the limits of our physical domination. Voice level is now moderate, head size is perceived as normal, and odor cannot generally be detected except among persons who use rather strong-smelling colognes or foods.

Social distance   At the close phase (4–7 feet), interacting individuals are not violating each others' personal space. The eye can now take in a far greater portion of the person, and the gaze tends to focus on one eye, the mouth, or the nose, and to shift back and forth between these focusing points. This is the distance most generally used by persons working together or socializing. It is still possible to dominate others at this phase by being able to look down on them.

More formal business is transacted at the far phase of social distance (7–12 feet). The full figure of the partner can be seen, but visual details are lost. Voices are louder, but shouting may have the effect of reducing social distance to personal distance, with the resulting problem of personal-space violation.

Public distance   At the close phase of public distance (12–25 feet) voices are loud, speech is formal, and interaction is impersonal. Fine details of the body are not visible, three-dimensionality is reduced, and only the white of the eye is clearly visible (it is now possible to view persons as objects, hence "don't shoot until you see the whites of their eyes"). This is the equivalent of flight distance among nonhumans. The far phase (25 feet plus) is used by public figures who do not wish to become personally involved with their listeners. Voices are exaggeratedly loud and nonverbal communication is simplified. The haranguing and gesturing of Adolf Hitler provides an extreme example, though Hall also cites the 30 feet of public distance which habitually separated J. F. Kennedy from his subordinates.

This classification should be tested by the experience of the reader. If correct, it supports Argyle's notion that there are optimum distances for different types of human interaction. Notably, at distances of less than two to three feet, uninvited interaction is a violation of personal space and will be opposed. Experiments by Albert and Dabbs (1970) and Lassen (1969) have confirmed this by discovering that both attention and interpersonal feelings of comfort are maximized when interaction takes place between strangers at points somewhat beyond the boundary of personal space.

Hall was careful to note that his findings chiefly applied to white, middle-class Americans. Indeed, he went on to describe in some detail the variations in personal-space behavior according to culture and other attributes. Hence, one of the chief problems in personal-space measurement is the variability of the personal-space zone.

The Variability of Personal Space

Both observation and experiment have confirmed that personal-space behavior varies with culture, personality, race, age, sex, psychiatric disorders, type of interaction, social influence, ego state, environment, and degree of affinity between interactors. It may also vary through time.

Culture and race   Hall (1959) describes in some detail the interactional problems created by encounters between Latin Americans and North Americans. In Latin America, interactional distances are physically shorter than in North America. Comfortable conversation distance for the Latin American may be so close as to evoke hostile or even sexual feelings in the North American, often leading to the latter's moving away. Failure to appreciate each other's cultural norms may result in the North American considering his southern counterpart to be pushy, while the Latin American may accuse his northern neighbor of being cold and withdrawn.

Cross-cultural studies of personal interaction began as long ago as 1926 when Bogardus demonstrated the different distances at which his subjects would tolerate members of various ethnic groups. More recent studies have shown that Arabs have smaller personal spaces, talk more loudly, are more apt to touch each other, and are more tolerant of crowded conditions than Americans (Hall, 1966; Watson and Graves, 1966). Sommer (1968) and Little (1968) found that interaction distances were not significantly different for English, Americans, Swedes, and Swiss, suggesting similar personal-space norms for Northwestern Europe and North America. The personal spaces of Mediterranean and Middle Eastern cultures (Greeks, Southern Italians, Pakistanis), however, were uniformly smaller. Some aberrations from this pattern appear in the slightly larger personal-space needs of the Germans and the Dutch. Cross-cultural studies suggested that at least some portion of the misunderstandings that occur between persons of different cultures may be due to unperceived differences in interpersonal-interaction distance norms. These clashes are most likely to occur where persons of different races or subcultures come into frequent contact. The evidence for ethnic differences in personal space among inhabitants of the United States is contradictory, however. Though Jones (1971) was not able to find such differences, three other series of studies report that pairs of whites, blacks, chicanos, and Puerto Ricans do exhibit differences in terms of comfortable interpersonal distance. Unfortunately, these results are themselves contradictory (Table 3.1).

TABLE 3.1

RACIAL DIFFERENCES IN PERSONAL SPACE

Author	Individuals Stand Closer Together ←——————→		Individuals Stand Further Apart
Willis (1966)	Whites	Blacks	
Baxter (1970)	Chicanos	Whites	Blacks
Aiello and Jones (1971)	Blacks/Puerto Ricans	Whites	

Where racially mixed interactions occur, distance requirements may be greater than when members of the same race interact. Leibman (1970), however, found that whereas white subjects were not influenced by the race of the experimental confederate, black females preferred the intrusions of black males rather than white in a personal-space intrusion experiment.

Age and sex   Leibman's study confirms further sex differences, in that the behavior of white females was influenced by the sex of the confederate.

Several researchers have concluded that females have smaller personal-space zones than men (Willis, 1966; Hartnett *et al*, 1970), and that when females interact with females they have smaller zones than males interacting with males (Sommer, 1959; Pellegrini and Empey, 1970; Horowitz *et al.*, 1970). In general, male-female pairs have smaller zones than nonheterosexual pairs (Kuethe, 1962a, 1962b). Jourard and Friedman (1970), using an experimenter who approached subjects until continuous eye-contact was maintained, reported that female subjects reduced the amount of self-disclosure of personal information, while males showed no significant increase or decrease.

The small amount of work on the age component of personal space indicates, as we have said, that children use more space as they grow older (Meisels and Guardo, 1969) and tend to maintain smaller distances from those peers who are liked than from those who are not liked (Guardo, 1969). Peers approach each other more closely than they approach those who are older (Willis, 1966), and eight-to-ten-year-olds are able to elicit personal-space responses in adults (Fry and Willis, 1971). Pederson (1973), however, suggests that few of these findings represent consistent trends.

Affinity As noted with the child experiments, the degree of familiarity between people influences interaction distances. Generally, pairs who are friendly exhibit smaller zones than persons who are not friends (Evans and Howard, 1973). Anger, or the wish to appear friendly, may result in the communicator moving towards the partner, though the latter has the option of moving away. Jourard and Friedman (1970) found that where an experimenter revealed personal details about himself, his moving closer to a subject increased the subject's amount of self-disclosure.

Social influence Those able to wield social influence are likely to be able to maintain enlarged personal spaces. Ancient kings avoided the touch of low-born subjects; in some cases all had to lower their eyes as the king swept by, so as not to invade his personal privacy. The Colombian author García Márquez, in *One Hundred Years of Solitude* (1970) demonstrates the inflated personal space of the rebel leader, Colonel Aureliano Buendía:

> . . . intoxicated by the glory of his return, by his remarkable victories, he had peeped into the abyss of greatness . . . It was then that he decided that no human being . . . could come closer to him than ten feet. In the center of the chalk circle that his aides would draw wherever he stopped, and which only he could enter, he would decide, with brief orders that had no appeal, the fate of the world.

Among nonhumans also, the amount of space that an animal can maintain between himself and others is an indication of his social position (Leyhausen, 1968).

Much research has been performed on the spatial aspects of social dominance in small groups. Several studies have shown that persons generally regarded as leaders claim certain seating positions, notably end seats at rectangular tables (Sommer, 1961; de Long, 1970). In studies of the seating arrangements of juries, Strodtbeck and Hook (1961) found that persons taking up end positions at the jury table would most frequently be chosen as foreman of the jury. Of course, it was also discovered that dominant, forceful, persons from upper socioeconomic classes tended to choose such positions to.

Personality   There is some controversy over the relationship between personality type and personal space. Though several studies suggest that introverts have larger personal-space zones than extraverts, similar studies have found no such relationship (Evans and Howard, 1973). Kleck (1969) has shown that Hall's preferred interaction distances are greater for physically disabled and epileptic persons than for physically normal persons.

Psychiatric disorders, in both children and adults, may have a strong personal-space component. Though this is denied by some workers (Meisels and Canter, 1970), others report that individuals with personality abnormalities generally need a larger area of personal space (Evans and Howard, 1973). Work with schizophrenics has produced contradictory results. On the one hand, schizophrenics, like infants, often appear to have some difficulty in distinguishing between themselves and the surrounding environment. Coupled with their frequent inability to relate to others as people rather than as objects, this feature would suggest the reduced importance of personal space in the schizophrenic. On the other hand, the apparent desire of the schizophrenic to avoid contact with other persons and to reduce sensory input would argue for a much larger personal-space zone than for normal persons. Hence, fight or flight reactions might be induced in schizophrenics at distances which for normal persons would not be felt as a violation of personal space.

Environment   As in the case of the schizophrenic, we often find ourselves in heavily crowded situations where the most efficient means of reducing violations of our personal space is to regard the violators as nonpersons. Subway commuters typically endure their daily journeys in an atmosphere of potential personal discomfort, which is offset by perceiving most other riders as objects. People using elevators also suffer potential violation of their personal-space zones. In elevators, persons who are comfortable at social distances (over 4 feet) are effectively placed within each other's personal-distance zones. Enclosed in a crowded metal cube, their flight reaction is effectively inhibited, and prolonged eye contact at such short distances would likely release aggression, resulting in severe embarrassment. The solution, as in the subway, is to stare at the floor, at the walls, or at the floor number indicator. Glass-walled elevators on the outside walls of buildings appear to induce a less tense atmosphere among their riders. The notion of persons as objects in crowded situations will be considered in greater detail in Chapter 7.

Ego state   Beside varying with age, personal-space size and intensity may vary through time on a short-term basis. Though detailed studies in this area are lacking, it is suggested that the individual's ego state or mood may affect personal-space behavior. As with nonhumans (Klopfer, 1969), human individuals may, during periods of increased stress, show a greater need to define and defend their personal space by warding off intruders in an emphatic manner. The opposite also occurs.

Personal Space and Environment

Human beings need privacy as well as interpersonal contact. Unmitigated contact with others may be as deleterious to the human personality as total lack of communication. Hence each individual needs to be able to withdraw from as well as to communicate with others. It is clear that the environment has a great part to play in supporting or hindering the fulfillment of these needs.

The relationship between environment and personal space may be approached by considering a classic study in this field. During the 1950s Robert Sommer worked in an elderly womens' ward in a Saskatchewan hospital. An economic windfall had enabled the hospital administrators to redesign the lounge wherein the women spent a considerable part of their waking day. The renovation involved newly painted walls, a newly tiled floor, new fluorescent lights, and new chrome chairs. The chairs were arranged in straight lines along the walls, though there were several rows back-to-back in the center. Around each column in the lounge four chairs were arranged so that each faced in a different direction.

This ward was regarded as a model institutional setting and won an improvement award. The administrators, men of tidy minds, were satisfied that they had improved the lot of the elderly ladies. The janitors were pleased because such a chair arrangement was conducive to rapid, easy cleaning of the ward. No doubt also the nurses and physicians were more easily able to attend to their patients than if the chairs had been scattered haphazardly within the room (Fig. 3.3a).

The ward physician, however, noticed that the mental state of the patients had not improved with the physical renovation of their lounge. Like bored passengers on the interlocked plastic chairs of airports, they sat day after day staring at walls, floor, or lights. Arranged shoulder-to-shoulder, they were unable to converse, for conversation requires eye contact and

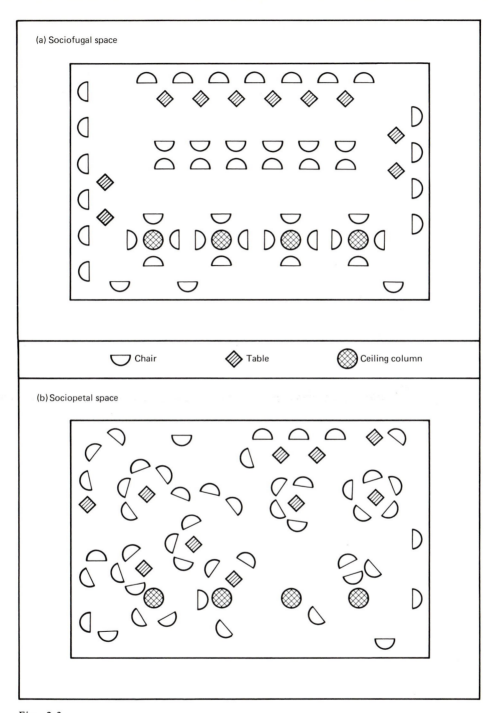

Fig. 3.3.

Sociopetal and sociofugal room arrangements.

mutual orientation of bodies toward each other for sustained audibility and comprehension. Over several weeks, with up to fifty occupants in the lounge, Sommer counted only one or two brief conversations per day. The institutional setting, by preventing suitable arrangements of the body for conversation, was gradually institutionalizing the patients, who withdrew more and more into their own private worlds. In Sommer's words: "They were like strangers in a train station waiting for a train that never came."

Moreover, the institutionalized women had no control over their environment (a concept discussed more fully in Chapters 12–14), whereas visitors in the visiting areas were prone to rearrange their chairs into small clusters so that they could face each other and sustain a comfortable conversation. The strong influence of environment on behavior (explored more fully in Chapter 8) resulted, for the elderly women, in a *sociofugal* environment, where individuals experienced only privacy. The noninstitutionalized relatives, however, were able to manipulate the chairs to produce a *sociopetal* grouping (Fig. 3.3b). When the lounge was rearranged in a sociopetal pattern, both brief and sustained interactions between the women increased considerably, magazine reading increased, and craft activities were developed (Sommer, 1969, 77–87).

Sommer's elderly women suffered compulsory privacy in a public place. Most people in the Western world are able to achieve some degree of privacy in their personal rooms, offices, workshops, or dens. Much of the day, however, is spent in public places such as large offices, schools, and workplaces. Persons using public or semipublic places require interpersonal contact at some times, or in some environments, and privacy at other times, or in other environments. Thus most of the research on personal-space-environment relationships can be conveniently divided into contact-seeking (sociopetal) situations and privacy-seeking (sociofugal) situations.

sociopetality: contact in public places

Sociopetality "is that quality which encourages, fosters, and even enforces the development of stable interpersonal relationships such as are found in small face-to-face groups" (Osmond, 1957). We might expect lounges, cafeterias, and sitting rooms to have some degree of sociopetality whereas long corridors, designed for moving people swiftly from place to place, would not. Some conclusions for environmental redesign based on psychosocial principles may be derived from studies of particular environments.

Institutional settings   Under this heading are included specialized and general hospitals, mental hospitals, old folks' homes, barracks, and similar environments. It is in the interests of economic and medical efficiency that sick individuals are removed from their warm, familiar, personalized home environments and placed in the large complexes we know as hospitals. The typical hospital has an air of crisp organization, if not regimentation, which is probably quite alien to the new arrival. Further, the recently arrived patient frequently finds his privacy needs assaulted when inhabiting large wards without screens between the beds. Sleeping in a large dormitory, eating in a vast restaurant, and perhaps spending the day in an enormous dayroom crowded with strangers, the patient may feel bewildered and insecure. On the other hand, to be bedridden in a single room may provide more privacy than one needs; privacy does not necessarily require isolation (Izumi, 1965).

Commenting on a newly completed geriatric complex, Osmond (1957) remarks:

> Old ladies don't sleep in groups of thirty and forty. They don't commonly eat in huge garish restaurants or sit about with 70 or 80 other old ladies. If they don't enjoy doing this when well and in the community, it is unlikely that they will like it any more in an old folks' home or a mental hospital.

Before the research work initiated by Osmond and others, it was commonly thought that patients isolated in single rooms would show signs of alienation and withdrawal from contact with the world, whereas patients in larger wards of 20 to 40 beds would enjoy sustaining social relationships with other patients. It has become apparent, however, that acute symptoms of personal isolation and social withdrawal occur frequently among patients in large wards. The sheer numbers of fellow patients, regimentation, and lack of privacy promote the withdrawal of the patient into his own private world from which he first ignores and then loses contact with his fellows. Osmond suggests that most patients would benefit from occupying four-to-six-bed dormitories with sliding partitions between the beds. This would permit individual control of the privacy-contact mix in the context of a small group, within which coping with one's fellows is usually easier.

Within institutional settings, lobbies and halls are chiefly designed for the efficient nonstop passage of people. However, studies in hospitals and similar institutions, and in retired persons' congregate housing, suggest that such spaces also have a social function (Lawton, 1974). Often, rather than use large spaces specifically designed as social areas, individuals tend to cluster in halls or, especially, close to entrances where there is much traffic. Sitting and watching others may be a valid form of social participation for many individuals, especially if they are impaired in some way. Lack of these privileges may lead to even further impairment because of lack of stimulation. Watching the world go by, however, is anathema to the administrators of many institutions, and in some cases chairs have been removed from lobbies and patients have been forbidden to loiter there. In view of the observed value of such social contact, however, Lawton suggests that all institutional buildings should have a lobby, through which much of the traffic goes, and which is provided with both fixed and movable seating.

Long halls are monotonous, often poorly lighted, and may be hazardous to locomotion. Yet, despite time-and-motion studies which have shown that staff transit time is far greater in hospitals with linear, rather than circular plans, long corridors continue to be the norm. Moleski, working with Lawton in the Philadelphia Geriatic Center, suggests that long corridors could be humanized by the creation of alcoves and the arrangement of furniture in conversation groupings at intervals (Lawton, 1974).

Noninstitutional settings   In this category are included studies of behavior which, although it may take place in institutional settings such as schools, involves far more freedom of choice in personal location than was accorded the elderly females of Sommer's study. In particular, studies have concentrated on small discussion groups, students performing tasks involving cooperation or competition, and cafeteria eating and conversational arrangements.

These studies suggest that certain seating arrangements are more suitable than others for particular activities. One of the more comprehensive investigations is that of Sommer (1969). Students were shown a diagram of a study arrangement consisting of a rectangular table with six seats (Fig. 3.4). Each was then asked to imagine that he and a friend were engaged in a certain activity, and to indicate on the diagram the best seating arrangement for this. Each student was then asked to explain the reasons for these choices.

1.   *Conversing.* Corner-to-corner and face-to-face arrangements were preferred. Explanations included references to the need for physical proximity and the possibility for sustained eye contact, the latter quality being notably absent in the seating of the elderly women described earlier. The corner-to-corner arrangement was valuable in that it provided the possibility for sustained eye contact, yet permitted each individual to look away from his partner when necessary. Sustained conversation rarely involves continuous eye contact, which may be interpreted as aggression. Rather, the eyes of conversing persons typically rove about each other's person and frequently look away.

2.   *Cooperating.* A side-by-side arrangement was by far the most preferred pattern for mutual cooperation. Such an arrangement facilitates access to communal tools and materials.

3.   *Competing.* Competing students, on the other hand, preferred a range of seating patterns which reduced the proximity of collaboration, but retained sufficient eye contact to stimulate competitive effort. This arrangement provides sufficient privacy for one's own work, yet permits constant monitoring of the progress or behavior of the competitor.

4.   *Coacting.* Student pairs asked to work separately at the same table naturally chose more distant arrangements, neither collaboration nor competitor monitoring being necessary. Here the aim was to reduce eye contact and facilitate privacy.

In all four conditions the face-to-face configuration was preferred by at least 25 percent of the subjects. It is difficult to arrange the four conditions in

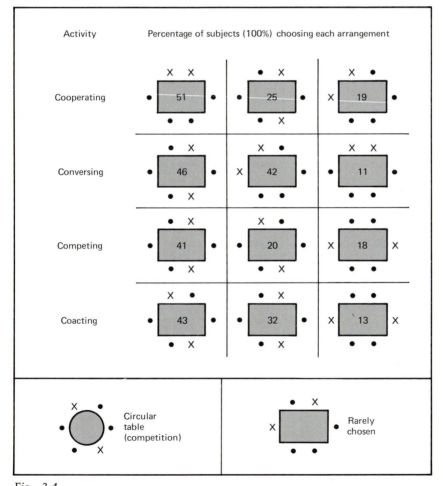

Fig. 3.4

Seating preferences at a six-chair rectangular table. (Redrawn from Robert Sommer, *Personal Space: The Behavioral Basis of Design,* © 1969, by permission of author and Prentice-Hall Inc., Englewood Cliffs, N.J.)

order of contact potential, for whereas the side-by-side position promotes maximum physical contact, the face-to-face configuration is best for eye contact. However, in terms of physical proximity there does appear to be a continuum from high proximity under conditions of cooperation and conversation to low proximity when competing or coacting. A very similar continuum was found when a circular table surrounded by six chairs was considered (Table 3.2). In this case, however, competing pairs chose more distant arrangements than coactors so as to reconstitute the typical face-to-face competitive configuration which at a circular six-seat table occurs best when each individual is flanked by two empty chairs (Fig. 3.4).

TABLE 3.2

SEATING PREFERENCES AT A 6-CHAIR CIRCULAR TABLE

	Percentage of Subjects Choosing Arrangement		
Condition	*Close* (students in adjacent chairs)	*Medium* (separated by one chair)	*Far* (separated by two chairs)
Cooperating	83	7	10
Conversing	63	17	20
Coacting	13	36	51
Competing	12	25	63

Source: Sommer (1969)

These typical adult seating arrangements have been confirmed by studies of behavior in real-world settings. However, a study of children showed that cooperating pairs sat side-by-side, while competing pairs and coacting pairs preferred the corner-to-corner arrangements. Few children sat face-to-face, but this pattern has been found to increase with age. Girls tended to sit side-by-side more frequently than boys (Sommer, 1967). Studies of adult eating arrangements in cafeterias suggest that corner-to-corner arrangements are most common among conversing pairs, followed by face-to-face; both these configurations confirm the questionnaire studies outlined above.

sociofugality: privacy in public places

As the opposite of sociopetality, sociofugality refers to situations which tend to separate people from each other. Sociofugal environmental arrangements are frequently sought by the occupants of public spaces. In relatively or potentially noisy, crowded situations, such as offices, libraries, and schools, we frequently feel the need to have a place of our own where environmental stimuli can be reduced and privacy assured.

These private places may be regarded as extensions of the individual's personal space. Thus an individual may even feel that his territorial rights have been invaded if another person enters the same room or study area. In institutional settings, for example, residents frequently occupy favorite chairs. Control of these seating spaces by the individuals concerned is tacitly acknowledged by other residents, nursing staff, and doctors. New residents may have difficulty locating an unpossessed vacant chair, for "owners" tend to take a dog-in-the-manger attitude and fly to the defense of their temporarily abandoned area of extended personal space. Such extended personal spaces, as territories, are often personalized and invariably defended. The vast range of literature on the defense of private spaces in a variety of public places attests to Western man's desire for privacy.

Bathrooms   Kira's study of the North American bathroom (1966) was intended to study everyday behavior in bathrooms with the intention of using the findings for comprehensive bathroom redesign. As such, it is a model for industrial design research. It also illustrates how little is known about human behavior in the most familiar situations. Design solutions for bathing, for example, had to include design features to facilitate body cleansing, tub ingress and egress, tub cleansing, and relaxation and play. Bathrooms, however, were found to be used for a wide variety of daily functions, from elimination and private hygiene to reading, daydreaming, and sulking. In many houses the bathroom has the only internal door which is lockable; it thus functions as an all-purpose refuge in an environment which tends to lack private spaces.

Physical arrangements are necessary to encourage this sense of bathroom privacy. The location of the entrance may be as important as interior furnishings. Victorian children in rural England were told never to let anyone see them approaching the entrance of the backyard privy; on entering, however, they were apt to be confronted by a framed biblical text such as "Thou God Seest Me." Security, as well as economy, provides a justification for the small size of bathrooms. Institutional settings, which lack the refinement of locks, or even doors, are the scene of privacy deprivation which can result in embarrassment or severe psychopathologies.

Access to bathrooms, and their degree of elaborateness, varies with culture and status. Limited-access facilities, such as executive washrooms, faculty washrooms, and first-class lavatories on airplanes are familiar examples. Bossard and Boll (1950) state that privacy norms are much less severe among persons of lower socioeconomic class, where several persons may use the various bathroom facilities at the same time. At the other extreme, upper-class persons typically have their own private bathrooms. Both groups were interested to learn that among the middle classes a strict, ritualized time-scheduling system operated whenever families shared a single facility.

Stresses encountered in this life-style may account for the excessive emphasis placed by middle-class house hunters on several facilities, and the popularity of "master bedroom and bathroom ensuite."

Offices   Having emerged from the bathroom, the office worker arrives at his place of work. A middle-echelon employee, he inhabits a large general office in which he has been allotted a fixed space containing a desk and other equipment. In such a situation, the individual generally comes to regard the space around his desk as being under his personal jurisdiction. It is, in fact, an extended personal-space zone, and is defended as such.

Personalization is frequently accomplished by idiosyncratic desk arrangements, photographs, and other personal impedimenta. Defense may involve the rearrangement of furniture such that the potential for visual and acoustical invasion of the territory is reduced. Filing cabinets, often quite tall, are good visual and auditory insulators, and thus serve as excellent territorial defenses. The author has observed a case where a less than competent functionary erected a barrier of reports, files, and computer cards along the front of his work space, the whole bulwark being taped securely to the surface of the desk.

Since World War II, operations research has sought means by which office work might be performed more efficiently and management decisions made more effectively. One aspect of this work has been an interest in environmental working conditions, culminating in the German concept of *bürolandschaft* (office landscape). Typically, the modern office area contains few internal walls or barriers and desks and other workspaces are aligned to facilitate communications patterns and work flow. To alleviate discomfort and disturbance, special floor coverings, insulation, and auditory stimulation of constantly varying pattern are introduced.

The trend to open planning in offices, justified in terms of work efficiency and social togetherness, may in fact be disastrous for both. Stea (1965) cites a case where a reduction in size and change in internal arrangement of a small group's office territory, coupled with removal of a file cabinet barrier to facilitate external supervision, resulted in both lowered morale and a decline in work efficiency. As in the institutional settings discussed earlier, regimentation and lack of personal control are potentially deleterious unless some counteracting force such as territorial manipulation is present. In *Office Design,* Manning (1965) describes a survey of environmental conditions and preferences in a new high-rise office building. Interviewees made a clear connection between the autocratic supervision system and the large general offices which fostered obsessional tidiness and a passion for useless symmetry. Section clerks felt uneasy when reprimanding subordinates, for large numbers of subordinates were within hearing distance. Rank and file clerks felt self-conscious when moving around the office and suggested that working in small groups would promote a friendlier atmosphere. The most frequent comment was: "You feel they've got you where they can keep an eye on you." When 2,500 employees were asked in what kind of office they would prefer to work, 27 percent had no preferences, 28 percent opted for the large open-plan arrangement, and 45 percent regarded a small partitioned office as the ideal. It is interesting to note that in most cases higher echelon employees enjoy greater privacy. Indeed, as Whyte (1956) points out, improved privacy is one of the major status symbols to which upwardly mobile business executives aspire.

Group learning environments   While the parents are employed in an office or other workplace, children and young adults spend much of their day in learning environments ranging from kindergarten to university graduate school.

A number of studies relating student participation in class to the individual's position within the classroom have been reviewed by Sommer (1969). Educators have suggested that classroom space zones can be recognized, each of which contains people who behave differently from those in other zones. For example, students at the rear of the classroom pay least attention, those at the front are the most interested, and those in the rear corner furthest from the windows show the greatest rates of absenteeism. It is likely that students choose locations which they judge to be appropriate to the type of behavior they wish to exhibit. Commonly, the more interested students in a straight-row desk arrangement choose front locations. In such cases, there appears to be a direct relationship between proximity to the instructor and degree of participation. Students in central positions are also psychologically closer to the instructor than are students at the sides and hence show greater participation rates (Fig. 3.5).

Another common seating arrangement is the seminar form, where students sit around a table and engage in group discussion. Here students seated directly opposite the instructor, and usually distant from him, participate more than those along the sides of the seminar table (Fig. 3.6a). Unlike the classroom arrangement, students occupying chairs next to the instructor rarely participate; from the instructor's point of view it is difficult to achieve eye contact with persons sitting on the periphery of his range of vision. Students sitting away from the table participate very little. Disinclination to sit close to the instructor is often so great that the chairs nearest the head of the table frequently remain unoccupied.

In the situation described above, the flow of discussion tends to follow a pattern whereby persons sitting opposite the last speaker are most likely to make the next contribution. This is termed the *Steinzor effect,* after the pioneering work of Steinzor (1950). Hearn (1957) found that interaction patterns depended upon leadership type. The Steinzor effect was most common in

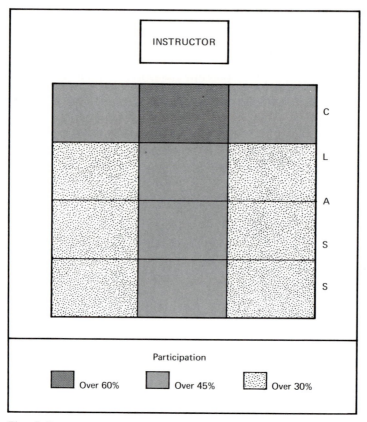

Fig. 3.5

Student participation in the traditional classroom. (Redrawn from Robert Sommer, *Personal Space: The Behavioral Basis of Design,* © 1969, by permission of author and Prentice-Hall Inc., Englewood Cliffs, N.J.)

leaderless discussion groups. Where a strong leader was present, however, communications were more frequently directed to an individual's side-by-side partner. It is suggested by Sommer (1969, 61) that where a strong leader is present discussants limit their eye-contact to their immediate area, whereas where no leader is present the eye may range anywhere without fear of making contact with the one person who can demand a contribution. This eye-avoidance effect is responsible for the difficulties group leaders often face in trying to catalyze a discussion among reluctant or ill-prepared students.

A further dimension in discussion group ecology is the right- or left-hand orientation of students with regard to the instructor. A study by de Long (1970) found that the dominant student in a seminar group took up a

position opposite the instructor. During discussions, students allying themselves with the student leader tended to be located on the leader's right, while
those on his left, though on the instructor's right, allied themselves with the
instructor (Fig. 3.6,b). These two sub-groups appeared to be aware of each
other's existence and, when the instructor withdrew from the discussion,
each suggested different policies for the continuation of the seminar. Subsequently, both groups rated the subgroup on the student leader's left lower
in leadership qualities. It is clear that more research is needed on left hand/
right hand symbolism (Winnick and Holt, 1961). These results do confirm,
however, the traditional Western view of the right (dextrous) hand as good,
superior, and dominant, while the left (sinister) hand is considered evil,
submissive, and inferior.

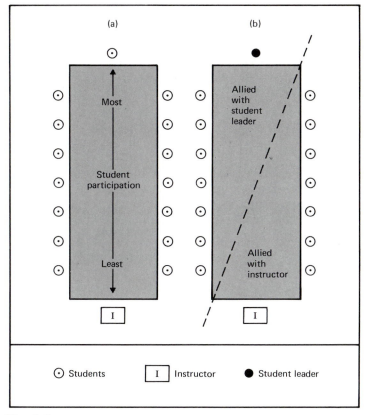

Fig. 3.6

Student participation in a seminar arrangement (b: after de Long).

Isolate learning environments   Most students, and a large number of workers in various fields, are required to spend a considerable amount of time in
isolated learning activities. The most familiar settings for such behavior in the
university are bedrooms, designated study areas, and libraries. Studying in
hall-of-residence quarters becomes a major problem when these rooms are
shared. Very frequently desk design and arrangement is such that only one
student can study comfortably at any one time. Hence the heavy use of vacant
classrooms and other spaces. Occupance of nondesignated areas for study
purposes may pose access problems for others. A student who occupies a
prominent position, facing the door, in a small lounge area or vacant
classroom is frequently able to keep intruders out by fixing them with an
annoyed stare as they enter. Thus a single person can successfully extend his
personal-space zone to room size.

More frequently, however, students study at high density in libraries
and study areas which are far from ideal. Here the problem of achieving
privacy in a public environment becomes acute. When the possibility of
distraction from the task at hand is great, the individual may practice
strategies of territorial *defense* or *offense*. Sommer (1966) asked students to take
up positions at a study table so that they would be "as far as possible from the
distraction of other people" (defense). Others were told to occupy positions
so as "to have the table to yourself" (offense). There was a striking difference
in the seating patterns chosen (Fig. 3.7). Students asked to take up defensive
positions overwhelmingly chose end chairs. An individual adopting this
strategy assumes that any subsequent occupation of his table will be at the
other end, far enough away for each to regard the other as a nonperson.
Offensive students, however, tended to choose middle chairs. This is an
effective tactic when room densities are low, but at periods of high demand
such an individual may eventually find himself surrounded. Observation of
library behavior suggests that defensive, avoidance behavior is more widely
used than offensive. Similar behavior is observed on park benches in public
places (Fig. 3.1).

One solution to the privacy problem in library study areas would be to
erect small barriers between study spaces. Even a painted line or a small
raised strip serves to identify territorial boundaries, thus enabling physical
proximity to be increased while psychological proximity is reduced. Undiffer-
entiated tables, however, are common in study areas. Where this is so,
observation and experiment (Eastman and Harper, 1971) suggest that people
prefer to sit alone. If this is not possible, people rarely sit side-by-side, though
when this arrangement is used, talking seems inevitable. Students also study
in groups, sharing materials with much talking and less reluctance to sit
side-by-side. Sex differences are apparent, newcomers being more inclined to
sit with someone of their own sex.

At high densities a problem emerges when the individual must temporarily leave his study space. Defending a temporarily vacated extended personal space requires the use of props for display purposes. Successful defense depends upon the intensity of space personalization. Typically, a coat, pocketbook, or open book with pencil and half-completed notes will hold a space longer than closed books, a careless pile of periodicals, or a newspaper. At low densities almost any marker is effective. When less personal items are used as markers, potential invaders frequently check the occupancy status of the space with someone occupying a nearby space. In a study by Sommer (1969) two-thirds of all neighbors defended a marked space even when the occupant had made no attempt to establish communication before departing. The neighbor effect, whereby neighbors feel obliged to protect temporarily vacated, marked spaces, diminishes with time.

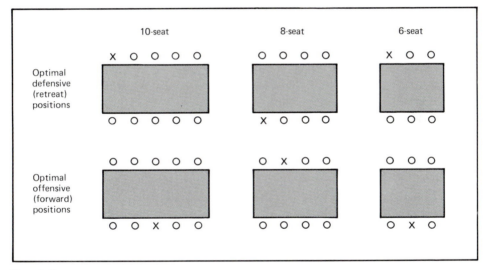

Fig. 3.7

Territorial defense and offense at study tables. (Redrawn from Robert Sommer, *Personal Space: The Behavioral Basis of Design,* © 1969, by permission of author and Prentice-Hall Inc., Englewood Cliffs, N.J.)

The implication is that an area of extended personal space, even when vacated, can remain under the absent owner's jurisdiction, which is usually supported by neighbors and generally accepted by intruders. In a cafeteria experiment, however, the experimenter either invaded marked spaces, took the space immediately adjacent, or occupied a seat opposite the marked space

(Becker and Mayo, 1971). In the latter condition, the occupants of the marked spaces returned to them. In the adjacent condition most returnees moved, and in the invade condition all did so. This study suggests that the markers, rather than staking out a fixed space which is valued and defended, serve rather to reserve an area which initially provides a comfortable distance between the self and other individuals. If this condition can be satisfied elsewhere, people in cafeteria situations will move rather than protest the loss of their original space. Further elucidation of the semantic and operational differences between extended personal space (a valued, fixed, defended *area* which can be lost) and personal distance (a spatial *relationship* which tends to remain constant) seems to be necessary.

Extreme environments   Much interpersonal spatial-behavior research has concentrated on extreme rather than everyday environments. Discussing territoriality aboard ship, Roos (1968) confirms Hall's (1966, 55) opinion that the serial use of beds by shift-workers is regarded as very objectionable. Hall suggests that this distaste arises from an individual's objection to another's body heat (hence the term *hot bunking* in submarines and *cama caliente* in Chilean mining camps). Roos, however, emphasizes the symbolic quality of the bed as personal territory, hot bunking being an invasion of virtually the only place a submariner can call his own.

Hot-bunking practices clearly require either compulsion or a high degree of compatibility on the part of the occupants. Altman and Haythorn (1967) investigated the latter quality in a study of the spatial habits of pairs of men socially isolated in a small room for ten days. Personality variables were measured by psychological scales and territoriality by observation of the usage of beds, chairs, tables, and the room generally, as well as occupation in solitary or joint activities. Beds, as fixed features, were rapidly adopted as private personal spaces, though evidence of chair and side-of-table territoriality soon followed. Where pairs were incompatible, higher levels of territorial behavior were apparent. Where incompatibility related to differences in dominance, territoriality was high though interaction was frequent. However, where incompatibility related to achievement motivation, withdrawal from interaction was more common. Complementary work by Rawls *et al.* (1972) suggests that persons with large personal-space zones have greater difficulties in task performance under crowded conditions than do individuals with smaller zones. This type of research is designed to provide criteria for choosing the participants for long-term submarine maneuvers, space vehicles, isolated arctic research stations, and other environments with severe space restrictions. It could also, of course, be of use in determining who is best suited to underground bomb-shelter environments in case of nuclear war.

Value for Design

The value of personal-space concepts for design has been suggested above in a variety of contexts. For example, economic pressures may result in raising densities in a study library. Personal-space solutions, such as physical or psychological barriers, may permit this measure by increasing the perceived distance between individuals. Similarly, an understanding of the relationships between room geography, morale, and efficiency could be of value in designing schools, offices, and working environments generally. An understanding of these concepts may be of great value in allocating personnel to environments of spatial restriction, such as space capsules, submarines, or new technologies designed to exploit the minerals of the ocean floors. At the very least, consciousness of personal-space behavior may be valuable to the individual in increasing his tolerance levels when experiencing the varied spatial vicissitudes of daily life.

There are both conceptual and practical objections to this view. As already noted, Becker and Mayo (1971) have pointed out the semantic and operational confusion between *personal space,* which is a spatial zone around an individual, and *personal distance,* which, as a process, is concerned with the interpersonal relationships which define the use of space. Evans and Howard (1973, 341) suggest that "it could be premature to conceptualize personal space as a unitary concept because of its considerable complexity." Leibman (1970, 209) regards personal space as "a catchall term for a number of variables with different conceptual and operational definitions." The confusion is compounded by the variety of measurement techniques used to provide data on this rather imprecise series of concepts. Clearly, personal-space research is still in its infancy, and its further elucidation will require not only more detailed research but also greater efforts in conceptualization.

From the practical standpoint, it is somewhat disillusioning to find Robert Sommer, the chief protagonist of personal-space research in the 1960s, stating that: "I look back upon the personal-space research with a sense of nostalgia" (1974a, 208). Sommer suggests that despite the quantity of recent research on personal space, it has not yet been demonstrated that buildings designed with the help of social scientists are more satisfying to the occupants than those built without the benefit of such help. However, as social scientists are only beginning to be involved on any scale in building design, no final judgment can yet be made. Hall (1971, 58) cautiously suggests that proxemics research "can never tell the designer how to design, only some of the things he should consider."

What is clear is that personal-space principles, if not yet fully proven in terms of spatial *design,* are very relevant to the problems of spatial *manage-*

ment. Knowledge of the interpersonal processes that guide behavior in libraries, classrooms, seminar situations, college dormitories, and offices should be of value in terms of the management of the physical environment so that it facilitates, rather than hinders, desired behavior.

Summary

1. Personal space is a bubble of territorial jurisdiction which surrounds the person. The drive to maintain personal space may be innate. The term is also used to refer to the behavior associated with this zone of privacy; *proxemics,* a term coined by E. T. Hall, is the study of personal-space behavior.
2. Personal-space behavior ensures the adequate spacing out of individuals within the group. It thus operates to reduce stress and promote personal integrity, privacy, interpersonal communication, and group cohesion.
3. The size and intensity of the zone vary with a large number of factors, ranging from the sex and ego state of the individual to environmental matters. One of the more important variables is cultural norms.
4. Among the variables influencing personal space is dominance or status. Territorial behavior may mediate dominance, as when a low-status individual is able to defend its space. However, wide territorial jurisdiction frequently enhances the power of the high-status individual.
5. Environmental configurations clearly affect interpersonal behavior, including personal space. Especially in institutional and other public settings, the environment may be manipulated to promote or hinder either interpersonal communication or privacy-seeking behavior (sociopetal or sociofugal configurations).
6. Although personal-space research faces problems of conceptualization and measurement, its principles should be of value in the management, if not the design, of environments which fit the behavior which is expected to go on within them. This should be of particular value in public settings which demand a mix of private and collective behaviors on the part of each individual.

Further Reading

HALL, E. T. (1966), *The Hidden Dimension.* Garden City, N.Y.: Doubleday, Chapters 10–12.

SOMMER, R. (1969), *Personal Space: The Behavioral Basis of Design.* Englewood Cliffs, N.J.: Prentice-Hall.

SOMMER, R. (1974), "Looking Back at Personal Space," in J. Lang, C. Burnette, W. Moleski, and D. Vachon (eds.) *Designing for Human Behavior,* pp. 202–9. Stroudsburg, Pa.: Dowden, Hutchinson, & Ross.

WATSON, O. M. (1970), *Proxemic Behavior: A Cross-cultural Study.* The Hague: Mouton.

4

MESOSPACE BEHAVIOR:
HOME BASE

We shall not cease from exploration
And the end of all our exploring
Will be to arrive where we started
*And know the place for the first time.**
T. S. Eliot

Unlike the mobile bubble of personal space, the territory known as home base by ethologists is generally static, though it may be relocated at intervals. The home base of any animal contains its nesting area, a secure position for performing vulnerable behaviors such as sleeping, raising young, and grooming. For the human individual, or the small primary group, such as family or household, the equivalent is the home, ranging from apartment to mansion. In many cases homes are not isolated but grouped in clusters. When the individuals within such clusters share a sense of belonging together, a group home base emerges. This collective expression of home base appears in the social territories of many primates and the tribal and clan lands of traditional societies. In the urban area, ethnic and small street neighborhoods, as well as gang turfs, are collective home bases, each of which encompasses a group of individual home bases. Mesospace behavior is therefore considered at both the individual (home) and collective (neighborhood) levels.

Home

Home is more than a house or an apartment. It is a structure or area in which an emotional investment has been made by an individual or small group. Few

---

* T. S. Eliot (1963), "Four Quartets: Little Gidding," in *Collected Poems 1909–1962*. New York: Harcourt Brace Jovanovich, and London: Faber and Faber, Ltd. Reprinted by permission.

individuals have more than one home. One may personalize and defend an office or work area, but these zones are ultimately invaded by cleaners, janitors, supervisors, secretaries, or other workers. The degree of personalization and defense of even an area regarded as home-away-from-home is rarely as intense as that of the home base.

Personalization of the home does not end with interior decoration. In suburban tract housing, where several thousand houses may share similar architectural styles, great efforts are made to individualize each house. Antique carriage lamps and cart wheels, plastic lawn fawns and flamingos, ceramic gnomes and huntsmen are all symbols of individualism, albeit conformist individualism. The naming of houses (Mon Repos, Iona House, Dunromin) is less fashionable today than before World War II. Personalization is extended into color schemes, garden arrangements, tree planting, and even garden sculpture.

Territorial principles suggest that space which is personalized is also defended. Boundary lines are important to the house owner, and may be actively defended to the point of litigation. Fences and walls are efficient territorial markers when their locations are agreed upon by both parties. In the words of Robert Frost, "Good fences make good neighbors." Unsocialized young children and pets, however, may not recognize fences or lot lines as boundaries. Home bases are often defended against these intruders, though rarely against wild birds. The latter may also intrude upon the apartment dweller, for in modern apartments the balcony alone provides opportunity for external personalization and defense.

Personalized and actively defended, the home frequently becomes the one sure refuge for the individual. Our emotional investment in this place is illustrated by a wealth of poetry extolling the virtues of home, a multitude of proverbs and sayings emphasizing this theme, and a range of glossy magazines (many with the word *home* included in their title) which confirm our preoccupation with home decoration, external appearance, comfort, and cooking. Accepted, commonplace phrases illuminate the meaning of home: home is imbued with emotion ("home is where the heart is"); its objective quality is less important than the feeling of belonging it imparts ("be it ever so humble, there's no place like home"); it is the symbolic hearth and source of our being ("the old folks at home") to which we constantly return. It is a refuge which we defend against the world ("every man's home is his castle"). Territorial principles suggest that our ability to defend increases with our proximity to home ("every dog is a lion at home"). Conversant with a subject, we are at home with it; secure in the fortress of a friend, we make ourselves at home.

It would be unfair to suggest that the home base is all "home sweet home." Shakespeare implies that "men are merriest when they are from home," and George Bernard Shaw stated: "Home is the girl's prison and the woman's workhouse." Moreover, folk wisdom and literature suggest that remaining at home may be stultifying for youth (Shakespeare's "home-keeping youth have ever homely wits"; Milton's "it is for homely features to keep home"). The same sources, however, remind us that only the traveler who has rejected "homeliness" by leaving home can fully appreciate the virtues of home. Many wish to go home to die.

Home, in fact, cannot be understood except in terms of journey (Tuan, 1974, 102). Travelers are temporarily homeless; they carry small articles and perform certain rituals which confer the feeling of home upon any temporary abode. Emigrants try to reproduce home. The painter Emily Carr refers to her father's creation of an English gardenscape in the nineteenth century British Columbia wilderness: "It was as though Father had buried a tremendous homesickness in this new soil." For women of her mother's age, homesickness was overwhelming: "it was extraordinary to see Canada suddenly spill out of their eyes as if a dam had burst and let the pent-up England behind drown Canada" (Carr, 1942). At the emotional minimum, home is a place to rest securely between journeys: "Home is for me . . . a fortress from which to essay raid and foray, an embattled position behind whose walls one may retire to lick new wounds and plan fresh journeys to farther horizons" (Maxwell, 1969, 210). More subtly, the traveler may indeed be seeking home. T. S. Eliot agrees with Jerry Moore that "Life is a constant journey home and I think that if I could be back where I started I'd be where I'm going . . . ."

From the above discussion it is clear that the home base is a territorial unit which provides the territorial satisfactions: security, identity, and stimulation.

Security   Security is obtained at the core of the home base, at the level of house or room. The rituals involved in entering another's home base, such as door knocking, bell ringing, and more elaborate apartment intercom behavior, have been compared with the recognition ceremonies of nesting gulls (Guhl, 1965). These security measures are of vital importance because the home base is used for sleeping, grooming, and reproductive behavior, all of which are activities which divert attention from outside threat.

Rapoport (1969) has suggested that home-base security involves a recognition of the sanctity of the threshold. Figure 4.1 illustrates the relationship between cultural norms, physical structure, and the permeability of the home base. It is hypothesized that the approach of a stranger to an unfamiliar private door raises the anxiety level of both stranger and occupant. The point of anxiety release on the part of both invader and home-base controller varies with lot layout, from the high surrounding wall of the Moslem dwelling, through the fence or low wall of the typical British lot, to the less defensible open planning of the North American subdivision. House architecture also expresses cultural differences in privacy seeking. In the Moslem case, the high wall pierced with few openings suggests a marked gap between the owner's public *persona* and his private personality. By contrast, the North American suburban lot, lacking fences and with large picture windows, is indicative of a culture that demands greater congruence between the individual's private and public lives.

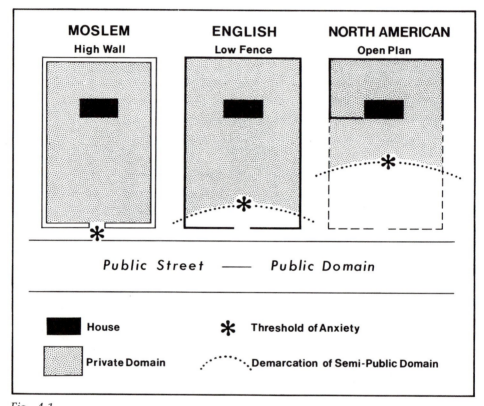

Fig. 4.1

Cultural variability in the sanctity of the threshold. (Redrawn from Amos Rapoport, *House Form and Culture,* © 1969, by permission of author and Prentice-Hall Inc., Englewood Cliffs, N.J.)

Identity   Identity and the individualism it implies are valued because of the implication of freedom of self-determination. The security of the home base allows personal identity to flower. Within the home, the individual may occasionally need a place to be by himself. Among the middle classes this need for privacy is expressed in the individual's jurisdiction over a room, usually a bedroom, but possibly also a workshop, den, or boudoir. When bedrooms are shared, as among poor urban families, the living room is often cited as a good place to be alone, as this room is used by the family only on formal occasions, as when strangers visit.

As has previously been suggested, the house as a whole, and especially its external appearance, is a major vehicle for expressing identity. Cooper (1974), using a Jungian psychoanalytic approach, sees the house as a symbol of the self. In poetry, literature, and dreams, houses are invested with human qualities. Jung suggested that the house is a universal, archetypal symbol of the self; Cooper states that the individual's house reflects how the individual sees himself. An example supports this contention. In a large suburban subdivision near San Francisco, Werthman (1968) noted that self-made, extraverted businessmen chose ostentatious mock-colonial houses with an emphasis on display. In contrast, professionals whose goals were directed toward personal satisfaction rather than financial success chose retiring, inward-looking styles. In another context, Cappon (1970a) delineates archetypal housing styles for introverts and extraverts, misanthropes and mixers (Fig. 4.2).

Other Jungian concepts concern the location of the threshold as symbolic of the owner's relationship with the rest of society. This clearly supports the discussion of Rapoport, above. Moreover, Jung and Cooper also see the house as sacred, giving man a fixed point of reference for structuring the world about him. The importance of this will be emphasized in the discussion of mental imagery in the next chapter. Adding further weight to these concepts, the philosopher Bachelard (1969) considers that, just as the self and the nonself are the basic divisions of psychic space, so the house and the nonhouse are the basic divisions of geographic space. Jung's relationship between home and identity extended to dreaming of himself as a house; the house he had built for himself he regarded as "a symbol of psychic wholeness" (Jung, 1969, 253).

Stimulation   Stimulation, the third of the territorial triad of satisfactions, is clearly gained by making, modifying, and defending the home base. Aggression or competition with neighbors, for example in terms of lawn smoothness, also provides stimulation.

housing preferences

This discussion of home has been concerned largely with houses rather than apartments. While reflecting the poverty of research on apartment living, this bias is also intentional. When asked to describe their ideal home, people tend to refer again and again to a rectangular, single-family structure standing in its own yard. The historical roots of this preference lie deep in the British and North American psyche (Handlin, 1972). Studies in Australia, Britain, and the

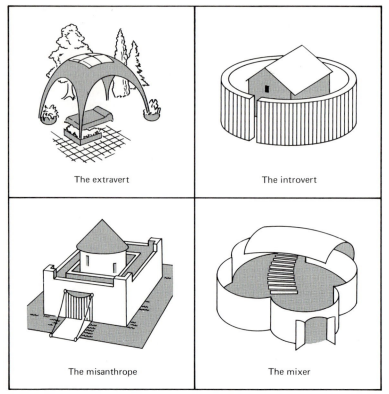

The extravert

The introvert

The misanthrope

The mixer

Fig. 4.2

Possible housing styles for certain personality types. The *extravert* communes with nature and the outdoors via enormous casement windows. The *introvert*, primarily concerned with his internal life and values, prefers the windowless courtyard. The *misanthrope*, past-oriented and seclusive, creates complex internal arrangements with soundproofing and outer defenses. The *mixer* produces cascading togetherness via a strong central plan, large open spaces, and a broad staircase. (Redrawn from "You're Living in the Wrong House," by Daniel Cappon, *Financial Post Magazine* 64 (24 October 1970), by permission of the publisher and author.)

United States, using people from all incomes and backgrounds, confirm this preference (Cooper, 1972). Apartments, the opposite of the free-standing ground-occupying house, tend to be rejected as structures suitable for family living. Studies of apartment dwellers have discovered that they also tend to prefer the private house as an ideal home setting (Michelson, 1968).

Nor is this preference simply that of white middle-class persons, though it may reflect the general acceptance of their standards as norms. A survey of urban blacks, Puerto Ricans, and persons of Italian, Jewish, Irish and White-Protestant backgrounds revealed that an overwhelming majority preferred to own single-family detached homes (Hinshaw and Allott, 1972). Moreover, neighborhood satisfaction varied with housing, from single-family, duplex, and garden apartments (60–65 percent) to buildings of over three stories (40–55 percent). A contemporary study by Ladd (1972) in Boston found that 54 of 60 low-income black youths interviewed wanted suburban housing. Analysis of childrens' drawings confirms the importance of the individual family house; even when drawing apartment blocks and castles, American children insist on adding peaked roofs and picture windows (Dennis, 1966; Rand, 1972; Fig. 4.3).

Attempting to elicit the preferred environments of respondents, Craun (1970) used a variety of techniques, such as asking respondents to rank photographs of houses in order of preference. The results confirmed the general preference for single-family detached housing. Respondents pre-

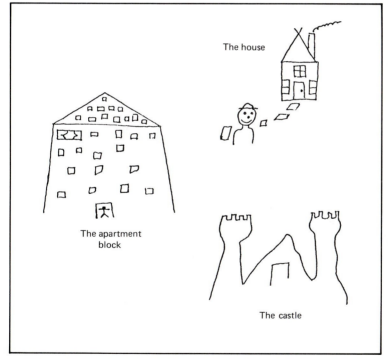

Fig. 4.3

The archetypal single-family house as revealed in children's drawings.
(Redrawn from *Environmental Design: Research and Practice*, EDRA Proceedings 1972, by permission of George Rand.)

ferred housing that appeared expensive, was highly complex visually, and which offered a high degree of family privacy. There were significant correlations between privacy and expensiveness, and between the least-preferred houses and those judged to be simple, economic, and public.

Total privacy, however, is not generally desired. Because of economic constraints, it is rarely available. The defense-security component of home-base territoriality recognizes that individuals and primary groups are units within larger groupings. Moreover, stimulation generally involves interaction with others. Identity also relates to man's desire to be recognized by others, a condition impossible in isolation. By acquiring a house, the individual expects to assume a position of respect within society, which may well measure him by his house and other possessions. In choosing a house in a particular area, the individual chooses a particular reference group with a set of norms to which he must conform. In other words, behavior in and around individual home bases is likely to be shaped and constrained by the accepted standards of the collective home base, the neighborhood.

The Neighborhood

Neighborhood refers to home base at the collective level. At its simplest, one's neighborhood is the geographic space in which one feels at home. This space generally contains the individual's core home base, the house, though this element may be lacking. Identification with the neighborhood as home, rather than one's house, is frequent among deprived children with unhappy home lives and with persons attuned to street rather than home life. Claude Brown, in his autobiographical novel *Manchild in the Promised Land* (1965) writes: "I always thought of Harlem as home, but I never thought of Harlem as being in the house. To me, home was the streets."

In other contexts, reference to one's neighborhood may mean little more than the vicinity of one's house which encompasses housing and persons of similar styles and life-styles. Neighborhood, however, has deep roots in the past, when cities were frequently divided into areas of functional homogeneity. The "shambles," the butchers' quarter of medieval European cities, finds its modern counterpart in the butchers', tinsmiths', and coppersmiths' streets which survive in Asian cities. Modern Western neighborhoods have lost their functional integrity. Nevertheless, the idea of neighborliness involves the maintenance of a healthy balance between two activities. Privacy seeking and respect for the privacy of others is matched by mutual support, especially in times of stress. This relationship is generally lubricated by a nodding acquaintanceship or other mutual recognition of each individual's right to inhabit the semiprivate territory known as the neighborhood.

Neighborliness implies an actor, or role (the neighbor), an activity (neighboring), and a geographic space (neighborhood).

neighbor

Neighbors, by definition, are persons who live in close spatial proximity to one's home base. They must be distinguished from both kinfolk and friends. With his kin the individual has a relationship prescribed by society. Kinfolk may not be liked but they must generally be acknowledged. The relationship is a blood or marriage tie which can be severed only by death or symbolic legal means. Friendship, in contrast, involves a chosen relationship which may be terminated bilaterally, with mutual consent, or unilaterally, when one person fails another in some way.

The neighbor relationship is neither prescribed nor chosen, but occurs because of spatial proximity. As a spatial relationship, it is terminated by moving away. The three relationships are not mutually exclusive, however. Considerable research in traditional working-class neighborhoods has pointed out that neighbors may often include kinfolk. In East London, for example, matrilocality was common in the 1950s; 51 percent of the married females and 25 percent of the married males surveyed lived in the same house or street as their mother (Young and Willmott, 1962).

Neighbors may also be friends, but the development of neighborship into friendship may be severely tested by the relocation of one partner from the neighborhood. In general, friends may be distinguished from neighbors in three ways. Whereas one's neighbors are physically proximate, one's friends may be widespread. The relationship with the neighbor is usually less intimate, personal, and involved. Moreover, while friendship is a private affair, the neighbor relation has collective social implications in a restricted spatial area.

neighboring

The act of neighboring is immensely variable. In many residential areas it may consist of little more than a curt nod or short greeting to neighbors of long duration. This has the effect of maintaining privacy while acknowledging the existence of the neighbor. In high activity neighborhoods neighbors exchange information and help, including the archetypal borrowing of a cup of sugar or three bottles of beer. Neighboring activity frequently peaks at times of crisis, such as a death, a fire, or the need for collective action against City Hall. In a village setting, "tragedies brought out all that was best in village life. Neighbours would flock to comfort the mourners, to take the motherless children into their own care . . . or to offer to lend or give anything they possessed" (Thompson, 1954).

Defending the neighborhood.
Protest against change in Victoria,
B.C. (Courtesy of Victoria Press.)

Keller, in *The Urban Neighborhood* (1968), provides a typology for the study of urban neighboring activity:

i)   *Content.* Neighboring may involve help in crisis situations, from borrowing a utensil to helping fight a fire. Information is also exchanged, especially regarding common problems such as garbage disposal during a municipal strike.
ii)   *Priority.* In rural areas neighbors appear to be less important than relatives, but more important than friends. With urbanization kinship remains important, but friends replace neighbors as sources of help and information.
iii) *Formality.* With increasing urbanization, the formality of the relationship declines.
iv)   *Range and depth.* Most urban dwellers do not know many neighbors, and rarely know these intimately. Zweig (1962) graded the intensity of neighboring in Britain from highest in villages, through moderate levels in old-established working-class areas in cities, to lowest in new subdivisions, especially where the houses were owner occupied.

v)   *Contact frequency.* Little is known of this dimension in urban settings, but it is suggested that frequency of contact is less than in rural
areas.
vi)   *Locale.* Contact may take place in the home, in the street, or in
some community facility such as a school or neighborhood bar.

the neighborhood

This is the general area in which neighboring takes place between resident
neighbors. Cast in the planner's mold as the neighborhood unit, it is a
concept of prime importance in city planning, and thus is considered in some
detail.

A neighborhood is basically a small, recognizable subunit of the city,
existing at a scale between the individual house and the city as a whole. In the
classic view, a neighborhood is a physically well-defined entity, with a selection of low-order amenities sufficient to satisfy the bulk of the inhabitants,
whose mutual interrelationships ensure a modicum of social control and
community feeling.

Early work on neighborhoods as social entities began with Park *et al.*
(1925) and McKenzie (1926) who founded the Chicago tradition of the *ecological
approach* to community studies. By relating the physical features of the city to
distributions of social groups and of behavioral and mental disorders, such as
delinquency and schizophrenia, they delineated natural areas of the city. No
attempt was made to discover whether these natural areas were perceived as
such by their inhabitants.

Building upon this work, which emphasized social and ecological relationships, the *planning approach* emphasized the importance of the neighborhood as a physical construct useful in the layout of residential areas. Again,
however, it was held that physical unit and social behavior would be spatially
coincident. Glass (1948) initially proposed two definitions for neighborhood.
The first regarded neighborhood as an *area* delimited by both physical characteristics and the social characteristics of its inhabitants. This is essentially the
Chicago School approach. The second definition regarded a neighborhood as
a *territorial group,* the members of which enjoyed primary social contacts on a
common ground. These definitions clearly overlap, and Glass suggested that
physical neighborhoods would correspond with social neighborhoods, as
defined by the catchment areas of schools, clubs, shops, and public facilities.
Unfortunately her survey found no such correspondence.

Despite the negative results of research-oriented planning surveys such
as those of Glass and Lock (1948), the neighborhood has been seen by many
planners as a distinct entity consisting of a variable number of residential
units and a selection of low-order facilities such as grocery stores, bars, post
offices, schools, and parks. Local residents make concentrated use of these

day-to-day shopping, educational, and leisure facilities, although for less frequent higher-order services, such as department stores, major cinemas, and stadiums, they must go beyond the neighborhood. The ethnic, cultural, and social characteristics of this ideal neighborhood are such that the inhabitants share a common set of standards. This, together with their concentrated use of local facilities, promotes a psychological unity whereby neighborhood inhabitants feel they belong together and to the area. Belonging may take the form of positive interaction and participation, or the negative form of banding together to resist external pressures, such as redevelopment or freeway building. This socially and psychologically united group inhabits an area which is marked off from the rest of the city by distinct, clearly recognized boundaries.

The neighborhood is thus both a formal entity (a physical unit) and a functional entity (a social unit). The insistence of some planners that it should also contain major work locations reconstitutes the early sociogeographical concept of Le Play (1855) that a spatial and psychological unity exists between place, work, and folk. Size is an important parameter, and there have been suggestions that all households should be within easy walking distance of central facilities, especially the school.

The Neighborhood Unit

It was the assertion that such neighborhoods exist and are beneficial to their inhabitants, rather than any demonstration based on research, that led to the concept of the neighborhood unit as a planning construct. The idea of the neighborhood as a valuable subunit of the city for planning purposes has taken strong root throughout the Western world. The modern concept of planned neighborhoods can be traced back to Ebenezer Howard (1898), who was concerned about the pathological effects and dreary uniformity of nineteenth century mass housing in Britain. It was given definition by Clarence Perry (1929, 1939), who popularized it among influential planners and architects such as Lewis Mumford, Le Corbusier, Clarence Stein, and Frank Lloyd Wright. Stein's *Towards New Towns For America* (1951) illustrates the practical response to the principle in the shape of a dozen experimental neighborhoods built between the two World Wars. Despite Perry's insistence on rather rigid formulae for determining such elements as density and the percentage of land devoted to open space, devotees such as Dahir (1947, 1948) suggested that planned neighborhoods would end the building of housing without consideration of social groupings, and in doing so would give people what they wanted.

The neighborhood unit was to be contained by definite boundaries (Fig. 4.4). In most cases, these were major arterial streets with heavy traffic. Within these boundaries, internal streets were to be less heavily used, mainly for access to individual homes or for servicing the shops and other facilities. The first emphasis, then, was on containment and safety. The latter was further promoted by the provision of a network of paths, so arranged that shoppers and children could reach stores and schools without crossing heavily trafficked streets. Accessibility by foot was a prime factor, and automobile use within the neighborhood was to be reduced by intricate street designs (walking via paths was quicker and easier); automobiles were mainly to be used as a means of entering and leaving the neighborhood. A pattern of local shops and open spaces served immediate needs. By constant contact with each other, neighborhood residents would develop a feeling of belonging.

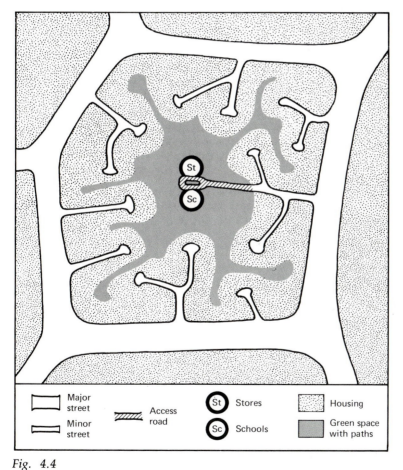

Fig. 4.4

An idealized neighborhood unit without through streets (reminiscent of Stein's Radburn Plan).

This physical plan, besides providing spatial order in the chaotic urban scene, was to have social and psychological ends. In a world of increasing insecurity, anonymity, and rootlessness, with high levels of residential mobility, the neighborhood unit was designed to encourage a return to face-to-face contact on a local basis. This would in turn encourage the growth of local loyalties, thus providing security, identity, and feelings of belonging. To encourage neighboring activity, various physical planning methods were introduced. Physical distance between residential units could be reduced either by increasing densities or improving accessibility between units. Recognizing that even people living close together may avoid each other, methods were found to reduce functional distance between households. These included the location of bus stops, the provision of communal sandboxes and playgrounds, and the sharing of lobbies, footpaths, and driveways. In many new communities planned on neighborhood lines, the erection of fences was actively discouraged in order to promote contact and allow people to meet as a natural by-product of their routine activities.

Elaboration of the concept by variety of planners resulted in the emergence, in planning theory, of a "standard unit which would provide a panacea for all problems of residential development and somehow fit all cases and needs" (Pearson, 1962). Precise statements regarding the philosophy behind the neighborhood unit are rare, but certain purposes are common to most plans:

1.   The unit would contain a population of predetermined size, "not too large to destroy personal contact and not too small to fail to afford variety and diversity" (Pick, 1941). Five thousand persons was a favored size, largely because of optimal elementary school sizes.

2.   Diversity would be achieved by a mix of income groups and housing types.

3.   The unit's diverse population would inhabit an unbroken tract of residential territory, with definite and recognizable boundaries.

4.   Within this area, sufficient amenities and facilities would be provided to make the unit self-sufficient in terms of day-to-day shopping and recreation.

5.   These facilities would be located at convenient (preferably walking) distances from each household.

6.   The grouping of the facilities would be such as to bring unit dwellers together on a daily or weekly basis, thus developing community identity and "a well-balanced community life" (Segal, 1948).

7.   By fostering community spirit at the local level, the neighborhood unit would, by "the conscious practice of democracy in small units" (Mumford, 1948), break down social barriers and provide a meaningful role for the individual in mass urban society.

This combination of social idealism and physical planning proved very popular amongst planners. The neighborhood unit is a relatively simple idea, apparently sociologically sound, readily conceptualized, and, theoretically at least, eminently manageable as a unit for filling the residential spaces of new towns. It was seen as an efficient and utilitarian means of distributing scarce resources, such as schools and parks, among the city's population. As a basic cell, it could be laid out over and over again until the new city became a mosaic of semiself-sufficient neighborhood units, bound together at the city level by economic and political ties.

Since the 1930s, the neighborhood unit has been widely used in planning new communities, particularly in Europe after the devastation of World War II. In Radburn, New Jersey, Stein laid out a radically new urban plan as early as 1929. Based on the now accepted principle of separation of pedestrian and vehicular traffic, the Radburn plan included a complete footpath, overpass, and bridge system, enabling pedestrians to walk from one end of the project to the other without encountering motor traffic.

European proponents included Le Corbusier in France, and Forshaw and Abercrombie's ambitious *County of London Plan* (1943) in England. Similar systems were advocated in the U.S.S.R. With the Dudley Report, *Design of Dwellings 1944*, the neighborhood unit principle was adopted for the new towns which forced planned change on the urban system of Britain after 1945 (see chapter 13). As the concept of new towns or satellite towns ringing old metropoli became entrenched in the 1950s, neighborhood units were used in planned communities ranging from Reston (Virginia) to Vallingby (Sweden), and from Sputnik (Moscow) to new Israeli settlements.

However, the rather unthinking use of the neighborhood unit principle, as if it were a recipe, generated both unease and protest. Neighborhood planning has been carried out in environmentally inappropriate areas, such as northern British Columbia, where Stein designed Kitimat on open-plan suburban lines much more suited to a mild midlatitude climate. Moreover, research studies have indicated that both the mechanistic view of the neighborhood unit as a basic planning cell and the idealistic socially oriented view of the neighborhood as community, invite criticism on both ideological and methodological grounds.

criticism of the neighborhood ideology

The neighborhood unit, defined as a physical unit with a distinct identity reflected in social interaction and based on common activity patterns, became a popular planning tool because it supported the cherished ideals of many planners. The face-to-face community aspect appealed in particular to middle-class planners brought up in an anti-urban tradition which made much of rural values (White and White, 1962).

A major feature of neighborhood planning theory has been the desire to produce social diversification in neighborhoods. Early workers saw the mixture of races and socioeconomic classes within the neighborhood as a means of reducing discrimination (Bauer, 1945). Recent work in racially mixed neighborhoods in Israel has shown that, in this context at least, the sharing of a neighborhood reduced racial prejudice (Soen, 1970). Others have suggested that homogeneous neighborhoods are the product of insecurity (Marcuse, 1969). An ethnically heterogeneous neighborhood would not only socialize but also acculturate children.

The social mixing ideal has frequently been related to the perceived virtues of rural life, where rich and poor lived close together and frequently used the same facilities. In the policies set out in 1947 for the building of Stevenage New Town, near London, the moral ideology of social intermixture was carried to an extreme (Orlans, 1952, 82):

> We want to revive that social structure which existed in the old English village, where the rich lived next door to the not so rich and everyone knew everybody . . . the man who wants a bigger house will be able to have it, but he will not be able to have it apart from the other houses.

The failure of such policies is discussed in detail in Chapter 13. This prim statement from Stevenage ignores the collapse of traditional village society in the twentieth century, and assumes that village people were satisfied with their prevailing social system. Community studies and personal accounts, however, confirm that village people were often dissatisfied and that strong social cleavages were apparent (Thompson, 1954; Blythe, 1970). Clearly, in the old South during the existence of slavery, both slave and master lived in close physical proximity. Socially, however, they were separated by a rigid dominance hierarchy. It is likely that the enforced legal equality of blacks has been a major factor in promoting racial segregation, physical distance having become a surrogate for social distance. General studies of community life in both Britain ((Frankenberg, 1965) and the United States (Stein, 1960) point out with a wealth of detail that the neighborhood cannot be viewed as a village in the city.

As most people prefer homogeneity, to live near people like themselves, the ideal of the socially balanced neighborhood is virtually unattainable. Mann (1958) urges that such ideologically based concepts be buried. Gans (1961a) proposes sufficient homogeneity to permit consensus, but enough heterogeneity to prevent undesirable inequalities in service provision which might occur between totally homogeneous neighborhoods. Social and racial balance in the neighborhood, then, is important only in terms of equal access to facilities. A recent model of neighborhood organization comprises homogeneous neighborhoods of a wide variety of sizes and patterns, sufficient to permit a wide range of life-styles in a highly mobile society (Hendricks and MacNair, 1970).

The chief burden of ideological criticism concerns the uncritical acceptance and application of the neighborhood unit concept. Although it may accord well with the planners' values, the imposition of this planners' solution upon people whose needs have not been ascertained cannot be condoned. An obvious requirement is research on human behavior and aspirations at the neighborhood level; Clarence Stein, a major proponent of neighborhood theory, was aware of this. Measuring neighboring activity is complex and difficult. Keller (1968) summarizes a number of methods for ascertaining the presence of neighborhoods. Perhaps the most important research approaches have been attempts to discover (1) the degree of localization of personal activity patterns, (2) residents' perceptions of their local residential environment, and (3) residents' satisfactions with neighborhood quality of life. These are discussed later. However, terminological confusion, notably over neighborhood, differing assumptions, and lack of comparability of research findings, have increased rather than reduced the prevailing confusion in the field of planning known as neighborhood theory. But there is a general consensus that the traditional urban neighborhood has declined in importance in the lives of many late twentieth-century urbanites.

the decline of the neighborhood

Although traditional neighborhoods were a normal element of urban structure in both Europe and North America before World War I, the decline since that period has been such that those remaining today exist "as islands in the sea of national society and culture" (Dentler, 1968, 47). Social, technological, and political changes have brought about the decline of the neighborhood as a vital force in the life of the individual.

Before World War I, many urban dwellers were first generation immigrants from rural areas, and naturally clung to their rural ways (Hoggart, 1957). Since that time urban values, notably with regard to both spatial and social mobility, have been absorbed not only by urban dwellers but also by residents of rural areas. Increased literacy, television, and transportation innovations have promoted this trend. Chief among the latter is the development of mass automobile use, which has liberated urban man from the local area and made possible the existence of many other settings for face-to-face contacts (Riemer, 1950). As Isaacs (1948b) has noted, "where you reside is not necessarily where you live." Moreover, traditional life-styles associated with occupational, ethnic, and racial groups have been greatly broken down since World War I. The traditional occupational hierarchy, for instance, has been blurred with the disappearance of a strong relationship between income and type of work.

Neighborhoods were once associated with work. Urban geographers have remarked on the survival of European city quarters associated with particular craft-related industries, such as watch- or gun-making (Vance, 1967). In general, however, workplaces have dispersed during the twentieth century and the worker typically travels some distance between home and place of employment. Craft-related jobs have been replaced by assembly operations which rely on easily interchangeable operators. Furthermore, industrial and office establishments operate on a scale quite unsuitable for placement within a neighborhood. Zoning regulations, finally, ensure a separation of place, work, and folk.

An ethnic neighborhood in the Bronx, New York. (Courtesy of Victoria Press.)

Social and institutional changes have also removed the underpinnings of the neighborhood raison d'etre. Increasing independence among young people and the related decline in importance of the extended family as a primary group are eroding even the matrilocal working-class neighborhood communities described by Kerr (1958) and Young and Willmott (1962). At the institutional level, the spread of service industries and public welfare facilities has reduced the need for neighboring activities. A cup of sugar need no longer be borrowed; the supermarket is open continuously and larger stocks are now kept at home. The mortician supplies aid at times of bereavement; the fire department appears when a conflagration occurs.

It is possible to conclude that the traditional neighborhood with high levels of mutual help and information sharing remains today only where certain circumstances prevail. These include ethnicity, poverty, lack of mobility, and a preference for kinship ties based on spatial proximity. In these areas, taverns are strong forces for social cohesion and resistance to change (Gottlieb, 1957; Richards, 1964). Such conditions are most frequently found in central city locations. Since the 1950s, however, many such neighborhoods have been destroyed by urban renewal policies (see Chapter 11).

antineighborhood views

With these considerations in mind, it is possible to take the stand that, as the neighborhood is a declining force in urban behavior, it should not be used as a planning tool. In a thorough examination of the neighborhood unit concept, Isaacs (1948a, b) suggested that a neighborhood unit of, say, 5000 people could not support the necessary facilities required by that group. Thus each family will be compelled to seek many services beyond the unit. Moreover, he suggests that the nature of the modern city, the essence of which is constant change and high levels of personal intercommunication and mobility, effectively prevents the formation of meaningful primary contacts and place loyalty at the neighborhood unit level.

A more extreme view is that of Meier (1962) who sees the city less as space than as the focus of transactions between individuals and groups. Given efficient communications, the spatial arrangement of the city as we know it, from central business district to suburban neighborhood, becomes obsolete (Meier, 1968; Gottman, 1970). Taking up this idea, Webber (1963, 1964a) suggests that the neighborhood should be discarded. He argues that the private motor vehicle has become an instrument of personal freedom which enables individuals to travel, at high speed and low cost, to any part of the metropolis. Just as the automobile and truck link together economic establishments which are spatially separated, so the urbanite can now rapidly communicate with friends whose residences are scattered across the metropolis. Mass ownership of telephones is a further support to this concept of wide-ranging personal contact. The end result is an increasing reliance on friends rather than neighbors, and the consequent decline of neighboring activities. Far from deploring the decline of the neighborhood, Webber regards the creation of the far-flung "community without propinquity" as a triumph for personal liberation from associations imposed by the friction of space.

Complementing this planner's view are a series of sociological works which point out that the city dweller is not only highly mobile but also prefers the anonymity available in the mobile urban society (Meyer, 1951). Thus the urbanite's activities have become divorced from his residential area and, being based on shared interests rather than physical proximity, are now diffused throughout the urban area (McClenahan, 1945; Riemer, 1951). To return to antineighborhood planners, there has been some feeling that planning for neighborhood activity is an outmoded concept based on nostalgia for rural life (Churchill, 1948; Dewey, 1950; Bauer, 1952).

Lee (1968) suggests that the antineighborhood viewpoint is that of a "dissenting minority," yet evidence from both planning practice and sociological research indicates that the viewpoint gained wide acceptance in the 1960s. New towns developed in the 1960s show much less evidence of neighborhood planning; Cumbernauld, a Scottish new town with a prize-winning high-density design, has no neighborhoods at all. Sociological work, moreover, confirms that social relationships bear little relation to planned neighborhoods (Mann, 1965). Yet the wide acceptance of the term neighborhood by citizens as well as planners demands consideration of the perceptions of neighborhoods by their inhabitants.

perception of neighborhoods

In examining and defining neighborhood, many workers have used size parameters. Some, such as Stein, Perry, and Mumford, have advocated an optimal size for the neighborhood unit. Mumford's (1954) ideal neighborhood unit would contain 5,000 persons of all ages and social strata, all within walking distance of a school which also serves as a community center. In view of the problems of facility duplication, however, neighborhood units have frequently been designed to contain as many as 10,000 inhabitants. In some cases, as in New York between the two World Wars, neighborhood planning became the organization of residential groupings of sufficient size to support a major school complex.

It is unlikely that the inhabitants of such units will ever develop a feeling of neighborhood identity. Clearly, the ideal of face-to-face contact is lost in units of 10,000 persons. Research in an old-established Boston neighborhood discovered that two-thirds of the inhabitants knew the conventional name of the area. In contrast, only 30 percent of interviewed residents in the British new town of Stevenage were able to name their neighborhood, despite the efforts of the development corporation to stimulate identity in each 10,000-inhabitant unit (Willmott, 1962). Other studies suggest that inhabitants have little conception of even 5,000-person neighborhoods.

Rather than the large units laid out by the planners, residents appear to perceive much smaller groupings, often no more than a few contiguous houses, as neighborhoods of social interaction. In the Stevenage study previously cited, interviewees who felt any place-related identity indicated areas of about 2,000 inhabitants, well below the size of the designated units. Studies in Philadelphia and Boston confirm that areas recognized as distinct on a city-wide basis were not recognized as neighborhoods by residents, who were more likely to distinguish one or two blocks, part of a street, or a small group of houses as the area they really knew and identified with (Ross, 1962; Herman, 1964). Keller (1968, 99) states: "Even a single street may be cut up into tight little islands where exclusive and often antagonistic groups form separate units, manifesting neighborly kindness and generosity within them but distance and hostility between them."

There is evidence from animal behavior studies of species as different as the howler monkey and Norway rat that the most effective use of resources is achieved by the aggregation of individuals into groups containing an average of 12 adults (Calhoun, 1966). Anthropological investigations suggest that among primitive groups such as the Kalahari bushmen, a group containing about one dozen adults is normal (Calhoun, 1973). Speculation on man's origins as a hunter suggest a group of 20 to 30 individuals as optimal for social control, adequate feeding, and a sense of identity fostered by frequent face-to-face contact (Morris, 1968). The same size group tends to coincide with an urban individual's range of friends and close acquaintances. Without drawing ethological analogies too finely, it is tempting to speculate that the small neighborhood islands, often no more than 8 to 12 houses, which are perceived by residents themselves, are natural neighborhood foci for the development of positive proximity-based relationships. Detailed studies of specific small neighborhoods have been made, most notably Kerr's (1958) five-year study of *The People of Ship Street,* in Liverpool, England, and Gans' (1962a) sympathetic investigation of the behavior of Italian-Americans in Boston, significantly entitled *The Urban Villagers.*

neighborhood satisfaction

Resident perceptions of neighborhood quality vary greatly according to conditions in both the physical and the social environment. Satisfaction, of course, depends upon perception and both individual and group value-systems (see Chapter 9). On the other hand, perceptions of good neighbors are related to satisfaction with the neighborhood (Michelson, 1970). Despite this complexity, several studies have linked neighborhood satisfaction to environmental variables.

One of the more important of these is traffic. In San Francisco three streets in an Italian neighborhood, varying chiefly in traffic density and the resulting noise, were compared (Appleyard and Lintell, 1972). The streets were identified in traffic terms as heavy (15,750 vehicles per day), moderate (8,700), and light (2,000). Resident type varied from predominantly long-established families with children in the light street to predominantly single renters in the heavy traffic street. Interviewees were asked questions regarding traffic hazards, stress, noise, pollution, social interaction, privacy, and home territoriality. Respondents from the heavy traffic street perceived higher levels of hazard and environmental degradation. More significantly, whereas friendship in the light and moderate streets extended across the street, an individual's friendship interaction on the heavy traffic street tended to be confined to one side. Light street residents had an average of 9.3 friends and acquaintances per person, whereas moderate and heavy traffic street residents had only 5.4 and 4.1 friends and acquaintances respectively. Yet more significantly, when asked to draw their home territory, light traffic street residents tended to include the whole street ("I feel my home extends to the whole block") whereas heavy traffic street residents included only their apartment, or at most, the apartment building, with no extension into the street ("It is impersonal and public"; Fig. 4.5). The authors suggest an environmental selection process, whereby families with children move away from heavy traffic streets, leaving behind those, usually single persons, who value accessibility. An earlier study in England also found that the perceived friendliness of the neighborhood varied with traffic type and intensity (Ritter, 1964).

Neighborhood satisfaction also varies in relation to service provision. A North Carolina study found that both blacks and whites rated good services, especially fire protection, as more important attributes of neighborhood quality than architectural features such as play areas, landscaping, and design for physical privacy (Sanoff and Sawhney, 1972). Most persons preferred housing arrangements involving single-family dwellings with an enclosed private area. However, the fallacy of policies which consider housing without its context was pointed out by the discovery that an individual's satisfaction with his dwelling was associated with his level of satisfaction with his neighborhood.

A study of New York college freshmen of varied backgrounds points out further variables related to the individual's perception of environmental quality; Table 4.1 indicates that white Protestants and Jews, high-income persons, and those living in single-family dwellings were more likely to be satisfied with their neighborhood than other groups. The questions asked relative to satisfaction included perceived friendliness of neighbors, safety, attractiveness, and suitability for rearing children. No question dealt with housing condition or the spatial arrangements of housing, which may account for the findings differing from a contemporary study which found no relationship between social status and neighborhood satisfaction (Yancey, 1971). A contribution based on research in England (Lee, 1968) suggests that an individual's involvement in the neighborhood was determined by his length of residence, age, house-type, location of husband's work, and number of children.

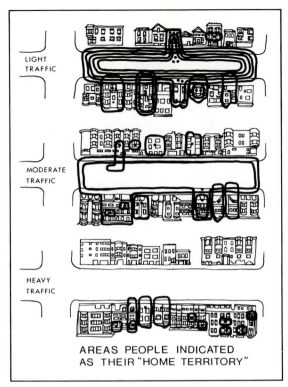

LIGHT TRAFFIC

MODERATE TRAFFIC

HEAVY TRAFFIC

AREAS PEOPLE INDICATED
AS THEIR "HOME TERRITORY"

Fig. 4.5

Home-base territories of residents of streets of varying traffic volume. (Redrawn
from D. Appleyard and M. Lintell, "The Environmental Quality of City Streets,"
Journal of the American Institute of Planners 38 (March 1972), by permission of
D. Appleyard and the *Journal.*)

TABLE 4.1
NEIGHBORHOOD SATISFACTIONS IN NEW YORK

| Group | Groups Satisfied with Present Neighborhood to Extent of: | | |
	45% or Under	46 – 59%	60% or Over
Racial	Black Puerto Rican	Italian Irish	White-Protestant Jewish
Annual Income	Under $5,999	$6,000–7,999	Over $8,000
House type	3–5 stories Over 15 stories	5–15 stories	Single-family Two-family Garden apartment

Source: Hinshaw and Allott (1972)

A Neighborhood Typology

The contrast between planners' neighborhoods of up to 10,000 people and residents' perceived social neighborhoods of as little as 8 to 12 houses has already been described. The existence of these two rather different concepts with the same name has bred much confusion, but has also led to attempts to integrate the two into an overall neighborhood typology.

In a comparative review of the neighborhood concepts of French, Greek, and English-speaking planners, Mann (1963) found that each author had produced not a single definition of neighborhood but a hierarchical ordering of neighborhoods of different sizes. This concept of smaller neighborhoods nesting within larger ones which provide a higher level of services accords well with the service hierarchies of the geographer's central place theory (Christaller, 1966). A hierarchy of planning units was suggested by Perry as early as 1929, and was subsequently modified by Blumenfeld (1948) who suggested a three-fold typology. Bardet (1951), studying a large number of both rural and urban places in Europe and Africa, also emerged with a three-fold typology. A three-level schema was produced by Lee (1968) after a detailed study of neighboring in Cambridge, England. The four typologies are compared in Table 4.2.

TABLE 4.2

COMPARISON OF NEIGHBORHOOD TYPOLOGIES

| | Number of Families per Neighborhood | | |
	First Order	Second Order	Third Order
Perry (1939)	5 – 10	50 – 150	500 – 1,500
Blumenfeld (1948)	6 – 12	50 – 100	100 – 500
Bardet (1961)	5 – 10	50 – 100	500 – 1,500
Lee (1968)	0 – 400	400 – 1,000	approx. 400 – 2,000

The typologies of Perry, Blumenfeld, and Bardet are quite similar. The small grouping of up to one dozen families is regarded as the maximum size for strong interpersonal relationships. At the 50–100 family scale, people can still be on first-name terms. Blumenfeld believes that the human scale, where children know each other, disappears in units larger than 500 families, and that there is little qualitative difference between 500 and 10,000 families.

Although the typologies of Bardet and Lee have been equated (Saarinen, 1969), the numerical discrepancy suggests that the first and second orders of Lee's schema are the equivalent of the second and third orders in the Perry-Bardet-Blumenfeld typology.

Lee's work was based on intensive interviews with a sample of housewives from various districts. These respondents were asked to draw a map of their neighborhood, to locate friends, kin, and acquaintances, to detail their travel habits, to express their attitudes toward their locality, and to provide the usual background factors of age, occupation, length of residence, and the like. Three levels of neighborhood emerged (Fig. 4.6).

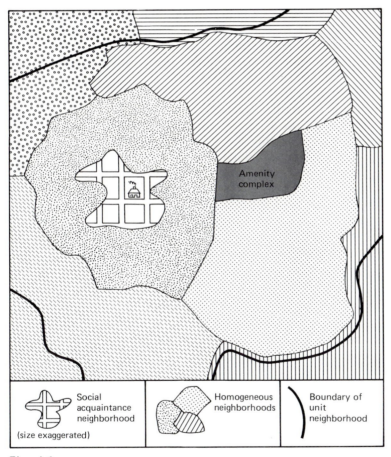

Fig. 4.6

A hierarchy of neighborhoods (after T. Lee).

1.   *The Social Acquaintance Neighborhood.* This corresponds to Blumen-feld's first-name level. Sheer proximity ensures that everyone knows everyone else, and the boundaries of the neighborhood are set by social interaction. The physical area involved is restricted to half a dozen streets, wholly residential except for corner stores.

2.   *The Homogeneous Neighborhood.* Here the boundaries are wider and are set by the quality of the houses and the type of people who live in them. The level of social interaction is low, but most residents are aware of each other, a feeling which results in social control through accepted group norms. It is a neighborhood of familiar strangers, described by residents as "people like us," but, more accurately, being composed of people who live in similar houses.

3.   *The Unit Neighborhood.* A larger area is involved, and both houses and population are heterogeneous in type. It contains a balanced range of amenities such as schools, churches, and stores. Friends and acquaintances are scattered, and the intervening spaces are filled with mutual awareness relationships.

The conclusion to be drawn from this research is that neighborhood planning must take place on at least two levels. Lee's *unit neighborhood* confirms the validity of the neighborhood unit as a means of planning the location of public amenities and facilities. Several reports provide practical models for amenity location (Higasa, 1960; Maw, 1971; de Vise, 1973). The neighborhood unit concept, however, seems to be less valid as a framework for social interaction, which typically takes place in smaller areas. Planning at the small neighborhood level should therefore be more concerned with the effect of physical environment on social interaction (see Chapter 8) and the provision of low-order amenities such as corner stores and tot lots.

the child-centered neighborhood

The reader will have observed that almost all discussion of neighborhoods is predicated upon the existence of families with children. Indeed, intensive research on the interactions between residents of single-family houses and nearby high-rise apartment dwellers has only recently begun (Wellman, 1972). Michelson (1970) suggests that apartment dwellers have far fewer local relationships than residents of adjacent houses. Persons rearing children, however, tend to prefer ground-level houses. These, because of sheer pro-pinquity, as discussed earlier, tend to be grouped together into small social interaction neighborhoods. Much research on the behavior of children supports the contention that such small neighborhoods are held together by a web of child-child and adult-child, as well as adult-adult, interrelationships. "Children are indeed the true neighbors" (Bell *et al.*, 1973, 176).

Margaret Mead (1966) argues that our foremost basic needs are privacy and the continuity of human relationships. The latter is very important for young children, and in building neighborhoods we should provide environments which enable children to learn about society, the nonhuman world, and danger. In particular, successful local playgrounds must provide movement, adventure, people, "and above all, danger" (Abernathy, 1968). Most writers agree that it is in the small neighborhood, beyond the immediate constraints of the family, that children become socialized rather than selfish beings. The small neighborhood is an appropriate arena for reinforcing desired behavior patterns (McKay, 1949).

There is also a consensus that childrens' needs are not sufficiently considered at the local level. Adult designers are insensitive to childrens' preferences (Bishop *et al.*, 1972). In particular, specially designed playgrounds which segregate children from the social life of the neighborhood are at best a partial solution. Children roam extensively and any area may be treated as a play area (Rosenberg, 1969). Jacobs (1961) emphasizes that city streets and sidewalks are often more interesting to children than designated play spaces. On the other hand, a preoccupation with providing play spaces for children may ignore the local recreational needs of teenagers and adults (Bangs and Mahler, 1970).

Clearly, the places in which children play should provide excitement, a constantly changing kaleidoscope of activities, and elements of both danger and security. Integration with adult activities may also be valuable; a survey in Baltimore found that unsupervised playgrounds had low levels of attendance (Dee and Liebman, 1970). A design solution which integrates all these facets is the concept of the neighborhood common, an area open to all neighborhood residents on the traditional village green principle (Linn, 1968). Similarly, and based on the twelve-house small neighborhood research previously outlined, Pahl (1970) proposes that, for every twelve houses in a new development, a half lot should be left vacant. This would act as a common meeting ground, functioning variously as an informal nursery, playschool, and sandbox; a base for older children who may, for example, erect a treehouse; a convenient spot for motorbike stripping and repair by teenagers; and a place where, in a communally built shed, the neighborhood's store of communal garden tools could be kept.

Such plans are idealistic in that they make assumptions concerning human nature. Problems would likely arise over sharing the cost of the plot. City councillors would probably deplore such areas as eyesores and as possible gathering points for undesirables. Moreover, there is no guarantee that the plot would even be used. In fact, it is probable that such a common would be taken over by a single subgroup of neighborhood residents, whether adults or youths. The history of commons and greens in English villages is one of unequal usage. Furthermore, over-use of such an area on the part of individuals with opposing goals could lead to environmental degradation and social disruption (Hardin, 1968).

The concept of the child-centered neighborhood is also valuable at the level of the larger amenity-oriented neighborhood unit. Bowden (1972) suggests that the neighborhood is a perceived area defined as "the territorial and perceptional range of advanced preadolescent males regardless of society or geographic location." The boundaries of a neighborhood are set by the activities of 9–12-year-old boys who lack the city-wide mobility of adolescents and adults, but are more free-ranging than girls of the same age. Younger children gain an awareness of neighborhood by association while older persons retain the preadolescent neighborhood definition into maturity. Adults may learn new neighborhoods primarily through the wanderings of children and pets. The choice of preadolescents of about 11 years of age is supported by Rand (1972) who states that only by age 10 to 12 have children fully assimilated the sociospatial order of the home, family, and world beyond.

This concept of neighborhood has not been verified by extensive research, but has important implications. The fact that busy traffic arteries, especially freeways, may be perceived as boundaries by preadolescent males supports the use of these as boundaries for the neighborhood unit. The neighborhood unit then becomes, as its first proponents suggested, a relatively safe, contained area for the raising of children. However, a second implication is that the neighborhood unit's core is not a central amenity (school and shopping) complex, but the home of each boy resident within it. In fact schools, supermarkets, and swimming pools, generally considered by planners as facilities both physically and socially central to the neighborhood unit, are commonly used as boundary designators. Preadolescent children often conceive of the area between home and school as their neighborhood, but not the area on the other side of the school.

Evidence in support of this assertion is found in Lee's suggestion that neighborhood unit shopping complexes should be positioned off-center, toward downtown, as residents appear to perceive distances toward downtown as shorter than equivalent distances in other directions (see Chapter 5). Centrally located amenity complexes would possibly cause residents of one unit to gravitate to a subjectively nearer complex in an adjacent unit, thereby disrupting the traffic patterns designed to preserve neighborhood unit integrity.

evidence for neighborhood survival

As a collective home-base territory the neighborhood should be both personalized and defended. There is evidence from graffiti that neighborhood personalization exists among preadults (Ley and Cybriwsky, 1974a). Adults widely accept such statements as "they have bought a house in a nice neighborhood." Neighborhoods provide identity, as when a street or district name is used to define where one lives.

Security and stimulation inhere in neighborhood defense. A number of studies support the contention that nearby residents will band together to collectively oppose perceived threats from the outside world (Gottlieb, 1957). Since the 1960s, in particular, neighborhood associations have been particularly strong in opposing freeway development. In a number of cities throughout North America, freeway building has been severely hampered because of citizen action which began at the local level. Organized neighborhood resistance to urban redevelopment has also become common (Lorimer, 1972). Increased government decentralization of services within cities, together with active citizen involvement in the planning process (see Chapter 14), may also promote a reawakening of neighborhood consciousness, notably where the ward system of voting operates or where community agitators are at work. Packard (1972) suggests that if such neighborhood consciousness is revived, we may avoid the consequences of becoming *A Nation of Strangers*.

The neighborhood unit, moreover, has reappeared as an element in the master plans of the latest new and expanded towns in Britain. Units proposed since 1967 vary from the traditional figure of 5,000 to the 8,000-person community of the Runcorn New Town Master Plan (Ling, 1967) and the 30,000-person townships of Greater Peterborough (Willis, 1969). Recognizing the mobility conferred by the automobile, planners appear to be favoring larger units as the basic building blocks of new communities. The urban unit of 30,000 to 70,000 people was proposed as early as 1949 by Tyrwhitt. Such a large size seems necessary because the 5,000 unit is probably too small to meet the amenity needs of the mobile modern family. The current need appears to be the facilitation of amenity choice for the individual on a city-wide basis. This presupposes that the individual's activity space covers the whole city, rather than a small segment known as a neighborhood, a subject discussed at length in the next chapter.

Summary

1. At the mesospace level, the human home-base comprises an individual core (the home) and a variable collective area around the core (the neighborhood).
2. Personalized and defended, the home provides security, identity, and stimulation. In particular, the house may be a symbol of the self.

3. Cross-cultural studies of both adults and children suggest a marked preference for the detached, single-family residence with private yard.
4. Theoretically, neighbors, neighborhood, and neighboring activity together form a sociospatial unit, recognized by residents and distinct from the rest of the city.
5. Traditional views of neighborhood coalesced in the planning tool known as the neighborhood unit, widely used in new residential developments since the 1930s.
6. Criticism of the ideology behind neighborhood (unit) theory, and the decline of the traditional neighborhood on which it was based, is supported by research on the activities, perceptions, and satisfactions of residents.
7. This research indicates that the neighborhood concept is immensely complex. "The neighborhood does not provide an easy rubber stamp for planning cities" (Bell *et al.*, 1973).
8. The neighborhood concept requires disaggregation into a hierarchy of three or four levels. Neighborhood planning should proceed on two levels at least, that of the small neighborhood for a balance between social interaction and privacy, and that of the neighborhood unit or larger community for the provision of accessibility to facilities.
9. A case exists for considering the chief function of the neighborhood to be the socialization of children. This requires further reshaping of the neighborhood concept.
10. Evidence suggests that neighborhood feelings exist in the 1970s, chiefly in terms of a response to crisis.

Further Reading

COOPER, C. (1972), "The House as Symbol," *Design and Environment* 3: 30–37.

KELLER, S. (1968), *The Urban Neighborhood: A Sociological Perspective.* New York: Random House.

LEE, T. (1968), "The Urban Neighborhood as a Socio-Spatial Schema," *Human Relations* 21: 241–68.

WEBBER, M. M. (1963), "Order in Diversity: Community without Propinquity," in L. Wingo (ed.), *Cities and Space*, pp. 23–54. Baltimore: Johns Hopkins Press.

5

MACROSPACE BEHAVIOR: HOME RANGE

How to describe a city? Even for an old inhabitant it is impossible: one can present only a simplified plan, taking a house here, a park there as symbols of the whole.[*]

Graham Greene

Most territorial mammals are unable to satisfy all their drives within their home base. At the human level, this was one of the arguments against the concept of neighborhood self-sufficiency. Beyond the home base the organism does not attempt to control the whole area covered by its wanderings, but asserts temporary jurisdiction over places where specific activities, such as feeding, working, or resting, occur. "All these places are connected by an elaborate network of paths, along which the territory owner travels according to a more or less strict daily, or seasonal, or otherwise determined routine. The areas enclosed by the pathways, though more or less familiar, are seldom or never used" (Leyhausen, 1965a, 249).

Home Range

Such an area is the animal's home range, defined as the area beyond the home base which is habitually traversed by the individual, but which is not personalized or defended except temporarily at certain spots. Home range is not a continuous area, but a network of public paths and public or semipublic nodes. A containing boundary around it is at best an arbitrary feature. In studies of human activity, the term *orbit* has been used as an equivalent of home range (Parr, 1965). In Chombart de Lauwe's (1965) hierarchy of social

---

[*]   Graham Greene (1971), *The Lawless Roads*. London: Penguin Books.

spaces, both home base and home range are subdivided into progressively larger overlapping areas which reflect increasingly temporary use of the urban area (Fig. 5.1).

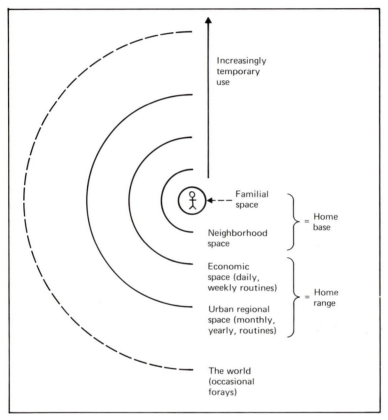

Fig. 5.1

Chombart de Lauwe's hierarchy of social spaces.

Each individual has his own orbit, but these individual orbits intersect along certain routes and in certain well-frequented locales; "even the most isolated elderly lady of an ethnic enclave occasionally meets an outsider" (Strauss, 1961). Yet people appear to know and use only limited sections of the city; other segments may be totally unknown or vaguely and erroneously conceived. From these observations three questions emerge.

1.   How much of the city does an individual use, and what factors guide the use of his *activity space*?

2.   How does the individual structure the city so as to find his way about therein, and how accurate are his images (*cognitive space*) of areas he does not frequent? In other words, does the citizen have a *mental map* of the city?

3.   How congruent are the individual's activity space and cognitive space? Are activity space and mental map mutually reinforcing features of the individual's behavior pattern?

Activity Patterns

An individual's activity space is the spatial pattern of his activity system. His *activity system* is "a flow of activities during some specified period of time . . . during which the person is engaged in the pursuit of his affairs" (Chapin and Brail, 1969). In activity-system terms, persons or firms are regarded as *behavioral units* which perform a series of activities, known as *episodes*, in particular *locales*. Attempts to discover the nature of the urbanite's daily routines have taken several forms, some related to time allocation only, others to both time and space (Lynch, 1972). The results produced vary in their value to the planner.

time budgets

Time budget work considers that the individual's daily or weekly routine can be broken down into a series of behavior categories, such as sleep, learning, eating, travel, work-related activities, recreation, and so on. The amount of time an individual spends in each activity is ascertained. Given standardization of categories, comparative studies of daily, weekly, and annual routines should be possible for both individuals and groups.

One of the earliest time-budget studies was carried out in the 1930s (Sorokin and Berger, 1939). With growth of interest in leisure activities and the quality of urban life in general, time-budget studies reemerged as a major research focus in the 1960s (Szalai, 1966). The basic methodology has changed little since Sorokin. Respondents are asked to record how they used their time during a specific period. The provision of a diary which can be completed on a daily basis reduces the problem of recall associated with the interview.

Activities are coded according to a predetermined classification. Defining the classification system involves treading a delicate balance between an enormously detailed activity set, which proves cumbersome to use, and a limited activity set which provides insufficient information. Two dissimilar examples of classification systems are provided in Table 5.1, and as several

TABLE 5.1

TIME-BUDGET CLASSIFICATIONS

Percentage of 24-hour Day, Puerto Rico Only	San Juan, Puerto Rico, 1957–8	Metropolitan United States 1960s (Chapin and Brail, 1969)
8.0	Work	Relaxation
1.3	School	Arts, hobbies, and sports
4.0	Travel	Reading
20.0	Personal service	Television and radio
42.9	Miscellaneous (including sleep, reflection)	In-home family In-home socializing In-home obligatory
2.0	Television/radio	
0.5	Shopping	Out-of-home discretionary
0.5	Reading	Out-of-home family
0.3	Meetings and parties	Out-of-home socializing
10.0	Dancing and drinking	Work-related
10.0	Play	Shopping and personal services
0.5	Ritual	Out-of-home obligatory

others are in use (Martineau, 1972), comparison of analyses is often hampered.

The Chapin-Brail classification is conceptually valuable because it makes three explicit distinctions which are fundamental to human behavior.

1. *Level of Interaction.* Activities are categorized according to whether the individual performs them alone, within the family group, or with others.

2. *Location.* As suggested in the last chapter, home and nonhome are basic divisions of geographic space. The first seven categories are mainly in-home activities.

3. *Obligatory/discretionary.* The individual may be compelled to perform certain activities. Others may or may not be performed at his discretion. In-home obligatory activities, for example, would include housework, while out-of-home obligatory activities include household errands and medical visits.

Obviously, the individual's activities within this framework vary according to his degree of subjection to cultural, environmental, and physiological constraints. Certain physiological constraints, however, such as the need for sleep and sustenance, are fairly constant among varied populations.

intensive investigation

The time-budget investigation typically generalizes its results from a representative sample of the available population. Other workers have attempted to study in greater detail the activities of single individuals. Barker and Wright (1951), for example, followed a single small child for a whole day, noting his activities and where and with whom they took place. Each episode of behavior generally occurs in an appropriate *behavior setting,* a concept further explored in Chapter 8. The results of such research appear in the form of vast schedules of behaviors, objects, spatial dimensions, people, and interactions.

Though of intrinsic and conceptual interest, this work is unlikely to be of value to the planner at present. The amount of data collected is enormous; there are major problems of comparison with other studies; and the physical difficulties involved in data collection are great. Leyhausen (1965a) and his research team attempted to make a continuous, uninterrupted day and night record of the activities of several domestic cats. He states: "It was an impossible job. To follow a single cat around day and night . . . and keep a record of all its movements, encounters, etc., requires at least three well-trained, physically fit, and inexhaustible observers."

the O & D survey

The time-budget survey may or may not include questions on the locales within which episodes of activity take place. Such information, however, is vital in assessing home range. One of the classic approaches to this problem is the *origin and destination* (O & D) survey, originally designed as a basic research tool for land-use and transportation forecasting, and pioneered on a large scale by such major operations as CATS (*Chicago Area Transportation Study,* 1959). As in the time-budget survey, a sample of city residents provides data on daily activities, including information on purpose of trip, trip duration, and the nature of the locale at both origin and destination (Mitchell and Rapkin, 1954). Outside the transportation-planning field, some efforts have been made to relate time budgets to land-use patterns (Chapin, 1965; Chapin and Hightower, 1965). The high cost of such studies, however, prevents their general use.

the human activity system

All three approaches to the human activity system have produced results which confirm the importance of the home base in the daily life of urban man. A survey conducted in Athens found that, on average, the urban Greek spent 81.1 percent of his time in his home or neighborhood (Table 5.2). Urban transportation studies in North America show that when the suburbanite leaves his home base, the major trip purposes are work, recreational and social, and shopping and personal business (Table 5.3). When all trips are considered, however, the dominant trip purpose is to return home, accounting for 43.5 percent of all trips in the CATS survey. From these data it appears that the home range of a typical urbanite, measured in time-budget terms, is largely composed of home, work, shopping, and recreational locales together with the necessary transport connectors (Fig. 5.2). Downtown is the single locale known to the majority of the urban population.

TABLE 5.2

ATHENIAN HOME RANGE

Locale	Percentage of 24-hour Day Spent in Locale
House	76.1
Community	5.0
Adjacent communities	5.1
City center	5.2
Remainder of urban region	4.8
Beyond urban region	3.8

Source: Pappas (1967)

In a major study of United States activity patterns, Chapin and Brail (1969) sampled 1,476 persons in 43 metropolitan areas. Respondents were asked to detail their time and space budgets for a single weekday. One general result was that if all obligatory activities are excluded from the typical adult's 24-hour day, only about five hours remain for discretionary activity, of which four (80 percent) are spent at home. The amount of discretionary time spent in the home reaches up to 85 percent for senior citizens, the unemployed, the fully employed, and those in the child-rearing stage of the life cycle. Part-time workers and young persons without children choose to spend less time at home, as little as 64 percent for young unattached persons. Income differences are also apparent; the affluent are more able to spend discretionary time away from home (Table 5.4). Income differences are especially apparent where the family is raising children, but working persons universally spend less discretionary time at home. Many other variables were considered as predictors of the likelihood of various activities being performed. The results indicate that attitudinal (e.g., satisfaction with means of access to activities) and environmental (e.g., distance from downtown) variables were not significant. Of greatest importance as activity predictors were sex, stage in the life cycle (age, family responsibilities, household size), and status (income, education).

TABLE 5.3

UNITED STATES SUBURBAN TRIP PURPOSES

	One-way Trips Outward Bound from Home	
Trip Purpose	Percentage Frequency (Smith, 1966)	Percentage Frequency (CATS)
Work	34	30
Recreation	21	22
Shopping	17	20
School	7	10
Others	21*	18**
	100	100

*   Includes 11 percent personal business.
** Includes personal business, serve passenger, eat meal, ride.

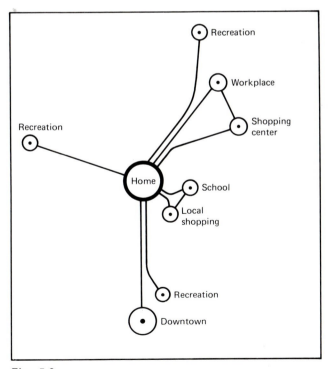

Fig. 5.2

The major elements of the urbanite's home range.

Turning from the national survey to the analysis of time allocation in a single city, Chapin (1971) found that the quality of life in Washington D.C., as measured by the amount of time spent in and the variety of discretionary activities, was somewhat higher than that of the nation as a whole. But the disparities in the use of free time between racial groups was large, blacks being clearly disadvantaged. More research is required in this area, notably with regard to suggestions made by several workers that residential segregation is related to the varying degree to which people from different parts of the city make use of downtown (Hardwick, 1974). Parr (1965) demands more comparative studies of orbits, suggesting that "the orbits of housewives and children are separating more and more from the orbits of husbands, single women, and working wives."

TABLE 5.4

INCOME AND HOME USE

Group	Mean Hours Spent on In-Home Discretionary Activities		
	All Respondents	Excluding Those with Family Responsibilities	Working Persons Only
The poor	5.06	5.26	2.87
The middle group	4.07	4.15	2.67
The affluent	3.77	3.64	2.73

Source: Chapin and Brail (1969)

the value of activity pattern studies

A major application of activity-system techniques is the delimitation of functional neighborhoods based on the actual movements of their inhabitants. In a study of a black ghetto in Raleigh, North Carolina, each respondent was asked to indicate, on a base map, the locations of his three best friends, closest relatives, place of work, primary shopping place, previous residences, neighborhood center, major neighborhood organizations, as well as his own residence (Stea, 1974). By drawing links between his home and the other activity nodes, and by aggregating the resulting collection of links, it was possible to discover groups of collections. Within each group, links were at a maximum; between groups, links were minimal. Functional neighborhoods, defined by one or more of the behavior criteria, were then produced by aggregating groups of linkages.

On a larger scale, a series of workers have suggested reasons for setting up national activity pattern surveys. Meier (1959) stated that as increasing leisure time permits an ever-widening variety of activities, cumulative time-budget data would provide an index of quality of life. Activity pattern analysis could throw light on why people move their residence locations (Chapin, 1968), could help set performance standards for designers (Pollowy and Bezman, 1972), and could be used in determining future land-use needs (MacMurry, 1971).

The concept has been applied most frequently to studies of leisure activities. Several activity-based models or typologies have been developed for the purpose of assisting the planning of accessible recreation sites (Maw, 1971; Burton, 1971; Janisova, 1971). The ability of people to predict their future behavior may be an important input to such models. Bull (1972) found that prediction errors were not related to social class, education, or age. Weather, however, affected predictions. Moreover, respondents overestimated their future leisure activities. The cost of general activity pattern surveys remains high, however, and inferences made from the study of a particular group of people in a particular time and space system are uncertain. It is suggested that the technique is most appropriate for "special projects to be installed at specific places for specific populations" (Bell *et al.*, 1973).

Cognitive Patterns

In moving through his activity space, the individual uses some system of navigation which allows him to move from point to point. Some systems are mechanical; many rodents run like clockwork trains along trails previously marked out by the deposition of urine (Lorenz, 1952). Long-distance animal navigation is complex (Carthy, 1956). Over short distances, however, where mechanical means are not used, and whether we are dealing with experimental rats moving through laboratory mazes or humans moving through the city, two approaches are possible. The stimulus-response approach of behaviorist psychology (Hull, 1943) would suggest that the individual, having initially learned his way by trial and error, proceeds in a given direction until a stimulus cue is perceived, such as a familiar building or the first decision point in the maze. The organism then responds by turning right or left and proceeding until it comes to the second cue, and so on until the destination is reached. Movement through space is thus viewed as a rather rigid sequence of learned operations.

The second strategy suggests that the individual is guided, not by a programmed series of responses, but by a generalized image of the environment. Constantly referring his present position to his image, which contains elements of both *distance* and *direction*, the individual is able to zero in upon the target. The generalized image theory allows for alternative route choices and considerable decision-making flexibility. Missing a specific cue does not mean that the individual becomes disoriented, as would happen in the sequence-of-operations strategy, for the image is replete with cues. Such an image, as envisaged by geographers and urban designers, is known as a *mental map*. Tolman (1948), basing his work on Lewin's (1936) topological psychology and studying the behavior of rats in mazes, suggested that these rodents navigate by means of such a *cognitive map*.

Interest in mental maps as a means of orientation in space began with Gulliver (1908) and Trowbridge (1913). The latter found people using two methods of personal orientation. The conventionally oriented based their judgments on objective systems such as map coordinates and compass directions. Egocentrically oriented persons, in contrast, used subjective or body-centered coordinate systems. Trowbridge also proposed a domicentric approach, where space is structured in relationship to the home base. Preferring the domicentric system, Trowbridge cited the frequent loss of compass orientation among soldiers on battlefields or when traveling long distances, "which unquestionably contributes to difficulty . . . in finding [the] way home in an unfamiliar region."

After Trowbridge, the concept languished. The work of Piaget on the child's conception of space (1948), the world (1963), and geometry (1964) did not deal with the geographic imagery of children. Except for Tolman, no significant progress occurred until the appearance of Boulding's *The Image* (1956). In this reflective, but seminal work, Boulding claimed:

> The first proposition of this book . . . is that behavior depends on the image. What, however, determines the image? . . . The image is built up of all the past experiences of the possessor of the image.

The suggestion is that space consists of a number of points embedded in a network of routes (Kaplan, 1973), a notion similar to the home-range concept. Several routes connect each point, and pass through other points. Direction involves moving toward or away from specific points, and regions of closely associated points can be identified. From these points, routes, and regions, however, emanates a confusing barrage of stimuli which impinges upon the observer. Thus man needs "a simplified model of the real situation in order to deal with it" (Simon, 1957), and a primary function of the brain appears to be the formation of spatial abstractions. The brain is therefore regarded as a selector, sifting the vast input of stimuli and retaining meaningful ones so that the complex overall structure of one's surroundings is simplified into a personal mental map (Carr, 1967). According to Lynch (1960):

Environmental images are the result of a two-way process between the observer and the environment. The environment
suggests distinctions and relations, and the observer — with
great adaptability and in the light of his own purposes —
selects, organizes, and endows with meaning what he sees.

The chief function of the mental map is to orientate the individual as he
proceeds through his regular activity patterns. Polanyi (1963, 11) asserts "I can
test the kind of mental map I possess of a familiar region only in action, that
is, by actually using it as my guide." It may also be useful as a base map for
further exploration, as a means of orienting others, and as a basis for our
aesthetic appreciation of the landscape as an artifact.

Only in the Soviet Union have psychologists devoted much attention to
mental mapping (Stea, 1974). Elsewhere, much work on cognitive maps at the
world, national, and regional levels has been done by geographers (Gould,
1966, 1967; Gould and White, 1968; Downs and Stea, 1973). There has also
been some concern with maps of imagined landscapes (Prince, 1971; Porteous, 1975). Our concern here, however, is with mental images of cities, a
study which has largely been the domain of planners, architects, and geographers.

the image of the city

Inspired by Boulding, and with a strong interdisciplinary background,
Lynch's *Image of the City* (1960) has proved to be the seminal contribution to
the study of cognitive mapping. The book merits detailed consideration
because of its conceptualization of images, its attempt to find methodologies
for both eliciting images from peoples' minds and for describing them, and its
concern with the practical application of imagery findings to urban design.

Lynch provides some terminological concepts which enable us to grasp
the nature of the image more easily. Like a printed page is visually perceived
as a related pattern of recognizable symbols, so a city's various parts should
be capable of being recognized and organized into a coherent pattern. Both
printed page and city would then be said to be *legible*. The quality in these
objects which endows them with the power to evoke strong images in any
given observer is termed *imageability*.

One's image of a city, regardless of the latter's degree of legibility, may
be analyzed into three components. *Identity* implies that a given object possesses individuality, is recognized as a separate entity, and can be distinguished from other items. *Structure* suggests that individual objects can be
related together and to the observer. A gate, therefore, may be identified and
related spatially and structurally to the observer and the garden beyond it.

But for full comprehension a third component, *meaning,* is required, for the gate is a means of getting in. Identity, structure, and meaning are clearly interdependent components of the image.

Image elicitation   Lynch used a series of image elicitation methods. Respondents were asked to draw a quick map of central Boston "just as if you were making a rapid description of the city to a stranger, covering all the main features." This method has been criticized on the grounds that a map drawn for a stranger would not necessarily coincide with an individual's personal image; there is likely to be an undue emphasis on routeways, for example. Respondents were also asked to list the elements of the city they thought most distinctive, from a doorknob to a region, and to provide detailed descriptions of a number of trips through the city. Other questions included instructions to locate, describe, and express any emotional feelings toward particular urban features. In contrasting the elicited maps with those of trained field observers, some significant differences were found, which supports the use of the sketch-a-map technique as a means of eliciting responses difficult to obtain by other means.

Image content   Lynch approached the problem of describing the maps and lists he elicited by analyzing their contents for repetitive element patterns. It was convenient to classify the elements into five types: paths, edges, districts, nodes, and landmarks (Fig. 5.3).

1.   *Paths* are movement channels, such as streets, railroads, transit lines, and walkways. For many people, paths are the predominant element. As people observe the city while moving through it, they are likely to structure other elements around their movement paths.

2.   *Edges* are linear elements not used as paths. They include outlines, such as the coast; barriers, such as walls; and "seams" which bind two regions together.

3.   *Districts* are regions of the city which are identified by some common character, and which the individual can enter.

4.   *Nodes* are frequently focal points where paths meet, as at intersections or transportation junctions. Or they may be places where there is a concentration of activity, as in squares or street corners. A node which is the focus and symbol of a district, such as a square with a fountain, is called a *core.* Nodes may be entered.

5.   *Landmarks* cannot be entered; they are external reference points which are distinguished in some way from a host of other possible landmarks. They may be accessible or inaccessible; a landmark to which the observer does not know his way is essentially "bottomless," as with the myriad golden domes and spires of many European cities. Landmarks may be local (storefronts, neon signs), distant (spires), or even outside the city (mountains). One of the prominent elements of the author's image of Victoria, British Columbia, is the mountain wall of the Olympic Range in Washington State. Such major fixed features may become direction referents.

Fig. 5.3

The five major elements of the mental map (after K. Lynch).

The way these elements are structured together as a mental map is illustrated in Fig. 5.4. Clearly, none of the element types exists in isolation. Elements overlap and pierce each other and form clusters or element complexes. A market square, for instance, is not merely noted as an area formally and functionally distinct from the urban matrix, but is seen as a node, the meeting-place of paths, defined by edges, and identified by characteristic landmarks. The mental map often consists of a series of such feature clusters, held together by a very legible intraurban transportation net. With modifications, Lynch's typology remains in use. For example, Stea's (1969) work suggests that the important elements of a cognitive map are points (arranged in a hierarchy), boundaries, paths, and barriers.

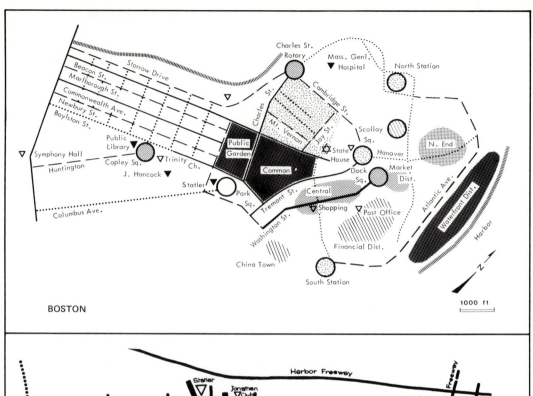

BOSTON

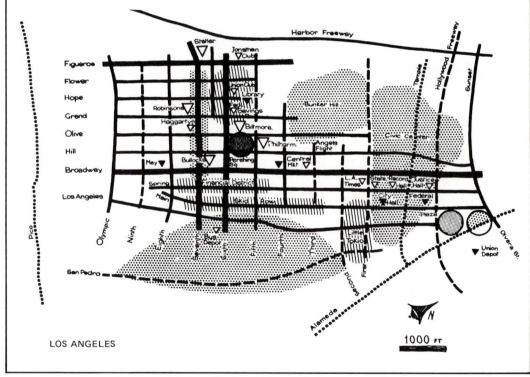

LOS ANGELES

Variations in image structuring Lynch found five major ways in which sketch maps were developed. Frequently, respondents would develop images along familiar lines of movement. Others would begin by drawing an enclosing outline, then filling in toward the center. Still others first laid down a basic repeating pattern, such as the gridiron street layout of Los Angeles. Some maps began with a few adjacent regions, which were then interconnected, and a few examples were totally oriented around a familiar node. There appeared to be two major variations, the path-oriented and the space-oriented development techniques.

This theme was taken up by Appleyard (1970), who found that the maps of 300 Venezuelan respondents were either dominated by *sequential* elements (notably roads), or *spatial* elements (landmarks, districts, nodes). The most primitive sequential map was fragmentary, consisting of fragments of paths or lists of elements unconnected with each other. The chain-type map was also simple but more schematic, treating all bends and turns as straight lines. With loops and branches from major arteries, the branch-and-loop map showed greater development. Network maps portrayed the most complete road system (Fig. 5.5). Similarly, the most primitive spatial maps were of a scatter pattern, showing unlinked elements, occasionally grouped into clusters. Mosaic maps portrayed districts with boundaries, and link maps interconnected these with schematic linkages which occasionally represented parts of the road system. Pattern maps were the most developed spatial type, involving a pattern of dominant features with fairly accurate boundaries. The types of map most commonly drawn were all sequential, namely, the chain (33 percent of respondents), the branch-and-loop (21 percent), and the network (15 percent). This reemphasizes the importance of paths in city imagery.

The value of the image As the individual's image depends strongly upon the legibility of his physical environment and in particular on the imageability of its various parts, it is probable that by manipulating the environment images may be strengthened. It may be more difficult to delete images. A study in England demonstrated that after-images persisted in elicited mental maps despite the disappearance of their physical counterparts from the landscape (Porteous, 1971). The images of a number of elderly inhabitants of two towns contained landmarks and other landscape elements which had long since been demolished.

Lynch felt that image studies would provide clues for urban designers so that cities might be made more legible. Greater legibility would result in

◀ *Fig. 5.4*

The Boston and Los Angeles images as derived from sketch-maps. (Redrawn and reprinted from K. Lynch, *The Image of the City,* 1960, by permission of The M.I.T. Press, Cambridge, Mass.)

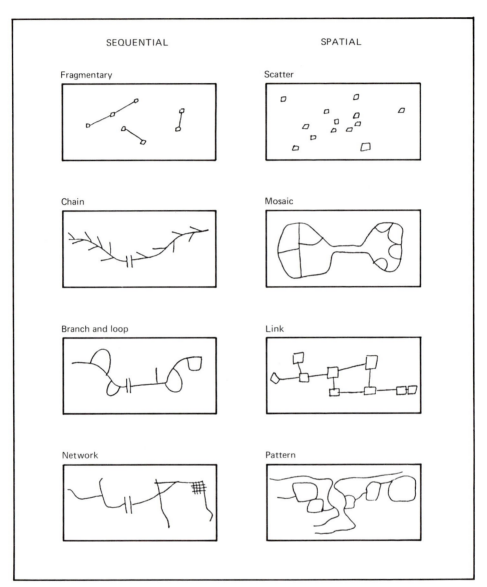

Fig. 5.5

Most frequent methods of structuring the city when drawing mental maps. (Redrawn from L. Rodwin (ed.), *Planning Urban Growth and Regional Development*, 1969, by permission of The M.I.T. Press, Cambridge, Mass., and Donald Appleyard.)

easier pathfinding on the part of both inhabitants and stranger alike. Streets, therefore, must be clearly identifiable, must clearly proceed toward a goal, and should be organizated into a visual hierarchy. Extreme legibility, however, could rapidly lead to boredom, as in the grid plans of North American small towns. The city must therefore be provided with a richly varied set of paths, edges, nodes, landmarks, and districts, providing for alternative choices, frequent minor changes (as in deciduous vegetation), and an element of surprise. Variety of urban form within an overall, coherent structure is of great importance in our aesthetic appreciation of the city.

personal and public images

Each individual builds up his own personal image which, because of his temperament and background, will differ from that of any other individual. Lynch's emphasis on the practical value of imagery study, however, presupposes that there is "a public image of any given city which is the overlap of many individual images" (1960, 46). It is likely that individuals belonging to a fairly uniform group in a specific area will not have mental maps which are entirely unrelated. Contrariwise, each unique map will interdigitate with others in varying degrees, so that an overall public image is apparent. Experience supports this view. Times Square, New York, is readily identifiable and fairly easily structured into the townscape by most habitués. Their methods of identification and structuring will vary somewhat. The meaning of Times Square may differ rather more greatly. Public images of Boston and Los Angeles (Table 5.5) are displayed in Fig. 5.4 where strength of symbol is related to frequency of mention by interviewees.

Despite the importance of identifying public images, however, much post-Lynch research has emphasized a variety of variables which appear to relate to individual and group differences in the perception and evaluation of the townscape. In part this is a reaction to Lynch's pioneer effort, which was based on interviews with only thirty respondents in Boston and a mere fifteen each in Jersey City and Los Angeles, all of whom were of the professional and managerial classes. In contrast, Klein's (1967) work on Karlsruhe covered 1,118 respondents of widely differing backgrounds. Klein discovered sex, socioeconomic status, and place of residence to be important variables affecting the way people viewed the city. Moreover, long-term residents had a broader view than newcomers, and those living nearer the city center had a narrower image than those living further away. A study of Chicago's Loop (Saarinen, 1969) showed that while all respondents included the grid street pattern and such landmarks as the Marshall Field store, Loop workers tended to have a narrower, more detailed image than students whose main activity nodes lay outside. Several variables are discussed systematically; they are all, however, interrelated.

TABLE 5.5

PUBLIC IMAGES OF DOWNTOWN BOSTON
AND LOS ANGELES

	Path	Node	Edge	District	Landmark
	Features Mentioned by 75 Percent or More of Respondents				
Boston	Commonwealth Avenue Cambridge Street Many fragments of streets	Scollay Square South Station	Charles River	Beacon Hill Boston Common Public Garden	Public Library State House Faneuil Hall Massachusetts General Hospital
Los Angeles	Broadway Sixth Avenue	Pershing Square Olvera Street	None	None (Bunker Hill, Civic Center etc. 25–50%)	Statler

Source: Lynch (1960)

Age and sex   Physiological differences and distinctive culturally assigned roles suggest that sex is important in terms of spatial imagery. Psychoanalysts assert that, when creating environments, girls design static enclosures, whereas boys are concerned with the externalities of buildings, with activity in unenclosed space, and with movement along paths (Erikson, 1964). In the *Chronicles of Narnia*, C. S. Lewis asserts: "girls . . . never can carry a map in their heads" (1970, 2, 114). In Venezuela, Appleyard (1970) found that females tended to draw area-based rather than path-based (sequential) maps, and were more prone to error. A study of Los Angeles demonstrated that mental map size, content, and directional bias differed according to sex (Everitt and Cadwallader, 1972). In particular, wives' maps of the home area (neighborhood) covered approximately twice as much area (1.3 square miles) as those of their husbands (0.7 square miles). Another Los Angeles study discovered that whereas husbands tended to use the coordinates of the base map provided when drawing their home area, wives made little or no reference to the available coordinate system and in fact appeared to be domicentric (Orleans and Schmidt, 1972).

Lowenthal (1961) states that children are unable to organize objects in space, to envisage places which are out of sight, or to generalize from perceptual experience. As such they are poor geographers. Research by Blaut and Stea (1971), however, indicates that even children under five years of age are able to read and map from aerial photographs. Among adults, the imageability of individual structures may vary with *age*. A study in England by the author found that whereas elderly persons' mental maps contained after-images of structures actually derelict or demolished, the cognitive maps of young persons tended to be dominated by new, highly visible construction projects. The data in Table 5.6 were gathered from a combination of respondents' sketch maps, verbal descriptions, and responses to the question "What first comes to your mind, what symbolizes [the town name] for you?" It must be noted that there were no new construction projects of great visual or emotional impact in Stourport or Goole.

TABLE 5.6

DOMINANT IMAGES OF FOUR TOWNS, 1968

Town	Respondents Reporting Overall Dominant Image	Respondents Under 35 Years Whose Dominant Image Was a New Construction Project	Respondents over 60 Years Whose Dominant Image Was a Landscape Element Derelict or Nonexistent
Runcorn ($n = 25$)	11 (new road bridge)	8 (new road bridge)	5 (canal and docks)
Ellesmere Port ($n = 25$)	10 (oil industry) 9 (civic center)	7 (new civic center)	2 (canal)
Stourport ($n = 20$)	16 (River Severn)	2 (new civic center)	1 (canal)
Goole ($n = 20$)	13 (dockyards)	0	0

Experience   In a study of the images of residents of the five boroughs of New York, Milgram *et al.* (1972) found that Manhattan had a high index of recognizability. As the cultural and entertainment core of the city, it attracts people from the whole region. Saarinen made a similar point in his work on the Chicago Loop. It is possible that the imageability of a structure may be due not only to its inherent qualities but to its degree of centrality within the city. Using a geographic accessibility model (Berry and Horton, 1970), it should be possible to test whether similar objects on routes of varying traffic use are equally imageable. This research has yet to be done, but in the interim Milgram provides a formula which expresses the degree to which any scene in the city will be recognized:

$$R = f(C \times D)$$

where R is recognition, C is centrality to population flow, and D represents social or architectural distinctiveness.

On the basis of experience, mental maps should be most detailed in areas most frequently used, notably around the home. This is especially so for females and for children (Anderson and Tindall, 1972), and is very marked when mental maps are elicited at the national scale (Gould and White, 1968). Experience may also be a function of length of residence. In "The Stranger's Path," Jackson (1957) shows that a stranger's view of the townscape may be highly selective and restricted.

Recent immigrants are also likely to have images different from those of long-term residents. In Ciudad Guyana, a new city in Venezuela, newcomers tended to produce sequential (path-oriented) maps rather than maps which emphasized spaces (Appleyard, 1970). Their maps were also more restricted in area, but were less prone to error than those of longer-term inhabitants, indicating a higher level of interest.

In the town of Ellesmere Port, England, an old dockland nucleus was encircled in the 1960s by tracts of suburban public housing built for families relocated from Liverpool. A study on the lines of Lynch revealed two separate public images of the town, with little overlap (Fig. 5.6). Persons working in declining industries and living in or near the urban core were familiar in detail only with the spatially coherent dockside zone of waterways, mills, and row housing, cut off from the rest of Ellesmere Port by canals and railroads. In contrast, the collective mental map of the recently arrived inhabitants of the peripheral public housing almost completely ignored historic Ellesmere Port. Highly legible elements were not spatially juxtaposed, but appeared as discrete entities, functionally linked. New housing estates, downtown, and places of employment such as peripheral oil refineries and auto factories were connected by bus and car trips wholly encircling, without including, the compact core. Such a nebulous image is frequently elicited from persons learning an unfamiliar layout. In this case, the existence of an immigrant image may presage further environmental learning or, more likely, a continued social division in a town which has been described as "the suburb of nowhere, the port without a soul [which], still struggling to find itself, lacks a personality" (*Liverpool Evening Express* January 21, May 6, 1955). Indeed, the mental map study indicates that Ellesmere Port has a split personality.

Socioeconomic class   Several studies have found differences in imagery on a socioeconomic class basis (Ladd, 1970; Orleans, 1973; Stea, 1974). In Los Angeles it was demonstrated that the known area of inhabitants from an affluent section of the city may be up to one thousand times more extensive than that of inhabitants of poorer areas (D.C.P., 1971). Appleyard's Venezuela study found several components of class to be significant variables. Automobile travelers produced more coherent, broadly based maps, whereas 80 percent of the bus riders' maps were fragmented, inaccurate, and indicative of repeated sequential journeys. Bus riders tended to be of low education, but persons of equivalent education traveling by car produced better maps,

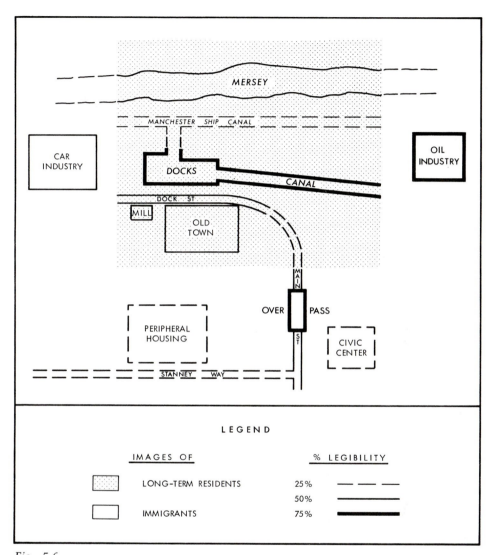

Fig. 5.6

Images of Ellesmere Port, England, 1968. (Reprinted from *Environment and Behavior* 3, No. 2 (June 1971), by permission of the publisher, Sage Publications, Inc.)

thus emphasizing the importance of transport mode in imagery formation. The most accurate maps were those of business executives and skilled workers, the least accurate those of housewives and professionals.

The poor showing of professionals is difficult to explain in view of the expected relationship between imagery capacity and education (Gulick,

1963). Many of the uneducated had never previously been asked to draw a map. In general, degree of connectedness between parts and accuracy of representation increased with education. Maps of the less educated were most clearly based on subjective experience and tended to describe their own journeys rather than the existing transportation system. The more educated groups drew the city more objectively and coherently. Their ability to visualize coherent patterns, however, could lead to error through inferring the existence of an absent element because of previous experience with similar layouts.

Using a single measure of social class, namely, occupational status, Goodchild (1974) surveyed 28 working-class and 22 middle-class residents of Market Drayton, England. The ability to remember details about imageable objects was independent of social class. Like Appleyard, however, Goodchild found that middle-class maps tended to cover a wider area and incorporate a more widespread road network than did working-class maps. It was concluded that middle-class people tend to conceptualize the environment in a clearer and more coherent manner than working-class persons. Moreover, middle-class people appeared to have a greater emotional investment in the environment. They tended to attach somewhat greater significance to townscape features of high architectural quality or historic interest, and were more concerned with aesthetic improvement than were working people. For example, working-class people placed more stress on items such as "plenty of work" and "near to shops and amusements," whereas middle-class people were more concerned with "attractive surroundings" and "preserving the environment."

Race and culture   A vast literature, partly summarized by Lynch (1960), Lowenthal (1961), and Tuan (1974), records the immense variety of views of the world held by different races and cultures. For example, it has been found that Samoans describe their total impression of a landscape, whereas Moroccans emphasize the details. The Trukese will differentiate the parts of an open space, but pay little attention to edges or dividing lines.

The world of traditional societies tends to be dominated by circular forms, whereas Western man lives in a built environment in which straight lines predominate. Experiments (Segall *et al.*, 1966) have shown cultural variations in susceptibility to optical illusions. These differences in perception and hence of imagery have practical consequences, notably in terms of cross-cultural contacts. From the point of view of pathfinding behavior, the differences between Japanese and American views of navigable space are illuminating (Hall, 1966).

North Americans tend to organize space on a coordinate plan. An extreme example would be an address such as 1729 J Street NE, which tells us in a technical fashion that the house is located in the northeast quarter of town, 10(J) blocks north of a main west-east line and 17 blocks west of a main north-south line. Furthermore, the house will be on the left side of the street about one-third of the way along the block. We thus define space by its edges, which are named paths, and give directions along them in terms of direction and distance. In contrast, the traditional Japanese concept of space involved naming not the paths or coordinates, but the spaces between them. United States troops arriving in Japan in the 1940s were bewildered to find many space names, but few path names. Moreover, Japanese houses were not numbered in spatial order along a street, but in the order in which they were built. Consequently, the Japanese mode of movement did not use a fixed linear route between points, but involved zeroing in on an area and then asking directions.

At a different scale, the difference between Japanese and European and American gardens is instructive. European gardens have traditionally emphasized straight lines, long vistas, and natural vegetation cut to shapes which provide symmetry and permit perspective views of the whole garden from a single point. The Japanese garden is one of winding paths, naturalistic vegetation, surprise views, and the varied textures of pools, paths, and stepping stones. It lacks vistas, and there is a cunning use of empty space, such as areas of raked gravel with a single rock, to express emotion. This general difference in spatial imagery between linear and space emphasis is best expressed in the *Tao Te Ching* of Lao Tse (1958):

> We put thirty spokes together and call it a wheel,
> But it is on the space where there is nothing that
>   the usefulness of the wheel depends;
> We turn clay to make a vessel,
> But it is on the space where there is nothing that
>   the usefulness of the vessel depends;
> We pierce doors and windows to make a house,
> And it is on these spaces where there is nothing that
>   the usefulness of the house depends.

Value system   The meaning people give to their images will vary according to their value system and personality, which in turn may be influenced by culture and social background. Firey (1945), studying central Boston, makes a strong case for group and neighborhood identity based on shared sentiment and symbols, whether dealing with a lower-class Italian area or the central-city island of the rich on Beacon Hill. In Toronto, the new city hall, with two curving walls 27 and 20 storeys high surrounding a central dome, was a rather startling design when built in the 1960s. Two studies of citizens' images of the building suggest that persons with a conservative value system reacted negatively to it, while those of a more liberal frame of mind saw it positively as an essentially progressive symbol (Bunting, 1967; Rockman, 1967).

The physical environment Despite recent emphasis on individual and group variability in image making, a considerable body of research supports the view that "perception and memory of the city . . . seem to be determined by the form of the environment itself" (Carr and Schissler, 1969). The structure of what is to be seen is probably of paramount importance in determining what is seen (Lowenthal and Riel, 1972). In a study of four English towns, the author found that towns which had accessible hilltop viewpoints within the urban area were more readily productive of cohesive images than towns which spread over flat terrain. Comparative town studies in the Netherlands indicate that the formation of an image is easiest where the town has a street plan with a regular pattern, a single dominant path, characteristic nodes, and unique landmarks (de Jonge, 1962). Further, the visual exposure of image elements identified by Lynch was found to be an excellent predictor of their relative dominance in the public image (Hassan, 1965). This renewed emphasis on the physical plan of the city, rather than on cognitive and individualistic differences, is heartening for the planner. Public or group images, rather than individualistic ones, are most useful for planning purposes.

cognitive mapping techniques

We cannot observe a mental map. However, "if a subject behaves as if such a map existed, it is sufficient justification for the model" (Stea, 1969). The problem becomes one of externalizing the image from the mind of the subject. Since 1960 Lynch's methodology has been used at several scales, in a variety of spatial contexts, and in relation to a number of different problems. Frequency of use alone testifies to its flexibility. However, a greater range of more accurate and responsive techniques has been demanded. Nongraphical scaling techniques and procedures drawn from psychophysics have been used on the premise that methods involving map drawing have rarely taken into account variations in drawing skill among respondents. Many respondents refuse to draw maps, or are reluctant to do so. Thus, a large number of rating scales have been developed for assessing the meaning of environments (Blasdel, 1972; Hershberger, 1972), together with several useful environmental image inventories (Kasmar, 1970; McKechnie, 1970).

More radical techniques have been adopted. Asserting that the sketch map is insensitive to what the respondent really knows, Wood and Beck created a graphic language for mapping which was used with apparent success with adolescent tourists in Rome, Paris, and London (Stea, 1974). The technique of toyplay (Blaut and Stea, 1971; Mark, 1972) has also been used. Here a street map of the city is provided, and subjects are expected to place named balsa wood miniatures of landmarks and other elements upon the map. This technique tests respondents' knowledge of absolute location and the location of elements relative to one another.

There has also been a tendency to use surrogates such as drawings, place names, photographs, and slides, as a means of eliciting responses to environments (Diaiso *et al.*, 1971; Honikman, 1972). Klein provided each of his 1,118 interviewees with a pack of cards with places and roads marked on them. Interviewees were asked to pick out those cards which represented city elements which they felt to be in the town center. Milgram's study of New York used photographs in a similar way. Two recent experiments, however, by comparing subjects' evaluations of buildings using the actual buildings, color slides, black and white photographs, and architectural models, have led to serious questioning of the photograph technique (Howard *et al.*, 1972; Seaton and Collins, 1972). Responses to simulations of the buildings were not the same as to the structures themselves. Color slides stimulated responses closer to those evoked by the real building than did the black and white photographs or architectural models.

In another technique evaluation, Rozelle and Bazer (1972) interviewed 52 residents of Houston, Texas, to determine how they saw the city, how they remembered it, and what they regarded as important about it. The three approaches produced different response patterns. Questions about what was seen produced references to landmarks, transportation routes, and general visual impressions; in short. the conventional cognitive map. Edges and nodes, however, were rarely mentioned. Questions on what was important elicited references to social, economic, and cultural elements of the city; no responses to this question related in any direct way to natural features of the environment, such as terrain, weather, or water-related features. When asked what they could remember about the city, respondents mentioned a synthesis of the "seen" and "important" characteristics. This research suggests that verbal tasks can elicit visual imagery similar to that produced by sketch maps. Moreover, the verbal technique is more flexible and seems to elicit a more complete range of responses, especially with regard to the meaning of city elements. These authors comment on the disparities between environmental richness and individual satisfaction, which Lynch regarded as a simple relationship. As Gulick (1963) had noted earlier, it is not sufficient to consider the city as a visual construct, for a city's elements, besides being visual phenomena, are also behavioral and social phenomena.

research trends

Cognitive mapping techniques, for better or worse, result in data which seem to reflect peoples' images of the city. The most obvious difficulty in comprehending what research in this area has produced, however, is the disjointed nature of the research and lack of an accepted terminology, largely the result of approaches from different disciplines. It is possible, however, to organize recent research trends in a spatial fashion: studies dealing with images of the city as a unit; research dealing with paths; and work on the intra-city image elements which are interconnected by paths.

The capsule image   An image of a city as a unit, without internal differentiation, may be termed a capsule image. Capsule images are common in slogans and folk myth; license plates on cars tell us that New Jersey is the Garden State. Desire for a capsule image of world renown is endemic in the United States, and small undistinguished towns seem prone to proclaim themselves Gateway to the South or Asparagus Capital of the World.

Chicago may be taken as an example of this boosterism (Kane and Alexander, 1965; Tuan, 1974). Chicago was once known as Garden City and Gem of the Prairies. This elegance lost, it became Hogopolis, Cornopolis, the Country's Greatest Rail Center, and the Hub of American Merchandising.

New York: an apocalyptic image for the "intellectual versus the city." (Courtesy of Victoria Press).

Hog Butcher for the World,
Tool Maker, Stacker of Wheat,
Player with Railroads and the Nation's Freight Handler;
Stormy, husky, brawling,
City of the Big Shoulders.*

A typical capsule image: Nanaimo, British Columbia. (Courtesy of Agnes Flett.)

Gleason (1972) explores romantic city images, and Strauss (1961) has painstakingly drawn together images of the American City from the writings of journalists, novelists, businessmen, academics, and others. Contrasting group views of the city are reported in telling detail by Studs Terkel in *Division Street: America* (1967).

Capsule images can easily become stereotypes. Further, whole cities may be recognized by a single stereotyped image, as with the Eiffel Tower or, more recently, the St. Louis Gateway Arch, expressly designed for its symbolic value. An image study of the twin cities of Kitchener and Waterloo, Ontario, found that the images people had of the towns varied significantly as a function of place of residence (Norcliffe, 1974). Residents in both cities recognized differences between Kitchener and Waterloo, and because of

---

*   "Chicago," from *Chicago Poems* in *Complete Poems of Carl Sandburg*. New York: Harcourt, Brace and World, 1950. Reprinted by permission.

serious factual errors in these it is suggested that loyalty and prejudice influence peoples' images of both their own and rival towns.

Stereotypes are generally associated with error and warped ideas (Fishman, 1956). Burgess (1974), however, proposing that they contain an initial grain of truth, designed an adjective checklist to measure stereotype images of Hull, England. Three hundred and sixty interviewees were consulted; half were residents of Hull, half were randomly drawn from other areas of England. No person in the latter group had personal knowledge of Hull or had conversed with anyone who had visited Hull. The city of Hull is one of the major fishing ports in Britain; a largely working-class port, it has undergone vast residential redevelopment because of extensive bombing in World War II. This was clear in the images of residents, who checked words such as docks (81 percent), ships (65 percent), and fishy (58 percent). These traditional elements were given higher scores by outsiders, however, with 90, 79, and 75 percent, respectively. Four distinct clusters of attributes were found (Table 5.7). Cluster IV, with low scores for both groups, suggests inappropriate image elements. Cluster I, with high scores for both groups, contains items true of most British cities (congested traffic) as well as the unique capsule image of Hull as a fishy, dockside town. Residents (Cluster II) perceive good qualities quite unknown to outsiders, but are also aware of disadvantages. This rather balanced view contrasts strongly with the outsiders' stereotype of Hull as the archetypal northern English city, cold, grey, dirty, and dull.

The view from the road   Within the city, paths appear to be the image elements most known to most respondents. Unless one has a working knowledge of paths one is unlikely to become acquainted with other elements such as nodes and districts. The role of paths in urban imagery formation was further developed in *The View from the Road* (Appleyard *et al.*, 1964). The authors describe a sequence of visual impressions registered by both driver and passengers of a moving automobile. The methods of analysis used, however, which included introspective analysis of the authors' own experiences, may not be reliable. Highway simulators are also suspect (Parr, 1965).

Carr and Schissler (1969) used the more objective technique of an eye-movement recorder which, mounted on the subject's head, was used to record the eye movements of subjects traveling along Boston freeways. Memory-testing interviews were also administered after the trip. It was found that drivers, passengers, and commuters all tended to remember the same things in the same relative order of importance. Drivers' memory reports, however, were the least detailed. Overall, subjects spent nearly two-thirds of their time looking off the road, but drivers tended to remember on-the-road items to a greater degree than did others. The driving task clearly focuses the driver's attention upon the road, whereas passengers are free to look around. Remembering was clearly based first, on what subjects actually looked at, and

TABLE 5.7

RESIDENT (R) AND NONRESIDENT (NR)
IMAGES OF HULL

Cluster IV (low scores for both R, NR)	Cluster I (high scores for both R, NR)	Cluster III (high scores by NR)	Cluster II (high scores by R)
Poverty	Docks	Unemployment	Good shopping
Affluence	Ships	Heavy industry	center
Modern	Fishy	Slums	Friendly
Derelict	Working class	Cold	Trees, parks
Aggressive	Large public	Smoke	Low wages
	housing estates	Drabness	Isolated
	Congested traffic	Grey	A garden city
	Redevelopment		Historic buildings

Source: Burgess (1974)

second, on the amount of time that the object was in view. The existence of objects and the amount of time they are likely to be in view are proposed as major factors in predicting the content of a traveler's mental map.

Road quality depends on a variety of factors. The sense of motion is largely a visual effect, and featureless, straight roads lacking landmarks are conducive to sleep, frustration, or excessive speed. Continuity appears to be an important feature in assessing the pleasantness of a road, as does the visibility of a sequence of goals, whether landmarks, intersections, or any feature such as a bridge or tunnel which results in an abrupt change in the trip sensation.

Little work has been done on implementing the suggestions made by various authors for making highways more legible as pathfinding devices and safer and more pleasurable to drive upon (Jones, 1972; Pollock, 1972). The essence of these suggestions is that driving quality is enhanced by the development of a visual rhythm within a time sequence (Theil, 1964a; Varming, 1971). Jackson (1956) noted that the mixture of land-uses along roads could be divided into work-related and pleasure-related activities. He contended that more leisure time was being spent in cruising along these thoroughfares, where businesses developed other-directed architecture to attract the passing public. This is confirmed by Goldberg's study of cruising (1969). Jackson suggested a more orderly grouping of land uses to reduce congestion and create lively, leisure-oriented fun-city strips.

Why spatial elements are imageable   Reasons for the imageability of nodes, edges, districts, and landmarks were first explored in a study of respondents' recall of their walks around a city block in central Boston (Lynch and Rivkin,

1959). The authors stated that open space was the most impressive feature of the landscape. Spaces were remembered because they were either clearly defined in form or made evident breaks in the general continuity. Sidewalks were remembered for their materials, texture, and state of repair. There was little unanimity about storefronts, signs, or street furniture. As animate objects, people and traffic were commented on, and both the presence and absence of vegetation provoked comment.

Lynch, however, was mainly concerned with identifying known image elements, rather than attempting to discover why they were known. The search for the reasons why buildings are imageable was systematized by Appleyard in a further study of Ciudad Guyana, Venezuela (1969). Almost 200 buildings in the city were scaled by trained urban designers for the presence of attributes of form, visibility, use, and significance. The environmental knowledge of 300 respondents was then tested by the Lynchean techniques of map drawing, verbal recall, and trip description. The results support some of the suggestions of Milgram but provide much greater detail.

Form Attributes.   As might be expected, movement proved to be a major feature which excited attention; even slight movements in the environment signal danger or provoke interest. *Contour,* defined as sharpness of boundary, isolated buildings from their surroundings and thus made them stand out. *Size* was related to isolation and singularity; a large school, for example, would be more likely to stand out in a residential area than in a downtown zone made up of many large buildings. *Shape* proved to be an imageable characteristic, especially in cases of very simple, very complex, or unique shapes. *Surface* brightness, coarseness, or complexity; *quality;* and the use of *signs* were less imageable attributes.

Visibility Attributes.   Visibility was related to viewpoints, especially *viewpoint significance;* even insignificant buildings at important intersections, bends, or other nodes may be highly imageable. The *immediacy* of a building to the viewing point or circulation system also drew attention. *Viewpoint intensity,* measured by traffic and pedestrian flows past particular points, was less important.

Use and Significance Attributes.   Areas with a high *use intensity* were very prominent in mental maps. *Use singularity,* describing the range of users and activities associated with facilities such as hospitals, cemeteries, and cock-fighting rings, was also a major factor, but *symbolism,* referring to political or historic significance, proved unimportant.

Further analysis of the cognitive maps suggested that the typical pattern of a citizen's knowledge of the city takes the form of three concentric zones.

Around the most-known area, which is the used zone, lies an unused visible zone with a hearsay zone beyond.

Image-Activity Congruence

Much of the above discussion has implied some degree of congruence between an individual's image of the city and his activity space. Milgram *et al.* (1972) state this relationship explicitly. Sex differences in mental maps, where the wife is more familiar with the neighborhood but less familiar with the city at large, may be the result of differing activity patterns. Household division of labor is still largely defined by sex roles, and many wives remain tied to the home base, especially if young children are present in the home. Working with children, Anderson and Tindall (1972) found that home-range size increased with age, and that the range of boys was always greater than that of girls. Individuals were found to have personal, peer-group, and family-based home ranges; their sketch maps generally represented the personal range.

Similarly, the discussion of differential images among long-term residents and newcomers in Ellesmere Port is strongly suggestive of image-activity congruence. Most of the long-term residents lived, worked, and shopped within the area portrayed by their public mental map. In the same way, newcomers located on the periphery tended to live, work, and shop there, and consequently produced a peripheral public image (Fig. 5.6). The only major point of contact between the two was downtown, and even this had both central and peripheral foci. Moreover, work on images which vary according to socioeconomic class, whether in North America, the Middle East, Venezuela, or Britain, strongly suggests that middle-class images are clearer, more detailed, and more coherent because middle-class persons have larger activity spaces than do working-class people.

Accordingly, the fact that poor people tend to have far more constricted images than affluent people has been attributed to the costs of spatial mobility (Orleans, 1973; Michelson, 1970). Appleyard (1969), however, attributed class differences in sketch map styles to education, and Ineichen (1972) has argued that the fact of home ownership alone makes people more aware of the public environment surrounding their home base.

cognition and activity

A number of studies have focused specifically on the relationship between image and activity patterns. Lee's study of neighborhood perception, described in the last chapter, was an attempt to fuse people's awareness space, or image, with their activity space in the overall framework of the neighborhood. Lee proposed that *neighborhood* was a salient experience for most individuals; rather than a vague feeling, it was easily described and readily portrayed in sketch maps. Working in Ohio, Zannaras (1969) came to similar conclusions. A large body of research on journey to work and shopping behavior also supports the concept of image-activity congruence. Sieverts (1969) has stressed the importance of the individual's activities in forming mental images. In studies of migration, Wolpert (1965) speaks of *action space* as the area both known and used by an individual. As activity spaces are largely route networks with occasional nodes, the image-activity congruence concept would suggest a similar mental map pattern. Mental maps have, in fact, been regarded as noncontinuous depictions of "space with holes" (Golledge *et al.*, 1972).

Several studies have noted the warping of distance in mental maps. Saarinen (1969) showed that respondents enlarged the boundaries of the mapped downtown core as distance increased between core and residence. A stretching effect may occur, where boundaries are extended in the direction of the respondent's home (Eyles, 1968). Although Lowrey (1970) tentatively suggested that urban residents' judgments of distance were closely related to geographic distances, Lee (1970) found that perceived distance varied with direction.

Earlier work on distance concepts had led to the formulation of Brennan's law, which stated that the catchment area of an urban store "takes the form of a semicircle on the side of the shop away from the centre of the town" (Brennan, 1948, 111). Lee confirmed that housewives were more likely to use their nearest shopping center if it lay in the in-town (downtown) direction from their homes (Fig. 5.7). Of a series of possible reasons for such behavior, it was proposed that urban residents have a mental image of the city which includes "a focal orientation, built up by the satisfactions of the center" (Lee, 1962, 662). Because of this, distances toward the center are perceived as being shorter than equivalent distances in an out-of-town direction. This was confirmed in an experiment (Lee, 1970), suggesting that Brennan's law of shopping behavior is a special case of a more general principle. Webber (1964b) has termed this phenomenon *the elastic mile*.

The strong emphasis on distance in the above-mentioned research implies that both mental maps and activity patterns may be heavily structured along lines of movement. Adams (1969) suggests that, given a city with major employment and retail foci at the center and with house quality increasing away from the center, the average urban resident's daily activity pattern will be sectoral (Fig. 5.8). Repeated trips to work in the center, to shops in downtown and in suburban shopping centers, and to peripheral recreation facilities, will reinforce his knowledge of home neighborhood, inner city, and outer suburbs *in his sector*. The remainder of the city, infrequently used, is unfamiliar. As a result of a sectoral activity space, the resident's mental image of the city will tend to be wedge-shaped, for activity patterns and awareness of the city have been shown to be strongly linked (Horton and Reynolds, 1971).

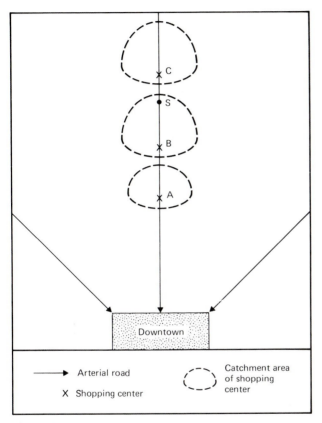

Fig. 5.7

Brennan's law of shopping behavior. Shopper *S* will probably shop at *B*, rather than *C*, although the latter is nearer.

One consequence is that nonregular behavior may be constrained by a city image developed on the basis of daily or weekly behavior patterns. The fundamental link between knowledge and behavior (Asch, 1952; Downs, 1970) may tentatively be expressed as follows:

$$\begin{array}{ccc}
\text{daily/weekly} & & \text{constraints upon} \\
\text{(regular)} \rightarrow \text{cognitive image} \rightarrow & \text{(nonregular)} \\
\text{activity pattern} & & \text{infrequent activities}
\end{array}$$

Though this model is crude, it reasserts that we are not dealing with economic man, with his perfect knowledge, but with real individuals with imperfect knowledge and a predeliction for "satisficing" behavior.

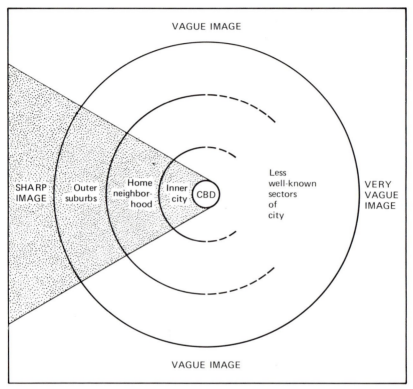

Fig. 5.8

The sectoral mental map concept (after Adams).

Adams attempted to prove the image-activity sectoral hypothesis by a study of intracity residential migration patterns. These patterns were indeed sectoral, but Adams did not attempt to elicit the mental maps of the movers. The need to demonstrate, first, the existence of sectoral mental maps, and second, that such images affect behavior, has been taken up by several workers.

A study of residential preferences in six Australian and New Zealand cities found that many residents disliked their home area and preferred other areas of the city which could not possibly be included within the same sector. On the whole, however, activity spaces were clearly constrained by distance and directional influences to produce sectoral cognitive maps centering around respondents' homes (Johnston, 1972). Further research in Christ-church, New Zealand, found that residents tended to perceive their home sector as a distinct area, and that residents were more familiar with their home sectors than with other areas. Moreover, residents in the same neighborhood tended to agree in their ratings of personal familiarity with a list of 48 suburbs. These findings strongly support the concept of sectoral mental maps based on regular activity patterns.

The second problem, that of investigating the relationship between (sectoral) mental map and less-regular activities, has received less attention. However, Adams' dependence on residential relocation as evidence of image constraints upon search behavior is hardly supported by a report that 30 percent of the residents of a surveyed suburb had found their houses during "casual weekend exploration" (Robinson, 1970). Such exploration is often regarded as recreation. Concentrating on recreation behavior, Mercer (1971) suggests that the sectoral mental map may not be anchored on downtown, based on regular daily behavior, but may instead focus upon recreation areas beyond the city which are visited weekly at most. Mercer reviews a number of studies which discovered wedge-shaped patterns of recreational travel be-havior based on road alignments. His own study of weekend trips and beach visits in Melbourne, Australia, provides further support for the sectoral model. Central city residents, however, had a much less directionally biased travel pattern than suburbanites, and hence are unlikely to have wedge-shaped images of the city. A great deal of work remains to be done on what de Lauwe has termed *behavioral space* (how people live and move), *knowledge space* (where they know alternatives are available), and *aspirational space* (where they would prefer to go were it possible) (Buttimer, 1969). Much of this, however, relates to nonregular behavior and as such does not fall within the compass of this book.

The Value of Image-Activity Studies

Mention has been made throughout the chapter of the value of studies of activity space and cognitive mapping; a brief summary is appended here. One major point is that if there is strong congruence between image and activity, as suggested by several studies, then more accurate *prediction* of behavior may be possible. This would obviously be of great value in both physical and social planning, from the laying out of transport lines to the location of new facilities and amenities which will be perceptually, as well as physically, accessible to their target populations.

Knowledge of seeing behavior, as suggested by the road studies, could help designers make roads more safe, more educative, and more pleasant to drive along. The *aesthetic* argument for image studies is strongly asserted by

Lynch. Steinitz' (1968) discovery that pedestrians have much clearer images than motorists suggests that planning for aesthetic satisfaction in cities should occur on at least two levels. The enclosed, large-scale, largely visual sensations of the motorist must be complemented by the intimate view of the pedestrian, who is also concerned with auditory, olfactory, and tactile sensations. Cullen (1961) in *Townscape* provides some examples of design solutions based on image aesthetics.

Improvement of city legibility could also be useful in improving the citizen's *quality of life* via enhanced awareness, interaction, and reduced stress. Carr (1967) proposes a series of strategies which could increase the exposure of people to a variety of environmental settings and potential interactions, stimulate and facilitate exploration, improve personal attachment to places, thus counteracting rootlessness, improve choice, and enhance the possibility of environmental manipulation by the individual. It might be possible, for example, to enhance the quality of the citizen's image of downtown, the single obvious locale for maximizing citizen interaction. Levels of sonic awareness may also be enhanced. Southworth (1969), after building up an auditory image of the city based on blind persons in Boston, proposes methods of sonic design which would both reduce and control noise and increase the informativeness of the soundscape. The very different perceptions of handicapped people have rarely been considered by designers (Vash, 1972). Duoskin (1970), a wheelchair designer, makes several suggestions to planners for making city navigation easier for the disabled.

Finally, one of the chief means of achieving experience and information in the city is personal mobility. Persons too timid to venture far from their home base lack a wide range of opportunity choices. The experience of the Minneapolis Rehabilitation Center, and duplicated in many American cities, is that poor people may not travel far because of difficulties of *orientation* (Hall, 1969). One of the most basic and important skills to be learned by inner-city dwellers is how to master the public transportation system. Understanding bus and subway systems may not be easy even for the college educated. The problem of orientation in a confusing environment may be illustrated by the difficulties encountered by a European blackbird which, confused by the topographical similarity of beams and struts in a bicycle shed, attempted to build fourteen different nests (von Frisch, 1974). Similarly, a species of wasp which marks its burrow with small landmarks becomes utterly unable to find its way home if these are removed (Carthy, 1965).

Orientation and pathfinding within the city are fundamentally necessary skills which might be enhanced by improvements in transport system legibility and the imageability of areas and nodes. In Lynch's study of Jersey City, one of the most memorable features of which proved to be the New York City skyline, poor legibility was strongly related to orientation difficulties. Route guide makers of the Roman Empire intuitively recognized that the only necessary features were a direction or goal, and a sequence of points between starting point and goal. This tradition is carried on in subway maps today (Fig. 5.9). For better direction finding in the streets, Carr (1967) has called for "information boards . . . at strategic points, preprogrammed to light up the quickest or most scenic route to any destination."

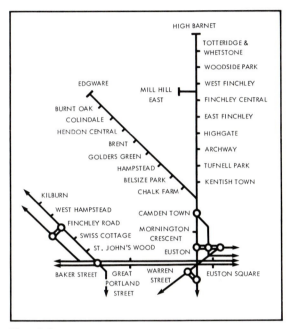

Fig. 5.9

Part of the London underground system map. For clarity, only direction and stops are identified. (Redrawn by permission of London Transport.)

Imagery research is a vital input into the design of even these simple navigational aids. In 1967, the town council of Goole, England, erected a large pedestrian information board in the major thoroughfare, with individual points of interest highlighted on a street map of the town. This base map, north conventionally at the top, showed the River Ouse on the right, and the western entrance of the town to the left (Fig. 5.10). In a survey by the author, however, all 20 mental map respondents ignored compass directions and drew the river to the left, the town entrance to the right. The information board was of use to visitors, but frequently misoriented residents. People adjusted to the board only with difficulty, usually trying to read what was to them an inverted mirror image of reality while, mentally, standing on their

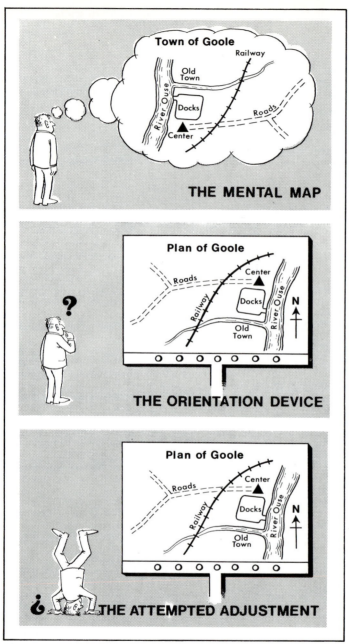

Fig. 5.10

Public versus official images of Goole, England: a case of misorientation. (Reprinted from *Environment and Behavior* 3, No. 2 (June 1971), by permission of the publisher, Sage Publications Inc.)

heads. This example supports the frequent assertion that planners rarely consider how inhabitants comprehend cities, and, when designing new environments, "usually structure them so that they read well at an altitude of 30,000 feet. The methods used by ordinary people on the ground are perhaps more relevant" (Appleyard, 1970).

Much of the above is speculation, for to date most imagery work has been descriptive. Practical application of imagery concepts and techniques to city design problems has rarely been attempted, notable exceptions being Appleyard's work in Ciudad Guyana, Venezuela and that of Lynch in Los Angeles. Studies in Mexico have been able to resolve several controversies among city planners. In one case, Guanajuato planners were unsure whether the city contained one or two major functional centers; the image study revealed three (Stea and Wood, 1974).

Overall, the imagery and activity studies of the last fifteen years have increased awareness of city structure. Using Lynchean analysis, some primary schools are teaching visual awareness to very small children (Bell *et al.*, 1973). Presumably, visually aware people will demand higher design standards. Bell laments, however, the failure to develop a design methodology, based on Lynch's work, which could be applied to the redesign of cities. It is perhaps too early for this at present. Moreover, several recent studies reviewed by Rapoport (1970) suggest that factual information for the designer may not be forthcoming because "the relationship between what is perceived and the nature of the environment is so complex that any simple, predictable relationship becomes difficult to establish". This complex relationship is discussed in greater detail in Chapters 6 and 9.

Summary

1. Home range is viewed as a series of activity nodes interconnected by paths. It has no effective boundary.
2. Time budgets and activity pattern surveys indicate that most discretionary time is spent in the home; they have some predictive value.
3. Activity space surveys indicate the importance of the nodes representing home, work, recreation, and shopping, and may be of value in allocating public facilities and amenities.
4. Individual orientation toward nodes and along paths in the city appears to be achieved through the individual's cognitive (mental) map of the city (an image). Cities are more or less *legible*, and structures more or less *imageable*.
5. Cognitive images are conveniently regarded as being made up of paths, edges, districts, nodes, and landmarks, or clusters of these phenomena.

6. Most individuals emphasize paths, and sketch maps tend to be drawn in a sequential manner.
7. There are strong individual cognitive map variations in terms of age, sex, experience, class, race, culture, and value system. However, the importance of the physical environment in map formation suggests that a public image exists, consisting of the overlap of individual cognitive images.
8. In spatial terms, research has tended to concentrate on the whole city (capsule image), paths, and other elements connected by paths. A variety of image elicitation techniques is available, from Lynch's sketch-mapping method to techniques derived from psychophysics.
9. There appears to be strong congruence between an individual's cognitive map and his regular activity pattern. Both may be wedge shaped, with the point of the wedge anchored in the city core.
10. Image-activity studies are valuable for behavior prediction, facility location, aesthetic improvement, personal orientation and pathfinding, and general design awareness.

Further Reading

CARR, S. (1967), "The City of the Mind," in W. R. Ewald (ed.), *Environment for Man*, pp. 197–226. Bloomington: Indiana University Press.

DOWNS, R. M. and D. STEA (eds.) (1973), *Image and Environment*. Chicago: Aldine.

LYNCH, K. (1960), *The Image of the City*. Cambridge, Mass.: M.I.T. Press.

STEA, D. (1974), "Architecture in the Head," in J. Lang *et al.* (eds.), *Designing for Human Behavior*, pp. 157–68. Stroudsburg, Pa.: Dowden, Hutchinson, & Ross.

II

ENVIRONMENT

6

ENVIRONMENTS

> *All aspects of the environment exist for us only so far as they*
> *are related to our purposes. If you leave out human signifi-*
> *cance, you leave out all constancy, all repeatability, all form.**
>
> *David Lowenthal*

Chapters 2 to 5 of this book were largely concerned with behavior. It is now time to place this behavior in context; behavior always occurs in an environment. Two levels of behavior exist (Tolman, 1932). At the *molecular*, or physiological level, involving stimulus receptors, impulse conductors, and motor (response) effectors, this environment is chiefly the organism's own body. At the *molar* level, behavior takes on its everyday meaning as some form of motor activity, comprising acts which are "more than and different from the sum of [their] physiological parts." Molar behavior takes place largely in the everyday environment of people, animals, plants, and things; this environment is also molar, since we are not considering the molecular structure of environmental objects and organisms but rather the objects and organisms themselves as *gestalts* or unit wholes (Craik, 1970).

Behavior Within Environment

Having surmounted this initial difficulty by regarding organism, behavior, and environment at the molar level, we encounter the problem of distinguishing between the three. Consider, for example, a person eating a

---

* David Lowenthal (1961), "Geography, Experience, and Imagination: Towards a Geographical Epistemology," *Annals of the Association of American Geographers* 51:241–60.

sandwich. At what point does the sandwich cease to be part of the environment and become part of the individual? If the meat in the sandwich is badly cooked, parasites may enter and multiply in the body. Are these intestinal parasites part of the environment or part of the individual? Theoretically, it is impossible to distinguish between the individual organism and the environment. Man may be regarded as a physical object describable in terms of size, shape, density, color, and other characteristics. In this respect he does not differ from any other environmental component. From a nonanthropocentric, ecological point of view (as far as it is possible to take such a standpoint):

> There is only the total environment, of which man is simply one kind of component in relationships with other kinds of components. Indeed . . . from a theoretical point of view . . . man does not exist except in his relationships with other kinds of components (Proshansky *et al.*, 1970).

The ecological perspective is largely a molar one, with an emphasis, for example, on social interaction processes rather than the physiology of the eye-blinks which form a structural part of such interaction. The molar view necessarily results in an emphasis on very complex relationships, so complex, indeed, that organism, behavior, and environment come to be regarded as a single system.

> The ecosystem . . . is an active, energetic composite . . . an intra-dependent activity network . . . It is not only the individual members of the system who act and react, but the total system "behaves" as a whole (Rhodes, 1972).

In this sense behavior is a property of the system rather than an attribute of the individual (Willems, 1973).

As living individuals, however, we are compelled by circumstance to make operational distinctions between the organism, its acts, and the environment in which these acts take place. Inability to distinguish one's self from one's environment is an indicator of mental disturbance. Psychiatric observations have shown that even normal individuals may suffer anxieties about losing the ability to distinguish between themselves and their environment (Klausner, 1971). From an egocentric viewpoint, then, the distinctions between self and environment are crucial. Man is not simply a found object in the environment but, like the beaver and the roots of a tree, is capable of influencing and even of transforming his environment.

Organism-environment-behavior relationships are best conceived in terms of a transactional model. Both organism and environment exist as complex systems, "each with properties of its own, yet both hewn from basically the same block" (Brunswick, 1957). The essence of the interrelationship between the two is a coming to terms across the boundaries between them. The primary mediating process in this coming to terms is behavior (Fig. 6.1). As in a simple stimulus-response model, bits of behavior and bits of environment may be hewn off the block and looked at as independent as well as interdependent items. From this simplistic model emerge two major issues. The influence of man's behavior on environment is considered in Chapters 12–14 in terms of urban planning. The influence of the environment upon the organism's behavior is explored more fully here.

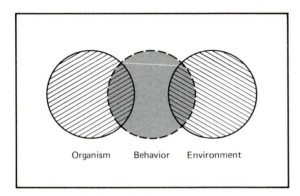

Organism   Behavior   Environment

Fig. 6.1

A transactional model of organism-environment relationships.

The Influence of Environment upon Behavior

If we cannot manipulate the environment for our own advantage, it may manipulate us. Tuan (1972) states that where man is to some degree liberated from the accumulated cultural baggage of his past and lacks concern for the future, he may be regarded as an organism potentially strongly subject to both biologic needs and environmental dictates. The concept of environmental influence on man has a long history (Glacken, 1967) and man's subjugation to nature has been regarded as one of the few major strategies for coping with human problems (Kluckhohn and Strodtbeck, 1961). Several behavioral models have been proposed.

environmental determinism

The concept of environment as dictator, directing man's actions in one direction rather than another, came to popularity in the late nineteenth century. The newly emerged theory of evolution favored the concept, for organic evolution was seen to operate through natural selection, whereby the fittest inhabitants came to occupy each particular place. The idea that climate, soil, terrain, and vegetation might control human behavior was eagerly grasped by historians who, preoccupied with the doings of great men, had previously disregarded these factors. Geographers were keen to seize this means of uniting the physical and human aspects of their discipline.

Moreover, the concept was not really new, but had a classical background. Aristotle's (1932) *Politics* suggested that the inhabitants of cold Europe were thereby active and brave but deficient in thought and skill. In contrast, the peoples of warm Asia were skillful, intelligent, and thoughtful, but indolent and without spirit. Neither too cold nor too hot, Greece maintained the principle of the golden mean by producing a race with the best qualities of both warm and cold regions. Such ideas were later to be carried to excess. The abbé Giraud Soulavie opined (Tatham, 1951):

> The inhabitants of basaltic regions are difficult to govern, prone
> to insurrection, and irreligious. Basalt appears to be an agent
> hitherto unacknowledged in the rapid spread of the Reforma-
> tion.

Equally extreme views of climatic determinism strengthened the feelings of superiority of active Europeans over the indolent inhabitants of warmer climes.

At a less general level, considerable speculation and research has been directed toward elucidating the influence of environment on specific behaviors, such as suicide. Among many other writers, John Milton frequently referred to the harmful effects of cold climates, and today folk myth asserts that high heat and humidity reduce initiative, while foehn (chinook) winds induce nervous tensions. Several studies cited by Thompson (1975) have found positive correlations between suicide rates and temperature, duration of sunlight, frequency of electromagnetic wave impulses, and the passage of both warm and cold fronts. Inverse relationships were found between suicide rate and precipitation, cloud cover, and barometric pressure. However, other studies have produced opposing evidence, and several have failed to discover any significant relationships between suicide rates and weather factors. Recent studies in Houston and Philadelphia deny such relationships. At best, evidence for the effect of weather upon suicide is inconclusive (Pokorny *et al.*, 1963).

The main tenets of environmental determinism, however, were enunciated long before the availability of reliable statistics. Determinism gained respectability with Ratzel's *Anthropogeographie* (1882, 1891) which propounded the thesis that the physical attributes of places determined the human actions that occurred within them. In the United States, as in Britain and Germany, the idea became firmly rooted. Semple, in her *Influences of Geographical Environment* (1911), illustrated Ratzel's thesis by showing how the varied landscapes of North America had conditioned the movements and behavior of those who pioneered and developed them. The concept was carried into the midtwentieth century by Huntington (1945), who saw climatic and physical factors as the *Mainsprings of Civilization,* and by Taylor (1951) who especially emphasized nature's control of behavior in extreme environments such as arctic and tropical deserts. Several modifications to the determinism theory were made, notably the concept of economic or cost determinism. Briefly, one may grow tomatoes in the Arctic because technology permits one to do so; however, the return on such a venture would invariably rule it out unless it was part of some larger strategy.

Determinism involves locking man into an invariable cause and effect system. Determinist writers employ "a heavy battery of causal verbs" (Sprout and Sprout, 1956). Sparse resources, for example, *drove* or *pushed* the British and Japanese to become seafaring nations. Geographical position *determines* a state's foreign policy. Other environmental influences *condition* behavior at all levels, and *lead inevitably* to certain outcomes. Less extreme environmentalists use such verbs as *beckon* and *influence.* Though the Sprouts (1957) regard much of this as rhetoric, the concept of nature's plan is alive in the arguments put forward by conservationist groups against the depredations of developers bent on ecocatastrophe.

environmental possibilism

The extreme views taken by many determinists provoked a reaction among proponents of free will as a major factor affecting human history. A series of French geographers and historians of the 1920s (Febvre, 1925) pointed out that history rarely repeats itself and that the same influences frequently produce different results on different occasions.

Possibilists saw the environment as the medium by which man is presented with opportunities. These opportunities may be realized or they may not; the important factor is the choice and effort of man. Extreme possibilists questioned whether human behavior was determined at all, provoking a strong possibilist-determinist controversy during the 1950s.

A modified possibilist view conceived the environment as the context of behavior which sets limits to the accomplishment of any attempted endeavor. The accumulation of technology, capital, and efficient organizational skills widens these limits and expands the range of effective choice. Before World War I, for example, international offense and defense strategies were based wholly on land and seapower. Hence, distance and penetrability of space had meanings which have become infinitely less restrictive since the development of long-range aerial vehicles after World War II.

environmental probabilism

The world of the determinist was one of inexorable, mechanistic laws. That of the possibilist was to a great extent lawless, and there was little attempt to discover regularities among the series of behaviors and objects which are the product of human will. Probabilism, a more moderate viewpoint which invokes common sense, asserts that lawful relationships exist between environment and behavior. Terrain, climate, and physiology do not dictate. Everywhere there exists a large number of latent opportunities and alternative possibilities for action or inaction. By detailed study of a host of individual examples some enduring relationships between behavior, organism, and environment may emerge (Prince, 1971). If these are accurate, they will be predictive in a probabilistic manner. Thus we may say: "Given an individual *A* with attributes *a, b,* and *c,* set in an environment *E* with characteristics *d, e,* and *f,* and with motivation for action *M,* it is probable that *A* will perform behavior *B."*

Probabilism opens up a large area of uncertainty concerning man's motivations, knowledge, and decision-making modes. Common-sense probabilism assumes that men are fairly knowledgeable, usually rational, and predominantly acquisitive. Using probabilistic models, it is possible to study individual as well as group behavior, as in several studies of the relationship between distance between partners' homes and the likelihood of marriage (Davie and Reeves, 1939; Gould, 1960; Morrill and Pitts, 1967; Mayfield, 1972). The individual's decision cannot be predicted, but his range of possible decisions and the probability of his making any one of them can be ascertained.

Types of Environment

The concept of probabilism suggests that environmental influences are rarely direct and obvious. Instead, they are mediated by cognitive variables. Clearly, people react to the environment only as they perceive it and cognize it in the light of previous experience. Action may therefore take place on the basis of an inaccurate image of the environment, such as a mental map. A distinction may therefore be made between the individual's *psychological environment,* which programs data and provides interpretations in reference to which decisions are made, and his *operational environment,* which sets limits to his actions once the decision is made (Sprout and Sprout, 1957).

Both terminological and conceptual problems have resulted from the use of the word *environment* in a wide variety of contexts. To many geographers, environment traditionally meant the physical world of landforms and climate. To architects, it is largely the structures built by man. Sociologists are concerned with an individual's environment as it consists of social groups made up of other individuals. Child psychiatrists and counselors may use the word loosely to mean the home background of the child. In attempting to add specificity to the concept, a variety of adjectival forms have emerged: social environment, molar environment, physical environment, home environment, psychological environment, behavioral environment, geographical environment, and others, are terms frequently encountered. A surfeit of these has led to alternatives such as ambience, context, surroundings, and milieu.

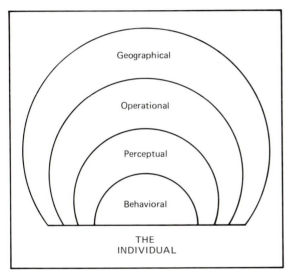

Fig. 6.2

A nested hierarchy of environments. (Redrawn from P. English and R. Mayfield (eds.), *Man, Space and Environment,* 1972, by permission of Oxford University Press and J. Sonnenfeld.)

In an attempt to rationalize the use of a single term to include everything from climate and psychiatric ward to peer group, Sonnenfeld (1972) suggested a nested hierarchy of environments (Fig. 6.2). The entire universe, external to the individual, is the objective *geographical environment.* Within this lies the *operational environment,* which consists of those portions of the world which impinge on man, whether he is aware of this or not. That portion of which he is aware is termed the *perceptual environment.* Awareness may be the result of present sensations or past experience, and may be derived at second-hand. The innermost level, or *behavioral environment,* is that part of the perceptual environment which also elicits a behavioral response toward it, or toward which such a response is directed. This model is reminiscent of the varied layers of activity space conceived by Appleyard, de Lauwe, and others, and reported in Chapter 5.

Sonnenfeld points out that all these subenvironments are regarded as nonreacting, that is, the environment makes adjustments not to man, but to any environmental disequilibrium caused by man. Anonymous people, especially if in large numbers, could also be regarded as a nonreacting environmental element. On the other hand, the model omits environmental stimuli born of interaction with others. In a reacting environment involving friends, lovers, teachers, workmates, and kinfolk, variables such as culture, social status, ethnic group, family affiliation, and life-style become important. All these factors are included in the Sprouts' generalized concept of *milieu*, which consists of all phenomena other than the environed unit's hereditary factors. The milieu includes all human and nonhuman tangible objects, the whole complex of social and cultural patterns, and the psychological environment of the environed unit's images of the milieu.

To operationalize these concepts, however, we must disaggregate milieu, add to Sonnenfeld, and provide a logical behavioral framework (Fig. 6.3). This framework suggests that:

1. *Stimuli* from the environment beyond the environed organism are perceived by the organism. *Perception*, in its strictest sense, refers only to the process of becoming aware, through the senses, of the existence of a stimulus. Perception is physiologically constrained, as with blind or deaf persons. It can also vary with experience, as where training may lead to heightened awareness.

2. The *percept* is then apperceived in the brain. *Apperception* is the process of interpreting something perceived in terms of previous experience. The interpreting mechanism involves a storehouse of cognized information, much of which ultimately derives from the organism's exposure to the particular behavioral norms of the series of social groups to which he belongs. The percept is matched with images already held; a landscape percept, for example, might be compared with a vast array of images in a cognitive atlas (Stea and Downs, 1970).

3. Once matched and understood, the percept becomes a *cognition*, something known by the organism. A cognitive map would be a good example of such an image. A cognition, of course, does not necessarily derive from the perception process, but may be self-generated, for example, by the imagination.

4. If a response to the initial stimulus occurs, it is made with reference to the cognized image. An overt response may not be made, however, in which case the image or construct is stored in the cognitive warehouse until reactivated by a similar stimulus at some later date.

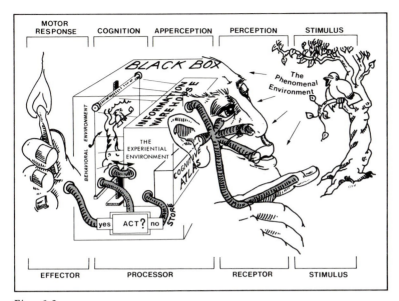

Fig. 6.3

A simple framework for cognizing the behavior-environment interface.

The most important point here is that action in the real world takes place on the basis of the cognitive image of the real world held by the individual. As noted in the previous chapter on cognitive mapping, Boulding stressed that imagery is necessary before purposive behavior can occur. To illustrate the point that, for the individual, the environment exists only as experienced and reconstructed in his brain, a short anecdote from Koffka's *Principles of Gestalt Psychology* (1935, 27) is in order:

> On a winter evening amidst a driving snowstorm a man on horse-
> back arrived at an inn, happy to have reached a shelter after
> hours of riding over the wind-swept plain on which the blanket
> of snow had covered all paths and landmarks. The landlord who
> came to the door viewed the stranger with surprise and asked
> him whence he came. The man pointed in the direction straight
> away from the inn, whereupon the landlord, in a tone of awe
> and wonder, said "Do you know that you have ridden across
> Lake Constance?" At which the rider dropped stone dead at his
> feet.

From the horseman's point of view, his behavior was riding-over-a-plain, not riding-over-a-lake. It was not the objective environment (Lake Constance covered in ice) but the horseman's cognized environment, an image in his brain, which guided his behavior.

Clearly, any action taken in the real-world environment depends not only on the nature of that environment but also upon the actor's personality. In assessing actions in the individual's *life space* (a concept similar to the activity space of Chapter 5), Kurt Lewin (1951) created the formula:

$$B = f(P, E)$$

where behavior *(B)* is a function of the person *(P)* and his environment *(E)*. It is on the basis of Lewin's *field theory,* interpreted by the geographer Kirk (1963), that the following model of three separate but linked environments is proposed.

the phenomenal environment

Lewin's term, this refers to the world of objects *per se.* Clearly, we operate in only part of it, but we may have knowledge of other parts. Organisms react not only to phenomenal objects, but also to imagination and food, sex, and other drives. None of these is part of the phenomenal environment, which consists of all external conditions or influences impinging upon the environed unit, whether or not he is aware of them. It is an environment of human, nonhuman, and inanimate objects, and for convenience may be divided into the *human environment,* which consists of people considered as objects (for example, strangers in street or subway), and the *physical environment,* which consists of all other objects. In architectural terms and in the context of city structures, the physical phenomenal environment is often known as the *built environment.* The phenomenal environment may be measured and quantified according to what are regarded as objective standards. Unmodified by perceptual experience, it is the same for all men.

For the sake of brevity, the term *environment* is used alone in later chapters; it should be taken to refer to the phenomenal environment. *External, built,* and *nonpersonal environment* are used in the same way.

the personal environment

The personal environment is Lewin's *P.* It contains two components. The first, following Lewin, is the *behavioral environment,* which is the image of the phenomenal environment held by the individual. First expressed by the psychologists Koffka (1935) and Lewin (1936), this concept has received considerable attention from geographers (Kirk, 1951, 1963) and in particular those in the fields of urban and resources planning (Craik, 1970; Golledge *et al.,* 1972). Cognitive maps are behavioral environments. As was learned from mental map studies, it is difficult, if not impossible, to elicit and measure an individual's behavioral environment with accuracy.

The behavioral environment, though based on perceived stimuli from the phenomenal environment, is also strongly influenced by the individual's personality, a complex of attitudes, beliefs, dispositions, preferences, and values. This storehouse of referrable information is the *experiential environment*, because it is built up largely from the experiences of the individual. As will be seen in Chapter 9, data from the experiential environment are also difficult to elicit. However, as it is based on experience, its content may partially be inferred from a study of the context of that experience.

the contextual environment

The apperception process involves the matching of perceptions with information already held in the experiential environment. The latter, as we have seen, derives from experience. Beliefs, attitudes, preferences, and other personality attributes derive not from the individual alone, but are largely colored by his experiences as a member of family, ethnic, social class, cultural, national, and life-style groups. This contextual environment, as a major input into the apperception process, has some effect upon the form of the behavioral environment and therefore on the individual's actions based upon his image.

Dividing the contextual environment into manageable sections is not easy. Clearly, *culture* (or subculture) is a major factor in one's behavior. A vast array of anthropological and geographical works suggests that culture is a fundamental influence on one's activities, from modes of war- and love-making to tastes in landscape and art (Lowenthal and Prince, 1965; Tuan, 1974). The particular life-style of an individual or group may be regarded as a subculture. As seen in mental map and activity studies, *social class* (measured by education, income, and influence) is another fundamental variable affecting both how we perceive and how we use space. A third major factor appears to be *stage in the life cycle*. Clearly, infants and senile people are heavily restricted in their behavior. Children suffer parental restrictions, but parents equally undergo many behavioral restrictions when in the child-rearing phase.

Strong support for these three dimensions is provided by the residential pattern analyses of psychologists (Tryon, 1955, 1958, 1967), sociologists (Shevky and Bell, 1955), and geographers (Murdie, 1969). With data on the social attributes of urban census tracts and using a variety of factor and cluster analyses known collectively as social area analysis, these workers have identified clusters of census tracts possessing similar configurations of demographic attributes.

Buying and locating a house is one of the major economic, psychic, and social investments of one's life. People appear to locate their residences in areas where they themselves conform to the demographic attributes of the existing residents. Parents in the child-rearing stage are keen to find a street with other children to act as playmates; they also look for neighborhoods with good schools and low levels of delinquency. Income constraints result in expensive view lots and seafront locations being taken by the rich. The movement of a *nouveau-riche* tradesman into such an area may be resisted on account of education, rather than income differences. Finally, racial, cultural, and subcultural differences transcend life cycle and social class factors. Black ghettos contain groups with varying income and educational levels. Segregation is a fact of life in most Western cities, but it obviously has many more dimensions than the racial segregation which has been such an emotional and legislative issue in the United States.

Since social area analysis was first developed in the 1950s, the technique has been used to derive residential segregation patterns for a large number of North American cities. The analysis isolates, from a vast array of demographic variables, those clusters of variables which account for most variation in the data being manipulated. In almost every case, the same three variables have been found to be the most important explicants of residential segregation patterns at the census tract level:

> *Life Level.*   Also known as social rank and economic status, life level is chiefly measured by education, occupation, and income.
>
> *Life Cycle.*   Also known as family status, or urbanization, life cycle concerns the age of household heads, ages of children (if any), and household size.
>
> *Life-Style*   Also known as ethnic status or segregation, life-style is a cultural attribute based on racial, ethnic, or national group.

Although the above analyses were conducted with aggregate data, it has been suggested that knowledge of an individual's life level, life-cycle stage, and life-style may provide sufficient data for a fairly good prediction of where he will live in the city, and possibly even of his likely behaviors and attitudes to life (Yeates and Garner, 1971).

The above statement is based on Berry's (1965) hypothesis that the three factors will tend to form three distinct spatial patterns in the city. Very briefly, it seems that minority ethnic groups, hemmed in by prejudice and zoning laws, tend to group in *clusters*. Based on the work of Hoyt (1939), whose analysis of a large number of cities found that high-income and low-income people tend to take up spatially polar opposite positions in residential terms, life-level groups tend to form *sectors* or wedges. Partly because of the outflow of young families to the suburbs, and the inflow of both old and young childfree persons to central-city apartments, life-cycle groups tend to locate in *concentric rings*. The existence of this very simplified triplex pattern was brought out most forcefully by Murdie's (1969) analysis of Toronto for both 1951 and 1961 (Fig. 6.4). By superimposing maps based on all three factors, Murdie suggested, homogeneous communities could be identified.

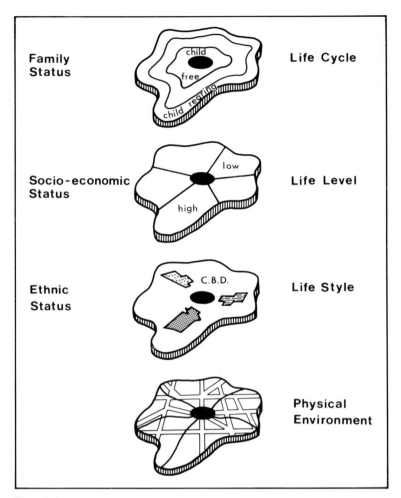

Fig. 6.4

Idealized model of urban residential segregation. (Redrawn from Robert Murdie, *Factorial Ecology of Metropolitan Toronto 1951–61*, 1969, by permission of the author and the University of Chicago Department of Geography.)

Relationships

In seeking to identify relationships between the phenomenal, personal, and contextual environments, the framework originally proposed by Craik (1972) is useful (Fig. 6.5). There is interplay between all three environments, resulting in six relationships.

The influence of the phenomenal environment upon personal (relationship *B*) and group *(F)* behavior has already been discussed in terms of the determinist-possibilist controversy. Further discussion of environmental determinism, where the phenomenal environment is the independent, and human behavior the dependent variable, will be found in Chapters 7 and 8. From the possibilist point of view, the individual is a major factor in influencing the environment *(A)*. He may also influence the social system *(D)*, and influence the environment thereby *(E)*. The individual's personal environments are discussed in Chapter 9.

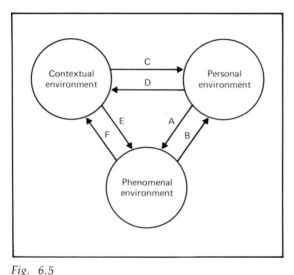

Fig. 6.5

Environmental interrelationships. (Modified from K. H. Craik, "An Ecological Perspective on Environmental Decision-Making," *Human Ecology* 1, 1972, p. 72, by permission of the author and Plenum Publishing Corporation.)

Finally, the contextual environment clearly has a major part to play in shaping the environment *(E)*. This has been a major focus for geographers and conservationists since George Perkins Marsh (1864; Thomas, 1956). The effect of the contextual environment on the individual *(C)*, however, is also very strong, and thus indirectly influences the environment *(A)*. These relationships are discussed in life-style, life-cycle, and life-level terms in Chapters 10 and 11.

Summary

1. Only in operational (and real-life) terms can we fully distinguish between organism, environment, and behavior.
2. Determinism, possibilism, and probabilism are the three major philosophical models for approaching the problem of man-environment interrelationships. Probabilism is probably the most useful.
3. Confusion concerning the varied meanings of "environment" may be reduced by careful consideration of the distinction between personal (behavioral and experiential), phenomenal (physical and human), and contextual environments.
4. The subjective behavioral environment, upon the basis of which we act, is a product of stimuli from the phenomenal environment modified by the experiential environment, which itself derives from the contextual environment.
5. Probable difficulties in measuring the constructs of the personal environment (discussed more fully in Chapter 9) emphasize the importance of the measurable contextual environment as an influence on individual behavior.

Further Reading

CRAIK, K. (1972), "An Ecological Perspective on Environmental Decision-Making," *Human Ecology* 1:69–80.

KIRK, W. (1963), "Problems of Geography," *Geography* 47: 357–71.

SONNENFELD, J. (1972), "Geography, Perception, and the Behavioral Environment," in P. W. English and R. C. Mayfield (eds.), *Man, Space, and Environment*, pp. 244–51. New York: Oxford University Press.

SPROUT, H. and M. SPROUT (1956), "Environmental Factors in the Study of International Politics," *Journal of Conflict Resolution* 1: 309–28.

7

THE PHENOMENAL
ENVIRONMENT: HUMAN

There was an old person of Stroud,
Who was horribly jammed in a crowd,
Some she slew with a kick, some she scrunched with a stick,
*That impulsive old person of Stroud.**

Edward Lear

Lear's impulsive old person perceived her fellow humans, crowded around her, as objects contributing to her discomfort. The environment in which we operate does not consist solely of ourselves and an arrangement of nonhuman objects; it also contains other people. Most often, the effect of other people on our behavior operates through a complex set of norms, or expectations, which are related closely to such personal attributes as sex, age, social class, ethnic group, and the like. In the modern urban world, however, we frequently regard other persons less as beings with the aforesaid attributes than as mere bodies. This is notably so in central-city situations, especially during the working day. It is estimated that in midtown Manhattan an individual could meet almost one quarter of a million other people within a ten-minute walking radius from his office. Clearly, he will know only a minute proportion of these, and can relate to only a few more as the familiar strangers he sees every day. The rest are objects which frequently impede his progress. In Tokyo, slick coats are sold to passengers on the subway to facilitate their progress through the hordes of other riders. On reaching the subway car, the rider is pushed into its congested interior by members of a special squad of pushers employed by the subway authority.

Though most people are able to adapt operationally to such situations, there have been many suggestions that such intense crowding may have

---

*   Edward Lear (1846), *A Book of Nonsense*. London: Simpkin, Marshall, Hamilton, and Kent.

deleterious psychological and physiological effects. Personal space is clearly violated. Complained one subject: "People get so close . . . you're cross-eyed. It really makes me nervous. They put their faces so close it feels like they're *inside* you!" (Hall, 1966).

The effect of other people on one's behavior does not wholly depend upon crowding and large numbers. Psychologists studying *social facilitation* (Zajonc, 1965) have found that persons at a convivial party, for example, will be stimulated to eat and drink more than if they were dining alone. Rats in crowded conditions behave similarly. In pubs and bars it has long been known that people in groups drink larger quantities than lone drinkers (Mass Observation, 1943). Sommer (1965), in a study of drinking in Edmonton, Canada, found that groups spent twice as long in the beer parlor than did isolates; the total amount of beer consumed varied directly with the amount of time spent in the pub. Of course, this may be accounted for by the hustling quality of Canadian beer parlors compared to the more leisurely and individualistic climate of the English pub or American neighborhood bar.

Beer drinking is directly related to urine production. Male public urinals often consist of a long line of open stalls. Observation over several years suggests that most males are careful to choose a stall which has at least one vacant stall on either side. The sudden occupation of an adjacent stall by another body may lead to embarrassment on the part of the sensitive (Goffman, 1972, 85), and in some cases to the abrupt termination of urinary behavior. This appears to be a case of crowding involving very few persons, and could be termed *social disfacilitation.*

Stimulus Deprivation and Overload

Other bodies of the same species, then, can affect an organism's behavior by their mere presence. The chief problem in this area is not social facilitation but the possibility that the presence of large numbers of one's fellows in a constricted space may lead to mental, physical, and behavioral ill-health. The suggested relationship between crowding and pathology has been so well publicized in newspapers and periodicals that it may attain the status of a modern folk myth.

Briefly, the argument runs as follows:

1.   By definition, urban areas exhibit very high population densities. This is especially marked if they are compared with rural areas, where man emerged and where he remained *en masse* until the twentieth century.

2.   These high densities are so great that individuals feel crowded. Crowding is perceived in the form of an overload of stimuli from the phenomenal environment impinging upon the individual. In part this operates via the reduction of territorial capability, especially at the personal-space and home-base levels.

3.   Overstimulation leads to physiological and psychological stress. In seeking to withdraw from the overstimulation of crowding situations, many individuals withdraw from society; hence the problem of loneliness in big cities, expressed in Riesman's *The Lonely Crowd* (1970). Withdrawal, in the midst of stimulus overload, leads to stimulus deprivation, which is also stressful.

4.   Stress, whether from stimulus overload or deprivation, manifests itself in pathologies such as mental illness, physical (psychosomatic) illness, or deviant behavior, ranging from excessive aggression in interpersonal relationships to extremes of deviance such as assault and rape.

A wealth of evidence, from concentration camp literature to psychological experiment, has been cited in support of this argument. Before detailing this, however, the nature of the alleged stressors, stimulus overload and deprivation, will be considered.

sensory deprivation

Most of the work in this area has been devoted to demonstrating the deleterious effects of drastic reductions in stimulation levels (Solomon *et al.*, 1961). Subjects have been placed masked, padded, and immobile in soundproof rooms, or totally immersed (with breathing apparatus) in tanks of warm water. By these means the senses of smell, touch, sight, hearing, and taste are reduced to the lowest possible levels. In such conditions of almost zero stimulation, and most notably when suspended in the water tank, the subject feels tactually only his supports and the mask, most bodily sensations having been reduced by the elimination of gravity. Besides this, he hears only his own breathing and some faint sounds from the water pipes.

After a few hours, subjects' thinking processes became disorganized. After about one day the borderline between sleep and wakefulness became less distinguishable. Later, subjects developed hallucinations similar to those experienced during mescaline intoxication. Some had paranoid delusions or seizures. Some of these more extreme effects were demonstrated in the film *The Mind Benders* (more subtle effects were demonstrated in *Fahrenheit 451*). Above all, subjects showed an extreme desire for stimulation; considerable periods were spent thrashing around in order to achieve this.

Similar results appear in cases where individuals have been inadvertently isolated, as when cast away at sea alone in a small boat. Lilly (1956) reviews autobiographical accounts of such occurrences, including polar camp and solitary confinement accounts. In almost all cases the solitaries withdrew into themselves, establishing an inner life so vivid that the individual's readjustment to society took much time because of the need to reconstitute his inner criteria of sanity. Christopher Burney, for example, when placed with other prisoners after 18 months solitary confinement, was afraid to speak in case he should appear insane (Burney, 1952). In general, persons undergoing prolonged isolation experience many of the symptoms of the mentally ill.

sensory overload

An experiment by Zuckerman *et al.* (1969) illustrates the difference between overload and deprivation. Subjects were exposed to sensory deprivation in the form of lying on a bed wearing gauntlets, in total silence and darkness. In the sensory overload condition they occupied the same cubicle, but this time were accompanied by two slide projectors, one filmstrip projector, one movie projector, two tape recorders playing three separate channels of sound through four speakers, and a strobe light programmed for three different rates of flash. All the machinery worked on a randomized basis to prevent any perception of sequence. A control group experienced the normal experimental room.

Subjects were asked afterwards to fill out an adjective checklist and to rate their degree of satisfaction with the experience. During the experiment, measurements of their heart rate, breathing rate, and galvanic skin response (GSR) were taken. Compared with the control group both stimulus overload and deprivation subjects showed high rates of hostility and adrenocortical arousal, a symptom of stress. Though there was little overall difference in heart rate, breathing rate, and GSR, there were significantly greater fluctuations in the overload condition. Most subjects gave more favorable ratings to the overload than to the deprivation condition. Other experiments have produced similar results.

an optimal level of stimulation

Organisms clearly exhibit a need for stimulation; overstimulation is usually preferred to understimulation. A large part of an organism's everyday activity is aimed at heightening stimulation levels (Wohlwill, 1966). Without adequate stimulation, the development and maintenance of normal behavior is impossible. There can be too much stimulation, however. This leads to the concept of an optimal level of stimulation (Fig. 7.1).

Optimal stimulation levels will clearly vary between individuals and groups. Helson's Adaption Level theory suggests that for any stimulus type the individual establishes an adaptation level (AL) which determines his response to any given stimulus of that type. Deviations from the AL in either direction will be evaluated positively, within a certain range (novelty), but beyond that range will become unpleasant (strangeness). Differences in AL may be illustrated by the rush-hour commuter, who may suffer no more arousal from his daily battle with traffic or subway than does his wife when taking a quiet bus ride through suburban streets.

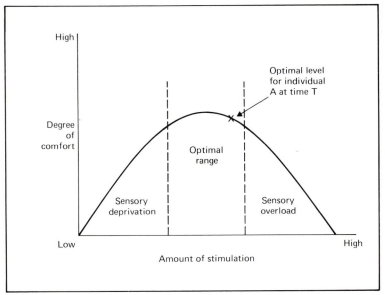

Fig. 7.1

The concept of an optimal level of stimulation.

The husband's evaluation of his experience, however, is still likely to be more negative than his wife's. Wohlwill argues that such surface adaptation to overload might in fact be hiding some of the cumulative effects of long-term exposure to overload. These effects might include heightened arousal thresholds, lessened frustration tolerance, or such an ability to cut off the outside world that the problems of lack of sensitivity or even deprivation may occur. Stress, whether hidden or manifested, frequently results, and may become a major factor influencing human behavior (Wolpert, 1966).

This brings us back to the possible stressing effects of the human phenomenal environment on individuals and groups. It is "quite conceivable that monotony and complexity may exist side-by-side in our urban environment" (Kates and Wohlwill, 1966). Evidence supporting the opinion that the sensory overload and deprivation conditions of city life induce stress which in turn results in illness and antisocial behavior will now be presented.

The Experience of Cities

Anyone coming from a small town or the countryside to live in a major city has experienced some degree of culture shock. Interpersonal relationships among the citizens of New York and Chicago vary significantly from those of Gopher Gulch or Telegraph Creek. The sheer number of people that the individual encounters encourages him to treat others as objects. These objects create frustration for the individual by impeding him or competing with him for scarce resources, such as cabs or breathing space on public transportation. The noise is intense; there is untidiness and clutter. The city seems endless, for it merges with the next city in a continuing sprawl.

Several popular accounts of this phenomenon have appeared. Newspaper stories such as "Crowding Makes Nasty People" (Guilion, 1971) and "Frustrations of the Metropolis Breed Rudeness and Insensitivity" (Kaufman, 1970) present common scenarios:

> Tensions on the subways. Predatory motorists and aggressive pedestrians. Argumentative cab drivers. Honking horns. Surly waiters, antagonistic clerks, querulous customers. Clash. Anger. Hostility.

Visitors to New York are appalled: "Sometimes people bumped into me without apology; . . . two people literally engaged in combat for . . . a cab; . . . drunks . . . were bypassed without a glance. People didn't seem to care about each other at all" (Milgram, 1970). These and other deviances are compared in *The Human Zoo* to the behavior of animals incarcerated in the prisons we know as zoos (Morris, 1969).

Interpersonal rudeness may perhaps be tolerated. However, it is also associated with a total disregard of persons who are defined as irrelevant to one's personal needs. This is most apparent in the area of bystander intervention during crises. People who would willingly help their home-base neighbors during crisis will stand idly by while strangers are publicly assaulted or beaten to death. In 1964, Kitty Genovese was stabbed to death during a period of over half an hour. The incident was witnessed by 38 respectable New Yorkers, none of whom responded to her cries for help nor even called the police. This well-known incident, and the many like it, illustrate the point that although Miss Genovese may have had an extended network of friends in the city, she also needed the assistance of strangers. If strangers are unwilling to help, Webber's world of community without propinquity (Chapter 4) is unworkable unless we travel nonstop between activity nodes in armor-plated vehicles.

Experimental studies have established the principle that the larger the number of bystanders, the less likely any one of them will intervene in an emergency. A similar principle operates in seminars, where the larger the group the less pressure each individual feels to contribute. Willingness to help in small crises is also low in cities. Small-town residents have been shown to be more likely to let strangers use their home telephone, provide street directions, mail a letter for a stranger, and do small favors generally.

It is also likely that in small towns a deviant act would arouse attention and be interfered with; the likelihood of its occurrence would also be less. Other factors are important, however. Zimbardo (1969) left an unattended automobile, license plates removed and hood opened, in each of New York's Bronx and Palo Alto, California. The Palo Alto car remained untouched for several days. Within 24 hours, however, the Bronx car had been stripped of all removable parts, and at the end of three days was merely a heap of metal. Much of the vandalism was performed by well-dressed white adults under the observation of several bystanders.

All this evidence suggests that city dwellers are in a constant state of anonymity vis-à-vis their fellows. Constant subjection to stimulus overload has bred norms of noninvolvement. So much observable deviant behavior occurs in cities that an individual who tried to help or interfere would be unable to keep his own affairs in order. Moreover, our welfare state system has provided such numerous assistance agencies, from policing to counseling, that personal involvement appears superfluous. Goffman, in *Behavior in Public Places* (1963) suggests that lack of civility in cities results from the breakdown of traditional patterns of interpersonal respect. Milgram (1970) blames this on sensory overload. Clearly, city life exposes us to an enormous amount of nervous stimuli, much of which we must block out, thus desensitizing us to the world. Further, in cities we grow to accept other people not as individuals, but as role players, such as bus driver, policeman, lawyer, shop assistant, or elevator operator. And our increased observation of deviance, by adaption, leads to a greater toleration of deviance.

Many of these ideas were suggested by the early sociologists. Simmel (1957), more than two generations ago, spoke of the intensification of nervous stimuli as a major feature of city life. City people, according to Simmel, lack spontaneity and are blasé. Wirth (1938) suggested that urban life hardens people to deviance and reduces meaningful personal interaction to the playing of "highly segmental roles." In order to support the evidence of subjective experience and the occasional associated experiment, more detailed analysis of urban behavior is needed.

Deviance and Pathology in Cities

It is generally thought that cities have proportionately higher incidences of deviance and pathology than do rural areas, whether measured by venereal disease rates, marital breakdowns, drug usage, lead poisoning in children, murder, unemployment, unfit housing, or mental health breakdowns. Lack of comparable data on an intercity basis, however, prevents an objective statistical analysis on a broad scale. Cappon (1970b), comparing Baltimore and Toronto with arbitrary thresholds of acceptability, found that rates of deviance and pathology in Baltimore were beyond the level of acceptability, whereas Toronto appeared far healthier. Others suggest that cities are no more unhealthy than the countryside (Srole, 1972). It is postulated, however, that unemployed or deviant persons may gravitate to the cities, because of the advantages of urban anonymity, perceived opportunity, and push factors in the nonmetropolitan environment. Despite the complex cause-and-effect migration system of push and pull, it is at least clear that it is in the larger metropolitan areas that the majority of the Western world's population now resides. Deviance and pathology in cities therefore claim our greatest attention.

physical pathology

Health is not the absence of disease, but a positive synthesis of fitness and creativity. Disease, however, is a positive indicator of lack of health. Medical geographers have been mapping the incidence of disease since Dr. Snow in the mid-nineteenth century shed light on the epidemiology of cholera by means of distribution maps of diseased residents and polluted public water pumps. Several atlases of disease, such as Britain's *National Atlas of Disease Mortality*, emphasize that diseases such as lung cancer, bronchitis, and tuberculosis have heavier incidence rates in cities than in nonurban areas (Howe, 1963).

Similar work has been done on an intracity basis, and McHarg's (1969) analysis of physical disease in Philadelphia is typical. Eight types of physical disease were chosen: heart disease, tuberculosis, diabetes, syphilis, cirrhosis of the liver, amoebic dysentery, bacillary dysentery, and salmonellosis. Incidence was measured per 100,000 population and mapped. The highest incidences of all diseases were in the center of the city, with a gradual reduction toward the suburban periphery. In relative terms, therefore, the central city was physically unhealthy, whereas the suburbs were fairly healthy. Other studies have revealed similar relationships between the poor physical environments of central cities and high disease incidence, but advances in medical treatment are reducing the differences between city and suburbs (Martin, 1967). Moreover, methodological techniques in such studies are suspect and generalizations to a wide array of cities cannot be made. Disease mortality atlases confirm this, showing that some cities (usually professional and cultural) are generally far healthier than others (generally industrial).

mental pathology

One of the most revealing studies in the field of mental disease in urban areas was performed by Faris and Dunham, who analyzed the distribution of residences of persons with mental disorders in Chicago and Providence, Rhode Island. Several types of mental disease and associated social pathologies were studied, notably schizophrenia, manic-depressive states, alcoholism and drug addiction, senility psychoses, and general paralysis resulting from syphilis.

In every case except manic-depressive states, the highest incidence of mental disease was found in the central-city core. Combining the rates for specific disease categories into a general insanity rate, Faris and Dunham (1939, 25) found that "the highest rates are clustered about the center of the city and the rates are progressively lower at greater distances from the center" (Fig. 7.2). A large number of subsequent studies, most of which support the center-periphery incidence dichotomy, have been reviewed by Dunham (1965).

A single psychosis will be singled out as illustrative of this pattern. Psychosis is a massive disintegration of the personality such that the individual cannot deal effectively with himself or his surroundings. Schizophrenia is regarded as the most severe psychosis; it generally causes life-long invalidism. The expectation of schizophrenia in the general population is approximately 1 percent, and "from many points of view it is the biggest single problem in the whole of medicine" (Richter, 1957).

Faris and Dunham found that the incidence of schizophrenia tended to occur in a pattern very similar to that of all mental disorders (Fig. 7.3). In more detail, the highest rates were found in high-rental apartment districts, skid row areas, and predominantly black areas. State hospital records showed a heavy concentration of admissions from the central city. Private hospital records included suburban admissions for the first time, but here again the highest rates were from the expensive apartments and hotels of the city center. One of the most recent studies, of Nottingham, England, confirms this pattern, for 68 percent of the patients lived within four kilometers of the city center (Giggs, 1973).

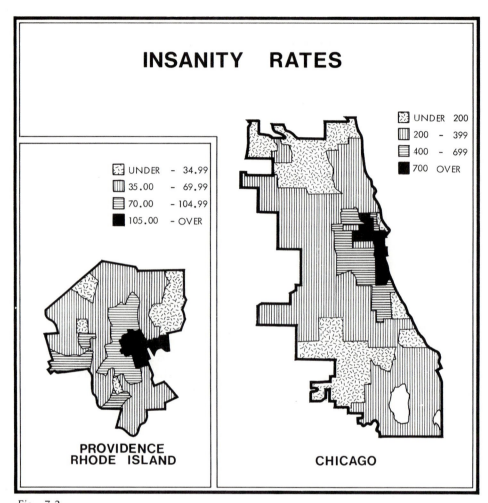

Fig. 7.2

Distribution of urban insanity rates, 1930. (Redrawn from Robert E. Faris and H. Warren Dunham, *Mental Disorders in Urban Areas*, 1939, 1965, by permission of the authors and The University of Chicago Press.)

social pathology

As might by now be expected, central-city areas show higher incidences of social pathology than do suburban areas. In Philadelphia, for example, McHarg (1969) mapped rates of homicide, suicide, drug addiction, alcoholism, robbery, rape, aggravated assault, juvenile delinquency, and infant

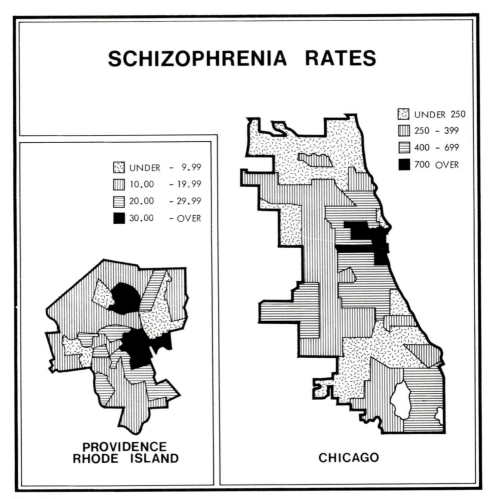

Fig. 7.3

Distribution of urban schizophrenia rates, 1930. (Redrawn from Robert E. Faris and H. Warren Dunham, *Mental Disorders in Urban Areas*, 1939, 1965, by permission of the authors and The University of Chicago Press.)

mortality (often an index of parental neglect). All showed the center-periphery dichotomy found in studies of physical and mental pathologies. Studies of crime and vice since those of Reckless (1934) in the 1930s have found these same high central-city incidences. Typically, city vice areas were found to locate in areas with high rates of other crime and social problems, immigrant and racial colonies, a disproportion of the sexes, large numbers of rescue missions and pornographic outlets, and the like. Even domestic quarrels to which the police are called occur more frequently in high-density areas (Ketcham, 1971).

Juvenile delinquency may be taken as an example of social deviance. From the Boston, Massachusetts, metropolitan data for 1966 it is clear that arrest rates vary with urban size, from an average of 15 per thousand in cities to 11 per thousand in towns. The only exception to this is in small coastal resort towns where visiting youths contribute to high arrest rates. The 1970 police statistics for the much smaller metropolitan area of Victoria, British Columbia, show higher rates of delinquency in the core municipalities (15 per thousand) than in the suburbs (8) and the semirural periphery (5). Several comprehensive reviews of delinquency confirm declining delinquency rates from center to periphery (Roucek, 1958; Shaw and McKay, 1942). Once again, however, there are many methodological problems involved in data comparison. One of the more obvious ones appears to be the greater leniency with which police treat suburban offenders, resulting in lower arrest rates. Moreover, the Boston figures clearly show that although larceny and auto theft rates were similar in both city and suburbs, city-center offenses generally tended to be of a more visible type, such as vandalism and running away from home. Finally, arrest rates cannot be equated with the occurrence of crime.

possible explanations

Most authors reporting the center-periphery dichotomy in incidence of social, mental, and physical pathologies have attempted explanations of the phenomenon. Unfortunately, though many correlative relationships have been found, unequivocal relationships of causality are rare. Two major explanatory tendencies are apparent, one concentrating on effects of the physical environment, the other on the human environment.

Physical environmental explanations generally involve pollution, considerations of overstimulation such as noise, or inadequate housing conditions. Urban noise is intense and of long duration; heavy center-city traffic may emit 90 decibels of unwanted sound. Constant exposure to such noise levels can permanently impair hearing. Rocket engines reach 150 decibels; experiments have shown that 160 decibels can kill rats and mice (Gordon, 1964). Noise may seriously disturb sleep by interrupting dreaming sequences; many people, notably those living near airports, exhibit mental fatigue from the effort needed to remain asleep despite noise (Bailey, 1972). Sudden noises can increase body tensions, adversely affecting blood pressure, heart rate, and the whole nervous system. Even noises that are not sufficient to disturb normal hearing can be emotionally upsetting (Farr, 1967). McHarg has also pointed out that the central city is not only noisy but heavily polluted, central Philadelphia having much higher incidences of settled dust, suspended dust, and sulfate content than peripheral areas. There are clearly established links between levels of physical and chemical pollutants, which are highest over city centers, and both physical and mental abnormalities (Esser, 1974).

Other workers have suggested a relationship between housing and pathology. Some have emphasized housing *condition* or quality. A review by Schorr (1963) concludes that housing condition clearly influences physical and mental health, especially where the housing quality is extremely inadequate. That this is feasible may be inferred from a recent survey of United States urban families on welfare (Harris and Lindsay, 1972, 43):

11.2 percent had no private use of a kitchen;

24.0 percent had no hot or cold running water;

22.5 percent had no private use of a flush toilet;

22.4 percent had no private use of a bathroom with shower or tub;

30.1 percent had insufficient beds for all family members;

24.8 percent had insufficient furniture to permit everyone to sit down while eating;

45.8 percent could not regularly provide milk for the children because of lack of money;

17.4 percent had occasionally kept their children from school because of lack of clothing or shoes.

Such factors can either promote or exacerbate physical ill-health. Moreover, emotional disturbances are also likely. Oscar Lewis (1959, 9), studying five families of different backgrounds in Mexico, remarked: "Where hunger and discomfort rule, there is little spare energy for the gentler, warmer, less utilitarian emotions and little chance for active happiness." And emotional disturbance or deprivation may result in social deviance.

The relationship between housing quality and health may best be tested by improving peoples' housing conditions and monitoring their health over a considerable period before and after the improvement. Reviewing forty studies of housing and health, Wilner and Walkeley (1963) found that 26 showed positive associations between housing condition and health. Their own study compared groups remaining in a Baltimore slum with others relocated to public housing. On the whole, improvements were not dramatic (Wilner *et al.*, 1962). Though neighbor relations and self-esteem rose, social pathologies did not diminish. However, physical health improved, especially among children, who thus had better school attendance records and achieved better grades. As we will discover in Chapter 11, however, the forced removal of slum families to public housing may have very deleterious effects upon their emotional lives.

If the relationship between housing condition and health is equivocal, that between housing *type* and health is more so. Faris and Dunham found that the greatest proportion of admissions to mental hospitals tended to come from collective living environments (apartments, rooming houses, residential hotels) regardless of class. Among British armed forces personnel in Germany, all other variables being equal, medical consultation rates for apartment dwellers were 57 percent above those of house dwellers (Fanning, 1967). Cappon (1971), however, finds no incontrovertible evidence that apartment living impairs mental or social health, but suggests that this is because we have not yet defined our terms or conducted sufficiently well-organized research.

One of the most obvious explanations of the high incidence of pathology in center-city tenements is poverty. It is in just such environments that the poor cluster. In a detailed review of the interrelationships between environment and health, Martin (1967) found that if overcrowding, air pollution, and poor socioeconomic conditions were eliminated, other factors were of little influence. In 1966, 48 percent of the nonwhite United States population had an income too low to provide an acceptable standard of living, whereas this was true of only 19 percent of whites (Starr, 1967). Comparing Harlem, a poor black area of New York, with the city as a whole, Clark (1967) found that rates of mental hospital admission, delinquency, and venereal disease were all higher in the ghetto. Poverty, however, cannot explain the high rates of mental illness found in high-income hotel and apartment complexes.

Perhaps a better explicant relates to the *human* environment. One quality shared by the inhabitants of ghettos, apartments, rooming houses, skid row, and residential hotels is social isolation. Faris and Dunham found that all areas with high insanity rates were characterized by high rates of social disorganization, notably persons living alone without family ties, one-parent households, and those with alcoholic or other problems. Moreover, high incidences of insanity were found among persons inhabiting areas primarily occupied by other races.

The relationship between social disorganization and mental health has been confirmed by several studies. McNeil (1970) suggests that being white, gainfully employed, educated, intelligent, and with a stable marriage promotes security; lack of any of these stabilizers may diminish the capacity to adjust, and the absence of several may lead to psychosis. In Chicago, senile psychosis rates were associated with tenancy. Elderly home-owners, often married, showed low rates, while single persons in rented rooms had high rates. As discussed in Chapter 3, excessive privacy and lack of interpersonal contact can be detrimental to health.

Controversy still remains over whether the physical environment of the central city itself creates the pathology, or whether those prone to exhibit pathological tendencies drift into the apartments and rooming houses of the urban core. There is ample evidence for both hypotheses (Sanua, 1969), but nothing conclusive in either direction. The drift theory, however, is shaken by studies which show that migrants frequently have lower mental illness rates than nonmigrants, and that schizophrenics may show a less than average propensity to move (Hollingshead and Redlich, 1958; Srole *et al.*, 1962). It has also been shown that the groups most affected by central-city problems are those least able to move, such as the poor and the black (Droettboom *et al.*, 1971).

It is possible, therefore, that a combination of physical, social, and economic factors may combine to form a milieu in which pathologies are likely to develop. In relation to psychoses, Giggs (1973, 71) states: "some social and environmental settings *may* create schizophrenia . . . and also precipitate schizophrenia in populations which may possibly be . . . constitutionally vulnerable." Attempts to isolate the physical environment as a cause, however, have as yet proved fruitless. Moller (1968) correctly describes the ghetto as an area of isolation and alienation with high rates of mental disorders. He infers that the squalid condition of the buildings causes the isolation which then results in mental disorder. This is unproven. However, it has been suggested that, as in hospital wards with large numbers of beds (Chapter 3), the high population densities of tenements, apartment blocks, and other collective living environments induce personal withdrawal from contact, or inhibit contact because few public places are available for meeting (Rosenberg, 1968; Michelson, 1970). Lack of meaningful contact thus results in isolation-based pathologies. It is possible therefore, as noted at the beginning of this chapter, that urban pathologies may be directly or indirectly due to the very nature of the city, namely, its high population densities and resulting feelings of crowdedness on the part of its inhabitants.

The relationship between large numbers of bodies in a constricted space and mental, social, and physical pathologies is complex. It is not normally possible to subject experimental subjects to excessively crowded conditions, although some information is available from prison camps and situations such as the Black Hole of Calcutta. Because of this problem, the initial work on the problems of high density living conditions was carried out on small mammals.

Crowding in Nonhuman Populations

One of the best-known animal migration patterns is that of the Scandinavian lemming. Every three or four years the lemming experience a population explosion which, despite the abundance of predators, can be assuaged only by migration. Lemming migrations cover the ground in a semicontinuous blanket, and migration through water inevitably results in mass death from drowning. However, many animals also die on land without obvious cause. During this period of rapid mass death, or population crash, the lemming become aggressive and may resort to cannibalism (Deevey, 1960).

The origins of population crash in lemming, rabbits, and other animals have been attributed variously to sunspot cycles, food supply problems, predator-prey relationships, and disease epidemics (Elton, 1924; Errington, 1956). All these theories have encountered contradictory evidence. Most notably, it has been found that food shortages cause gradual rather than rapid population adjustments. Many incidents of population crash, moreover, have occurred when food supplies were plentiful (Barnett, 1964). The most recent explanation, based on observation and autopsies of lemming and various other species undergoing population crash (Christian, 1950), suggests that death in such situations is largely due to metabolic disturbances (Dubos, 1965). Convulsive seizures, internal hemorrhaging of major organs, lesions in the brain and the adrenal glands, and endocrine imbalance, particularly in sugar levels, are common. These are symptoms of shock or stress; the adrenal glands, in particular, regulate growth and the body's fight-or-flight defense mechanism. In emergencies, the adrenals respond to stress by overworking and becoming physically enlarged. It is suggested that the stress of high-density living, including constant tension because of the inevitable invasions of personal space, exhausts the adrenopituitary system whose hormones regulate body functions.

A single example of high-density effects is provided by Christian's work on James Island, Maryland (1960). Five deer released on the island in 1916 had built up a population of about 300, a density of one per acre, by 1955. Between 1955 and 1957 several deer were shot and a detailed histological investigation of their internal organs was performed. In the first three months of 1958 over half the deer population suddenly died, and after other die-offs the population stabilized at about 80. The carcasses recovered from the 1958–60 crash showed no evidence of infection or starvation; on the contrary, the animals were fat and sleek. The most notable changes were that animals from the post-crash population were larger, and had adrenal glands up to 81 percent smaller in weight. The precrash population, animals with hyperactive, swollen adrenals, were clearly in a state of shock or stress, presumably caused by overcrowding.

physiological effects of crowding

Based on the evidence from wild populations that high densities (crowding) result in metabolic disturbances followed by population crash, many experiments with laboratory animals have been carried out. Christian continued his work, using rats in the Philadelphia zoo. A small breeding population in an environment replete with food, water, and litter soon bred beyond the spatial capacity of its environment, resulting in population crash.

A series of experiments by Myers *et al.* (1971) is illustrative of the physiological changes induced by the stress of high density. Using wild rabbits, the first experiment varied the size of the living space, but kept the population density constant (Fig. 7.4). Despite the fact that the number of animals in the smaller living spaces was reduced to keep density constant, the most detrimental effects occurred in the smallest living space. Aggressive and sexual behavior increased. Reproductive capacity was lowered, however, with reduced ovulation rates. Moreover, there was significant deterioration of liver, spleen, kidney, and adrenal glands. In the smallest living spaces the young were severely stunted and, though sexually active and very aggressive when adult, possessed enlarged adrenals and other attributes of ill-health.

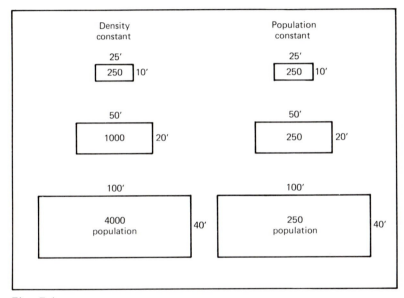

Fig. 7.4

Hypothetical examples of constant population and constant density conditions in crowding experiments.

In the second series of experiments living space was again varied, but in this case the population was held constant. This had the effect of increasing or decreasing density as space size was decreased or increased (Fig. 7.4). There was a great improvement in the quality of individual animals as density was reduced. On the other hand, increased density resulted in marked physiological and reproductive changes (Table 7.1). There was an increase in spermatogenesis, ovary size, and mammary gland weight, but a decline in the number of ovulations. Successful pregnancies were fewer, numbers born per pregnancy larger, but the weight of both embryos and nestlings was much reduced. Mortality of the young more than doubled when space was reduced from four units to one, and the high mortality rate of young born in the latter condition continued even when they were removed to improved conditions. Myers (1971) concluded:

> The "density syndrome" in mammals is a reality . . . it is not a response to group size *per se* but to some form of spatial restriction, either in the form of space itself or some configuration of animals behaving in space.

TABLE 7.1

PHYSIOLOGICAL CHANGES IN WILD RABBITS

| Variable | Population Constant: Living Space Varying | | | Significant Difference? |
	4 Space Units	2 Space Units	1 Space Unit	
Ovulations	1.15	0.77	0.75	Yes
Successful pregnancies (%)	85.00	87.10	79.90	No
Embryo weight (gm)	25.21	19.70	16.61	Yes
Mean litter size	4.55	4.50	4.95	No
Nestling weight (gm)	122.54	100.73	85.86	Yes
Mortality of young (%)	4.00	9.00	9.80	Yes

Source: Myers *et al.* (1971)

behavioral effects of crowding

Myers and his associates kept careful records of the changes in behavior which were induced by crowding. Emphasis on the behavioral effects of crowding, however, is associated with the work of Calhoun (1962, 1966, 1973). He first established a small population of wild Norway rats in a quarter-acre enclosure, and by eliminating all possibility of predation or disease and providing abundant food, left only the animals' behavior toward each other as a factor that might affect population increase. From the observed reproduction rate 5,000 adult individuals were expected after 27 months. The population, however, stabilized at 150 adults. The population control mechanism was high infant mortality, probably resulting from the stresses of enforced social interaction.

Similar experiments were then carried on under controlled laboratory conditions. In smaller indoor cages protected rodent populations were allowed to expand freely, or, by removing excess infants, were kept at levels approximately twice the size at which stress could be detected (Watson, 1970). The consequence of such crowding was most apparent among the female rodents. Many could not carry their pregnancies to full term, or did not survive delivery. Many more, after giving birth, seemed unable to perform normal maternal functions. The effect of this on infant mortality was exacerbated by sexual deviation and cannibalism. Among both sexes pathological togetherness resulted in extreme forms of social facilitation, with some rats being able to eat and drink only alone, while others were transformed into social drinkers.

Abnormalities were also common in the male population. Those males which remained most normal were the aggressive, dominant animals which emerged successfully from the inevitable status struggles of the crowded pen. Even these, however, occasionally went berserk, attacking females, juveniles, and weaker males. The latter tended to fall into three behavior categories:

1. *The pansexuals.* Compared with the dominants, the activity level of the pansexuals was only moderate. Their title derives from their inability to distinguish appropriate sex partners; they made advances indiscriminately to males, juveniles, and females not in estrus. Their competition for dominance with the dominant males resulted in frequent attacks. In contrast, the two other groups had entirely resigned from the status struggle.

2. *The somnambulists.* These passive individuals ignored, and were ignored by, all other rats. Fat and sleek, they were totally divorced from rat society, existing as social isolates engaging in no other activities beyond food consumption.

3. *The probers.* These were the most active males of all. Hyperactive, hypersexual, and often homosexual, they were also cannibalistic. Ignoring all normal courtship rituals, they would run down females in packs.

Rodents in normal conditions do not behave in this deviant manner. "It is obvious that the behavioral repertoire with which the Norway rat has emerged from the trials of evolution and domestication must break down under the social pressures generated by population density" (Calhoun, 1962).

Such a behavioral breakdown into pathological deviance Calhoun termed a *behavioral sink*.

Similar results were obtained with other laboratory animals such as mice (Calhoun, 1966; Marsden, 1972). Marsden recounts the building of a mouse utopia of 16 high-rise apartment environments with abundant food and nest materials and total freedom from predation or disease. The population was allowed to grow until it reached 2,200, which is about half the theoretical maximum and about 15 times the optimum number of adults. As expected, a behavioral sink developed and each individual began to treat other mice as objects rather than individuals. Physical contact was necessary to generate any interaction; "other mice at slight distances away were hardly mice" (Calhoun, 1973, 24). After several years, deviance levels, including infant mortality, were so great that there remained no normal males or females capable of reproduction resulting in healthy young. Almost the whole population eventually became passive somnambulists, with no courtship, no sex, no territorial defense, no activity beyond self-centered feeding and grooming. Consequently, the population became wholly adult. Zero population growth was reached and passed; as adults aged and died, the population began to fall. At last report the population had fallen from its 2,200 maximum to less than fifty, all destined to die out without heirs.

mechanisms

The obvious analogies between human and animal population growth, and the scenario of a final mouselike end to the human population, which are so frequently drawn, necessitate an investigation of the mechanisms operating in the behavioral sink.

Davis (1971) suggested that there must be some optimum population size in every species which permits the normal functioning of physiological processes. When animals are crowded, a variety of stimuli excites the central brain mechanisms to stimulate the hypothalamus, which releases the pituitary hormone ACTH. This in turn stimulates adrenal activity, which results in a variety of behaviors designed to cope with stress. It is thought that the stimuli are largely of the sensory overload type, based not simply on animal numbers but on the arrangement of animals in relation to space.

One of the most feasible explanations of the behavioral sink is that increased density upsets the normal social system which depends on a fine balance between territoriality and dominance. In many animal societies social organization involves a well-defined dominance hierarchy or pecking order. Status in the hierarchy depends upon initial anatomical and physiological differences among individuals, which are exaggerated as the initially larger individuals grow proportionately even larger through their greater access to food. Acceptance of the hierarchy by both dominants and subordinates ensures social stability and a reduction of the tensions that might erupt did every animal not know and accept its place. A major requirement for the formation of a stable society based on hierarchical dominance is that every individual be acquainted with all others.

Dominance, however, is not absolute. A dominant animal may attack an encroaching subordinate, but will rarely pursue it into the area recognized as the subordinate's territory. In fact, subordinates battling on their home ground may frequently vanquish more dominant animals, a home-base effect mentioned earlier in Chapter 2. Thus territory mediates dominance. The exertion of territorial influence, however, can occur only if two conditions are met. The first is sufficient space for each individual to possess a territorial base. The second is the maintenance of individual distance (personal space) between the individuals.

High-density living clearly violates many of these social norms. As populations increase, the individual's opportunity for meeting another individual at frequent intervals, as would occur in a normal situation, is drastically reduced. Consequently, each individual increasingly finds itself operating in an anonymous mass of other bodies. Lack of recognizability ensures that a stable hierarchical system cannot be set up, or if set up, breaks down. Moreover, individual personal-space norms are increasingly violated as animals find it impossible to maintain individual distance between each other. The maintenance of personal jurisdiction over an area of space similarly becomes impossible. At all three levels of territoriality there is disruption: personal space is violated; the control of a home base is almost impossible; and beyond the home base normal activity patterns are increasingly frustrated by the deviant behavior of others.

A major consequence of the general abolition of territorial behaviors and the breakdown of the social hierarchy is the rise of the tyrant. Dominance becomes all-important; having no territorial base, subordinates can be continually attacked. They provoke attack by their inability to escape encroaching upon their superiors. When attacked, they have little chance to flee. Calhoun describes the situation in his behavioral sink as a status-struggle. Certain portions of the experimental pen were easily defended because they could be approached only by ramps. In these sections the most dominant males, together with their harems, foregathered in relative spatial comfort. These animals remained the most normal of the whole population. The rest were crammed into the remaining portions of the pen at excessive densities, and exhibited all the abnormalities of the behavioral sink.

The mechanism, then, appears to be that high-density conditions reduce personal privacy; the consequence of this stressful situation is social collapse. One result is increased hostility, at least in the initial stages. These mood changes are regulated by neurohormones (Moyer, 1971), released by stress which may result directly from sensory overload (Davis, 1971; Evans and Eichelman, 1974). A further result, found also among humans whose personal space is violated (see Chapter 3), is poorer performance of normal tasks. This is probably associated with mobility. Calhoun found that higher-ranked animals were much more mobile than others, which accords with human activity pattern investigations reported in Chapter 5. One of the final results is total aimlessness and quiescence, a state which seems close to the *anomie* which Durkheim (1951) associates with many human inhabitants of cities, especially the suicide-prone. Bronfenbrenner (1974), discussing alienation in the United States, has linked increasing infant mortality, juvenile delinquency, violent crime, juvenile suicides, and divorce rates with changes in family structure, which themselves relate to stress on mothers, apartment living, and the breakdown of the social fabric of the neighborhood.

If these human parallels can indeed be safely drawn (a point explored later in this chapter), some further issues drawn from animal studies will have direct relevance to the human situation. First, it is clear that in natural conditions all animal species have some form of population control mechanism, by which they achieve *homeostasis* (population balance). In artificially crowded conditions these homeostatic mechanisms overreact to the extent of population destruction, rather than producing a simple return to equilibrium. The species *homo sapiens* appears to have liberated itself from the homeostatic chains which originally bound it, with the result that its population threatens to overrun the food resources available to maintain it. Moreover, this population increasingly crowds itself into high-density conglomerations known as cities, where the stress diseases (e.g., heart disease) take an increasing toll (Selye, 1956).

Further, human crowding into cities is associated with accelerated change, the increasing diversity of stimulation, and the rapid emergence and extinction of new behaviors (the hula hoop, streaking). It has been suggested that "our problem is tempo, not density" (Bell and Tyrwhitt, 1972). If carried too far or too fast, this increasing overload of sensory input could result in mass *Future Shock* (Toffler, 1970). The growing numbers of pathological deviants and the increasing preponderance of social withdrawal have been described by Esser (1972). Esser suggests that such a result could come about because of the physiological limitations of the human brain.

The greatest potential for horror, however, emerges from the work of Keeley. Working with mice born in normal conditions (a control), born in crowded conditions, and born in crowded but raised in uncrowded conditions, Keeley found marked behavior differences. Individuals born in crowded conditions were less active and slower to respond to stimuli than were the control group. Moreover, mice born in crowded conditions but raised by uncrowded nurses were equally as slow, and their survival rates were just as low as those born and raised in a crowded situation. Keeley's experiment demonstrated that the stressing factors are passed from mother to offspring not through the milk, as had previously been thought, but through the placenta from mother to embryo. Abnormal levels of stress-related hormones are therefore thought to result in offspring with abnormal behaviors. And what is more important for the long-run operation of society, "while the mother could respond perfectly well to high-density stress, her offspring could not" (Keeley, 1962, 45).

Crowding in Human Populations

There has been much observation of human crowding in slums, ghettos, prison camps, and the like. According to Leyhausen (1965b):

> Nearly five years in prisoner-of-war camps taught me that over-
> crowded human societies reflect the symptoms of overcrowded
> wolf, cat, goat, mouse, rat, and rabbit communities to the last
> detail . . . all differences are mainly species-specific . . . the basic
> forces of social interaction and organization are identical.

Biderman *et al.* (1963) collected details of historical incidents of extreme overcrowding, including prisons, emigrant ships, and slave ships. Solzhenitsyn (1973) is only the latest of a series of writers who have described the crowded horrors of concentration camps. All such observations, however, are confounded by the conditions that produce the crowding or are produced by it, including the presence of an oppressor, poverty, disease, and inadequate environmental conditions other than spatial restriction.

The criticism that intervening variables have not been taken into account applies to all observation studies, including Barker and Gump's (1964) finding that students in small schools have higher rates of direct participation in group activities than students in large schools. As early as 1930 Plant observed that crowding challenges the child's individuality, reduces his self-reliance, and increases his cynicism. The crowded child needs constant immediate gratification and is overly gregarious. Schorr (1963) suggests that much of this may be true also for crowded adults.

In overcrowded conditions relationships between both adults and children are likely to be less than optimal. Goodwin (1964, 4) defines overcrowding in slum conditions as:

> never a moment of privacy for husband and wife to build an
> emotional life together, never a night's sleep unbroken by cry-
> ing, fretful children in a crib next to the bed, in the kitchen, in
> the living room, never more than 15 feet away . . . it's nowhere

> to go to rest and relax . . . it's nowhere to drink a glass of beer
> . . . it's no place to cook three meals a day . . . and no place to
> serve them . . . it's nowhere for children to do homework . . .
> it's nowhere to pretty up to call one's own . . . it's children sent
> out to the streets . . . anything to get a minute's peace . . . but
> no way to get it.

In such situations it is not surprising that parents, like the crowded rats, are likely to be irritable and inefficient. Children, in turn, find home an unattractive place and take to the streets, thus increasing the potential for social deviance (Galle *et al.*, 1972).

A more objective approach to human crowding studies is provided by statistical surveys. New York is frequently cited as a crowded, stressful environment inhabited by aggressive individuals and with high rates of social, physical, and mental pathologies. The Midtown Manhattan Study conducted by the Cornell Medical School compared midtown Manhattan (between Park Avenue and the East River, 59th to 96th Streets) with the whole of Manhattan and the other boroughs (Langner and Michael, 1963). The mean density of the midtown area was about 600 persons per acre, four times that of Manhattan as a whole, ten times the Bronx and Brooklyn, and 130 times Staten Island. A sample of 1,910 inhabitants was interviewed by psychiatrists and social workers. Comparing the boroughs and midtown, the latter was found to have twice the rate of suicide, tuberculosis, accidental death, and juvenile delinquency, and three times as much alcoholism. Twenty percent of the sample were considered so mentally incapacitated as to be indistinguishable from mental hospital patients, and only twenty percent of the total appeared free of mental disease.

As no data on physical environmental variables were gathered, a causal relationship between density and pathology cannot be assumed. A series of correlation studies of the type originally popularized by Faris and Dunham has found that density tends to correlate with social disorganization (Schmitt, 1957, 1966; Winsborough, 1965; Mitchell, 1971). Correlations, however, are ambiguous and can merely provide a direction for further research. Accordingly, the most recent approach to the study of human crowding has taken the form of experimentation.

Some experiments have defined crowding in terms of group size (Hutt and Vaizey, 1966; Ittelson *et al.*, 1970a; Griffit and Veitch, 1971). The general result of these experiments has been to demonstrate that members of larger groups are more aggressive and asocial than members of smaller groups, regardless of environment type. However, the environment is important; 32 separate classes were asked their opinions of a single classroom (Sommer and Becker, 1971). According to local fire codes, the optimum capacity of the room was 25 students, with a maximum of 31. However, classes of 20 considered themselves crowded, and as class size increased, satisfaction fell and the number of complaints rose.

Other studies have kept group size constant, but manipulated the space available (Freedman, 1971; Freedman *et al.*, 1971). Task performances in a small room were quite as efficient as those of subjects in a large room. In conditions of reduced space, however, interpersonal relationships among females were far more friendly than among males. These sex differences with space reduction have been confirmed by other experiments with schoolchildren (Preiser, 1972). When Loo reduced room size to about a third of its original area, aggression declined. The children, however, isolated themselves by playing with fewer other children. "Enforced isolation may be the child's way of blocking out stimulation which is too physically encroaching. Playing in solitude may be the child's way of increasing psychological distance from others when physical distance is limited" (Loo, 1972, 352).

Fundamental Problems

The design implications of density studies, whether of rats or humans, and whether experimental or correlational or observational, are obvious. If high densities are directly productive of pathological behavior, our fundamental concepts of city building will require radical rethinking. No such direct link has yet been proven, and the presumed crowding-overload-stress-pathology relationship has been attacked on several grounds.

culture

People appear to live satisfactorily at high densities in Japan and China. In a comparative study of the United States and Hong Kong, Schmitt (1963) demonstrated that high-density living does not necessarily engender urban pathologies. Density varied considerably in the United States, from 62 persons per acre in Seattle to 450 in Boston and New York. Thirteen census tracts in Hong Kong, however, had over 2,000 persons per acre. In terms of room density, many Hong Kong residents are living at densities which allow only 24 square feet of interior space per person (Lai, 1974). Indices of pathology, however, indicated that it was not high-density Hong Kong but the low-density United States which qualified as a behavioral sink. Mortality was on the whole considerably lower in Hong Kong. Moreover, the rate of hospitalization for psychiatric disorders was less than one tenth of that reported for the U.S.A. The serious crime rate was half, the murder rate one sixth, and the juvenile delinquency rate considerably lower than corresponding American figures. Similarly, murder, rape, and robbery rates in Japan are far lower than comparable American rates, and life expectancy is somewhat higher. Yet the overall density of Japan is more than twelve times that of the United States, and the number of persons per room considerably higher.

High density: public housing in Hong Kong. Though these units typically allow only 130 square feet of space per family group, in appearance they closely resemble public housing projects in Singapore, Europe, and North America. (Courtesy of Hong Kong Government.)

Cultural factors accounting for these remarkable differences include social expectations, long established traditions of tolerance of high-density living, extreme family cohesiveness, natural gregariousness (Chaudhuri, 1959), and fewer vehicles per capita. A suggestion by Biderman *et al.*, (1963) that pathologies result from overcrowding only when the crowded persons lack optimism and group organization seems to apply well to Hong Kong. Where high densities are a necessary condition for survival, they can clearly be tolerated. The design of the built environment is also important. The Japanese place greatest emphasis on designing interior spaces, leaving exterior and public areas unkempt. The chief features of interior design are simplicity and discipline, reflecting the values inherent in the Japanese lifestyle (Hall, 1966; Michelson, 1970). Further, the public environment is more readily comprehensible because even heavy industrial processes are readily visible (Smith, 1970). Internal delight and external legibility combine with an emphasis on collective unity, rather than on independent individualism, to reduce personal stress.

High density: a street scene in Kowloon, Hong Kong. "Crowding" or cultural norm? (Courtesy of Hong Kong Government.)

the extrapolation trap

If cultural differences are so great, there is no need to belabor the problems inherent in extrapolating from the behavior of other mammals to that of man. In a conference on this topic during 1969, Brereton (1971) exclaimed: "In this conference we extrapolate from rats to man, from cats to man, from mice to man." This tendency towards zoomorphism, or ethologism, has been explored by Callan (1970).

Rats are used because they are cheap and easily manipulable. Getis and Boots (1971) argue that as the behavior of rats is predominantly stereotyped and reflexive, rather than cognitive, studies of rats have little relevance for man. Stea (1973), however, argues that rats have strong cognitive abilities, as shown in maze learning via mental mapping. Others criticize animal experiments because the animals are confined and thus unable to escape (Dempsey, 1972). Studies of activity patterns, however, show that many people living in ghettos, for example, have activity spaces restricted to only a few blocks. Though the human-nonhuman controversy continues (Alland, 1972), there is support for the relevance of animal studies in evidence which shows similarity of both biochemical (Marsden, 1972) and social structure (Callan, 1970) between *homo sapiens* and other mammals.

causality in human studies

Some of the problems associated with studies of human crowding have been cited above. We are clearly constrained by the nature of the beast; it is generally impossible to sacrifice human subjects for the weighing of their adrenal glands. Moreover, there is no agreement on what constitutes a pathology, for normality is not an absolute but a relative term (Duhl, 1963; Gad, 1973). Many workers have drawn conclusions from positive correlations between physical density and tabulated data on mental and physical illness and deviance rates. However, correlation studies, by their very nature, cannot indicate causal relationships. Indeed, when characteristics such as social class, ethnicity, and residential mobility are held constant, very few correlations remain statistically significant. Observations, on the other hand, are subjective and thus suspect. For example, Chombart de Lauwe's (1965) observations on optimal densities are merely culture-bound.

Nevertheless, on this rather insubstantial evidence, coupled with animal studies, a modern folk-myth concerning the evils of crowding has emerged. After an intensive review of the relevant literature, Zlutnik and Altman (1972) found that most references to the evils of crowding, if not based on animal research or correlations, were based solely on opinion. Their conclusion was that rigorous human data concerning this important social problem simply did not exist. A contemporary review by Stokols (1972) comes to the same conclusion. Gad (1973) argues convincingly that although it is possible to conceptualize the link between crowding and stress, we have as yet no sound explanation of how stress is transformed into pathologies. Although it is widely accepted that stress may cause physical illness, there is no evidence for a causal link between stress and social pathologies. All four authors demand further research and provide conceptual bases and research strategies to guide future work.

definition of terms

Before rigorous research on human crowding can be contemplated, there must be some agreement on terminology and concepts. A great variety of meanings is attached to the words *density* and *crowding*. At its simplest, density refers to the number of social units per unit of space. Even here, however, only two-dimensional space (area) is generally considered, rather than volume. And the area usually considered is ground area. Yet density measured in floor area is more obviously meaningful in Manhattan than ground area alone. Further, on a city scale there is confusion between gross density (the whole area considered) and net density (residential areas alone considered). All these definitions consider density as an absolute measurement. But densities may be defined by the roles played by the participants in conjunction with the physical setting. For instance, one hundred people in a small cinema is acceptable, but one hundred people in front of oneself on the golf course would be intolerable. With this concept, known as role density (Loring, 1956) or use-crowding (Chapin, 1951), we move to a consideration of crowding.

Most recent workers in the field have distinguished between density and crowding. *Density* is usually regarded as a physical condition of limited space, without behavioral connotations. It is a descriptor only. *Crowding*, however, refers to a situation in which the restrictive aspects of limited space are perceived by individuals exposed to them. Stokols (1972) further suggests that high density is not a sufficient condition for the arousal of crowding stress; for crowding to occur there must be some form of disruption in the individual's social relation with others in the immediate area. Others offer similar interpretations. Desor (1972) proposes that being crowded means "receiving excessive stimulation from social sources." Proshansky *et al.* (1970) suggest that a person will feel crowded by others to the extent that they restrict his freedom of choice. The recognition of a discrepancy between what one wishes to do and what one is able to do is also important in subjective feelings of crowding (Wicker, 1972a). In these terms a large room containing two lovers and a voyeur, though objectively a low density situation, may be perceived as crowded by two of the three participants; "two's company, three's a crowd." High densities, of course, can induce feelings of crowding by rendering an individual's personal space vulnerable to frequent intrusion.

This redefinition of crowding, while conceptually valuable, is not readily operationalized in large-scale studies. While psychologists continue to refine the relationships between density and crowding in small-scale experiments (Choldin and McGinty, 1972; Esser, 1974), the sheer labor involved in personal interviewing suggests that less precise or surrogate measures will remain in use whenever attempts are made to study crowding phenomena at neighborhood, city, or regional scales. In their investigation of historical high-density situations Biderman *et al.* considered crowding to occur only when individuals had less than 10 square feet of living space per person. At this extreme, there may be a feeling of crowding for all persons. Nevertheless, personality differences in crowding perception are likely to be apparent, most notably because individuals vary greatly in their experience of and expectations of spatial restriction.

inside versus outside density

Dealing with less extreme situations Schmitt (1966) distinguished between micro-level crowding, defined as persons per unit space within a residential unit, and macro-level density, defined as persons per unit space in a larger area, such as a neighborhood or census tract. Having already distinguished between crowding and density on an objective-subjective basis, however, Schmitt's terms would better be renamed *inside density* and *outside density*. On relating persons per room and persons per acre to several social disorganization indices for Honolulu, Schmitt found that outside density was the more significant variable. This finding is supported by a study of Toronto school children, for though internal density was not related to achievement, the number of families per block was (Michelson, 1970). On the other hand a Chicago study found no relationship between outside density and pathology, but a strong relationship between the latter and number of persons per room (Galle *et al.*, 1972). Similar equivocal results have been described elsewhere (Miller, 1961; Rosenberg, 1968).

These studies have all the inherent problems of correlational studies. Moreover, even persons per room is a crude measure, for it fails to specify the ratio of usable interior space per person. Further, it also fails to take into consideration a host of variables such as income or competence, which account for high-income families living satisfactorily at high densities (e.g., New York's upper East Side) while low-income families living at lower densities suffer distress. Other variables rarely considered are duration of the density condition, possibility of escape (e.g., to a country cottage), and degree of personal control over both the physical and human environments.

Based on the research which stresses inside density as a probable pathological agent, it is possible to take the stand that cities with high outside densities are quite habitable as long as each family has the amount of internal living space it requires. Both Jacobs (1961) and Whyte (1968) support 'this view, and structures such as Safdie's Habitat in Montreal have proved that satisfactory living at high densities is possible if privacy and family space are guaranteed. On this basis, new high-density urban designs of a utopian character have been put forward (see Chapter 13). Similar conclusions have been reached from studies of satisfactory high-density environments in Japanese cities (Smith, 1970; Canter and Canter, 1971). These authors suggest that the East Asian model might be one approach to the solution of the apparent high-density problems of the Western city.

Summary

1. The presence of other bodies of the same species affects an individual's behavior even though he regards them as objects rather than persons.
2. It is suggested that the crowding of individuals together at high densities results in stimulus overload and feelings of stress, which are manifested in mental, physical, and social pathologies.
3. Experiential evidence suggests that stimulus overload and withdrawal from contact are common among city inhabitants.
4. Studies of mental, physical, and social pathologies indicate higher incidences in high-density central-city cores than in low-density suburbs. Both the physical and human environments have been cited as major explicants of this distribution; it is clear that there are strong correlations between pathologies and social disorganization.
5. High-density conditions (crowding) result in severe behavioral and physiological disturbances in mammals. Sensory overload, partly in the form of territorial breakdown, results in social disorganization.
6. Observation studies, correlation studies, and experiments have so far been unable to demonstrate direct causal relationships between density and pathology among humans.
7. The problems inherent in the density-pathology relationship are complex. They include extrapolation from other animals to man; failure to consider intervening variables, notably culture; the impossibility of making causal inferences from correlation studies; and terminological problems, including the definition of crowding, density, and pathology.
8. At present, it is possible to conclude little beyond the fact that density itself does not induce stress or pathologies. It is the conditions of density and the nature of the participants which are of most importance.

Further Reading

ESSER, A. H., ed. (1971), *Behavior and Environment: The Use of Space by Animals and Men.* New York: Plenum Press; Chapters by Leyhausen, Davis, Myers *et al.*, Ellenberger, and Calhoun.

GAD, G. (1973), "Crowding and Pathologies: Some Critical Remarks," *Canadian Geographer* 17: 373-90.

WILNER, D. and R. P. WALKELEY (1963), "Effects of Housing on Health and Performance," in L. Duhl (ed.), *The Urban Condition* pp. 215-28. New York: Simon & Schuster.

WOHLWILL, J. F. (1966), "The Physical Environment : A Problem for a Psychology of Stimulation," *Journal of Social Issues* 22: 29-38.

8

THE PHENOMENAL
ENVIRONMENT: PHYSICAL

We shape our buildings, and afterwards our buildings shape us. *

Winston S. Churchill

Propinquity does it . . . †

Mrs. Humphrey Ward

A person's behavior is influenced by three interdependent sets of factors: his genetic endowment, his experience of interaction with the environment, and the existing phenomenal environment (Studer, 1969). The first two of these phenomena sets cannot be influenced extensively by architects or planners. In this book the experience factor is treated in Chapters 9–11. A biogeneticist is required for control of the genetic endowment. The designer, however, is able to exert strong influence on the shape of the existing physical environment, and has some influence over the human phenomenal environment (Chapter 7).

One of the major beliefs of designers has been that quality of physical design is important for man's well-being and happiness. A number of social scientists support this view. Proshansky *et al.* (1970) suggest that although the surroundings remain neutral and enter our awareness only when they deviate from what we have adapted to, they may still influence the behavior of the environed unit; "to be unaware of an environment is by no means to be unmoved by it."

---

* Winston S. Churchill, quoted in R. K. Merton (1948), "The Social Psychology of Housing," in W. Dennis (ed.), *Current Trends in Social Psychology.* Pittsburgh: University of Pittsburgh Press, pp. 163–217.
† Mrs. Humphrey Ward (1888), *Robert Elsmere,* Book 1, Chapter 2. London: Smith and Elder.

Degree of environmental awareness and the extent of environmental control may vary according to environmental type. Hall (1974) distinguishes between organic space (personal space), semifixed feature space, and fixed feature space. Semifixed feature space includes those objects in the environment which may be moved to facilitate the desired behavior pattern. Thus persons may alter a sociofugal arrangement of chairs into a sociopetal layout to provide a suitable setting for conversation (Chapter 3). Whether a particular item is semifixed, of course, depends upon the competence of the individual to alter it. This in turn may vary with culture; the Chinese, for example, treat furniture as fixed features, so that to move one's chair may affront one's host. Fixed feature space is space which is normally an unalterable part of the individual's phenomenal environment, including walls, doors and windows, street patterns, and complete urban layouts.

Major Areas of Man-Environment Interaction

This chapter deals with fixed feature space and its influence on behavior. Some behaviors appear to be fully determined by the physical environment. For example, at a traffic intersection, one tends to obey traffic signals. This, however, is a learned response, does not hold for everyone, and thus is a probability relationship (Chapter 6). More subtle environmental influences have been claimed by designers, including the determination of friendship patterns by housing layout and the strong influence on the learning process exerted by the physical environment. Some psychologists engaged in behavior modification have made similar claims (Proshansky *et al.*, 1970). In this connexion the 1960s saw the reemergence of environmental determinism at a much smaller scale level than previously, notably the determination of behavior by the subtle arrangement of walls, rooms, buildings, and grounds.

To consider attempting to modify human behavior by manipulating the physical environment assumes that a consistent relationship exists between environment and human response. Though individual differences and cultural traits will clearly result in behavior variations, several workers have found strong influences of design upon behavior. The effect of environment upon people, however, is not a simple, direct relationship, but a complex, systemic interaction. Gutman (1966), for example, suggests that the physical layout of a housing tract may influence the relationships of that community with the rest of the city, social life within the area, family life, and mental health. More generally, Ittelson (1960) has distinguished seven major areas of man-environment interaction, all of which interrelate in a complex manner. These are the following.

the perceptual area

The concern here is with how the phenomenal environment influences our perception of it. This has been explored in Chapters 5 and 6 and will be further considered in Chapter 9. There is evidence that the physical environment has some influence on the formation of attitudes.

the expressive area

The colors, shapes, and symbolic meanings of the environment are relevant here. There is a strong indication that colors influence moods (Dreschler, 1960; Wenner, 1964). The very words used by interior designers confirm this; reds and browns are rich, active, and warm, while blues and greens are cool and soothing, hence the extensive use of pale greens in hospitals and similar settings. People generally estimate rooms painted in light colors to be larger than dark-colored rooms. Activity levels in warmer-colored rooms, however, are often higher, and Bechtel (1967) speaks of color-induced activity.

the aesthetic area

Man's aesthetic appreciation is both expressed in and influenced by the environment. A controversy concerning varying aesthetic preferences for complexity or simplicity is outlined in Chapter 9. Aesthetic appreciation clearly varies with culture; in Western cultures, complexity appears to be preferred. "Variety is not the spice of life, it is the very stuff of it" (Heron, 1957). Fitch (1965) relates aesthetic decisions to both biology and the physical environment. By using a *hodometer,* an electrical system for automatically recording the number and location of footsteps across a floor space (and thus the duration of standing behavior), preferences for viewing art objects in museum settings have been objectively measured (Bechtel, 1967).

the instrumental area

This concerns the tools and facilities provided by the environment. Perception of these is vital; the presence of many minerals was long known to native groups which had neither the means nor the motivation to use them. Studies of open-plan schools show that students use a greater variety of tools in such open environments than in schools with a traditional classroom structure (Durlak *et al.,* 1972).

the ecological area

The ecological area considers overall patterns of spatial organization and how far these are environmentally influenced. It is the area most strongly related to the deterministic studies outlined in Chapter 6. This area subsumes many of the others, and generally deals with behavior on a larger scale.

the adaptive area

This area considers the extent to which the environment hinders or aids our activities. Though a very wide and complex area of study, it is of vital importance in terms of survival and satisfaction. It clearly overlaps into the instrumental area. Of great importance are the relationships between the physical environment and learning, environmental control, and movement behaviors. The importance of these for human survival and environmental competence compels the more detailed investigation below.

the integrative area

The integrative area is concerned with the relationship between environment and social groupings. This is important at all levels of interaction from dyad (two-person) relationships to the crowding described in Chapter 7. As some form of association with others appears necessary for mental, as well as social health, this area receives detailed consideration after the ensuing discussion of the adaptive area.

The Adaptive Area

The degree of environmental influence on overt behavior will vary with the behavior type. Human movement, for instance, is often environmentally influenced, especially among children. A cold room causes people to move jerkily. Open spaces prompt children to rush about and play (Tuan, 1972). Interdigitation with other areas is seen in Gibson's (1958) suggestion that human perception depends upon locomotion possibilities. Traffic patterns in New York's Guggenheim Museum are clearly constrained by the building's snail-like gallery structure.

street environments

Though there is a considerable amount of work on the distribution of people in parks and recreation settings (de Jonge, 1967), there is little information on pedestrian street behavior (Goffman, 1972). Though not an institutional setting, the street pattern is a fixed feature which generally defies manipulation by the individual. Wolff and Hirsch (1970) have shown that sidewalk pedestrians cooperate to prevent collision, adopting sidewalk rules and changing walking styles in relationship to their fellow walkers. There have been some studies of behavior in shopping malls, which are generally provided with benches, trees, and other physical artifacts. A study by Preiser (1972), for example, found that such artifacts had observable radii of attraction in which specific behaviors took place. Movement was usually direct from entry to exit, and group behavior was less tied to physical artifacts than was solitary behavior. In particular, solitary purposive behavior, such as reading, requires some space sheltered from the mainstream of circulation. Stilitz (1969) noted that such shelter is most frequently found in the vicinity of columns, edges, niches, and corners.

Such niches are important for a variety of behaviors. An irregular sidewalk building line has been found valuable for childrens' play and for providing high levels of environmental imageability (Jacobs, 1961; Lynch and Rivkin, 1959). Such niches also provide activity spaces for street people of various types, from vendors of goods to bootblacks. Beggars fall into this category by having the same paradoxical location demands; to achieve their goal requires exposure to the passers-by, yet self-preservation on the crowded sidewalk requires shelter from pedestrians.

A study, by the author, of beggars in Santiago, Chile, illustrates the relationship between sidewalk ecological niches and behavior. Five possible niches were available. Beggars could choose to exhibit themselves immobile on the sidewalk, could move along it, could take up positions along the building line, could retreat to the shelter of an alcove or recess, or could withdraw into the safety of deep entrances and arcades (Fig. 8.1.).

Of 47 begging units containing one or more persons, 74.4 percent chose the wallside position, and no more than 4 (8.5 percent) chose any other niche (Table 8.1). Collapsing the Table 8.1 data into wall/nonwall terms, a Chi^2 test showed a significant difference between the distributions of blind, crippled, and aged beggars. Using other statistical techniques (Goodman and Kruskal, 1954), significant differences were found between the distribution over all five niche types of the blind/nonblind, crippled/noncrippled, and aged/nonaged. In conjunction with Table 8.1 one may conclude that while the majority of beggars favored the wall as a site for operations, there was a tendency for the aged to withdraw, and for crippled persons to occupy exposed positions. The blind were the only group containing ambulatory members, and the only group to occupy all five niche types.

TABLE 8.1

NICHE CHOICES OF SANTIAGO BEGGARS

Infirmity	Ambulatory	Exposed	Wallside	Recess	Hidden	Total
Blind	2	1	24	1	1	29
Crippled	0	3	4	2	0	9
Aged	0	0	7	1	1	9
Totals	2	4	35	4	2	47

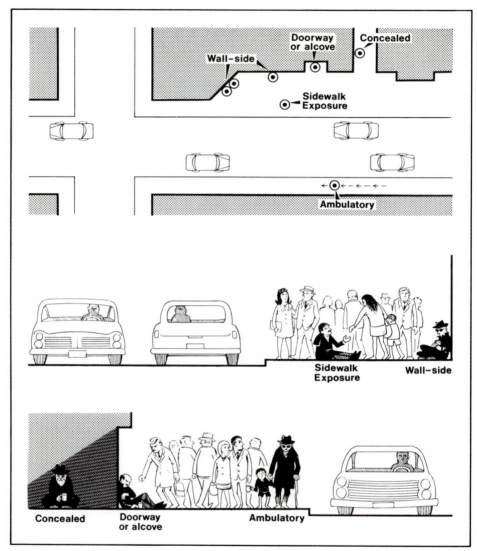

Fig. 8.1

The niches available to beggars on the sidewalks of Santiago de Chile.

An interpretation of these results must invoke the individual's degree of environmental competence. The aged, the group most likely to fear the bustling sidewalk crowds, exhibited the highest degree of withdrawal from exposure. In contrast, the blind, 41 percent of whom played instruments or sang, were able to take up the wallside positions which appear to be the best compromise between exposure and withdrawal. Most cripples, however, are unable to sing or play instruments, and none did so. Consequently, the crippled beggar's ability to attract attention may be reduced to exposing himself to public view. Competition at the wallside by the more adept sonic entreaties of the old and blind may therefore have forced some of the crippled, relying on visual impact as a means of entreaty, to the center of the sidewalk. In the case of begging, then, the physical environment in no way determines behavior, but permits a variety of behaviors, the choice of one of which depends to some extent on individual competence.

home environments

Physical environments also influence activities by the extent to which their components are fixed or moveable. An important feature here is the effect of architectural constraints on the placement of furniture within rooms. A pilot study carried out in Victoria, British Columbia, suggested that as many as two-thirds of the occupants of apartment towers have more or less identical furniture arrangements because of the location of doors, openings, windows, and electrical outlets. This clearly has social effects in terms of conversational and other groupings. Around the home, physical arrangements can clearly make the individual self-conscious about performing his everyday activities. Lilian Beckwith (1973, 26) describes her parents' new home in an English working class row housing environment:

> Mother had made curtains . . . so that she would not have to work under the scrutiny of curious neighbours whose windows overlooked us from across the narrow road. The living room was overlooked by more neighbours from across a back alley and the kitchen window stared straight on to a high red brick wall which enclosed a small red brick yard [with] barely enough space for me to swing a skipping rope . . . The outside lavatory . . . had no window at all [and] if you left the door open [for light] you were exposed to the view of neighbours . . .

Parr (1971) has asked whether the use of such unheated outdoor toilet facilities in various climates may have led to geographical differences in personality development.

Kuper found that physical constraints in English duplex housing led each householder to place his beds in such a way that their heads were adjacent, separated only by the common party wall (Fig. 8.2). The effects of such architectural constraints may be far-reaching. In Kuper's study the party walls were only lightly insulated and easily penetrable by noise. Neighbors were often compelled to reduce their desired activities in order not to disturb

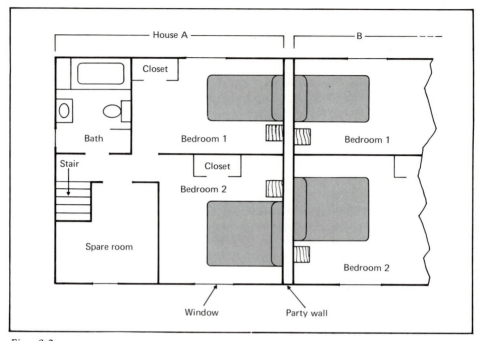

Fig. 8.2

Furniture arrangements on either side of the party wall, second floor. (Redrawn from L. Kuper (ed.) *Living in Towns,* 1953, by permission of the University of Birmingham, England.)

the occupants of the next house; radios and television, for example, could be clearly heard through the walls (Fig. 8.3). This was most embarrassing in adjacent bedrooms, with beds lying head-to-head (Kuper, 1953):

> You can even hear them use the pot; that's how bad it is. It's terrible . . . I hear them having a row in bed . . . You sometimes hear them say rather private things . . . It does make you feel a bit restrained, as if . . . *you* must say private things in a whisper [and] walk tiptoe into your bedroom at night . . .

The problem here is that not only is the individual disturbed by noises emanating from next door, but he also feels that he must restrain his own behavior. As some may not be able to adapt fully to this, there is a possibility of induced stress.

Rosow (1961), in a similar vein, considers housing *livability,* defined as that organization of space which best accommodates the needs of the occupants. He finds many examples of nonconforming usage, where the occupant uses the space in a way not envisaged or planned for by the architect. The archetypal example is the teenager's room with a designed-in desk space, and the teenager sprawled with his books across the living-room floor. Sauer and Marshall (1972) provide six examples of how architects were able to alter existing house plans to better accommodate the actual activities of the occupying families.

Fig. 8.3

The perils of the party wall: an Andy Capp cartoon by Smythe. (Reproduced by permission of Daily Newspapers Ltd.)

work environments

Similar changes in office layout (Chapter 3) have been found to influence work efficiency (Wells, 1965; Duffy, 1969; Roizen, 1969). Ruys interviewed 139 female workers in windowless offices in Seattle. Of these, 87 percent preferred to have windows and 47.5 percent thought that the lack of windows had deleterious effects upon either themselves, their work, or both. The reasons given for these perceived effects were 30 percent physical reasons and 70 percent psychosocial reasons (Table 8.2). No individuals said they preferred not to have windows, and only 0.8 percent indicated that not having windows might be less distracting.

The implications of this for the design of work spaces is obvious. Bell *et al.* (1973) note that at the room scale of analysis most research concentrates upon work efficiency, notably in industry, offices, and schools. Office studies have discovered that modern office landscaping may not fulfill expectations of increased efficiency (Brookes, 1972), and that office remodelling, while reducing dissatisfaction, is unlikely ever to reduce it to negligible proportions. A variety of procedures is being developed for the better evaluation of office efficiency and worker satisfaction (Wells, 1967; Sloan, 1972; Davis, 1972).

TABLE 8.2

REASONS FOR PREFERRING WINDOWS

Reason	Percent Response	
No daylight	14.3	PHYSICAL
Poor ventilation	15.7	
Want to monitor weather	14.3	
Want view, especially of distances	15.7	PSYCHOSOCIAL
Cooped up, isolated, claustrophobic	20.0	
Depressed, tense	20.0	
	100.0	

Source: Ruys (1971)

Hospitals are also undergoing evaluation. One of the major goals of the hospital has been to isolate the sick from the community (Lindheim, 1966). Until recently, therefore, hospitals have often been designed as fortresses. Within the hospital, efficiency of care seems to be linked strongly to physical design (Souder *et al.*, 1964). Three major designs are in general use: the single corridor, the double corridor, and the radial plan (Fig. 8.4). Each design has its proponents who stress its advantages in terms of staff efficiency and patient care. However, until recently there have been no studies which have compared simultaneously the effectiveness of these designs.

Trites *et al.* (1970) compared the three designs in terms of efficiency and staff satisfaction. Considering a series of work activities, from travel time within the hospital and direct patient care to nonproductive time, it was clear that the single-corridor design was the least desirable and the radial design was to be preferred. The latter was important in reducing travel time; in both double and single corridor units the extra travel cost was estimated at $77 more per bed per year than in the radial units. Time saved in travel was mostly spent on patient care. There were no clear-cut conclusions from the satisfaction questionnaire completed by nurses. However, staff were found to have fewest accidents and least absenteeism in the radial design, with highest rates for both factors in the single-corridor design. When asked which design they would prefer to work in, nurses overwhelmingly chose the radial layout. Physicians had the same preference.

The patient must also be considered. As noted in Chapter 3, size of bedroom seems to directly influence behavior. A survey of three psychiatric

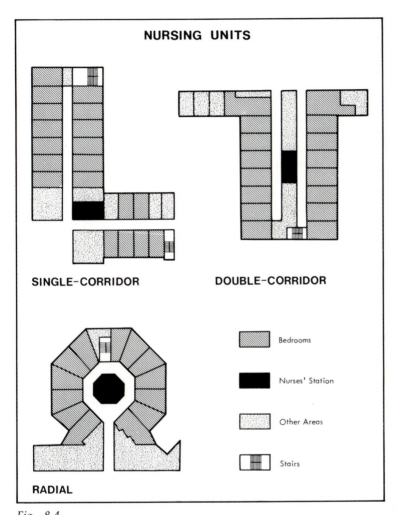

NURSING UNITS

SINGLE-CORRIDOR   DOUBLE-CORRIDOR

Bedrooms

Nurses' Station

Other Areas

Stairs

RADIAL

Fig. 8.4

Three types of hospital design. (Redrawn from "Influence of Nursing-Unit Design on Activities and Subjective Feelings of Nursing Personnel" by D. K. Trites, *Environment and Behavior* 2, No. 3, December 1970, by permission of the author and Sage Publications Inc.)

hospitals suggested that most patients treat their bedrooms, regardless of size, as if they were private rooms (Ittelson *et al.*, 1970b). On the other hand, patients in small rooms seem to have the greatest freedom of choice in terms of activities. The inhabitant of a multioccupancy room is limited in this respect; his environment "almost forces him into isolated passive behavior." Such a person typically spends up to three-quarters of his in-room time lying on his bed, whether asleep or awake. The authors conclude that the lack of privacy in the multioccupancy bedroom promotes rather than reduces personal and social problems.

learning environments

Learning efficiency and learning satisfaction in the school environment are of vital importance in the development of competent, socialized adults. There is a growing feeling that where we learn may be of considerable importance in retaining what we learn. The experience of designers and teachers supports this view. A study cited by Hall (1974) found that although administrators were reluctant to provide students with individual study spaces (perhaps because of symbolic status connotations), 80 percent of the students preferred small study spaces and 85 percent wanted to study alone. Sommer (1970), studying 23 college campuses, however, found that there was no ideal study environment; students were found studying in libraries, residences, cafeterias, lounges, classrooms, laboratories, and outdoors. Environmental manipulations by space managers were important in terms of study ease; very frequently, opening hours and furniture arrangements are considered solely from a maintenance rather than a study function viewpoint. Air conditioners may provide noise distraction and illumination conditions may be in-

Classroom organization: the traditional classroom. (Courtesy of Victoria Press.)

adequate. Cameron and Wheeler (1963) describe a math classroom so dim that it was known as the Black Hole of Calculus.

In Chapter 3 the physical arrangement of the classroom was discussed in terms of student participation. Richardson (1967) has referred to the symbolic value of the traditional classroom with the teacher's desk alone at the front. This layout is valuable only for certain kinds of learning and in some cases may inhibit communication and control. Disillusionment with the traditional classroom has grown with the realization that during the lengthy learning day the child may require different environmental conditions, whether of humidity, temperature, decor, or furniture arrangements. This recognition of learning as a dynamic process has led to attempts to manipulate the physical learning environment so that the child's learning advances with optimum speed and minimum stress. Since the 1950s there has been a concerted move toward open-plan classrooms, where the walls as well as the furniture are removable or capable of rearrangement in a variety of desired patterns.

Open planning clearly encourages greater physical activity by students. Objections include the possibility of increasing noise and decreased privacy, and thus greater distraction. A study of student satisfactions, however, suggests that open-plan schools are superior to traditional ones in terms of privacy (Brunetti, 1972). Open space may also provide a superior acoustical environment through lowered reverberation conditions. Moreover, a direct

Classroom organization: the open-plan classroom. (Courtesy of Victoria Press.)

relationship between noise level and distraction has not yet been fully established. Students are able to screen out much background noise, although they appear to find social conversation very distracting in both open space and conventional space. Very few studies in this area, however, have attempted to relate physical environmental conditions to how well children actually learn. In a review of the relevant literature Drew (1972) finds little agreement, except that environmental *complexity* may have important implications for learning.

learning and environmental complexity

Working with nonhumans, psychologists have found that animals raised or placed in enriched environments tend to have problem-solving abilities superior to those of similar animals exposed to less rich environments (Thompson and Heron, 1954; Rosenzweig, 1966). Even when mature rats were placed in a visually enriched condition their learning capacity improved (Krech *et al.*, 1962). Both humans and nonhumans appear to prefer complex, visually rich environments (see Chapter 9).

Wohlwill (1966), however, rejects the straightforward "the more the better" assumption, and states that the success of such efforts is not surprising "in view of the impoverished level of stimulation provided by the typical laboratory environment." Further, enrichment via the introduction of plastic cubes and balls, puffs of air, and noises into the animal's environment is only a caricature of the sensory bombardment available in the city. A key concept here is that of the optimum level of stimulation (Hebb, 1955; Leuba, 1955; Berlyne, 1967), as noted in Chapter 7. This concept asserts that an inverted U-shaped relationship exists between environment and behavior (Fig. 7.1). Just as there can be too little stimulation, so there may be too much. An approach such as "the more the better" cannot account for the deleterious effects of high stimulation levels on slum children.

In pursuit of optimal stimulation levels, much recent school design has emphasized the minimization or maximization of environmental stimulation. Windowless classrooms reduce external stimulation. Although there is much controversy over their effectiveness in improving the learning process, Wools (1969) noted that there is no significant difference in learning rate when windows are replaced by solid walls. Following this line of thought, it has been found that learning ability may increase with continuous sensory deprivation (Vernon and Hoffman, 1956), and that errors were fewer in the less rich environment (Vernon and McGill, 1957).

However, there has also been a practical trend toward an emphatic enrichment of the child's internal or classroom environment. Many modern classrooms are replete with noise, tools, posters, paintings, mobiles, and multifarious activities. The assumption is that environmental richness is conducive to learning. A study of a year-long classroom enrichment program, however, found that children's performances were not enhanced (Busse *et al.*, 1972). On a number of performance measures the control groups surpassed the performance of groups from the enriched environment. The experimenters suggest: "There can be too much of a good thing."

In this context Trabasso (1968) has argued that:

> there is some danger in enriching a learning environment — perhaps we might do better as teachers to impoverish the environment by displaying only those objects, words, or relationships that are to be learned.

In other words, by making the environment dull and the task interesting, the child would become more task-oriented. It was found, for example, that brain-injured children learned more and learned faster when the windows of their rooms were covered, and when the children sat in front of a blank wall and were exposed to a small portion of reading material through an opening.

In order to investigate the conflicting claims of environmental impoverishment and enrichment, Carole Porteous (1972) exposed children to a learning task in an environment which was sufficiently flexible to permit the rearrangement of soft furnishings, posters, and mobiles to give distinct levels of environmental complexity. Students were found to learn best in the low-complexity and least well in the high-complexity environment. Children were found to spend more time looking at the environment, rather than the task, in the high-complexity condition (Fig. 8.5). Of course, several replications of the experiment would be required to discover whether adaptation occurred and the environmental display became effectively less noticeable. Moreover, there was no significant correlation between inattention to the task and performance level. When a child is looking around the room it is impossible to assess whether he is attending to the environmental displays or whether he is rehearsing the learning task. Clearly, a design decision for or against enrichment of the traditionally bare classroom or the impoverishment of many modern classrooms will require much more research on the lines proposed by Porteous.

The Integrative Area

In the realm of social interaction, designers have made "imperious claims" that the layout or plan of the physical environment will have profound effects upon behavior (Gutman, 1966). For most thoughtful designers, the *site plan* is not simply a mechanistic tool for the laying out of the building structures of

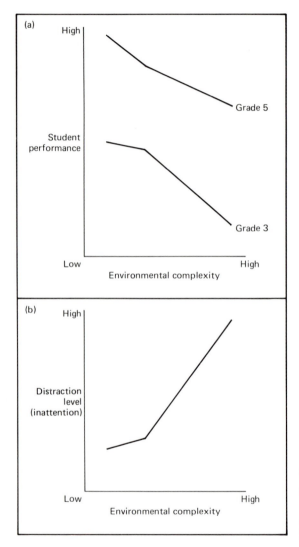

Fig. 8.5

Environmental complexity, attention, and student performance. (Redrawn by permission of Carol Porteous.)

fixed-feature space, but also conveys a social purpose. The site plan is clearly a social symbol. Open space, green lawns, mature trees, culs-de-sac, and private community facilities symbolize status and wealth. Site plans also appear to have a profound effect upon the occupants' communications network. It has been claimed that the site plan can determine one's friendships. Before venturing into this controversial area, however, the effect of the physical environment on interaction in institutional settings will be considered. Whereas the inhabitants of a subdivision may be able to erect a fence, dwellers in institutional environments are usually unable to manipulate their environment. This lack of control is of major concern if physical environment does indeed determine behavior, and especially so when it is realized that "few buildings are ever neutral; they tend to be for you or against you" (Cameron, 1963).

confinement environments

In involuntary confinement situations the confined person is compelled to remain in a space which is separated from the outside world by a barrier over which he has little control. Adjustments are necessary on entering, during one's stay in, and on leaving the confined environment. Ellenberger (1971) has described the deleterious effects of being committed to either semi-isolation or the company of a host of strangers in hospitals, monasteries, mental hospitals, homes for children and the elderly, prisons, and prison camps. Frequently the trauma of commitment to such institutions exacerbates the disease which commitment was meant to cure. In addition, mental hospital inmates often become institutionalized and are unable to cope with the outside world when returned to it.

The prison inmate, on the other hand, is relieved of almost all possessions and provided with a spartan living environment. Sykes (1958) suggests that in a materialistic Western society this attacks the deepest layers of personality. In many institutions there is an unfulfilled demand for privacy but a fear of solitary confinement (Frame, 1961). On the other hand, observation of space flight crews and arctic research station inhabitants suggests that sensory deprivation combined with security and boredom may lead to violence (Robinson, 1972). In prisons the effect of crowding is added (Gilbert, 1972; Sommer, 1972).

Research by Glaser (1964) has contradicted previous suppositions concerning prison socializing. Normal prison and detention center architecture involves dormitories in youth institutions, but small cells for adults. Glaser suggests, however, that dormitories promote the spread of criminal attitudes far more among younger inmates than among adults. It seems, therefore, sensible to provide the juvenile offender with private quarters for those parts of the day when he is not participating in a supervised program.

In greater detail, there appears to be more reading in cells than in dormitories, and cell inmates also tend to spend more time in out-of-cell activities such as eating, physical culture, and art. The possibility of using the physical environment to influence prison behavior has been investigated by Ricci (1972), who suggests that building spaces which conform more closely to activity patterns will have a therapeutic effect. The physical environment imparts messages to its users. An administration's statement of its confidence in the inmates' ability to act as responsible citizens will not be regarded positively by inmates compelled to use long rows of doorless toilets (Izumi, 1965).

learning environments

Learning environments should not be built solely to promote traditional learning activities in classrooms, libraries, and study areas. The British Oxbridge tradition, following the Greeks, saw formal learning as an interaction between tutor and student while engaged in walking, drinking, or smoking. As an extension of this, the student was expected to gain as much intellectual stimulation informally from his fellow students as from his tutor. Such interaction clearly requires spaces in which to interact. Students recognize this need (Sommer, 1970), but administrators frequently do not (Cameron, 1963):

> few colleges in America have sought self-consciously to provide physical surroundings calculated to maximize . . . congenial and informal contact.

An open room with a coffee pot may be all that is needed to promote social interaction and provide the setting for vigorous intellectual debate.

Clem *et al.* (1974) came to similar conclusions after studying interaction patterns in traditional fixed-plan and modern open-plan schools. In the fixed-plan school the class tended to work in large groups or as individuals engaged in identical teacher-initiated activities. In the open-plan school, there was much more small-group behavior, peer instruction, and student-initiated activity. The open-plan school facilitiated the use of physical resources and the use of the teacher as a resource as well as an instructor. The study concluded by suggesting that the open-plan school was better able to achieve the goal of learning via the presently fashionable methods of learning by doing, peer group instruction, and child-oriented learning.

residential environments

Compared with confinement and learning environments, residential areas would seem to be sufficiently complex as to preclude the determination of voluntary behavior by the physical environment. It is in just such environments, however, that most of the work on the determination of social interaction by the physical environment has been carried out. Strong relationships between friendship patterns and the distances functionally separating habitations have been found in studies of barracks (Blake *et al.*, 1956), student housing projects and dormitories (Priest and Sawyer, 1967), and suburbs.

Before exploring these in detail, however, the notion of propinquity (proximity, nearness) must be clarified. Marriage choices, voting behavior, and racial prejudice reflect propinquity; power and leadership are distributed by it. When architects draw up site plans, the location and orientation of houses may also specify future relationships because of the locations and orientations the occupants are thereby compelled to take up. The concept most generally expressed is that physical proximity will render friendships or interactions more likely with persons whose dwelling units are close to one's own. *Physical proximity,* the measurable physical distance between units, however, is only one type of proximity. *Functional proximity,* perhaps more important, concerns the distance between units taking into consideration possible lines of movement. This is a measure of potential accessibility. Clearly, the house next door may be physically proximate, but if surrounded by high walls, barbed wire, and electronic surveillance devices it is functionally much more distant than a normal house a block away.

Many early studies of the determination of social interaction by architectural design were performed soon after the end of World War II in student housing environments. The classic study is that of the Westgate veterans' housing project on the Massachusetts Institute of Technology campus (Festinger *et al.,* 1950). Two distinct housing types were available. Westgate comprised small prefabricated single family homes grouped around courtyards. Westgate West consisted of several military barrack buildings with five apartments on each of two floors, all leading out to communal balconies rather than on to a central hallway (Fig. 8.6).

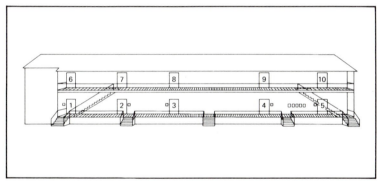

Fig. 8.6

Diagram of a Westgate West building, M.I.T. campus. (Reprinted from L. Festinger, S. Schachter, and K. Back, *Social Pressures in Informal Groups,* with permission of the publishers, Stanford University Press. © 1950 by Leon Festinger, Stanley Schachter, and Kurt Back.

In Westgate, friendships were found to be a function of physical proximity. Residents were likely to make friends with persons in the same court, and within the court with those living physically closest to themselves. Architectural determinism did not operate in the same way in Westgate West, at least for residents of the upper floor. Lower-floor residents had a choice of five stairways (one each) to ground level. Upper-floor residents shared two stairways, one at each end of the upper-floor balcony. This system brought second-floor residents into frequent contact with the inhabitants of the end apartments on the lower floor, but not with centrally located lower-floor residents. Friendships were made on the basis of functional rather than physical proximity.

Similar results were produced by a study of dormitories at Princeton (Case, in Michelson, 1970). Here the crucial element in social interaction appeared to be the placement of lavatory facilities. By physiological necessity students were compelled to travel to these clustered facilities, thus promoting interaction nearby. There was much contact between residents of dormitory sections which shared lavatory facilities and little interaction between sections that did not. In a second building the same facility provoked interaction, but in this case vertically between floors (some floors had no toilet facilities) rather than horizontally along floors. Case concluded that 70 percent of the friendships in the former building and 76 percent in the latter building were influenced by architectural design.

Porteous (1968) compared friendship formation in two halls of residence in the University of Hull, England. Hall A was horizontal in design, with two separate wings, each with two floors. It stood off-campus in its own grounds and contained a dining hall. In contrast, Hall B was vertical in design, comprising eight floors. It stood on the university campus, had no grounds of its own, and had no dining facilities as it was adjacent to the Student Union building. Seventy-five percent of the students from each hall were randomly sampled as respondents and were found to be fairly homogeneous with respect to sex (male) and age (19–20 years). There were no significant differences between the halls with respect to major subject, extraversion or neuroticism (based on personality tests), or social class. In each case students chose their hall, but had been randomly assigned to rooms within the hall.

In both halls friends were likely to be studying the same subject, have the same social interests, be of similar age, be in the same academic year, and be of the same social background. Locality of origin was not important. Proximity proved to be an equivocal factor. In Hall A, 73 percent of friends were in the same wing; overall, however, physical proximity was of no importance for 76 percent of friends were not on the same corridor. In Hall B, only 44 percent of friends were on the same corridor; physical proximity was not statistically significant as a friendship-influencing factor.

Sociability indices were also derived by asking respondents to estimate the number of people in their hall, to give the number of residents with whom they were acquainted, and to give the number of acquaintances on the same corridor. Residents of the horizontal hall (A) were far more accurate in their estimations of the total resident population (Table 8.3); the range for the vertical hall (B) demonstrates wild inaccuracies. Respondents from both hall groups stated that they were acquainted with about one-quarter of the total

TABLE 8.3

ESTIMATES FOR HALL POPULATION

Hall	Actual Population	Percentage Giving Correct Estimate (within 10% error)	Range of Estimates
A	160	95	140–180
B	100	63	70–250

Source: Porteous (1968)

residents. However, 68 percent of Hall B students recognized over 90 percent of the inhabitants of their corridor, with only 12 percent for Hall A.

It is likely that hall design influenced hall knowledge as revealed by the sociability indices. Hall A, while having long corridors which probably prevented strong acquaintanceship at the corridor level, also had a dining hall, recreation facilities, and grounds. Communal use of these probably permitted more efficient scanning of fellow residents and more frequent contact with a wide range of fellow students. In contrast, Hall B had almost no communal facilities and consisted of short corridors leading to a central elevator shaft. Functionally, contact and scanning potential were much reduced and Hall B residents, while knowing most of their fellow residents on their short corridor, were unlikely to know people from the hall at large. Further questions confirmed that interaction in Hall B was corridor oriented while that in Hall A was hall oriented. In particular, Hall A friends tended to eat together and hall friends were also reported to be university-wide friends; in contrast, Hall B showed a much lower level of coincidence between hall friends and university friends.

In terms of the potential for community spirit, this research supports the horizontal design of Hall A, for Hall B, in which the author lived, showed a remarkable lack of unity. However, the demand for community spirit on the part of hall administrators is value-laden. European universities, especially in Germany, have concentrated on providing lecture halls, libraries, laboratories, and ceremonial halls; students are expected to find their own board and lodging (Hsia, 1967). The English collegiate tradition, however, emphasizes communal living, less to provide housing or even promote sociability *per se*, but rather to encourage a total learning environment. Colleges in North America have followed both patterns.

In this connection the case of the University of Victoria, British Columbia, is instructive. The design of student residences, especially those grouped into colleges to which students belong and to which they are expected to show allegiance, involves the identification of social goals. The goals of the designers of Lansdowne and Craigdarroch colleges included the promotion among both residents and nonresidents (who also belonged to a college) of a sense of identity, and the fostering of friendly relations not only between students but also between students and faculty members of the college.

A study of interaction behavior, however, found several areas of mismatch between architectural design, actual behavior, and the goal of community interaction. Television rooms, housing at best a passive form of interaction, were universally crowded and judged by students to be too small. Communal areas, such as games rooms, lounges, and study libraries were frequently underused because the presence of one or two persons engaged in study was sufficient to inhibit the entry of others (see Chapter 3). One respondent complained: "Someone is always reading in there. No one feels in the mood for socializing when someone is reading in the room." Even if lounges contained no persons indulging in studying behavior, they remained largely unused. A typical response was: "I don't like the atmosphere; it's too big to meet anybody." Among inmates of the same sex, most interactions appeared to be initiated, if not sustained, in communal washroom and kitchen areas. Salinger's epic of adolescence, *The Catcher in the Rye* (1951), corroborates this finding.

Further, the possibility of inducing community spirit was reduced in Craigdarroch College by its division into four separate blocks, two housing males and two housing females. Questionnaire studies demonstrated that the average inhabitant of one of these blocks would be likely to have some form of acquaintanceship with 90 percent of the residents of the same floor and 35 percent of those in the same block, but with only 11 percent of those in the adjacent block of the same sex, and a mere 5 percent of persons in the two adjacent blocks of the opposite sex. Though sex is a major variable here, it is likely that the physical separation of the four halls hinders social interaction on the college level and promotes the formation of small-group rather than college-wide loyalties. In terms of student-faculty relationships, the location of faculty offices at the end of a closed-corridor system inhibited interaction. In contrast, Lansdowne College appeared to enjoy more sustained relationships between staff and students because of a spatial link between faculty offices and a student lounge area, a plan which invites, rather than inhibits, communication. Nevertheless, and partly in response to student pressure, the university terminated the college system after only a few years' operation, the halls reverting to their housing and informal socializing functions.

The present trend in student housing is away from high-density, corridor-type arrangements to complexes of suites which, by providing a sense of smallness, intimacy, and support, are perceived to be better social environments (Heilweil, 1973). Bickman *et al.* (1973) found that students were less ready to engage in helping behavior in high-density sites than in low-density environments (see also Chapter 7). Whereas corridor-type living environments appear to be associated with intellectuality, achievement, and independence, suites are more associated with attitudes of social involvement and support (Gerst and Sweetwood, 1973). Valins and Baum (1973) go so far as to suggest that corridor-type dormitories are environments of sensory overload, are considered overcrowded by their inhabitants, result in personal withdrawal from interaction, and may be considered analogous to a behavioral sink. Suites, such as an arrangement of three rooms housing four students, however, are not the complete answer to the student housing problem. Although privacy is increased, the likelihood of roommate incompatibility is also increased if students are randomly assigned to the suites (Corbett, 1973). Considerable communication and cooperation between suite-mates is required for the enjoyment of maximum benefits from suite living.

Studies of student housing, however immediately relevant to the readers of this book, are perhaps less important than studies of residential subdivisions if only because many readers will sooner or later leave the one environment for the other. The Westgate study was, in effect, a study of a residential subdivision rather than a hall of residence. A similar study, with similar results, was carried out in a similar social and physical environment by Caplow and Foreman (1950). The chief feature of these studies was that awareness of others, which often ripened into friendship, was based largely on the orientation of house doors.

A contemporaneous study by Kuper (1953) emphasized the importance of door orientations and thus of functional rather than physical proximity. The auditory problem of party neighbors in these side-by-side duplexes has already been mentioned. Party neighbors were both physically and auditorily proximate. However, because of door orientations, side neighbors were functionally closer than party neighbors (Fig. 8.7). People tended primarily to use their side doors, which faced into the narrow strip of land between two adjacent duplexes. This threw them into visual contact with side neighbors; the latter were more frequently regarded as friends than party neighbors whose doors were functionally further away. Merton's (1948) study of a planned industrial town in the United States confirms the importance of door orientations. For example, considering across-the-street friendships only, 74 percent of these were among people who both had doors facing the street, while only 4 percent were among people both of whom were without doors facing the street.

Whyte's (1956) observations of social interaction in Park Forest, a young executive-professional suburb of Chicago, brought out further aspects of functional proximity. The latter was intensified by the siting of lawns, the orientation of doors and windows toward each other, and the sharing of driveways. In addition, the suburb was child oriented, so that mothers would gravitate for kaffeeklatsching to those houses with the best possibilities for the surveillance of children at play. Barriers to interaction were created by wide streets and rear fences. Whyte also found that each court or micro-neighborhood tended to have its own style of neighboring, such as parties, picnics, churchgoing, and the like. Carefully noting neighboring activity and location in 1953, he obtained the same data for the same months in 1956. In the interval there had been a large turnover of residents, and neighboring activities had changed. However, despite these changes in both residents and activities, Whyte found that the same houses tended to be grouped together by interactive links.

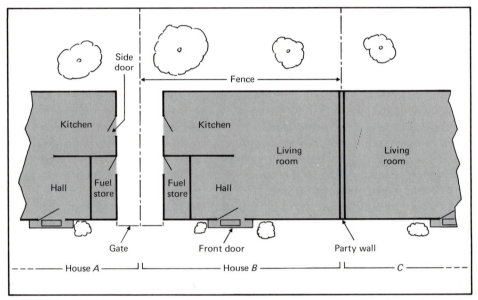

Fig. 8.7

First (ground) floor plan, side-by-side duplex housing in England (after Kuper).

Whyte asserted that this phenomenon was induced by functional proximity. He came to further deterministic conclusions, stating, for example, that persons living in the center of a block are more likely to have high levels of neighbor interaction than persons living at the corners of a block. For this reason he suggested that introverts should occupy end and extraverts central positions. Should these types occupy unsuitable positions, the one would feel the neighborhood to be too pushy, the other would find it too unfriendly. Based on his observations, Whyte (1956) believes that the designer of a residential environment has the power to determine social relationships by means of site plan manipulation:

> In suburbia friendship has become almost predictable . . . it is possible deliberately to plan a layout which will produce a closeknit social group . . . certain kinds of physical layouts can virtually produce the "happy" group.

If architects can specify our social relationships as just described, the consequences for personal freedom are great. As noted earlier, residential propinquity is an important factor in voting behavior and even in choosing a marriage partner. All the studies previously mentioned have discussed the various consequences of design-determined interaction. At a rather banal level, neighbors appear to emulate each other in a "keeping up with the Joneses" fashion, so that the diffusion of luxury appliances in micro-neighborhoods can be both mapped and predicted (Whyte, 1954). Whyte also developed the concept of the tyranny of the small group, which permits little deviance from its norms. In Westgate, opinions and attitudes on local issues varied from clique to clique. To deviate from these opinions was to risk ostracism by the group. Persons who do not fit into the general pattern of the residential area, such as minorities or single persons in suburbia, are generally not included in the web of friendship (Tomeh, 1964). In studies of Levittown, Gans (1967) found that working-class people felt out of place in a middle-class setting. Small-group tyranny includes the constant observation by others of one's behavior, especially in court and cul-de-sac layouts.

Further, high intensity of contact, as determined by the environment, does not inevitably lead to friendship but may produce friction between neighbors. Kuper (1953) reports a long-term quarrel between side neighbors which resulted in their avoiding each other at their side doors, "a considerable feat, involving reconnaissance every time the housewife plans an exit from her house." Many residents in such layouts have reduced functional proximity by means of walls, trellises, or symbolic fences. This protection is impossible with party neighbors, and the physical and auditory intimacy suffered by dwellers in such arrangements may have drastic results. In 1972, for example, one such resident in Warwickshire, England, shot all his party neighbors to death (*Sunday Times Magazine,* 15 July 1973). The neighbor family had provided an atmosphere of constant harassment for three years, including such activities as tearing down boundary fences, making threats, hurling abuse, and creating such high noise levels all night that sleep in the bedrooms on the other side of the party wall was impossible. Because of such provocation the neighbor was found guilty of manslaughter on the ground of diminished responsibility.

the problem of propinquity

Despite much evidence, based on detailed research, that physical and functional proximity determine neighbor interaction and friendship formation, this concept has not remained unchallenged. Research in some communities, for example, has not supported the concept of door orientation as a determinant. In Levittown Gans (1967) found that predictions of interaction based on door orientations could not be confirmed by observation of interaction activities.

Most of the criticism, however, has been directed at the assumptions made by researchers who came to the conclusion that functional proximity determines relationships. In particular, it may have been remarked upon by the reader that one outstanding characteristic of all the studies previously cited is that the groups studied were extremely homogeneous. Single students, married war veteran students, the industrial workers of Kuper and Merton, and the organization men of Park Forest were all largely homogeneous groups in terms of social status, income, education, and stage in the life cycle. In particular, tests of student characteristics frequently fail to discover any significant differences in socioeconomic class or other variables between groups of students. Gans (1961b) therefore suggests that architectural design will influence positive interaction only if there is substantial group homogeneity. In a review of relevant studies, Rosow (1961) comes to the same conclusion.

Homogeneity, of course, will not occur in terms of all possible characteristics. However, in suburban environments it is probable that ethnicity and religion are less important than similar position in the child-rearing stage of the life cycle. Homogeneity is enhanced if there is substantial agreement on child-rearing methods. The homogeneity of a neighborhood is clearly a perceptual phenomenon, that is, it must be perceived to exist by the inhabitants. In this respect Tomeh (1969) found that the greater the perceived homogeneity of residents, the greater their participation in neighborhood activities. It is therefore necessary to add a third proximity type to the proximity typology.

Social proximity refers to residents' perceptions of each other in terms of attitudes, opinions, and social characteristics. People are socially proximate if they appear to be alike in terms of one or more important characteristics such as age, class, or cultural group. Social proximity is expressed in the phrase: "We're all alike in this neighborhood." Low degrees of perceived social proximity in low-income settings, notably public housing, help account for the low intensity of neighboring in such environments.

A second type of homogeneity concerns not social characteristics but common needs and mutual motivations. A review of relevant research suggests that when people are brought together for the first time, as in the occupation of a new suburban subdivision, considerable social solidarity springs up (Rosow, 1961). At such a time, most people are faced with a variety of similar tasks, such as lawn making. Mutual assistance appears to be given readily and, assuming homogeneity (social proximity), by the law of least effort (Zipf, 1949) close neighbors are more likely to help each other than residents living further away. Some of these mutual relationships may ripen into lasting friendship.

A number of researchers, however, have found that, as time passes, the intense neighboring activity gradually declines along with the general emergencies of residential relocation. As people become settled, they have more time to select friends from a wider area and in doing so they frequently decrease contact with immediate neighbors. In Gans' Levittown study, quite intense neighboring occurred when residents initially moved in. After two years, however, only 31 percent of the residents had the majority of their friendships located on the same street. Intense neighboring, it seems, will tend to be continued over a lengthy period of time only if strong needs for mutual assistance remain, as in the case of a suburb with a high resident turnover rate. It is therefore possible to add a fourth proximity type. *Instrumental proximity* refers to mutual feelings of a need for cooperation. As discussed in Chapter 4, this is a minor component of low-intensity neighboring.

Given these modifications of physical and functional proximity, we may now assess the possibility that planners are able to determine friendship and sociability by means of the site plan. On the whole, there is general agreement that functional proximity may be an initial cause of an intensive positive relationship. However, it is not a sufficient condition for friendship, and tends to operate only where there is evidence of strong instrumental and social proximity. Even then, with time, relationships with immediate neighbors tend to become of lesser importance in an individual's overall web of friendship. The key concept appears to be resident homogeneity, but as yet there is little agreement with regard to what kind of homogeneity (e.g., child-rearing practices, political beliefs, religion, race, etc.) is most conducive to spatially determined friendship.

A recent series of studies (Yoshioka and Athanasiou, 1971), however, suggests that important homogeneity factors in the friendship-distance equation are the stage in the life cycle, social status, ethnicity, and social attitudes. Propinquity appears to be important in maintaining friendships among women who have little in common besides the life-cycle stage (especially the stage involving young children). At greater distances, however, the maintenance of friendship requires social homogeneity; "propinquity may overcome status differences, but not life-cycle stage differences" (Athanasiou and Yoshioka, 1973, 61). These results, based on detailed research, tend to support Gans' (1961b, 1967) hypotheses which were based on observation. Gans, however, also asserted that homogeneity was more important than propinquity in determining the intensity of relationships. In contrast, Athanasiou and Yoshioka found that people did tend to have a high proportion of their more intense relationships in the immediate vicinity of their home. The authors are careful to state, however, that much more research on a wide variety of living environments is required before we can attempt to "write the equation which specifies the probability that A and B are friends based on the distance between A and B and the similarity of A and B on other variables" (Athanasiou and Yoshioka, 1973, 63).

It is clear that planners *can* create functional proximity and, by orienting doors and windows, can manipulate visual and social contacts among neighbors. By their arrangement of house types builders can specify income homogeneity in a particular area; real-estate companies can also guide people to areas of high social proximity. What none of these manipulations of functional and social proximity can achieve, however, is the formation of lasting friendships and an atmosphere of community (Chapter 4). A series of populations selected for homogeneity, which simultaneously occupied a new housing estate in Scotland, were able to form only small internally interacting groups, without connecting links and therefore with little sense of community (Hole, 1959). Moreover, simply by arranging for frequent visual contact between neighbors the designer cannot guarantee whether the relationship produced will be friendly or unfriendly; all he can specify is that it will initially be fairly intense. The question of whether planners *should* exercise such manipulatory powers is left for the reader to decide, though a related general discussion of planners versus people is raised in Chapter 12.

The Behavior Setting and Determinism

Hole's study noted that lack of community feeling was probably caused by the absence of places wherein contact could be made. This need for a recognized interaction space was brought out in Willa Cather's novel *My Ántonia* (1918). The early peopling of parts of Nebraska involved Bohemian and Scandinavian immigrants occupying the rural areas and rather more urbane New Englanders in the towns. As the adults of each group despised the other, and as no acceptable place existed for the young people of both groups to meet and mingle, there was no possibility for the intermarriage so necessary for the operation of the American ethnic melting-pot. When a traveling circus came to town, however, the tents "brought the town boys and the country girls together on neutral ground," no doubt to their mutual satisfaction.

The need for neutral ground as a meeting place for hostile groups or strangers was recognized early by the sociologist Simmel (Spykman, 1925). In public housing projects social interaction often occurs informally in laundry rooms rather than formally in the community center. In student halls of residence, as we have seen, washrooms and kitchens are preferred over lounges. In factories it is the water fountain and in ships the galley which often become the focus of sociability. The pathologies associated with rooming house districts (Chapter 7) may be reinforced by isolation caused by the fact that rooming houses rarely have a common meeting place where friendships may be initiated and maintained (Zorbaugh, 1929). Modern apartment blocks may induce similar problems. Informal snacking areas near libraries and classrooms may aid both sociability and peer learning among students; "if you can't rub elbows, it is hard to rub minds" (Cameron, 1963).

Spaces recognized by their users to be primarily suited to certain kinds of activity, whether or not designed as such, are known as *behavior settings* (Barker and Wright, 1955; Barker, 1968; Gump, 1971; Wicker, 1972b). A behavior setting is a stable combination of behavior and phenomenal environment which possesses the following properties:

a) a recurrent behavior pattern;

b) a particular phenomenal environment; and

c) a specific time-period; with

d) strong congruence between behavior and the phenomenal environment.

With respect to (d) Gump (1971) states that behavior settings are above all the scene of synomorphy (shape similarity). There is a strongly synomorphic relationship between an object for sitting upon (chair), and the sitter's behavior (posture). This approach therefore stresses the goodness of fit between environment and behavior, which appears to have a positive value for the maintenance of the stream of life.

Although time passes and the identities of participants change, there is an essentially persistent and characteristic behavior pattern in a library which differs from that occurring in a fast-food outlet, a drugstore, or a football game. Barker's painstaking study of a small Midwestern town identified 884 public behavior settings. He also identified 198 behavior genotypes (programmed behavior patterns which were not interchangeable). Thus, "if the town were abandoned by its present inhabitants and resettled by people of totally alien culture, they would require 198 instruction books and/or training programs to reconstitute the behavior environment of Midwest" (Barker, 1968, 116).

In its rejection of the one-way determinism of behavior by physical environment and its inclusion of the human environment, the behavior-setting concept becomes an important focus for research on the obviously complex interplay of environment, personality, and behavior. A series of research methodologies and research studies have appeared (Barker, 1968; LeCompte, 1972, 1974). One of the more interesting concerns the differential effect of school size on behavior. In comparison with students from large high schools, their counterparts in small high schools were found to be less sensitive to individual differences in behavior, to see themselves as having greater functional importance, to have more responsibility, to have six times more experience in leadership and 2–5 times more activity participation, to be more tolerant, and to be under greater pressure to perform (Barker and Gump, 1964). On the basis of thirty years of research Barker (1968, 4) states:

> it is possible to predict aspects of childrens' behavior in known settings . . . more adequately from knowledge of the behavior characteristics of the setting than . . . from knowledge of the behavior tendencies of the particular child.

Several theoretical approaches tend to the conclusion that the phenomenal environment influences behavior in behavior settings (Wicker, 1972b). The nature of the influence, however, is as yet poorly understood. It is unlikely to be direct physical determinism. It is more likely to be a function of early socialization and learning. We teach children to be quiet and reverent in church, to sleep in bedrooms, to eat in dining rooms, and to play in parks, yards, playgrounds, and designated areas of the family home. As these are general social norms, the performance of x activity in setting X is usually rewarding, whereas the performance of y could well result in some form of punishment. Moreover, as the individual plays his various roles in society and family (e.g., teacher, bus passenger, lover, parent), every role requires an appropriate role setting (Goffman, 1963). Attempting to play role z in setting A may have disastrous consequences, hence an "important property of a building is its ability to provide the appropriate setting for its users" (Canter, 1969).

The concept of the behavior setting, although extremely difficult to operationalize, seems to be a reasonable probabilistic compromise between the chaos of possibilism and the structured extremes of determinism. As amply demonstrated throughout this chapter, direct determinism of behavior by the physical environment is difficult to assess. Between the stimulus of environment and the response of behavior there is a strong screen of personal and social variables (Chapter 9). Gans (1961a, b) has drawn attention to the importance of age, sex, class, and culture in mediating environmental influences on friendship formation (see Chapters 10–11). Moreover, most of the studies which concluded that friendship was determined by design involved socially homogeneous respondents such as lower ranks of the armed forces, students, and the inhabitants of one-class suburbs. Thus social and instrumental proximity come into play.

A further intervening variable is the *environmental competence* of the individual actor. Lawton (1970a) has put forward an environmental docility hypothesis which suggests that the greater the degree of competence of the organism, the less the proportion of variance in behavior due to the phenomenal environment. Clearly, the extreme docility of the inmates of schools, prisons, mental institutions, hospitals, old peoples' homes and the like justifies the heavy research emphasis on these areas. Free-ranging adults appear to be less docile (White, 1959). Competence, however, is not an absolute quality. An individual's competence is likely to vary according to the behavior setting and his role within it (Kelly, 1972).

In summary, it is clear that the physical environment is likely to determine behavior only in extreme cases. In everyday life we should rather look upon the physical environment as *facilitative* rather than as determinative. In probabilistic terms, the physical environment permits a range of behaviors. However, the individual's choice of a particular behavior is likely to be conditioned by the behavior setting. And behavior in the behavior setting is a learned response, itself largely conditioned by the contextual environment and modified by the individual's experiential and behavioral environments, all of which are discussed in Chapters 9–11.

Summary

1. Social scientists have asserted, and many designers believe, that fixed-feature space has a determining influence on behavior. Environmental determinism has reemerged on the more subtle, small-scale level of rooms, buildings, and neighborhoods.
2. Environmental influences are rarely direct, however. There are at least seven major areas of man-environment interaction, all of which interrelate in a complex manner.
3. Studies of the adaptive area in street, home, work, and learning environments suggest that the form of the physical environment may considerably aid or hinder human activities. There are strong links between design and both work efficiency and neighbor tolerance.
4. In learning-environment design a controversy over optimal stimulation levels exists. Though the practical trend is toward the maximization of classroom stimuli, experimental results indicate that learning is facilitated by a reduction in general environmental stimuli and an emphasis on task-oriented stimuli.
5. Studies of the integrative area in student residences and several types of housing environment appear to indicate that proximity (physical and functional) is an important factor in neighbor interaction and friendship formation.
6. In student halls of residence different designs can foster residence-wide loyalties, small-group loyalties, or promote withdrawal from interaction.
7. The orientation of doors, windows, driveways, and other physical features is important in initiating contact between the inhabitants of residential areas.

8. Functional proximity, however, tends to operate in fostering sustained interaction only where there is *instrumental* or *social* proximity between residents. Both imply homogeneity, and it is suggested that the most important homogeneity-specifying variables are social class and stage in the life cycle.

9. Though the planner may be able to determine initial contacts by site-plan manipulation, he is unable to specify the direction of the relationship, i.e., friendliness or hostility.

10. Determinism of behavior by the physical environment is a one-way process which fails to take into account the complex interplay of environment, actor, and behavior. Both social characteristics and personal attributes, such as competence, mediate environmental influences.

11. The behavior-setting approach, which considers the complex fit between environment and behavior, is a more valid probabilistic mode of viewing behavior-environment congruence.

Further Reading

BARKER, R. G. (1968), *Ecological Psychology*. Stanford, Calif.: Stanford University Press.

FESTINGER, L., S. SCHACTER, and K. BACK (1950), *Social Pressures in Informal Groups*. New York: Harper.

GANS, H. (1961), "Planning and Social Life: Friendship and Neighbor Relations in Suburban Communities," *Journal of the American Institute of Planners* 27: 176–84. See also his *People and Plans*, New York: Basic Books (1968).

WHYTE, W. H. (1956), *The Organization Man*. Garden City, N.Y.: Doubleday, Chapter 23.

9

PERSONAL ENVIRONMENTS: BEHAVIORAL AND EXPERIENTIAL

> *All men have the stars . . . but they are not the same things for different people. For some, who are travelers, the stars are guides. For others they are no more than little lights in the sky. For others, who are scholars, they are problems . . . But all the stars are silent.**
>
> The Little Prince

As defined in Chapter 6, the individual's personal environments are two in number. The behavioral environment is his image of the immediate real-world phenomenal environment. His experiential environment is the mental storehouse containing the sum of his experiences, including behavioral environments of the past, and thus roughly coinciding with his personality. A neopossibilist argument would be that the individual's view of the world, being based not only on inputs from contextual and phenomenal environmental experience but also on fantasy and imagination, is sufficiently different from that of any other individual to demand a major study effort in the light of its behavioral consequences (Lowenthal, 1961; Tuan, 1974). The concept of human exceptionalism has had considerable impact on the social sciences (Klausner, 1971) and most recently in geography (Relph, 1970). There is a theoretical gulf between those social scientists who assert that societies are made up of behaving individuals (most ethologists, for example) and those who believe a society to be "a superorganic whole which often operates by rules which are independent of any given individual at any given moment" (Pfeiffer, 1971). We will first concentrate on the exceptionalist, individual-centered point of view.

---

*   A. de Saint-Exupéry (1943), *The Little Prince.* New York: Harcourt, Brace and World.

The Individual

A wealth of evidence supports the view that the individual, rather than the group, is the most meaningful entity for study in terms of man-environment interactions. Personal space is clearly an individual experience; every individual will react somewhat differently to crowding. At the meso-space level, home and neighborhood have different meanings for different people. Using two independent measures of an individual's mental representation of the environment (sketch-mapping and verbal-association tests), Moore (1974) found that there were consistent differences between individuals of the same age, sex, and intellectual level. Our attitudes to life clearly reflect individual differences in physiology and biochemistry.

decision making

It is on the basis of our personal environments that we make decisions which are translated into actions. These actions take place in the phenomenal environment and therefore have consequences for objects and other individuals. In an unmotivated state the inactive individual can be described by a set of personal functional variables (mental and physical abilities, value system), a set of personal structural variables (age, income, occupation, etc.), and a set of existence variables (location, orientation) (Golledge *et al.*, 1972). Decisions occur when the individual is motivated to make them, either by self-generated needs or external stimuli.

Decisions to act usually result in some form of interaction with the phenomenal environment. Carr (1967) has put forward a five-phase summary of the man-environment interaction process which holds for any level of planful interaction from personal planning to national planning.

1.   *The Directive Phase.*   This concerns the determination of the individual's needs, desires, and purposes.

2.   *The Intelligence Phase.*   As was suggested in the discussion of cognitive maps, the phenomenal environment consists of a myriad of To Whom It May Concern messages from which the individual selects those which concern him (Wiener, 1964). According to his idiosyncratic predilections, the individual perceives and remembers the environment, creating his personal behavioral environment from it.

3.   *The Planning Phase.*   Using the model of the real world developed in the intelligence phase, a plan is made. Inputs to the planning phase come also from past experience, changes in the phenomenal environment (and thus in the behavioral environment), and feedback from ongoing activity.

4. *The Action Phase.* When plan is converted into action, the importance of nonpersonal environmental influences becomes apparent. The form and content of the phenomenal environment supports some activities and hinders others. It is the individual's perception of these constraints and supports which guides his actions.

5. *The Review Phase.* Feedback from the phenomenal environment permits assessment of the rewards obtained from the action. This assessment may be used in evaluating the possibility of other, future actions. Knowledge resulting from action adds to the meaning the phenomenal environment has for us. Closely linked with these meanings, we create a personal system of values associated with the nonpersonal environment.

In traditional societies lack of complex technology and closeness to nature ensure that the process of decision making, action, feedback, and environmental alteration is immediate, continuous, and adaptive. In urban-industrial societies, the intricate network of decisions affecting the phenomenal environment is excessively complex and as yet incompletely analyzed. As many far-reaching decisions, from declaring war to redeveloping central cities, are made by powerful individuals or small elite groups, it seems important that we should know on what basis these decisions are made. The ultimate bases, of course, are the behavioral and experiential environments of the decision makers.

Growth of interest in the personality assessment of decision makers whose actions are likely to influence the common phenomenal environment has arisen because of three parallel developments (Burton, 1971). Increasingly, the public demands a greater share in decisions which will affect the environmental quality of their personal and collective action spaces. Governments, increasingly aware of this trend toward participatory democracy, have recognized the need to improve upon the old method of assessing public preferences by means of biased constituency feedback and personal intuition. In universities there has been growing interest in behavioral aspects of the man-environment system, and in particular in trying to see the world from the respondent's, rather than the researcher's, point of view. This *phenomenological* posture has involved the creation of methods for tapping the personal environments of the individual decision maker.

We are all decision makers all of the time, and the decisions we make are based as much upon our personalities as upon the facts of the situation. Personality comprises "the natural and acquired impulses, and habits, interests, and complexes, the sentiments and ideals, the opinions and beliefs" of the individual (Drever, 1964). It is a complex entity which manifests itself in the form of value orientations, social attitudes, intellectual abilities, dispositions, and other personality traits. Recent research on personal decision making has tended to emphasize three major components: perceptions, attitudes and values, and preferences and satisfactions.

Perception

In Chapter 6 perception was defined in the strict neuropsychological sense as the process of becoming aware of a stimulus. In common parlance, however, and increasingly in environmental psychology, architecture, and geography, the verb *perceive* and the noun *perception* are applied to the behavioral environment. Thus the personal image one has of the phenomenal environment is said to be one's perception of the environment. Tuan (1974, 4) regards perception as "both the response of the senses to external stimuli and purposeful activity in which certain phenomena are clearly registered while others recede . . . or are blocked out." Schiff (1971, 7) emphasizes the distinction between neurological definitions of perception and *social perception* which is concerned with "the impression one has of . . . stimuli, as that impression is modified by the perceiver's past experience in general, his previous experience with that same or similar stimuli, and the individual's state at the moment he is viewing the stimulus of interest."

In the remainder of this book this common interpretation of perception will be used. We must bear in mind that in this sense a perception is part of the behavioral environment as defined in Chapter 6, being made up of an externally generated stimulus (a percept) modified by the experiential environment. Following Schiff, the term perception is reserved for instances in which there is or was an actual external stimulus to perceive, and which was perceived directly by the individual. Sets of beliefs based on events not experienced by the individual, or personally experienced at some time in the past, have been incorporated into the information storehouse of the experiential environment, and are more accurately referred to as beliefs, cognitions, values, or attitudes.

individual variations in perception

That perception varies with the individual is a commonplace. Two individuals with different past experiences and present wants may become aware of the same external stimulus, receive the same image on the retina, and yet perceive the image differently after it has been processed by the brain. This concept is best illustrated in a painting by Erhard Jacoby (Fig. 9.1). In Jungian psychoanalytic terms, we are surrounded by something completely unknown and unknowable, represented by the grey background of the painting. Looking at the same urban scene, the man, woman, and child each perceive it somewhat differently. The child's image is foreshortened and lacks detail. The woman is concerned with nearer objects, specific people, and certain signs. The man's view is broader and deeper and involves different objects, people, and signs. It must be emphasized here that we are concentrating upon individual rather than group (sex and age) differences.

Fig. 9.1

Individual differences in visual perception. (Copyright Erhard Jacoby, from Carl G. Jung, *Man and His Symbols,* London: Aldus Books.

Several properties of the individual contribute to differences in perception, physiology being of great importance. One of the more interesting accounts of the relationship between physiology and perception is Edwin Abbot's *Flatland* (1884). In this early science fiction work the hero is a square whose world, Flatland, is wholly two-dimensional (Fig. 9.2). Led by a three-dimensional sphere, which he is quite unable to perceive as such, Square is taken to Pointland, the Abyss of No Dimensions. Pointland has a single inhabitant, who occupies his whole world, which has no length, breadth, or height. This single inhabitant is the One; for him "space is Me." It is impossible for Square to make contact with the Point, which is unable to perceive anything but itself. In Lineland, which has the one dimension of length, the king is surprised to find Square entering his linear kingdom in the perceived form of a superfluous point. He is even more surprised when Square, passing across the king's unilinear line of vision, apparently falls off the world. Passing from Lineland, where "space is length," and through his home

territory of Flatland, where "space is length and breadth indefinitely prolonged" and only lines can be perceived, Square reaches Spaceland, where
space includes the third dimension of height. Convinced of the reality of
three-dimensionality by Sphere, Square then loses Sphere's friendship by
postulating fourth- and fifth-dimensional lands. Unabashed, Square returns
to two-dimensional Flatland, proclaims the coming of the Third Dimension,
and is promptly clapped into a lunatic asylum.

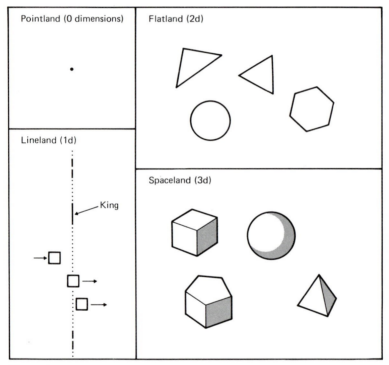

Fig. 9.2

Lands of three, two, one, and no dimensions (after E. Abbot). Note the King of
Flatland perceives the Square as a point which appears and disappears from his
world.

Our perceptions clearly depend upon our physiological abilities, notably
our capacities for sight, taste, smell, hearing, and touch. The individual
perceives the world through all the senses simultaneously. However, compared with many animals, who operate in a landscape of odors or sounds,
humans rely extensively on vision. And whereas tasting, smelling, touching,
and even hearing require some degree of involvement with the stimulus

object, vision may readily occur without evoking an emotional response. "The world perceived through the eyes is more abstract than that known to us through the other senses" (Tuan, 1974).

Learning, experience, and habituation are also important. Infants soon acquire the ability to see three-dimensional objects, but experience is needed for the full development of three-dimensional vision. This ability is probably not innate. Persons blind from birth learn to inhabit a visionless world and can operate successfully in it. Some congenitally blind persons have been given their sight in adulthood via surgery. Such persons are usually unable to recognize by sight the objects they perceive instantly by touch. Indeed, they have to be taught to perceive the differences in light and shade which are necessary for the visual perception of solid objects.

However, just as we learn to perceive, we may also unlearn. A given stimulus may at first produce a strong response. When the same stimulus is repeatedly presented, the original response may eventually decrease or disappear. The individual is then said to be habituated to the stimulus. On entering a room reeking with cigarette fumes a nonsmoker's olfactory sense may be strongly assaulted. After spending some time in the atmosphere, however, and with his attention directed elsewhere, he may find that his initial discomfort has disappeared because of adaptation. In the same way, persons habituated to noisy working conditions would feel upset if the noise were suddenly to cease.

Meaning and value of the stimulus are other factors. Schiff (1971) recounts experiments in which children were asked to estimate the size of poker chips. When the chips were given as a reward for performing a task, and could then be used to buy candy, their size was greatly overestimated. When the rewards ceased, size overestimation decreased, rising again when the rewards were reinstated. The size estimations of control groups which did not receive rewards did not vary significantly.

the stimulus object

It may appear somewhat deterministic to suggest that the nature of the stimulus has a major influence on perception. Chaudhuri (1959, 22), however, observes that although art critics have long noted that traditional Oriental art is linear, whereas Western art is plastic, "they do not seem to have realized that this distinction [is] related to the natural appearance of the visual phenomena to the peoples of the two worlds." He goes on: "We see the world as it dictates our way of seeing."

This concept is supported by a cross-cultural study of perception of a variety of geometric optical illusions (Segall *et al.*, 1966). In particular, there were differences in perception between persons brought up in the carpentered, rectangular world of technological societies and those inhabiting the

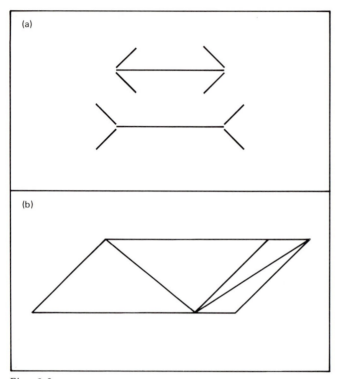

Fig. 9.3

Visual illusions: (a) the Muller-Lyer illusion, (b) the Sander parallelogram illusion.

rounded world of traditional societies. In the Muller-Lyer illusion (Fig. 9.3a) both crossbars are of equal length. People deriving from an environment with a predominance of right angles were more likely than others to pronounce that the lower line looked longer. Similarly, persons from highly technologized societies were more likely to perceive the Sander parallelogram (Fig. 9.3b) as a three-dimensional surface with the shorter left-hand diagonal appearing longer than that to the right. Note that images appear on all retinas as two-dimensional, nonrectangular surfaces; their interpretation as three-dimensional rectangles is of obvious value in an urban setting. Tuan suggests that because urban people, and especially those in cold climates, spend much of their lives in rectangular environments, they are likely to perceive the world in a somewhat different way from rural dwellers and inhabitants of warmer climates.

Traditional Stimulus-Response (S-R) theory in psychology defined perception as a response to an outside stimulus which, producing further stimulation within the organism, eventually results in an appropriate overt response to the stimulus. "What the subject might be said to be inwardly experiencing . . . is of no consequence" (Allport, 1955, 53; Koroscil, 1971). Ignoring the apperceptive and cognitive processes, S-R theory originally concentrated on observable data only, namely, the stimulus object and the subject's response. Considerable criticism by proponents of Gestalt (Koffka, 1935) and information-based (Gibson, 1966) theories of perception has led to increased concern with subjective experiences to the neglect of the stimulus object.

Current thought has seemingly abandoned the original belief that perception is largely determined by the characteristics of the stimulus object. Stimulus determination has given way to the concept of stimulus information, a wide range of potential inputs to which people may attend. Different people, however, will attend to different aspects. The only recent return to a modified stimulus determinism is Carr and Schissler's conclusion, reported in Chapter 5, that the physical environment is the most important single factor in perception. Designers, who have long held this view intuitively, will find this comforting in view of recent demands that they recognize individual differences in perception when designing for clients' personal needs (Lang *et al.*, 1974, 86).

nonpersonal environments

If the architect is designing for a single client, as was his traditional role, individual perceptions could readily be taken into account. More frequently, however, modern architects must produce designs which please committees, and buildings which are used and commented upon, often to some effect, by large numbers of people. It is clearly impossible to take into account the individual perceptions of the myriad user-clients as well as the paying client. Hence design researchers have sought to find regularities in group perception.

Whorf, in *Language, Thought and Reality*, suggests that language and perception are intimately related; each person is locked into his particular language group's way of perceiving the external environment. According to Whorf, English-speakers tend to analyze the world in terms of things linked together by space. Even nonspatial items are spatialized imaginatively for our better understanding (Whorf, 1956, 146):

> I "grasp" the "thread" of another's arguments, but if its "level"
> is "over my head" my attention may "wander" and "lose touch"
> with the "drift" of it, so that when he "comes" to his "point"

we differ "widely," our "views" being indeed so "far apart" that the "things" he says "appear" "much" too arbitrary, or even "a lot" of nonsense.

In contrast, the Hopi analyzes his world in terms of events rather than things. He has little of the imaginary spatial metaphor which so colors the language of English-speakers.

To bring this point home, subcultural meaning and vocabulary differences among English-speakers are common. For example, the sentence:

I was mad about my flat

can be interpreted several ways. An urbanite from southern England would be pleased with his apartment. His counterpart from northern England would be angry about his apartment. And most North Americans would be angry about a punctured automobile tire. In Chapter 5, the importance of culture and social attributes such as socioeconomic class in forming mental maps was stressed. The culture-boundedness of time perception (Hall, 1959) and space perception (Hall, 1966; Rapoport, 1969) has also been made clear recently.

Attitudes and Values

Whereas *perceptions* require an actual external stimulus, *attitudes* exist in the experiential environment of the self. Perceptions are more transitory than attitudes and less stable, for attitudes are built up from a long series of perceptions. Moreover, perceptions are generally of specific stimuli; attitudes involve the organization of a set of feelings and beliefs. Attitude, in general parlance, usually refers to an individual's feelings about the attitude object, or, more generally, a view of the world. Attitudes imply considerable experience and a degree of firmness of opinion; they involve expectation of further experience and provide for a response to that experience object when perceived.

On the basis of this definition, and the definition of perception in the previous section, we may distinguish perceptions from passive beliefs and active attitudes by examples from Saint-Exupéry's fable *The Little Prince* (1943):

1.   The Prince, newly arrived from a distant asteroid, climbed a Saharan mountain to survey the strange planet known as Earth. On reaching the top he looked around and exclaimed: "What a queer planet. It is altogether dry, and altogether pointed, and altogether harsh and forbidding" (Perception).

2.   Attempting to find some of the human inhabitants of Earth, the Prince asked a desert flower, which had once seen a caravan pass by, for directions. The flower replied, "Men? . . . one never knows where to find them. The wind blows them away. They have no roots, and that makes their life very difficult" (Belief).

3.   The same question asked of a fox resulted in a different answer, for the fox was actively involved in stealing chickens and, in consequence, in being hunted by man. "Men," said the fox, "They have guns, and they hunt. It is very disturbing" (Attitude).

The fox's behavior, moreover, is conditioned by his *values*. He tells the Prince, "It is only with the heart that one can see rightly; what is essential is invisible to the eye." When told by a businessman that a newly invented thirst-quenching pill would save him 53 minutes every week to spend as he liked, the Prince replied, "if I had fifty-three minutes to spend as I liked, I should walk at my leisure toward a spring of fresh water."

Clearly, while attitudes are organized sets of beliefs based on perceptual experience, attitudes may themselves be components of an individual's *values*, which together interrelate to form his *value-system*. Rokeach (1970) contrasts attitudes, which each focus upon a specific object or situation, and values, which each refer to a desirable end state of existence or mode of behavior. Values, as generalized standards, transcend attitudes toward individual objects. A person may thus have many thousands of attitudes, but only a few dozen values.

The problem of differentiating between perception, attitude, and value is great, and is not made easier by the variety of definitions of each proposed by psychologists and others. Moreover, all three develop as a result of experience. Further complexity is introduced by statements to the effect that attitudes affect perception, perceptions affect attitudes (Schiff, 1971), and values determine attitudes (Rokeach, 1970). An involvement scale may aid elucidation; we have perceptions *of*, beliefs *in*, attitudes *toward*, and preferences *for*. The latter two are perhaps more active than the former.

One point of considerable agreement is that attitudes contain cognitive, affective, and behavioral components (Krech *et al.*, 1962). The *cognitive* component concerns beliefs about the attitude object (banning smoking in public places will improve environmental quality); the *affective* component concerns the individual's feelings about the attitude object (being in the same place as smokers is unpleasant); and the *behavioral* component is a predisposition to respond to the object (decision making with regard to leaving the room, asking smokers to stop smoking, etc.).

People tend to keep affective and cognitive components internally consistent. Lack of consistency, however, may not be perceived by the individual. When it is so perceived, the individual is said to be in a state of

cognitive dissonance, and this may be followed by attitude change. The organizing of consistent feelings (affects) and beliefs (cognitions) into a system is
thought to predispose the individual to react in a particular way to the object
of the attitude. It is this behavioral component, a "state of readiness"
(Allport, 1935) or a "disposition to respond" (Campbell, 1963), which is of
most interest to urban planners and designers.

From this argument it has been inferred that if we can only discover an
individual's attitudes toward an object we may predict his behavior, whether
a verbalized posture or a motor response, in relation to that object. To this
end a vast battery of techniques for eliciting attitudes from the experiential
environment have been created by social psychologists (Thurstone, 1928;
Edwards, 1957; Fishbein, 1967). Two components of attitude are generally
measured. Attitude direction refers to whether the attitude is positive or
negative; attitude magnitude refers to the strength of the attitude. Measurement is usually by some form of scaling technique. Table 9.1 illustrates the
form of an attitude questionnaire using a Likert scale and shows how responses provide data on both direction and magnitude.

TABLE 9.1
SCALED ATTITUDE QUESTIONS

Building more freeways will reduce traffic congestion.	Strongly agree — Agree — No opinion — Disagree — Strongly disagree
The ghetto violence problem is now being tackled effectively.	Strongly agree — Agree — No opinion — Disagree — Strongly disagree

As with perceptions, attitudes are also the product of experience and
will vary with individual differences in such areas as physiology, training,
and exposure to a range of phenomenal environments. Culture also plays a
major role in attitude and value determination. The overwhelming example
here is the clash between the Eurocentric attitudes of white imperialists and
the vastly different value systems of the black, red, and brown colonized
peoples. No detail is required here; the point is summarized in Lederer and
Burdick's *The Ugly American* (1958) and was given greater direction and
magnitude by the Australian Aborigine who reportedly greeted the Captain
Cook Bicentenary with the words: "Fuck your Captain Cook; he stole our
land" (Brookfield, 1973).

Preferences and Satisfactions

Assuming that the accurate elicitation of attitudes and perceptions were possible, would the environmental designer have sufficient information to produce buildings which fitted his clients' needs and wants? From the considerable body of empirical research on environmental preferences and satisfactions, it is possible to infer that these have been regarded as more direct approaches to the problem of providing behavior-supportive physical environments. There is an intimate link between *preferences* and *attitudes*. According to Rokeach (1967) and White (1966), attitude always involves a preference, which is the attitude's affective component. Preference is also related to *satisfaction*, which results from the evaluation of repeated perceptions and the achievement of goals, and which in turn becomes an input into attitude formation. If one receives a high level of satisfaction from performing a certain behavior toward a certain stimulus object, it is likely that this particular stimulus object will be preferred to one which produces less intense feelings. One's attitude toward the first object is likely to become positive and strong.

Increasing demands for public participation in planning have resulted from the failure of planners to intuitively recognize the preferences of the public (Sewell, 1971a). Several techniques have long been in use for assessing public preferences. These include public opinion polls, referendums, voting at several governmental levels, public hearings, letters sent to newspaper editors or public officials, and the statements of a variety of pressure groups (see Chapter 14). In-depth studies of preferences by social scientists could help correct some of the inherent biases of these traditional assessment techniques. Several house-type preference studies were reported in Chapter 4 and Gould's work on mental maps, mentioned in Chapter 5, was predicated upon the environmental preferences of his subjects.

Preferences, like attitudes and perceptions, vary with the individual and his experiences. During the socialization of the individual he is taught cultural preferences, as in the dietary preference contrasts between the United States and India. Membership of a social group also implies group preferences, for example, in type of music. However, in terms of preferences for landscapes, Sonnenfeld (1966) distinguished between native and non-native. Natives' preferences are usually biased in favor of the landscape they inhabit; though not completely satisfied with his environment, the native is likely to have adjusted to it by virtue of extended residence. The non-native, on the other hand, is far less likely to be satisfied with what he perceives to be an inadequate landscape. The fact of his greater mobility and experience set him apart from the native. Moreover, the non-native is less involved with the landscape, and his judgment of it tends to contain a larger aesthetic compo-

nent. The virtue of this native/non-native distinction in assessing environmental preferences and satisfactions is its broad applicability, the chief biases
being not culture or social group but rather environmental experience and
personality.

Value for Planning

The value of perception, attitude, and preference studies for planning lies
first, in discovering regularities and consistencies in behavior from empirical
studies, and second, in sensitizing planners to individual and group differences. The large number of studies in mental mapping and the controversy
over their value in urban design were reported in Chapter 5. Other than
these, the major body of environmentally oriented perception work has been
in the field of natural hazard perception (Burton and Kates, 1964). Variations
in hazard perception were found to be dependent on the relationship of the
hazard to resource use (for example, farmers are more aware of flood hazards
than are urban dwellers), the frequency of occurrence of the hazard, and the
level of personal experience. A person using a resource frequently threatened
by flooding and with some experience of flood devastation will tend to have a
heightened perception of flood hazard. This hypothesis has been generalized
to studies of drought, urban snow hazards, landslides, tidal waves, and
storms (Craik, 1970; Saarinen, 1971). In terms of response to such problems, it
has been shown that the responsible engineers and public health officials
have very narrow perceptions of both problems and solutions (Sewell,
1971b).

Attitudes toward the environment have been studied in a variety of
ways, from analysis of historical documents (Holsti, 1969) to the experimental
procedures of social psychology. Past attitudes, and historical changes in
attitudes toward rural landscapes and the urban scene have been documented by Lowenthal (1968), Lowenthal and Prince (1964, 1965) and Tuan
(1974), among others. The clash between pastoral and urban values in American life, "the machine in the garden," has been extensively studied (Lowenthal, 1962, 1964; White and White, 1962; Marx, 1964).

Research on the attitudes of contemporaries has, like perception work,
been largely focused on resource problems, with surveys of attitudes toward
air pollution, water pollution, aircraft noise, recreation, and wilderness preservation. Lee (1966) has noted the influential role of attitude in stress conditions such as extreme cold or heat; the comatose desert nomad, lying in the
shade of a wrecked vehicle, will survive better than the European whose
cultural attitudes demand that he do something.

A considerable body of research suggests that value systems have a
profound effect upon perceived housing quality, choice of activity, and set-

tlement patterns (de Lauwe, 1960, 1965; Jonassen, 1949; Rapoport, 1969). In his pioneer study of symbolic values in Boston, Firey (1945) has demonstrated how sentiment and symbolism have prevented the attainment of economic efficiency. Boston's central business district (CBD) is constricted in its expansion by Boston Common and adjoining gardens covering in total over 48 acres, and by the residential enclave of old, rich families on Beacon Hill (Fig. 9.4). Studies of the CBD phenomenon by economic geographers (Murphy, 1966) have shown that CBDs tend to expand in the direction of general urban growth and, in doing so, convert adjacent land uses into CBD land uses. During the 1950s and 1960s there was also a tendency to provide them with urban freeway links at the expense of nearby residential neighborhoods and parks. Beacon Hill and, to a greater extent, Boston Common, lie athwart the predicted expansionist path of Boston's CBD; in purely economic terms such areas would be more economically efficient if redeveloped to highways, parking areas, offices, and specialty stores. As both are loaded with historic, cultural, and personal associations, however, they are jealously protected by active citizen groups and their redevelopment is unlikely ever to occur.

Firey's study encompassed a third region of central Boston known as the West End. A low-income Italian ethnic neighborhood, it had a unity of

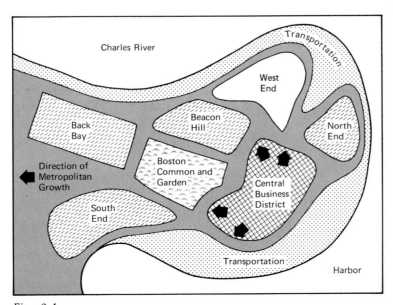

Fig. 9.4

Value-laden central Boston districts restrict central business district growth. (Note: this is the author's mental map, districts and edges only.) The West End is now converted to CBD uses.

sentiment and was as symbolic of cherished values to its inhabitants as were Boston Common and Beacon Hill to the general populace. Lacking city-wide appeal, however, the West End was razed and redeveloped from the late 1950s onward. The Italian-Americans, with their home- and neighborhood-oriented values, were relocated at some psychological cost to many individuals (see Chapter 11). They were replaced by an apartment and office complex catering to higher-income groups. Those who made the decision to redevelop the West End operated wholly on economic values, and in particular, desired the improvement of land use on the CBD fringe in order to raise the city's tax level (Gans, 1959).

That values influence environmental preferences was shown by Ross (1961), who found that people moving from a house in the city center to the suburbs stressed aesthetic reasons, while those moving toward the city center stressed convenience. Michelson has demonstrated that housing preferences also relate to such value dichotomies as: instrumentalism (roughly, convenience of access) — expression (aesthetic values); and group-mindedness — individualism (Table 9.2). From this it appears that the single-family house is valued as a locus for private family activity; the *"doing* orientation" refers to the value placed on activity and accomplishment, such as the home handyman syndrome. At the further end of the continuum, high-rise apartments are not valued as places for privacy or home activities. Rather, the stress is placed on convenience (instrumentalism) and aesthetic beauty (expression).

Michelson suggests that people evaluate such housing types with different yardsticks according to the type of housing, rather than the individual's personality type; whether people like high-rises or not, they look for expressive and instrumental qualities in them. In a similar way, private open space is associated with family activities, regardless of the size of the space. Preference for house type and lot size, however, follows personal value orientation. Those who value convenience highly tend to prefer small lot sizes; those who value individualism highly are likely to prefer larger lots.

Deriving data from environmental displays by means of photographic representations, several workers have studied preferences for neighborhoods (Wilson, 1962; Lamanna, 1964; Michelson, 1966). Peterson (1967) has suggested that neighborhood preferences can be predicted. As discussed in Chapter 4, single family houses are generally preferred for family living, and neighborhood preferences and satisfactions depend upon individual perception of environmental quality.

the value of complexity

The importance of perception and preference studies may be illustrated with reference to a major problem in the design field, the simplicity-complexity dimension of any particular design. A considerable body of research, re-

TABLE 9.2

PERCENTAGE CITATION OF VALUE ORIENTATIONS

| | House Type Evaluated | | |
Value Orientation Cited	Single Family	Duplex, Row House, Low-Rise Apartment	High-Rise Apartment
Instrumentalism	7	10	26
Expression	7	49	48
Group-mindedness	8	2	5
Individualism	63	33	13
"Doing orientation"	15	6	8
	100%	100%	100%

Source: Michelson (1970)

viewed by Craik (1970), indicates that peoples' preferences are generally related to intermediate amounts of stimulus complexity, whereas exploration (for example, voluntary exposure to an environmental display) increases with increasing complexity. These findings are relevant to the aesthetics of urban design. As noted in Chapters 7 and 8, some attempt has been made to ascertain optimum levels of stimulation (Fiske and Maddi, 1961). These clearly vary with individual differences. Persons of an ascetic temperament, most notably religious mystics and writer-adventurers such as T. E. Lawrence and A. de Saint-Exupéry, prefer the naked expanses of deserts to the crowded luxury of cities. Urban writers of this inclination, such as Camus, prefer enclosed spaces to be as bare as possible.

Design theorists have frequently clashed over the problem of complexity or simplicity. Those of the picturesque school, deriving from eighteenth and nineteenth century views of aesthetics, hold that complexity is essential for continued interest and satisfaction. Extreme examples of this attitude include Victorian Gothic and the turn of the century Picturesque Eclectic house style. Here the architect was left free to combine shapes and textures from all sources, whether Egyptian, Romanesque, or Gothic, in the one building (Gowans, 1964; Lewis, 1975). Later twentieth-century architectural critics have scorned such complexity, and modern design theory favors simplicity and clarity. Modern architects tend to favor broad, simple lines in the Mies van der Rohe tradition, so that every modern metropolitan center is now graced by scores of indistinguishable glass cubes.

Psychologists, however, have suggested that several dimensions relating to complexity of design are important in providing attention-getting stimuli (Berlyne, 1960; Wohlwill, 1966). *Variation,* as in freeway or suburban housing layouts, will reduce boredom and monotony. *Novelty* is of value in retaining attention. *Surprisingness* will arrest the observer and possibly prove pleasing. *Incongruity* will heighten attention. Certain designers and critics, more concerned with townscapes than with individual buildings, have long emphasized the importance of variation and surprise in architecture (Cullen, 1961; Johns, 1965; Nairn, 1965). Reviewing the thinking of a variety of designers, philosophers, artists, and urban critics, Rapoport and Kantor (1967) reject the modern architectural tradition of simplicity, clarity, and control. They suggest that all that a contemporary glass-and-steel office building has to say to the observer is revealed at a glance; there is no range of meanings and possibilities for the individual to perceive, select, and organize to his satisfaction.

High architectural complexity. Gingerbread mansion in Victoria, B.C. (Courtesy of Victoria Press.)

A review of psychological research on both humans and nonhumans supports this hypothesis. Krech *et al.* (1960) placed three matched groups of rats in contrasting environments of visual enrichment, visual impoverishment, and a standard control condition. The environments differed only in the amount of available perceptual stimulation. Whether mature or young rats were used, rats in the enriched environment improved more in brain weight, problem solving, and learning ability than did rats in the other two conditions. Munsinger and Kessen (1964), exposing 617 college students to random visual sequences, concluded that adults prefer variability and uncertainty in their stimulation. Similarly, Berlyne (1958, 1960) demonstrated that both adults and infants prefer complexity of stimulation.

Low architectural complexity. Headquarters, Canadian Imperial Bank of Commerce, Toronto. Architects: I. M. Pei and Page and Steele. (Courtesy of Hugh Philip Massey.)

Three conclusions may be drawn. First, adults, infants, and laboratory animals have a fundamental perceptual preference for ambiguous, complex, visual patterns. Second, both lack of work on the other senses and experiments comparing several senses suggest that vision is dominant in human perception (Arnheim, 1965; Rock and Harris, 1967; Victor and Rock, 1964). Third, and most important, Rapoport and Kantor have put forward the notion that for each individual there is an optimal perceptual rate. Too few and too simple stimuli lead to boredom; too many and too complex stimuli lead to saturation and chaos in comprehension. In this connection Thiel (1964b) supports the above-mentioned views of Sonnenfeld that environmental appreciation varies strongly on the native/habitué-non-native/tourist dimension.

If the optimum perceptual rate varies with the individual, then buildings and townscapes must be sufficiently complex to provide a variety of stimuli, only some of which are perceived by any one individual. Human preference for high levels of complexity suggests that modern glass slab buildings will prove boring to most urbanites. Rapoport and Kantor therefore propose that "building in open-ended, complex, involved, allusive ways is . . . more psychologically satisfying than the traditional simplicity . . . sought by many designers." The demonstrated need for perceptually rich surfaces rather than broad smooth ones has in part been responsible for the public's disdain for minimal art and architecture. The architect Venturi (1966) has recognized this in his designs, which often contain one level of meaning for the user and another for the cognoscenti.

Problems and Limitations

The value of attitude, perception, and preference studies is manifold. From the scientific point of view, careful comparison of overt behavior and elicited verbal responses may result in the possible classification of individuals according to similarity of overall patterns of behavior. In planning terms, individual and group enlightenment may be achieved by discoveries that perceptions of both problems and solutions differ between individuals and groups. This is especially important in the designer-client and public official–general public relationships. Knowledge of a particular individual's or group's attitudes and values, and their antecedents, may be a powerful input into planning. At the very least it may result in a more humanistic approach to planning for others on the part of sensitive designers. Public preference elicitation, however, would seem to be of greatest value for urban planning. It is difficult to argue against the viewpoint that on ethical grounds people have the right to be consulted about plans and decisions which not only may profoundly affect their way of life, but which they are also paying for through public funds. Of course, there may be considerable discrepancies between what people want and what they need; on a subjective basis, however, what they want is what they need. The inevitable clash between what people prefer and what urban designers and administrators believe they want, or think they should have, is considered in Chapter 12.

   This discussion of the practical value of perception, attitude, and preference studies, however, presupposes that we have adequately conceptualized these constructs, that we have sufficiently refined the techniques available for eliciting them, and that the practical and philosophical problems of going direct to the individual for his perceptions and opinions have been overcome.

   On the conceptual level, there remains a great deal of confusion over the exact meaning of such terms as *attitude, perception, satisfaction, preference,* and *value.* We are told that they influence each other; they often appear to be parallel or overlapping in meaning. This conceptual circularity does not bode well for future studies unless clarification can be made. Moreover, it is

difficult to fit them, in any kind of logical sequence, into the flow of hypothetical processes through which environmental inputs pass before culminating
in behavioral output.

The measurability of attitudes, perceptions, and the like is also in
dispute. It should be emphasized that attitudes and perceptions are in no
sense real, that is, they have no physical dimensions which can be measured.
They are invented constructs, necessary as intervening mental variables to
explain the relationship between the two sets of observable, measurable
variables known as environment and behavior. The only means of measuring
the covert psychological processes of the brain is by measuring observable
behavior, whether verbal or overt.

Study of overt behavior via *Unobtrusive Measures* (Webb *et al.*, 1966)
allows the individual to express himself fully (Proshansky, 1946; Webb and
Salancik, 1970). The objectively insoluble problem is how to interpret the
responses. In contrast, studies of verbal behavior generally involve rating
scales, as noted earlier in this chapter (Thurstone, 1928; Osgood *et al.*, 1957).
Their popularity is due to ease of administration and capacity for standardization, the latter often leading to spurious notions of objectivity. Several major
problems, however, are inherent in asking people to verbalize their attitudes,
perceptions, and preferences.

Bias is inevitable. Questionnaires usually introduce a foreign element
into the normal social setting. The very attempt to identify and measure
phenomena such as attitudes may condition the response. Respondents may
respond to a question on building complexity even though they have never
previously thought about the issue. In this way attempts at verbal elicitation
"may create as well as measure attitudes" (Webb and Salancik, 1970, 317).
The experimenter-effect is difficult to avoid. Respondents may gain directives
for questionnaire response from the experimenter's facial or body postures;
they may respond as they perceive the interviewer would like them to
respond. Semantic problems also introduce bias. Perception studies themselves suggest that the same word means different things to different individuals and also to the same individual in different contexts. This poses
problems of interpretation, especially when trying to measure interest, concern, or awareness. People may be aware of, but not concerned about, a
particular problem. Residents, for example, are often less vociferous about
coastal oil pollution than are visitors.

A further fundamental problem concerns the data derived from such
procedures. There is a tendency to attribute more to these data than the
measurement procedure can possibly deliver (Proshansky, 1974). The fact
that questionnaires and other techniques elicit data on attitudes from individuals does not necessarily mean that the individuals actually hold these
attitudes, or that the attitudes have any permanence beyond the moment of
elicitation, or that they are in any way significant in influencing how the

individual behaves. "Only the naive believe that two 'strongly agrees', one 'disagree', and an 'I don't know' make an attitude" (Webb and Salancik, 1970, 318). Given these disclaimers, the usual approach taken has been the pragmatic one that attitudes are what attitude scales measure (an operational definition).

The application of attitude-, perception-, and preference-eliciting techniques on a scale large enough to provide major input into planning decisions would also result in severe practical problems (Sewell, 1971b). As all these phenomena change rapidly over time, the information produced may be redundant before it can be used. Thus one-shot surveys would likely give a biased view, so that costly continuous monitoring would be necessary. However, such a continuous barrage of questionnaires or interviews is likely to result in an increasing unwillingness to participate on the part of the public. This is especially the case where, as in the Canadian Maritime provinces, respondents perceive few practical results or are dissatisfied with decisions made on the basis of data previously collected. The lack of personnel skilled in administering such surveys not only prevents information being collected or introduces bias when unskilled persons are used, but may further exacerbate feelings of hostility on the part of overinterviewed respondents. Low-income residents of urban renewal areas have now been assaulted by several generations of urban planning and social science students in every university town from Boston/Cambridge to Victoria, B.C. Their inability to perceive the value, if any, of such exercises may result in self-disenfranchisement when yet another interviewer, but this time from the city planning department, appears at the door.

the problem of prediction

Of fundamental importance to any scientific endeavor is the problem of prediction. Though of intrinsic interest, information on perceptions, attitudes, and preferences must be of some value for planning if it is to be worth the social and economic cost of producing it. For example, it should be possible to predict behavior from attitude, which, it should be reminded, has been defined as a "state of readiness" (Allport, 1935, 799). The very words used by researchers dealing with the relationship between attitude and behavior (determine, mediate, predispose, influence) suggest some degree of predictability.

Concentrating on the attitude-behavior relationship, much research has emphasized the discrepancies between verbalized attitudes and overt behavior. The classic study was that of La Piere (1934), in which he accompanied a Chinese couple to a number of restaurants and hotels across the United States, all of which gave them exemplary, nondiscriminatory service. La Piere later sent letters to the proprietors of these establishments asking them about the acceptability of Chinese guests. He received almost uniformly negative replies. Eighteen years later Kutner *et al.* (1952) obtained similar results with blacks as experimental subjects (de Fleur and Westie, 1963). In a review of the discrepancies between attitude and behavior in both Europe and China, Tuan (1968) found marked differences between the philosophy identified with a people and the actions they undertake. Clearly, to expect a correspondence between verbal behavior (attitude) and overt behavior is to make an inferential leap of some magnitude.

Several studies, however, have found consistencies between attitude and behavior (Bruvold, 1973; Fendrick, 1967; Willits *et al.*, 1973). It is therefore suggested that discrepancies have resulted when attitudes have been measured toward inappropriate stimulus objects, as, for example, toward Chinese or blacks in the La Piere study, as opposed to particular Chinese or black individuals (Fishbein, 1967). Moreover, verbal behavior has fewer consequences than overt behavior so that the individual is free to express any reasonable attitude unless he perceives immediate commitment to a behavior. Further, the behaviors studied may be unrelated to the attitudes expressed. A research review by Murphy and Golledge (1972) thus expresses a qualified support for attitudes as predictors, especially in cases where the subject is familiar with the concept or stimulus, level of controversy is low, and the interference of social norms minimized.

It is clear, however, that we must not look to attitudes for direct prediction of behavior. An attitude is predispositional, but not prescriptive; the individual carries the attitude with him to a situation, but it does not necessarily result in overt behavior even when an appropriate stimulus is presented. A variety of other influences operate on behavior, including the phenomenal environment itself. "Attitude, no matter how conceived, is simply one of the variables in the complex regression equation we use to predict behavior; we cannot expect it to do much" (Weissberg, 1964, 424). It was because of this complexity, together with the concept's internal inconsistencies, that Harvey (1969) rejected attitude as an explanatory variable in spatial studies, while others have cautioned against a too simplistic view of attitude-behavior determinism (Golledge *et al.*, 1972).

The Individual and the Group

In discussing perceptions, attitudes, and preferences, attention has focused largely upon the individual. All individuals, however, are members of one or more of a series of groups, ranging from the family to the species *homo sapiens* (Fig. 9.5). In varying degrees our egocentrism is tempered by ethnocentrism or anthropocentrism. Our egocentrism can never be fully realized because the individual depends upon others for support. Ethnocentrism, in contrast, can achieve realization in group self-sufficiency. Tuan has discussed the relationship between perceived centrality and feelings of superiority. Common human traits, however, such as the fundamental dichotomies of up-down, left-right, front-back, center-periphery, and open-closed, ensure that we view the world anthropocentrically (Lowenthal, 1961; Tuan, 1974). We are unable to appreciate the odorscape of a cat or dog.

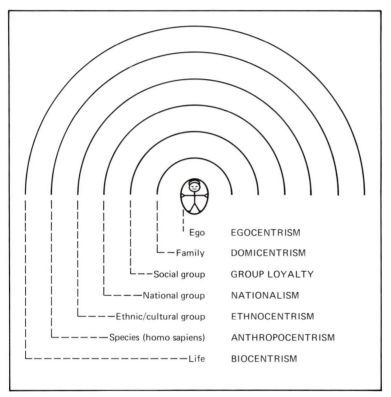

Fig. 9.5

Group memberships and orientations.

At a less fundamental level, but perhaps more influential in everyday life, the individual also belongs to a series of social groups, including age, sex, class, culture, and life-style. These groups have behavior norms, and may therefore be expected to have group attitudes, preferences, and the like. As attitudes and perceptions derive from experience, and as the latter may be heightened by training, it is possible to assume that such group norms grow out of common experiences during childhood socialization.

The studies of determinism discussed in Chapters 7 and 8 frequently reported intergroup rather than interindividual differences in behavior, attitude, and preference. Individual value systems, which affect attitudes, are very much a product of group norms. In Chapter 6 it was found that persons belonging to similar age, social class, and ethnic groups tend to cluster together, resulting in residential segregation. On the basis of group segregation, behavior may be predicted; in both the United States and Britain, for example, differences in political affiliation and participation have been found between the (poorer) inhabitants of central cities and the (richer) inhabitants of suburban peripheries (Cox, 1968). Studies of perceptions, attitudes, and preferences reveal that strong generalizations can be made on a group basis. Even the concept of an individual optimal perceptual rate, which arose from the complexity-simplicity debate, has been challenged by a laboratory study which found a *consensual* point of visual preference among humans as opposed to a random preference among individuals (Rapoport and Kantor, 1967).

Two of the most fundamental groups are culture and sex. Sex is a basic physiological variable, dividing most of *homo sapiens* into two fairly distinct groups. Though the experience of hot and cold is subjective, in general men are more sensitive to cold than women. Males are generally heavier and more muscular than females, who are more sensitive to the sensations of touch and smell than are men. Sonnenfeld's (1967) study of the environmental preferences of both natives and non-natives of Alaska showed that while males preferred rough landscapes with water, females preferred warmer, vegetated environments. The sex difference was greater among Inuit (Eskimos) than among whites.

This influence of culture upon sex roles is everywhere apparent, and perceptions of and attitudes toward the environment may vary greatly according to sex. For example, Inuit male hunters' cognitive maps are accurate in shape, with much detail of coastal configurations. In contrast, female maps are accurate in distance and direction, consisting of a series of points each of which is the location of a settlement or trading post (Carpenter *et al.*, 1959). Mental map differences by sex were described for Western societies in Chapter 5; it must be noted, however, that among certain subcultural groups, such as high-income cosmopolites and counterculture street people, such differences are greatly reduced.

The cultural and subcultural groups to which we belong strongly mold our opinions and activities. That the structuring of value orientations and spatial behavior according to cultural norms is an invaluable input into the design process is a view expressed most recently by Hall (1974) and Zeisel

(1974). Indeed, culture can influence perception to the extent that hallucinations or perceptual illusions become not personal idiosyncracies but normal cultural traits (Tuan, 1974).

Because of these group regularities, it is suggested that while the methodological tools for extracting attitudes, perceptions, and preferences are being sharpened, practitioners seeking behavioral design input would do well to consider group norms as a basis for behavior prediction. People manifestly act in a predictable fashion according to group membership. In locating their homes, so full of symbolic meaning (see Chapter 4), individuals conform to group behaviors, resulting in the typical residential segregation pattern in Western cities. Further, data on groups rather than individuals are far easier to obtain, and much can be derived without resorting to interviews. Finally, despite individual differences in perception and attitude, it is clear that it pays most of us to see most of the external environment in the same way most of the time. Lowenthal (1961) suggests a strong degree of congruence between individual perceptions, group perceptions, and what is there. In the Sprouts' words: "the fact that the human species has survived (so far) suggests that there must be considerable correspondence between the milieu as people conceive it to be, and as it actually is" (Sprout and Sprout, 1956, 61).

The above are a range of conceptual and practical reasons for the study of the contextual environments of the individual as well as, or even instead of, his experiential and behavioral (personal) environments. This is largely an aggregative, probabilistic stance. The probabilistic models which derive from it may be able to predict within a more or less calculable margin of error what a group's reaction toward a given stimulus is likely to be. Our daily lives involve myriads of predictions of this type, and it is because of these normally expectable behaviors that society continues to function. Probabilistic models, however, do not pretend to predict the behavior of specific individuals. If this is important, better research methodologies for the elicitation of attitudes, perceptions, and preferences are required. Because of the present doubtful quality of these, Chapters 10 and 11 follow the probabilistic line of thought by discussing individual attitudes, preferences, and overt behavior in terms of the three major dimensions outlined in Chapter 6, namely, life-style, life cycle, and level of life.

Summary

1.   Decisions regarding action in the phenomenal environment are based on the personal environments (behavioral and experiential) of the decision maker. Research has emphasized the importance of perceptions, attitudes, and preferences.

2. Perceptions, mental images of the phenomenal environment, vary from individual to individual according to physiology and experience. Though the nature of the stimulus object is of obvious importance, cultural and other group biases are evident.

3. Attitudes spring from a series of perceptions organized and interpreted by the experiential environment. As attitude is thought to have a behavioral component, attempts have been made to predict behavior from attitude.

4. Preferences are related to both attitudes and satisfactions. They may be the most valuable inputs into a participatory form of the planning process.

5. The complex interplay of perception, belief, attitude, value system, satisfaction, and preference is the guiding force in human activity. Knowledge of consistencies between attitudes, values, and preferences may aid the designer in providing the kind of environments people want. The complexity-simplicity debate suggests that, in architectural terms, people have generally been given what they do not want.

6. The present state of the art, involving confusion in conceptualization, the need for technique refinement, and the practical and philosophical problems of studying the individual, does not favor heavy reliance on personality assessment studies in urban planning.

7. Until such refinements are made, and the tools of assessment and prediction sharpened, planners should place more reliance on studies of groups (the contextual environment) than on studies of the individual (personal environments).

Further Reading

MICHELSON, W. (1966), "An Empirical Analysis of Urban Environmental Preferences," *Journal of the American Institute of Planners* 32: 355–60.

PROSHANSKY, H. M. (1974), "Environmental Psychology and the Design Professions," in J. Lang *et al.* (eds.), *Designing for Human Behavior*, pp. 72–80. Stroudsburg, Pa.: Dowden, Hutchinson & Ross.

RAPOPORT, A. and R. E. KANTOR (1967), "Complexity and Ambiguity in Environmental Design," *Journal of the American Institute of Planners* 33: 210–21.

TUAN, Y-F (1974), *Topophilia.* Englewood Cliffs, N.J.: Prentice-Hall.

10

THE CONTEXTUAL ENVIRONMENT: LIFE CYCLE AND LIFE LEVEL

Crabbed age and youth cannot live together. *

William Shakespeare

O let us love our occupations,
Bless the squire and his relations . . .
And always know our proper stations. †

Charles Dickens

In Chapter 6 it was suggested that an individual's stage in the life cycle and his level of life were major factors influencing his behavior. This chapter discusses the relationship of both factors to the residential environment at all three levels of territoriality, though concentrating primarily upon the home base.

Life Cycle

Knowledge of an individual's stage in the life cycle involves data on both his age and his family status. Age alone is insufficient as a predictor of the need for residential space; a single person and a household head with a spouse and three dependent children will have very different housing needs. Some sociologists suggest that stage in the life cycle is a more important variable than socioeconomic class in influencing the way in which people spend both time and money (Abrams, 1964).

---

* William Shakespeare (1954), *The Passionate Pilgrim* xii, in *The Complete Works.* London, Odhams Press.
† Charles Dickens (1901), *The Chimes: a Goblin Story,* Second Quarter, in *Christmas Books.* New York: Scribners.

One of the earliest categorizations of meaningful stages in the "strange eventful history" of an individual's movement from birth to death was provided by William Shakespeare in *As You Like It.* Although some of his seven ages of man are no longer relevant, Shakespeare emphasizes the importance of environmental competence as a criterion for categorization. Clearly, the puking infant, whining schoolboy, and senile person "sans everything" are environmentally docile (Chapter 8). A second criterion is family responsibility. Despite much assault, the institution of marriage and associated child rearing remains strong, and with it comes the responsibility for providing an adequate child-raising environment.

In a British study, Abrams found that 46 million of a total population of 52 million could be allocated to one of eight life-cycle stages (Table 10.1). The remaining 6 million belonged to minor categories such as middle-aged and older persons who were either unmarried or married but without children. In the North American context, Lansing and Kish (1957) used a similar categorization, although they omitted dependent children as a separate category and carefully distinguished between married and single older persons. The latter is important in that in most cases one spouse (frequently the male) predeceases the other.

As the individual moves through the life cycle he frequently changes his residence type and location in accordance with changing needs. About 20 percent of the United States population changes residence annually. An average family will move eight or nine times in its lifetime. These moves are not predominantly income-related moves to houses in better districts, for Rossi (1955) has estimated that five of the eight moves of the average family are related to the changing composition of the family. Simmons (1968) has charted these life-cycle related moves, which are detailed in Table 10.2.

Move 1   The individual has little control over moves made during his childhood, even though such moves may be made on his behalf. For example, parents frequently move to residential environments which have reputable schools and suitable playmates for their children.

Move 2   On leaving the parental nest the postadolescent makes his first independent move to an environment chosen by himself. Typically this involves a rejection of the child-oriented environment established by Move 1.

Move 3   Marriage may entail another relocation, although the type of accommodation may differ little from that occupied during the premarriage state. Typically we are dealing with two people who formerly had separate establishments but who now come together to occupy a single dwelling, frequently an apartment.

TABLE 10.1

STAGES IN THE LIFE CYCLE

Stage	Age Group	Percentage of Total Population
1. Infants and schoolchildren	0–14	26
2. Young unmarried	15–24	12
3. Young married, no children	15–34	3
4. Young married, with children	15–34	12
5. Middle married, with children	35–44	11
6. Older married, with children	45–64	5
7. Older married, children gone	45–64	18
8. Pensioners	65+	13
		100

Source: Abrams (1964)

TABLE 10.2

RESIDENCE CHANGES AND LIFE CYCLE

Age	Stage	Move Number
0	Birth	
10	Child	1
	Adolescent	
20	Maturity	2
	Marriage	3
30	Children	4
40		
50	Children mature	
60		
70	Retirement	5
80	Death	

Source: Simmons (1968)

Move 4   The production of children, however, frequently requires relocation to a residential environment similar, in many respects, to that which the individual left in Move 2. Typically, more space is required than was needed before children arrived on the scene.

Move 5   Children, however, mature and eventually leave the parental nest (Move 2). The amount of space occupied by the parents may now prove excessive, especially if one of them predeceases the other. Elderly persons may therefore seek yet another housing type more suited to their changed space needs. In many cases this will resemble the environment they chose in Move 2, and which their children chose in *their* Move 2.

Significant moves, then, cluster around three meaningful phases in the life cycle: setting up one's first independent residence with possible locational change upon marriage (Moves 2 and 3); a lengthy child-rearing phase (Moves 4 and 1); and a readjustment to a childfree state after one's children have left the parental home (Move 5). Habitat selection occurs with several criteria in mind, including stress generated by the present environment, and the perceived advantages of other environments, which may include greater convenience to jobs or urban facilities, greater privacy or opportunities to engage in certain activities, or more appropriate space needs. The need to control an appropriate amount of living space seems to be of vital importance in generating residential relocations (Rossi, 1955):

Space for children: suburban dwellings. Note the emphasis on both private and public recreation space. (Courtesy of Victoria Press.)

Mobility is the mechanism by which a family's housing is brought into adjustment to its housing needs . . . substantive findings stress space requirements as the most important of the needs generated by life cycle changes.

Given that mobility and choice in habitat selection are economically possible (minorities and the poor are considered in Chapter 11), how far do the typical relocations outlined above result in the occupation of different environments in different locations by the various life-cycle groups? In other words, do modern Western cities exhibit life-cycle segregation in residential terms?

As outlined in Chapter 6, life-cycle patterns in North American cities form a series of concentric rings with the childfree toward the center of the

Convenience for the childfree: downtown dwellings. An inner city neighborhood in Victoria, B.C. is being ringed by high-rises and penetrated by low-rise apartments. Individual houses (foreground) may become surrounded by apartment complexes. (Courtesy of Ian Norie, Department of Geography, University of Victoria.)

city and those engaged in child rearing toward the periphery (Fig. 10.1). Alonso (1964, 230) has likened these typical moves to a convectional circulation pattern, whereby the young and childfree old flow to central-city apartments and the child oriented flow back to single family residences in the suburbs:

> It is . . . instructive to follow the location of middle-class families through their life cycle: the young couple lives in a central apartment, moves to the suburbs as the family grows, and returns to the center after the children leave home, thus reflecting their changing space-preferences with changing family size.

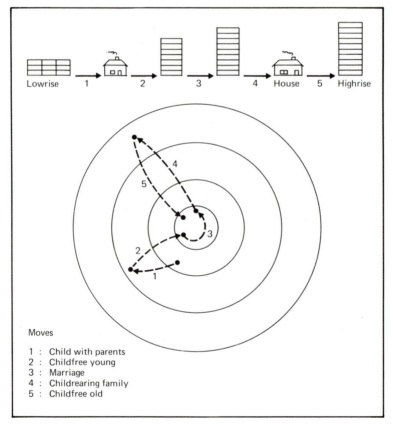

Fig. 10.1

Life-cycle–related relocations in the North American city.

Specific reasons for making such moves, together with a detailed discussion of the problems of adjustment to various living environments, are discussed in the sections below.

the child-rearing stage

Before the advent of mass transit in the late nineteenth century, and especially before the mass automobilism of the twentieth, cities were dense, compact areas with a heterogeneous mixture of land uses in close juxtaposition. In this physical environment the basic social unit was the family, which often included three generations and many persons from lateral family branches. Work was often located in or near the home. Many individuals lived in neighborhoods with strong kinship webs and on marriage did not venture far from the parental home. In the twentieth century, personal mobility has enabled many persons to escape the inner city which is increasingly seen as incompatible with healthful child rearing. As families were able to move out to the urban periphery, the strong ties between home and work, home and kin, and home and community were broken. Through time, then, the family has changed from an extended, open unit with strong local ties, to a stripped-down, nuclear family unit which increasingly turns inward in the face of a larger, more anonymous society.

The modern nuclear family, having shed its original ties to work, kin, and place, has become largely a child-rearing unit. Despite the increasing numbers of one-parent families, communal living experiments, and alternative child-rearing modes, the two-parent family has shown surprising resilience as a child-rearing unit. As poor housing conditions contribute very strongly to the maladjustment of children (Wilner and Walkeley, 1963), selection of an appropriate child-rearing environment is critical.

Child-oriented suburbia   In Chapter 4 it was found that single-family housing was highly preferred by several ethnic groups, including the white majority in North America, as a child-raising environment. The highly suburban landscapes of North America, Australia, and New Zealand express in concrete form the aspirations of previously space-restricted European immigrants. Single-family housing in good condition is found, for historic, spatial, and fiscal reasons, on the suburban periphery of cities. The essence of suburbia is land-use homogeneity, with a strict separation of residential, industrial, and commercial land uses. Individual home bases are physically separated by arrangements of driveways, grass, and trees. Within the home base there is frequently sufficient space for recreation both indoors and outdoors. In fact, the suburban backyard is probably the most intensively used type of recreation area in any urban region; an Australian research project on backyard recreation activities is ongoing (Halkett, 1975).

Land-use homogeneity, the separation of houses, and large amounts of private indoor and outdoor space together promote freedom of choice of activities, privacy, and safety for children. Compared with central-city environments, suburbia is also relatively free from overt crime, vandalism, fast traffic, and pollution (Chapter 7). It is not surprising, then, to find that the chief reason given by persons moving to the suburbs is that suburbia is "a good place to raise children" (Whyte, 1956; Wattel, 1958; Eaton, 1970; Hardwick, 1974). In a Toronto study, 90 percent of the respondents chose the single-family house as the best place to raise children, achieve privacy, and "most easily do the things you want to" (Michelson, 1970). Michelson (1967) also found that few married people with children wished to exchange detached homes for apartments. On the contrary, Rossi (1955) stressed family space requirements as the most important of the needs generated by life-cycle changes; thus "large families renting small apartments are the most mobile of all households, especially when they are in the earliest stages of the family cycle."

Suburbia, with its image of country living with easy access to urban delights, is clearly the chosen domain of the modern nuclear family, which has increasingly become a standardized package of two parents and two or three children. According to Michelson (1970), the typical suburban house with its extensive yard promotes child rearing in several ways:

1.   Self-contained housing without party walls or very close neighbors permits freedom of expression within the home base. The problems of auditory annoyance, visual proximity, and the need for excessive self-restraint in duplex and multiple-dwelling environments were explored in Chapter 8;

2.   Direct access to private open space maximizes the parents' opportunities for child control. Picture windows looking onto a private yard permit surveillance, from indoors, of children's outdoor activities;

3.   Regardless of the size of the space, people tend to associate private open space with active family pursuits.

The value of these attributes is emphasized by a brief analysis of the problems of child rearing in high-rise apartments. The apartment may have many party walls, with neighbors not only on both sides but also above and below. Consequently, parents must constantly inhibit childrens' activities, especially if these are noise generating. There is little available open space for childrens' play within an apartment block. Moreover, the absence of interior windows prevents the surveillance from the home of children playing in the corridor. Children engage in play activities in corridors, on stairwells, in elevators, or in outdoor playgrounds at ground level, none of which can be supervised from the home. From a height of several stories it is difficult to distinguish children at ground level, let alone control them. Apartment play areas are often poorly designed. Children raised in apartments may thus be overexposed, without adequate supervision, to the external environment. At the other extreme, solicitous parents may overinsulate the child from the local environment, thus potentially lowering his capacity to cope with it at a later date. There seems to be little neighbor interaction in family apartments; the informal social networks that provide a modicum of child protection and control in suburbia lack suitable semipublic spaces, such as front lawns, sidewalks, and driveways, in which to develop (Yancey, 1971).

The lack of private and semipublic open space is perhaps the greatest problem in apartment child raising. Only garden apartments and town houses have adequate front lawns and backyards. High rises have only public open space, and this is often restricted to entrance lounge and car park. The restrictions placed on children in high-rise environments have led Gregoire (1971) to liken Parisian high-rise projects to "modern concentration camps" which threaten the liberty of children. In this connection recent research studies have suggested that private open space is a greater generator of neighbor interaction than shared public open space (Fanning, 1967; Michelson, 1970). Clearly, one needs a socially acceptable reason to enter and stay in public open space. The identity and security conferred by territorial control over private open space, however, is conducive to more frequent use of it and more frequent and acceptable stimulus seeking in relation to the owners of adjacent private open spaces. Private open spaces promote neighboring, and neighborhood interaction provides a suitable socializing situation for children (Chapter 4).

Adolescents in suburbia   An environment designed for environmentally docile children, however, becomes inappropriate as children reach adolescence. Jacobs (1961) advocates high-density environments with mixed land uses for all children. This is clearly necessary for teenagers who, lacking the personal mobility of their parents, find that the homogeneous land uses of suburbs provide them with "nowhere to go" and "nothing to do." The teenager becomes increasingly dissatisfied with the child-oriented suburban setting, and this dissatisfaction is the prelude to Move 2, the individual's first attempt at habitat selection.

"The move to the suburbs . . . creates behavior changes of a largely negative type for the adolescent" (Gans, 1963). One adolescent reaction is the formation of teenage gangs, though gangs occur in all types of residential environments. Gangs have been regarded as highly structured primary groups with organizational independence, some degree of permanence, and the capacity to generate a subculture which is transmitted to new members. Alternatively, the gang has been characterized as an informal, short-lived, secondary group which lacks organization and which has few expectations of its members (Myerhoff and Myerhoff, 1964). There are clearly many types of gangs, from the inner-city organizations specializing in violence and various illegal activities to relatively innocuous associations of like-minded adolescents seeking the dramatic and exciting (Thrasher, 1927; Margolis, 1961; Yablonsky, 1962, 1964).

One frequently observed feature of gang life is its need for territorial expression (Klein, 1966). Ardrey (1966, 339) draws perhaps too close an analogy between the teenage gang and animal societies such as the baboon troop:

> the delinquent . . . creates directly from his instincts the animal institution of territory. In the defense of that territory his gang evolves a moral code, and his need to love and be loved is fulfilled. In its territorial combats, the gang creates and identifies enemies, and his need to hate and be hated finds institutional expression. Finally, in assault and larceny, the gang and its members enjoy the blood and loot of the predator.

The analogy, nevertheless, is striking; the popularization of the theme, as in *West Side Story*, dramatic; and the social problem both real and pressing.

A distinctive feature of gang structure is that the composition of the gang, or of its individual cliques, depends less upon functional roles than upon such space-related variables as residence patterns, attendance at common schools, and the close proximity of several heavily used meeting places. In Webber's "nonplace urban realm" (Chapter 4), the gang yet remains a community strongly based upon propinquity. Juvenile gang members may not have regular access to motorcycles or automobiles; the gang territory is restricted in size by reliance upon other means of locomotion. Thus gangs and their subcliques are apparently generated and perpetuated on a chance basis, favorable factors being a suitable neighborhood age structure and a fairly high population density. Where gang territories abut against each other, heavy use of territorial marking, such as graffiti, is often made (Ley and Cybriwsky, 1974a).

As an example of teenage adjustment to residential space, the behavior of the Burnside Gang in Victoria, British Columbia, has been investigated (Porteous, 1973a). This gang inhabits a medium density area of single-family, duplex, and row housing which straddles major highways and contains several streets lined with commercial developments (Fig. 10.2). The gang was found to have a fluid membership of approximately 60 youths, with a core clique of 25 members. This core group exhibited the greatest consistency in the initiation of and participation in gang activities. Of this 25-member clique, 17 were male, and an equal number were from families whose male head was employed in a white-collar occupation.

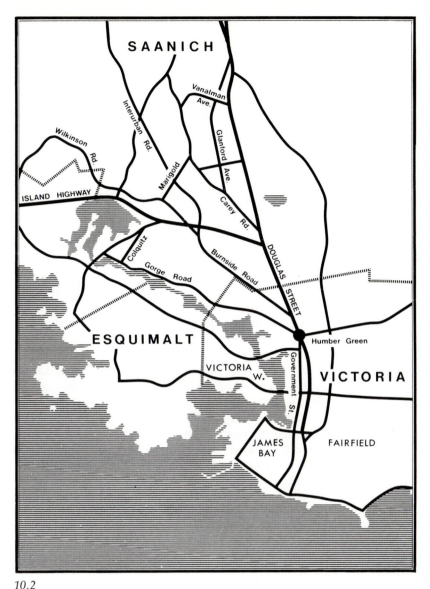

10.2

The Burnside gang: physical environment. (Reprinted by permission from *Western Geographical Series*, 5, 1973.)

In attempting to describe such a group's activity space, the elements of fixed-feature space are of great importance. Fixed-feature space consists of all environmental components not directly manipulable by the group, which in the case of juveniles comprises the bulk of their physical environment. Use of fixed-feature elements, however, may be voluntary or involuntary. For gang members, the involuntarily used fixed elements are chiefly home and school, which absorb at least two thirds of each weekday. Figure 10.3 illustrates the distribution of the residential home bases of the core clique. A circle of 1.5 miles diameter, based somewhat arbitrarily on a half hour's walking distance and described from the mean center of distribution of the residences, contains seventy-six percent (19) of these residences. No residence is more than 1.25 miles from this mean center, confirming the 1.5-mile diameter circle as an initially useful attempt to describe the outer limits of the gang turf. Although five schools exist in the vicinity, gang members attended only two of these; a junior high school (13 members) located close to the residential mean center, and a senior high school (12 members) approximately one-half mile distant, but easily accessible from the majority of the gang members' residences.

Gang members are able to exercise a greater degree of choice in terms of workplaces and meeting places, although these again are usually adult-created, fixed-feature elements. Twenty clique members (80 percent) had part-time jobs. As the Burnside area is primarily residential, only two work-places (8 percent) fell within the 1.5-mile diameter circle. Most workplaces are either in downtown Victoria or on major streets leading from downtown to the Burnside area. In terms of meeting places, however, the gang's activity space was sharply restricted to their immediate locality, with all six meeting places, together with the two schools, lying well within the circle. Of six major meeting places identified, only one was a residence. The five others comprised a drive-in diner, a youth-oriented drop-in center, a drive-in out-door theater, a park, and a secluded position beneath a railway bridge. With the schools, the bulk of these meeting places form a compact core area of gang activity adjacent to the residential mean center and located centrally within the 1.5-mile circle at a point where several major streets intersect with the interurban highway (Fig. 10.3).

A final parameter chosen for study was the distribution of delinquent acts performed by the gang over a period of several months. Such acts involved minor offenses, such as shoplifting, setting fires, destruction of property, breaking and entering, and the consumption of alcohol. Some of these activities were carried on in downtown stores, but eighty percent (12 of 15) were committed within the 1.5-mile circle.

Clearly the objective social space of the Burnside Gang cannot be contained within a single all-embracing boundary line. However, discounting workplaces, which involve gang members acting in isolation, it is evident that a territorial core may be demarcated around which residences, schools, and meeting places are located, and within which most delinquent acts are committed. This core area may be objectively defined as the area immediately surrounding the mean centers of distribution of residences, meeting places, and locations of delinquent acts (Fig. 10.3). The remainder of the area within the 1.5-mile circle, together with a small area outside it which encompasses the major roads leading to downtown, may be regarded as a less heavily used

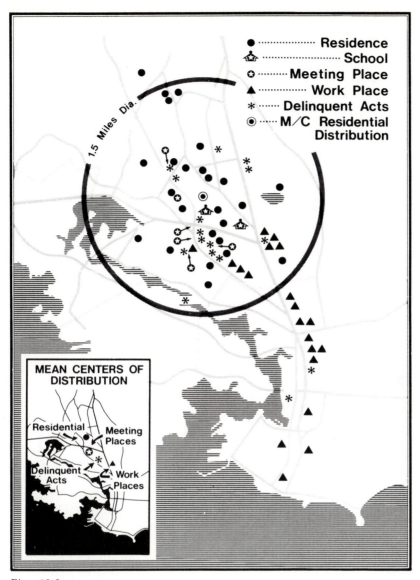

Fig. 10.3

The Burnside gang: activity space. (Reprinted by permission from *Western Geographical Series*, 5, 1973.)

fringe area of the territory. Like most political, socioeconomic, and biological entities, the teenage gang turf consists primarily of a central core and an outer frame.

The second part of the investigation involved an imageability questionnaire. Each of the 25 members of the core clique was asked to indicate, by drawing a continuous boundary line on a prepared street map, his conception of the gang turf. He was then asked to locate and name any townscape elements which were distinctive to him; these were, in general, landmarks with unique qualities or those rendered memorable by long and frequent association. Finally, the respondent was asked to rank in order of importance the six meeting places identified in the objective study.

It was predicted that the cognitive maps, though varying in areal extent from respondent to respondent, would all contain the gang core area and that landmarks closest to this core area, such as the diner, would be mentioned more frequently and ranked as of greater importance than landmarks on the fringe of the turf. For correlational purposes, previously gathered data on sex and school attended were supplemented by data on length of residence in the Burnside area, a variable hypothesized to be of some importance in terms of cognitive mapping.

Preliminary sorting of the boundary line maps indicated a wide range of conceptions of the areal extent of the turf (Fig. 10.4). The most extensive area reached east to the commercial strip on the edge of downtown, southward to the Gorge waterway, and westward and northward into the semirural suburban fringe. The smallest area comprised most of the gang's core area, including both the junior high school and the diner. All of the twenty-five subjects included most of the objectively defined core area, and all of those whose boundaries extended significantly beyond it perceived the Gorge waterway as an absolute southern barrier and the Douglas Street highway as a major eastern boundary. No such boundary consensus was apparent toward the north and west. The maps were grouped according to areal extent (Table 10.3), which suggested a negative correlation between size of turf and length of residence. The correlation coefficient, however, was merely -0.145. Further, Chi^2 analysis showed that the variables sex, school attended, and length of residence had no significant influence on size of territory. The mean turf size of the whole group was 1.8 square miles. A circular area of this extent would have a diameter of approximately 1.6 miles, which closely conforms to the arbitrarily designated diameter of 1.5 miles used in the study of objective social space. A circle of 1.6 miles diameter contains an equivalent number of elements to that of 1.5 miles and thus confirms the value of this figure as an assessment of the range of the gang.

Ranking of the six meeting places noted in the objective study elicited the data in Table 10.4. From this it is clear that the diner was of greatest collective importance to the gang as a meeting place, followed by the two schools (which, however, split the gang into two age groups during school hours). The drop-in center, located some distance from these major meeting places, was considered no more important than the outdoor theater and little more important than the residence of one of the gang leaders. When asked to note landmarks on the prepared map, gang members added little to the

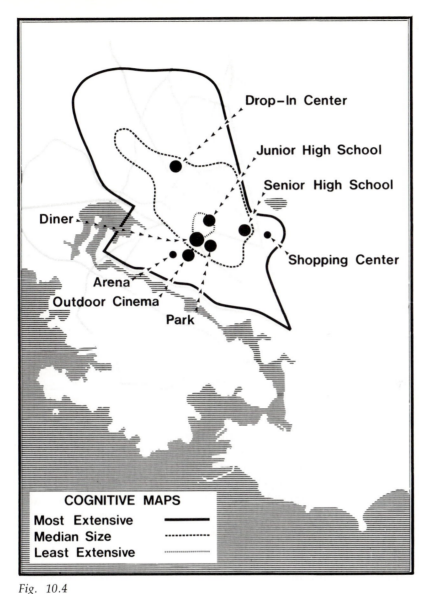

Fig. 10.4

The Burnside gang: cognitive maps. (Reprinted by permission from *Western Geographical Series* 5, 1973.)

landmarks already analyzed as meeting places in the section on objective social space, although girls took greater pains in map production and tended to place landmarks more accurately than did boys. Only eight landmarks were noted by at least two respondents, six of these corresponding with the above-mentioned meeting places, including the two schools. All of these

TABLE 10.3

COGNITIVE MAPS BY AREAL EXTENT

n = 25	Area Type	Mean Size (square miles)	Mean Years of Residence of Respondents
9	small	0.6	13.8
7	medium	1.6	11.7
9	large	3.1	10.7

Source: Porteous (1973a)

TABLE 10.4

RANKING OF MEETING PLACES

Meeting Place	Ranked First (number of times)	Mean Rank (1–5)
Drop-in center	1	3.44
Diner	15	1.60
Schools	7	2.72
Outdoor theater	0	3.40
A gang leader's residence	2	3.84

Source: Porteous (1973a)

landmarks were mentioned by at least one third of the respondents. Two additional landmarks, a shopping center east of Douglas Street and a sports arena on the fringe of the turf, were also mentioned. By far the most distinctive landmark (mentioned 23 times, compared with 11 references to the second most-mentioned landmark) was the diner, which the objective study had identified as a central focus within the core of the turf. Analysis of variance, however, demonstrated that the demographic variables previously mentioned had no significant influence upon the number of landmarks noted.

An overall correlation analysis also found no significant relationships between cognitive map size, landmark content, landmark ranking, the mention of individual landmarks, and social background variables. However, interesting relationships were observed between the landmarks themselves. The junior high school correlated strongly with both the senior high ($r = .510$; $p < .01$) and the park ($r = .557$; $p < .01$), while the latter correlated weakly with the drop-in center ($r = .428$; $p < .05$). Finally, the shopping center correlated strongly with the arena ($r = .702$; $p < .01$).

By adding frequency of mention scores and thus interpolating the centrally placed diner, which had no strong correlative links, and by arranging all these landmarks on a spatial basis, an admittedly rough conception of the gang's territory may be gained (Fig. 10.5). The diner forms the *central focus* of a *core area* in which well-frequented landmarks are highly correlated. The core is surrounded by a *peripheral zone* in which less frequently mentioned landmarks are also highly correlated.

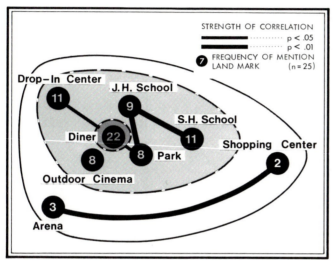

Fig. 10.5

Schematic representation of gang territory. (Reprinted by permission from *Western Geographical Series* 5, 1973.)

Planning Implications.   In Greater Victoria attempts to reduce the incidence of delinquent acts, to provide juveniles with neighborhood meeting places of their own, and to form a bridge between youth and the adult world have involved plans for setting up a series of drop-in centers throughout the urban area (*Victoria Daily Times,* 17 December 1969). A drop-in center is an informal version of the older church- or otherwise adult-sponsored youth group. Like the latter, it requires physical plant in the shape of a meeting place and a variety of leisure equipment. Unlike an adult-organized club, however, the drop-in center does not require a membership commitment, is less formally organized, and has no adult leader beyond an adviser, often a university student, chosen by the drop-in group itself.

Meeting places are to be provided by the municipalities. In the case of the Burnside Gang, the creation of the drop-in center noted by survey respondents as a common meeting place was a project of the youth program of Saanich municipality. Given the availability of suitable land or buildings, a major spatial issue is the location of the drop-in center (Fig. 10.6). One school of thought stresses the cohesive nature of the gang, which may possibly be a valuable force if directed into activities which result in adult-approved goals. According to this view, youth centers should be located centrally within the gang turf, in the core area most familiar to gang members. On the other hand, disapproving attitudes toward gangs, or a desire to reduce their territorial nature, would support the location of drop-in centers at border positions between adjacent gang turfs, where rival gangs may meet and mingle and, hopefully, lose their mutual hostility.

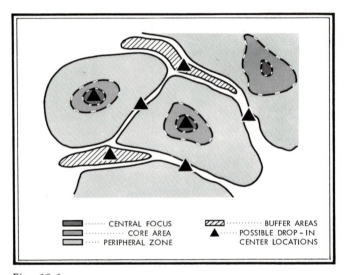

Fig. 10.6

Possible drop-in center locations. (Reprinted by permission from *Western Geographical Series* 5, 1973.)

Little evidence exists as to the merits of either course of action. The Burnside Gang, however, showed considerable hostility when a proposal was made to start a youth center less than one-half mile distant from its own meeting place. Lacking data on the spatial experience of various youth-center locations, one might favor the central location on accessibility grounds. A city-wide survey of this nature could provide a fairly accurate map of turf meeting places, central cores, peripheral zones, and neutral buffer areas between rival gangs. Armed with such data, the proponent of either centrally or peripherally located youth centers would at least be cognizant of the location of center and periphery and thus be better equipped to make accurate locational decisions according to his or her philosophical disposition.

the childfree stages

Child rearing requires space, particularly private open space, and much of the child-raising family's time is spent in the home (Chapter 5). In the pre- and post-child stages, however, control of large amounts of space may be disadvantageous. The elderly may be unable or unwilling to cope with a large house and garden, while those who have not yet produced children may regard extensive household chores as restrictive of their freedom. Moreover, both the childfree young and the old who have already launched their children into independence have positive needs for amenities and facilities which are not felt to the same extent by child-raisers. While the childfree young often value frequent use of central city cultural and entertainment facilities, the childfree old, in addition, value easy access to stores, hospitals, and clinics. Both groups rate access to goods and services more highly than do families with growing children (Michelson, 1970).

Accessibility to urban facilities usually means centrality within the urban area, and because of high land costs centrality is associated with apartment blocks. Though most older people would prefer to live in a single family house (Michelson, 1970), their accessibility needs require many of them to occupy center-city apartments. In a case study of seven high-rise apartment buildings in central Edmonton, Canada, apartment units were found to be occupied by married persons without children, persons living alone, and unrelated sharers (Smith and Hayter, 1974). In accordance with management policies, there were few children below the age of 19. Apartment occupants readily fell into two distinct categories:

1. Young childless adults, either married or unattached, who had histories of high residential mobility and expected to move again in the future. They viewed their apartment as but one step in a series of moves and most aspired to home ownership associated with raising a family.

2. Older childless adults, who had moved much less frequently, formed the bulk of the hard-core renters. Their move to the apartment from their family home frequently occurred after the death of a spouse. They did not anticipate future residential changes.

Apartment blocks are tending to specialize in accommodating primarily young or old tenants. A study in Chicago has found that whereas the young wanted space for socializing within the building, the old were more concerned about the quality of the building itself (Hall and Wekerle, 1972). Minor groups occupying apartments included those who had never married and middle-aged childless couples.

Apartment location within the city emphasizes the occupants' demands for centrality and accessibility. Apartments are typically located on the downtown fringe, along major arterial roads, and close to parks and waterfronts (Murphy, 1973). Apartment growth in the last decade has been spectacular; in Canada, for example, apartment dwelling starts have consistently outnumbered single family dwelling starts since 1966. On the supply side, rising land costs, taxation policies, and technological changes have favored apartment growth. On the demand side, the postwar baby boom has increased demand for rental accommodation, and there is some evidence of more permanent changes in housing preferences in the shape of delayed childbirth and married couples who choose not to have children.

As noted above, apartments are generally regarded as unsuitable environments for raising children. There is a considerable general feeling, however, that apartments are unsuitable for all groups and may even induce pathologies (Chapter 7). Faludi has outlined some prevalent anti-apartment public attitudes. Apartments are said to give rise to social conflict between nearby house occupants and apartment tenants who have no respect for neighborhood life. Lack of aesthetic quality in apartment blocks lowers the property values of adjacent houses. High population densities overload streets and utility lines. Though there is little concrete evidence to support any of these objections, a bias against apartment living remains prevalent. Yet apartments have been recommended even for ,child-raising on the grounds that the quality of childhood life is determined less by the physical environment than by the economic, social, and cultural traditions of the family (Faludi, 1963).

Because of the antihigh-rise bias, coupled with economic constraints, there has been a recent tendency to build horizontal multiple units (town housing, row housing) or low-rise, medium-density apartment blocks. Although the high rise permits more economic land utilization and greater amounts of public open space, the horizontal multiple unit in particular provides private outdoor space and thus a greater territorial support for individuality, especially where units can be entered directly from the outside. Again, people choose such units on the basis of life-cycle stage. A recent suburban apartment study found that the typical row house and garden apartment was occupied by a young family which was hoping eventually to move to a single-family dwelling (Saanich, 1972). Occupants of medium-density low-rise apartments, in contrast, were past the child-rearing stage and had no plans to move back to a single family dwelling. Comparing high-rise and low-rise occupants in Kansas it was found that high-rise inhabitants tended to be older, to have fewer children, to have fewer friends within the building, and to be more hostile and more alienated (Boyd, 1965). Although there is no concrete evidence that the physical environment was a causal factor, it was apparent that the low-rise complex had far more semipublic places where persons could interact.

the elderly

The social aspects of aging are too complex to be reviewed here. Two major views are apparent, however. While some researchers maintain a positive approach to old age (Cummings and Henry, 1961; Streib, 1970), aging is more frequently viewed in a negative manner. As noted above and in Chapter 7, one of the chief problems of the elderly is that of social isolation in a youth- and family-oriented society (Carp, 1972). This is chiefly associated with a series of losses sustained by most elderly persons. At age 50-65 the children leave the home; age 65-75 is characterized by loss of occupation, a lower income level, and possibly the deaths of spouse and friends; age 75-85 frequently brings loss of sensory acuity and health. There is also a severe loss of roles formerly played in society (Rose, 1965, 193):

> There tends to be a movement from head of household to de-pendent, from lack of awareness of psychological dependency to poignant awareness, from a rise in prestige to decline, from hav-ing a meaningful life role to having to search for a new role, and from being an active person to being a partial invalid.

As Simone de Beauvoir (1972) has noted, modern industrial society con-demns old people to decrepitude, poverty, and loneliness, in the face of which they are expected to display serenity so that their juniors will be spared guilt feelings.

Loss of physical competence, loss of a place in the nuclear family, and the need for accessibility to central services are among tendencies which propel elderly persons into apartments or congregate living environments, all of which tend to increase personal isolation (Chapters 7, 8). Isolation is enhanced by the declining mobility of elderly persons. It is generally agreed that older persons, like children, are environmentally docile (Pastalan and Carson, 1970). Several studies of the mobility of the elderly have shown that older people express displeasure with their inability to get about (Carp, 1970; Jones, 1975). The unwell, the poor, and those who do not drive have the greatest mobility constraints. City-center residents tend to go out more often and to be fairly well satisfied, despite the fact that few have cars. In terms of home range, Barker and Barker (1961) compared the number of behavior settings used by persons of different ages in similar communities in both the United States and Britain (Fig. 10.7). It is notable that in both cases an individual's range was greatest during the age period 18-64, but after 65 fell back to the level of the adolescent.

Gerontological research, however, frequently lacks a spatial or en-vironmental component. A recent publication on planning for the elderly, for example, has little to offer on the relationship between the elderly and the physical environment or on the impact of various types of dwelling arrangements upon the elderly (Kent *et al.*, 1972). Yet in view of the problem of role loss and social isolation, dwelling type and location may be critical.

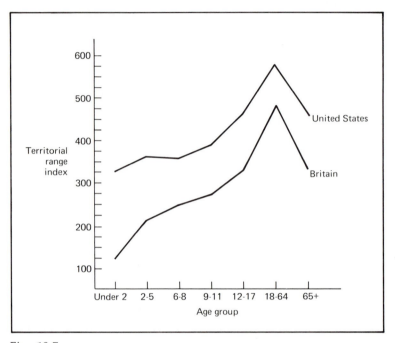

Fig. 10.7

Home range versus age in Britain and the United States (data derived from Barker and Barker, 1961).

Two schools of thought are apparent, the major issue being whether the elderly should be *segregated* in large, homogeneous concentrations, or *integrated* into society by scattering them in small groups throughout the whole urban area. Proponents of integration, whether within apartments or at the neighborhood level, suggest that although most elderly persons want their own accommodation, they would prefer to live near their families. Older persons could serve useful functions, such as babysitting, which might help them retain their personal integrity. The integration of older persons with young child-free and child-rearing persons also satisfies a long-held desire among planners to produce balanced communities (see Chapter 12).

However, as older persons lose work and other roles, the importance of friends and neighbors in their lives increases. Social interaction is essential to mental health, and older persons are better able to form friends with persons from the same social class and age groups. Several studies have established that where aged persons live among other older people, their levels of interaction increase dramatically (Rosenberg, 1970). According to Rosow (1967, 64):

> There is a threshold effect in which minimally half the dwelling units in a residential setting must have an older person before strong neighboring patterns are stimulated and interaction is significantly intensified.

The need for high concentrations of the elderly also occurs because the elderly often reject, and are rejected by, other life-cycle groups.

Much evidence, therefore, supports the view that elderly persons of low environmental competence are most likely to benefit from a policy of segregation into a concentration of people at the same life-cycle stage. This is especially true for people, often of lower socioeconomic class, who have a history of restricted activity space (Rosow, 1967). It is also important for persons who have lived in neighborhoods with little neighboring activity (Michelson, 1970). In contrast, those with histories involving a wide-ranging activity pattern, with friends scattered throughout the city, as well as those who are well-integrated into a neighborhood with strong community feeling, will be less likely to benefit from age-segregated housing. Working class and ethnic districts in which the extended family still survives will also house elderly persons who derive most satisfaction from integration.

For the more environmentally docile many types of age-segregated housing are available, ranging from detached or attached housing arranged around a central facility or courtyard to congregate living, where all live under one roof, and the geriatric complex, which provides a total housing and recreational environment complete with qualified institutional care. Age-segregated housing improves the efficiency of delivery of services and care, and improves the accessibility of the aged to community facilities. While cushioned against the slights and insults of a bustling world, the elderly are afforded greater opportunities to make friends. In several ways social isolation is reduced.

The simple provision of age-homogeneous housing, however, is insufficient to solve the problems of social isolation among the aged. At the microspace level, the internal arrangements of the housing unit are important, and at the macrospace level, the relationship between the age-segregated unit and the rest of the city is critical.

Taking the latter point first, it is desirable that the age-homogeneous unit should not be isolated from the everyday activities of the city. Scandinavian nations pioneered the concept of the old-age community, one of the best-known examples being the Gamles By (Old Peoples' City) in Copenhagen. But the inhabitants of such age-homogeneous institutions can frequently become inward looking, with days of boredom broken only by eventful funerals. Such establishments have been regarded as ghettos for the aged, with a typical internal orientation toward four standard facilities: the chapel, the recreation room, the dispensary, and the morgue (Benoit, 1974). It is clear that the age-homogeneous community will be of little benefit to its inhabitants unless it is an open community with ready access, if only visually, to the multifarious activities of the city. Old people do not necessarily want to gaze at acres of peaceful green grass. One of the chief social events for old people is the act of shopping; several studies have shown that old people want convenient access to stores, buses, health services, parks, libraries, and the like (Jones, 1975). Old people are also interested in children, and the location of an age-homogeneous complex opposite a school is likely to elicit a favorable response.

Within the residence, design should be such that privacy and interaction are facilitated. A series of studies by Lawton (1972) emphasizes the point previously made in this chapter that social interaction is facilitated by territorial control of private space with access to semipublic open space. In one experiment in the Philadelphia Geriatric Center, two traditional four-bed rooms were remodeled to form six private bedrooms, each opening on to a small common space, which in turn was separated from the main hall by a half-wall. This new environment allowed the individual to choose privacy, or to sit in the semipublic area which provided visual access to the main hallway where most ward activity occurred. The remodeling radically changed space occupancy patterns. Patients occupied their rooms during 96 percent of the prealteration observation periods, but only to the extent of 43 percent after alteration. Patients also more than doubled their use of the hospital area beyond their semipublic domain, this increase in home range providing them with necessary exercise and social intercourse. In other studies the importance of hallways, lobbies, and other semipublic space for socializing was noted; such spaces are especially valuable as locations in which persons suffering some impairment may simply sit and view ongoing activities.

The debate on the integration or segregation of the aged is still far from resolved. Proponents of integration cite the sense of personal worth felt by the aged in societies which still have three-generation families living in the same house. The aged still have an important economic housekeeping function in communally oriented societies such as Israel's kibbutzim (Wershow, 1969) and the Soviet Union (Geiger, 1968). Such roles have been rejected in the Western world with the result that elderly persons living in couples or alone in an integrated arrangement are likely to feel more isolated than in an age-homogeneous setting. A study by Poorkaj (1972), however, found that residents of an age-segregated environment with vast recreational opportunities had no greater morale than integrated residents who used senior centers or disengaged residents who did not use such facilities. Studies of the relationship between morale and activity (Messer, 1966; Teaff *et al.*, 1973) suggest that the degree of individual environmental competence or docility should be a major factor in deciding whether integration or segregation is most suitable for an aged individual (Lawton, 1970b).

Life Level

Life level is, in a sense, a measure of environmental competence based on wealth. Better known as social class, it is so commonly associated with income in North America that the term *socioeconomic group* has been coined as a euphemism. Life level is generally measured by income, education, and occupation, attributes which tend to intercorrelate highly. It is manifested in both physical and intangible ways, ranging from the house type occupied and the automobile owned to the degree of prestige or status enjoyed by the individual within his community. Life level has important consequences, for it is experienced throughout life in terms of who participates with whom, who is acceptable to whom, and who marries whom (Beshers, 1962). "Friendships are formed primarily between persons with similar status characteristics" (Rosow, 1967). In Chapter 5 it was found that persons of different classes not only had different home ranges but also had important differences in their cognitive maps.

Almost every research worker has proposed his own categorization of life level (Warner *et al.*, 1957; Michelson, 1970). The most generally recognized differences, however, are between lower, middle, and upper classes.

> **1.** *Lower Class.* Regular blue-collar employment is a major criterion here, usually, but not always, involving only moderate education and income levels. This group is often known as the working class. Below this is a low-income group with little education and which comprises individuals who frequently lack steady jobs.
>
> **2.** *Middle Class.* Lower-middle-class persons also work for others and may enjoy education and income levels no greater than those of blue-collar workers, but, having white-collar employment, frequently exhibit a very different life-style. Upper-middle-class persons have higher levels of education, comfortable salary or professional fee incomes, and may be self-employed.
>
> **3.** *Upper Class.* This involves either or both of great personal wealth or aristocratic lineage, thus affording high levels of education, where needed, and ready access to positions of power and prestige.

These are not rigid class lines. Finer distinctions can be made, and several groups may not fit the pattern exactly. Low-echelon university faculty, for example, are upper middle class in terms of education and occupation, but have incomes at the blue-collar level. Their individual life-styles frequently fit none of these categories. Further, the great overlap in income between blue-collar workers and lower middle-class white-collar salaried employees emphasizes the importance of life-style in accentuating social differences.

Social-class differences are acknowledged throughout society, and nowhere more so than in residential location. Here the status differences of office and factory are repeated in residential terms. Although much attention is paid to racial segregation (Chapter 11), residential segregation by social class is one of the fundamental realities of cities in the Western world. Though some residential areas remain immortally of one particular class stamp (Forward, 1973), others radically shift in class atmosphere as groups leave or invade. Despite these changes, all large cities continue to comprise a wide range of social-class areas, with higher areas, peripheral areas, and coastal zones preempted by the rich. A large number of studies have shown that the chief criterion in residential segregation is occupational status (Duncan and Duncan, 1957; Wheeler, 1968). Persons with occupations furthest from each other in status terms (e.g., bank president and garbage collector) are located furthest from each other in residential terms.

As an illustration, the pre–World War I residential segregation patterns of Vancouver, British Columbia, are of interest, especially as the class differences of that era still persist. At the turn of the century Vancouver was dominated by Eastern Canadian businessmen associated with the timber industry and the Canadian Pacific Railway. These industries demanded labor, which quickly became radical and unionized. The two groups, known respectively as the *lotus-eaters* and the *loggers*, took up very different residential locations involving spatial segregation and street patterns which strongly reflected their ideologies (Gibson, 1973, 67–9). The loggers' residential sector in South Vancouver was laid out on a rigid grid pattern with very small lots. Street misalignment was common, and there was no clear relationship between the residential lots and open spaces. In contrast, the lotus-eaters of Point Grey enjoyed a naturalistic, curvilinear street plan, with a clear relationship between residential lots and urban open space. Whereas South Vancouver's townscape was merely utilitarian, Point Grey had a pastoral ambience, with a conscious use of land planning to project images of patriotism, civic order, and material progress.

Besides house location and street pattern, the type of house occupied is also strongly related to life level. In Britain, where the class struggle is manifested in fierce competition for the use of the housing stock, life-level classes have been translated into housing classes (Rex and Moore, 1967). Seven major classes of housing are distinguished, arranged in a descending hierarchy of prestige and having a distinctive spatial distribution in the city:

1. Outright owners of large houses in desirable areas;
2. Mortgage payers who own whole houses in desirable areas;
3. Public housing tenants in publicly built housing;
4. Tenants in publicly bought slum housing awaiting demolition;
5. Tenants of a whole house owned by a private landlord;
6. Owners of a house bought with short-term loans who are compelled to let rooms in order to meet repayments;
7. Tenants of rooms in rooming houses.

These categories reflect the peculiar social ambience of Britain, where approximately 30 percent of the population lives in public housing. Rex and Moore state that occupation of one of the above housing classes is a strong predictor of a person's interests, associations, life-style, and social class. People are not, however, permanently restricted to any one housing class, and persons living in types 7, 6, 5, and 4 tend to aspire to types 3 and 2. In North America, where public housing shelters a much smaller proportion of the population, aspirations are almost universally toward type 2.

As in life-cycle stage, the process by which segregation occurs is selective residential mobility. A series of research studies suggests that segregation occurs not simply because of income differences but because of an active desire on the part of all classes to exclude social inferiors (Walinsky, 1964). More subtly, there is a general tendency for persons to identify themselves with others of equivalent or higher rank and to differentiate themselves from those of lower rank; "for high-ranking occupations, this is evidently a matter of excluding others, while for low-ranking occupations, it is a matter of including themselves" (Feldman and Tilly, 1960). The measures taken by higher ranking persons to ensure class homogeneity in their home area are many and varied (Keller, 1966, 504):

> They include economic and financial selection due to the inability to purchase or rent homes in such areas, outright refusal to lease or sell to "undesirables," social ostracism of unwanted newcomers by oldtimers, and, as a desperate last gesture, the abandonment of the area by the old residents who thereby lower the value of the area they leave behind while raising it in the area to which they move.

This raises the question of whether personal mobility between life levels involves spatial mobility from one class-homogeneous area to another. Lipset and Bendix (1959) suggested that only a small proportion of North Americans ever leave the social class into which they were born. This means that people who change their residence, whether for life-cycle or other reasons, will tend to move to another area occupied by the same social class. If an upward or downward movement in the class hierarchy is achieved, however, there will be corresponding residential movements. But such movements rarely involve relocation beyond areas occupied by the next higher or next lower class. In *Plainville, U.S.A.*, West (1945) notes that only two men moved all the way through the social-class system in a single lifetime.

A study of Rhode Island confirms this view of strong life-level constraints on residential movement (Table 10.5). The largest figures in the matrix form a diagonal and indicate that most moves are made to areas of similar class standing. Away from the diagonal, percentages decline along the columns, demonstrating that most across-class moves are made to the nearest upper- or lower-class levels. Finally, a general tendency for upward mobility is indicated by the decrease of the diagonal figures toward the low-class areas, and the fact that percentages on the left side of the diagonal (moves from lower to upper) are generally larger than those on the right of the diagonal (moves from upper to lower).

TABLE 10.5

RELOCATIONS AMONG SOCIAL AREAS (in %)

Social Areas (Origin)	Social Areas (Destination)				
	1 (High)	2	3	4	5 (Low)
1 (High)	63.8	12.0	11.3	8.2	4.7
2	8.2	51.0	20.6	13.3	6.9
3	6.1	18.8	50.4	16.7	8.0
4	5.1	13.0	21.0	52.7	8.2
5 (Low)	4.1	13.2	17.3	17.4	48.0

Source: Goldstein and Mayer (1961)

Residential relocation is influenced by economic, social, and spatial factors. One of the most important *spatial* factors is the distance between home and work. In general, higher-status people appear more willing or able to endure and pay for long journeys to work than are lower-status people. Decisions to relocate far from the worksite have important social consequences. De Lauwe (1960), analyzing the time budgets of numbers of working people, found that leisure-time activities, the conjugal relationship, the amount of time spent playing with the children, and hence parent-child relationships, are all affected by the length of the journey to work. *Economic* constraints obviously limit the locational choices of the poor, while enhancing the choicefulness of high-status life. *Social* constraints operate to selectively filter people out of areas which are marginally mixed. In Kuper's cul-de-sac (Chapter 8) one family in three had moved within four years. The bulk of these moves occurred for status reasons. Among the middle classes, significant hierarchical career changes may be followed by residential relocation. Promotion is often followed by a move to a "better" area. A pilot study in Victoria, British Columbia, suggests that the attainment of promotion and tenure by university faculty correlates positively with residential relocations from lower- to higher-status residential areas. Analysis of real estate advertising in the same city has shown that real estate agents are important in helping to fit house purchasers into socially suitable areas.

class differences in housing attitudes

Moving one's residence from one homogeneous life-level area to another of different rank means far more than a mere physical relocation. It may involve, either before or after the event, a major change in attitudes toward the housing environment. And changed attitudes may presage changes in lifestyle, activity patterns, and the like. In fact, "upward skidding demands a value shift" (Cameron, 1963). In Chapter 5 it was found that persons at the lower end of the life-level scale had smaller activity spaces and more restricted mental maps than persons of higher status. This income-related feature accounts for the observation that working-class persons are more *local* in their activity and friendship patterns, while persons of higher status are more able to take a *cosmopolitan* stance involving community without propinquity (Merton, 1957; Rosow, 1970).

This is not to suggest that people of different social classes have different environmental needs or preferences. Indeed, in the discussion of home base in Chapter 4 it was found that all classes and races had a strong preference for single-family homes. The images projected by advertising in Britain and the United States reinforce this positive attitude toward the single-family dwelling (Sinton, 1960). In a series of studies cited by Michelson (1970) preferences for such features as house type, lot size, accessibility, and neighborhood atmosphere did not vary according to life level as measured by occupation and education. The greatest variations were related to life-style and stage in the life cycle. In general, the standard preferences are for the environments typically enjoyed by higher-status persons. It is the physical limitation of low income which prevents lower-status people from achieving the levels of environment to which they aspire.

Income, occupation, and education, however, not only influence the quality of housing that a person will occupy but also have a significant part to play in influencing what that housing will mean to its occupants (Fig. 10.8). A three-level typology is suggested.

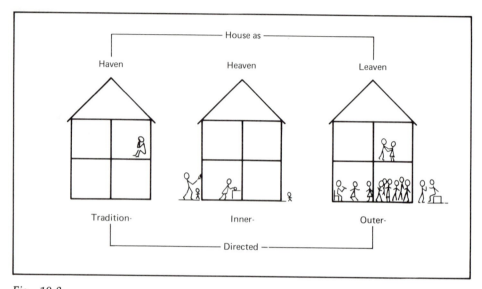

Fig. 10.8

Basic housing orientations. (Note: an individual may combine values from all three orientations.)

House as haven   Rainwater (1966), concentrating on the lower end of the lower-class spectrum, asserts that the outside world presents a constant and all-encompassing threat to the poor. Strauss (1961) found that many black immigrants to cities look upon their street and block as an island in a sea of threat. Many of these threats are inherent in the physical structure of both dwelling and neighborhood, and include rats, cold, poor construction, and plumbing and electrical hazards. Other threats are human in origin, and include physical and verbal violence and the problems inherent in family, neighbor, and institutional interaction. On the whole, such people regard the house as a *haven*, an oasis of safety and security in a threatening world. This is a case where an upgrading of the physical environment, if unable to change social behavior, would at least eliminate many nonhuman dangers (Montgomery, 1966).

Many blue-collar workers, however, have incomes similar to those of the lower middle classes. Differences occur in the way this income is expended, and it appears that level of education is the important factor in explaining segregation between groups of similar income status (Collison, 1960; Tilley, 1961). Whereas the blue-collar worker is likely to spend more of his income on consumer durables, such as cars and televisions, a white-collar worker with the same income is more likely to spend a greater proportion of his income on housing. Having attained a higher educational standard and regarding his occupation as of higher status, he is at pains to spend up to one-third of his income on housing in order to be able to live close to higher-income members of the middle class and thus maintain a gap between himself and the blue-collar worker. Many working-class persons are simply not sufficiently concerned with housing quality and symbolism to the extent that they will spend over one quarter of their income for housing alone.

House as heaven Since World War II, however, there has been a steady influx of higher-income working-class persons into the suburbs, where higher-quality housing is expected (Berger, 1960). These, together with lower-middle-class people who are paying a considerable portion of their income for housing, tend to be house-centered (Clark, 1966). Whereas lower-class people are tradition directed and more concerned with physical safety, this group consists of financially insecure, inner-directed persons who may regard the house as *heaven*. They have left the noise, dirt, and crime of the central city for the expensive suburbs, and tend to lavish much time and attention upon their chosen home base. The home-handyman syndrome is common.

House as leaven Persons of higher status tend to be more outer directed. They have fewer problems of physical safety or financial insecurity. Consequently, the house is neither a haven, a refuge from the world, nor a heaven, toward the betterment of which much activity is directed. Rather, the house is *leaven*, an operational base for people who are concerned largely with their role as catalysts in society. These community-centered persons are the group most likely to press for the upgrading of the environment beyond their own particular home base.

social-class integration

It will be noted that it was not possible to ascribe the three housing orientations described above exactly to the three social-class levels used in this chapter. There is now increasing overlap, in both attitudinal and residential terms, between lower and middle, and middle and upper classes. In the nineteenth century persons of different classes lived spatially closer together. Differences between classes were much more institutionalized than now, especially where property qualifications were necessary for voting. Moreover, though physically close together, the different classes were clearly distinguished by their capacity to pay for living space, whether arranged horizontally or vertically. In the egalitarian atmosphere which followed World War I, social distance between classes gradually became blurred, and had to be replaced by physical distance, hence the growth of residential segregation.

A strong belief among planners, however, has been that socially balanced neighborhoods should be created wherever possible (Chapter 4). The difficulties involved in age integration have already been mentioned in this chapter. Classes are even more difficult to intermix on a residential basis. Indeed, Keller (1966) has noted that although it is possible to find persons of different ethnic group, culture, and religion living close together, this occurs only where social class is relatively homogeneous. Further, it has been found that stable residential mixtures of races, such as blacks and whites in the United States, are possible only where social class is fairly uniform. "In short, racial differences in behavior are imaginary, but social-class differences are real" (Wolf and Lebeaux, 1968, 109).

In several cases where social-class mixing has been somehow engineered, the result has not been meaningful interaction between classes but rather the opposite. Gutman (1963) and Gans (1963) both found that working-class persons quickly became social isolates when living in a predominantly middle-class milieu. Gutman suggested that working-class wives lacked the social skills necessary for intimate interaction with middle-class wives. They tended to leave social integration attempts to their husbands, and were thus isolated during weekdays. Gans (1963, 190) found that working-class wives and others who deviated from accepted norms did not "suffer from pressures to conform, but from a shortage of like-minded people in their surroundings." In Gans' detailed study of Levittown, it was found that although there were mixtures of social class on the large neighborhood level, at the small neighborhood level (a block, or about 12 houses) social homogeneity tended to prevail. Even in projects where lower, middle, and upper classes are mixed fairly equally there are problems of the control of facilities and open space by a single class, of noise, and of time-scheduling, especially where different classes tend to keep different hours (Boeschenstein, 1971). Strong social and psychological barriers appeared between the class-homogeneous sections of a mixed housing project in Brookline, Massachusetts, barriers which were substantially broken down only by children.

Finally, Keller asserts that social-class mixing at any neighborhood level is just as likely to lead to hostility as to social integration. Imagine a mixture of house as heaven, leaven, and haven people in the same neighborhood, with the community-centered group agitating for costly community facilities such as libraries and tennis courts. There is likely to be an intense clash of interest. House as haven people will probably not become heavily involved. House as heaven people, however, being inner directed, conscious of the existing costs of mortgages and taxes, and home oriented in terms of activity patterns, will be likely to oppose any facilities or improvements that might result in added financial burdens.

Groups with different educations, incomes, occupations, activity patterns, social norms, and attitudes are unlikely to agree except on very basic issues. Like life-cycle segregation, life-level segregation continues to intensify in Western cities. If all classes were environmentally competent, could be guaranteed equal access to urban facilities and an adequate standard of housing quality, and had recognized areas for interaction when needed, there would be no moral reason for planners to attempt to reverse these trends. Planners have, however, attempted such social engineering on a large scale, and this will be discussed in Chapter 13. The social integration of the very poor, and of racial minorities, both of which groups have distinct life-styles which do not conform to the mainstream of social norms, is a somewhat different issue and will be discussed in the next chapter.

Summary

1. Life-cycle stage, measured by both age and family status, is a major factor in residential relocation. Habitat selection is strongly influenced by space needs, which substantially depend upon whether the family or individual is in a child-rearing or childfree stage.
2. Single-family dwellings, especially in suburbia, are highly preferred by most social groups as the ideal child-rearing environment.
3. The suburban environment, unlike the apartment complex, permits freedom of expression and adequate surveillance of childrens' outdoor activities. This is achieved by the control of private and semipublic outdoor space, which is generally associated with family activities.
4. The land-use homogeneity and child-oriented atmosphere of suburbia, however, is found unsatisfactory by adolescents. These may develop strongly territorial teenage gangs, communities with common activity patterns based on both spatial and social (age) propinquity.
5. Both the childfree young and the childfree old rate accessibility to urban facilities, and thus centrality within the urban area, higher than do child-rearing couples. At this stage in the life cycle people are more likely to occupy apartments than single-family houses.
6. A controversy rages over whether environmentally docile aged persons should be residentially integrated or segregated into age-homogeneous communities. Much research favors age segregation, but only if the internal structure of the residence affords a range of choice on the privacy-interaction continuum. Further, age-homogeneous environ-

ments should be so articulated with the city as a whole as to provide easy access, whether physical or visual, to a wide range of city activities.

7. Life level, or social class, measured by education, occupation, and income, influences the individual's choice of housing type and location within the city. A change of social class generally involves residential relocation in societies which stress upward mobility.

8. Although members of all class levels typically aspire to single-family housing, the house has a different symbolic meaning for each class group.

9. The mixing of persons of different life levels in the same residential area has rarely led to meaningful interaction across social classes. It is just as likely to lead to class hostility or the isolation of one class group.

10. In Western cities the trend toward increasing homogenization of residential areas in terms of both life cycle and life level continues unabated. *Ceteris paribus,* there is no moral reason why planners should regard age and class segregation as a problem.

Further Reading

CARP, F. M., ed. (1972), *Retirement.* New York: Behavioral Publications.

GANS, H. J. (1961), "The Balanced Community: Homogeneity or Heterogeneity in Residential Areas," *Journal of the American Institute of Planners* 27: 176–84.

GANS, H. J. (1962), "Urbanism and Suburbanism as Ways of Life," in A. M. Rose (ed.), *Human Behavior and Social Processes,* pp. 625–48. Boston: Houghton Mifflin.

ROSOW, I. (1967), *Social Integration of the Aged.* New York: Free Press.

11

THE CONTEXTUAL ENVIRONMENT: LIFE-STYLE

Life-style is a more subtle personal characteristic than life level or stage in the life cycle. It is also more difficult to measure, although a combination of income-expenditure and time budgets (Chapter 5) would probably provide useful data. Such data are important because life-style is "one way of doing things" chosen from a variety of possible ways of life. Unfortunately, the cost of eliciting these data is great, and all the more so in view of the necessity for frequent monitoring because of rapid life-style changes.

Varieties of Life-Style

An individual has many life-styles to choose from. The choice will vary according to the individual's personality; because of the difficulties of personal assessment outlined in Chapter 9, however, it is fortunate for designers that regularities in life-style choice are apparent. For example, the peculiar life-styles of the groups variously known as beatniks, flower children, and hippies were embraced by persons of varying age and class backgrounds despite their usual association with the middle-class youth cult of the 1950s and 1960s.

---

* Sarey Gamp, in Charles Dickens (1901), *The Life and Adventures of Martin Chuzzlewit*. New York: Scribners.

On the other hand, persons of similar age, family status, and life level may exhibit very different life-styles. Bell (1965) suggests three major life-style designations. *Familism* involves a strong orientation toward child-rearing; the alternatives are *consumerism,* where the acquisition of material goods is a major force, and *careerism,* the pursuit of an occupation to the exclusion of other interests. Even these may be further broken down, however, because of different age, class, or aspirational backgrounds. Two adjacent houses, for example, may be inhabited by first, a male who drives a large Chevrolet, brings home a six-pack of beer, and watches football on the television, and second, a male who drives a small Volkswagen, brings home a bottle of Chilean wine, and goes out to play badminton or squash. Other fine distinctions have been made between *localism,* where individuals restrict their range and interests to their local area, and *cosmopolitanism,* where the individual may operate in all spatial contexts from local to international (Merton, 1949). The judgmental standards of members of these two groups are likely to be very different, the first tending toward the subjective and personal, the second toward more objective and universal standards.

These distinctions are not exclusive categorizations. They should rather be viewed as extremes on continua, with an infinite variety of intermediate points. Moreover, life-style types may be successfully combined and may indeed be mutually reinforcing. Familism and careerism are commonly combined, most notably among managerial groups in business where a stable family background may be looked upon as a career asset.

The career implied above, of course, is primarily a male career. Traditionally females have been less prone to careerism and, until recently, career women have often avoided, or had to give up, the child-oriented responsibilities of familism. More recently, the childfree professional couple has emerged, with both husband and wife devoted to their careers and with no tendency toward familism.

Recent studies have brought out other fine distinctions in life-style orientations (Michelson, 1975). There appears to be a clear distinction, for example, between professionals, who frequently seek housing in the city core, and managerial persons of similar income, who prefer suburban housing. Moreover, it appears that it is the managerial male who feels child-oriented, and family-oriented, while his wife frequently feels merely isolated and withdrawn, despite a stated preference for the suburban life-style.

Further distinctions are apparent, and the reader can no doubt create his own life-style typology. One further example is appended. A strong life-style distinction may be made between a husband and wife who spend most of their out-of-home discretionary time together, and a couple whose ways part on leaving the threshold. The latter is a common phenomenon in English working-class life, associated with a strong division of labor in the home and exemplified by the widely syndicated cartoon strip *Andy Capp.* Andy and

Florrie habitually meet only at home. Andy's home range includes home, pub, football matches, pigeon racing, and the welfare office. Florrie seems largely confined to home, shopping, and bingo. Several sociological studies have confirmed this as a normal English working-class life-style (Bott, 1957; Mogey, 1956).

Of greatest interest in these studies are the life-style contrasts between inner city and suburbs. Suburban people were found to have a much weaker division of labor between husband and wife, and tended to enjoy their recreation time together. Even more significantly, several workers have observed that the relocation of families from inner city to suburbs may induce the taking up of a new life-style. Young and Willmott (1962), for example, found that people relocated from central London to suburban public housing became more intensely devoted to familism and consumerism. Voluntary movement to the suburbs may result in little life-style change, however. Berger (1960), studying the life-styles of affluent automobile workers in suburbia, found that they did not take on the stereotyped suburban life-style of conservatism, church attendance, the joining of associations, and a dedication to upward mobility. Gans (1963) refutes the concept of the suburban environment's capacity to induce new life-styles. On the contrary, he suggests that many people move to the suburbs because they wish to change their life-styles. The changes they make on arrival in suburbia, far from being induced by the environment, are in fact long-anticipated changes. This in turn suggests that the anticipated life-style could not adequately be operationalized in the inner city, and that the suburban environment provides the optimal physical setting for such a life-style.

The physical environments provided by the inner city and the suburb appear to be conducive to different life-styles. Stress may occur when a particular life-style must be carried out in an environment to which it is unsuited. The most obvious distinction between inner city and suburb is density. The inner city is characterized by high inside and outside residential densities, space restrictions, older housing or new high- and low-rise apartment blocks, lack of open space, inadequate public facilities, and high incidences of pollution and pathologies (Chapters 7, 10). In contrast, the suburbanite enjoys low density, which permits large private open spaces around and between dwellings, newer single-family houses or multiple dwellings with private open space, adequate public open space and facilities, and low incidences of pollution and pathologies.

Concentrating on the spatial differences, it is possible to make some tentative connections between physical environment and life-styles. Those whose life-styles tend toward careerism and consumerism are likely to value convenience and accessibility to services and facilities, and thus centrality, more than the child-oriented. They will therefore be found to a greater extent in central-city apartments than those persons devoted to familism. Many families are, however, raised in the inner city; at this point two rather gross stereotypes may be presented.

1.   *Inner-city familism* is generally associated with low income levels. Such persons frequently belong to extended families, where many relatives live in the same neighborhood and substitute for friends. These inner-city neighborhoods have a close-knit social network with intense neighboring associations. Life-styles are person-oriented, communal, and local in a high-density environment of mixed land uses (small industries, corner stores).

2.   *Suburban familism* is associated with higher income levels, the nuclear family, and an emphasis on friends rather than neighbors or relatives (Chapter 4). Suburban neighborhoods have a loose-knit social network in an environment of homogeneous low-density residential land uses. Life-styles emphasize individualism and are more thing-oriented and cosmopolitan.

According to Jacobs (1961), inner-city neighborhoods are socially more healthy because high densities and mixed land uses promote frequent interaction and permit constant surveillance of the activities of the street, thus reducing the opportunity for deviance. A heavy use of public spaces is also promoted, and Jacobs cites the high degree of helpful contact between persons inhabiting such inner-city neighborhoods. The other side of this coin is the lack of intimate social control in suburbs. Indeed the suburbs have been heavily criticized in terms of both social cohesion and cultural mediocrity (Riesman, 1958), despite the fact that people still prefer to live therein (Vernon, 1962).

Segregation and Ghettoization

Suburban people tend to live in housing which is fairly new, largely single family in type, far from the city core, and designed for the automobile. The populations of such areas are fairly homogeneous, and compared with the city as a whole tend to be younger, married, have higher incomes, and more white-collar jobs. Child-rearing is an important preoccupation (Duncan and Reiss, 1956). Gans (1962b) argues that these characteristics are either spurious or of little significance for the way of life of the inhabitants. Yet we have seen in earlier chapters that there is a strong aspiration among many life-cycle, racial, and social groups for single-family housing in such settings, especially where child rearing is involved. Because of prejudice, the prevailing social system, income constraints, and other problems, however, large numbers of people must bring up their children in other, perhaps less suitable environments. In middle-class eyes the least suitable of these nonsuburban environments are the ghetto and the slum.

People occupying ghettos and slums are effectively residentially segregated from the rest of society by virtue of color, ethnicity, religion, poverty, or a combination of these factors. Lieberson (1963) has suggested two types of segregation:

1.   *Voluntary segregation,* which occurs where members of a particular group view the residential proximity of other members of the same group as desirable. For reasons of sentiment or symbolism "birds of a feather flock together."

2.   *Involuntary segregation,* where a group is regarded as undesirable by a more powerful group, which then enforces segregation by social, economic, and political means.

Religious and racial ghettos are clearly of the second type. Slums, often containing people racially similar to the most powerful group but economically and culturally below notice by them, may be of either type.

Stokes (1962) has produced a simple model of the slum. He distinguishes between slums of hope, where the resident feels positive attitudes toward self-betterment and employment, and slums of despair, where residents have negative estimates of future improvement possibilities. Because of social and economic factors, slum dwellers may be members of an escalator group (which possesses the wherewithal for upward mobility if attitudes are positive) or a nonescalator group, which cannot move upward because of caste, religion, color, or other variables. Clearly, four slum types emerge:

1.   *Slums of hope containing escalator classes.* These are usually whites. Economic growth should aid their upward mobility.

2.   *Slums of hope containing nonescalator classes.* Basically as employable as group 1, this group must break down some barriers, whether linguistic, ethnic, or racial, before upward mobility can occur.

3.   *Slums of despair containing escalator classes.* These are people equivalent to those of group 1, but who have lost hope. Increased job opportunities will not solve the problem, and job retraining and social reconstruction are required.

4.   *Slums of despair containing nonescalator classes.* This is the most difficult type, consisting of despairing people who are not socioeconomically assimilable. Many nonwhite ghettos are of this type.

The above formulation presupposes that slum residents basically desire to leave the slum. Other discussions of urban ways of life (Seeley, 1959; Gans, 1962b; Suttles, 1968) suggest that while many persons are indeed temporarily or permanently trapped in the inner city, notably the poor, the emotionally disturbed, nonwhites, the aged, and the downwardly mobile, others choose to live in inner-city environments. This latter group includes the unmarried and childless (Chapter 10), cosmopolites who locate with regard to central-city cultural facilities, and ethnic villagers, who practice voluntary segregation. However, those who choose to live in the inner city do not necessarily live in slums, or would not call their environment a slum. Slum seems to be a particularly middle-class designation.

What is clear is that inner-city dwellers are exposed to higher levels of pathology and deviance than suburban dwellers. In Chapter 7 it was found that rates of physical disease, mental disorders, and social deviance are greatest in the inner city, declining toward the periphery. Crime rates (Wolfgang, 1968), poverty, civil disorder and riot (Lessing, 1968), and drug abuse all follow this pattern. Key variables which relate strongly to all these pathologies are degree of social disorganization and poverty, measured by income, children not living with parents, marriage instability, education, unskilled males in the labor force, dilapidated housing, and persons living alone (USOEO, 1966; Smith, 1973).

A multivariate approach to the problem of defining slums, ghettos, and the like involves the simple technique of overlaying a series of maps, each depicting a single variable. Lessing's (1968) study of the social context of the Watts Riot in Los Angeles is a good example (Fig. 11.1). The Watts area was found to be one of the areas of Los Angeles with the highest crime rates, population density, and school dropout rates, a heavy concentration of blacks, and a high degree of poverty. Similar studies in Philadelphia (McHarg, 1969) and Gainesville, Florida (Dickinson *et al.*, 1972) confirm that the simple graphic overlay technique is capable of identifying the social-problem zones of the city, almost all of which are inner-city areas.

In most cases the inhabitants of these areas, whether they enjoy living in them or not, have no choice in the matter. There is a growing literature on *ghettoization,* the process by which social groups are spatially segregated to their own disadvantage (Baran and Sweezy, 1966; Rose, 1969; Elgie, 1970). Muth (1969) outlines as many as eight theories of slum formation. The result of residential segregation is segregation in many other areas of living. If different social groups do not live near each other, they cannot "associate with each other in the many activities founded on common neighborhood" (Myrdal, 1944, 146). There is little opportunity to see other groups in social contexts which could possibly reveal their common humanity; rather, lack of contact promotes stereotyping. Residential segregation therefore has a dynamic quality which tends to be self-perpetuating and a reinforcer of prejudice. Three examples of ghettoization are provided.

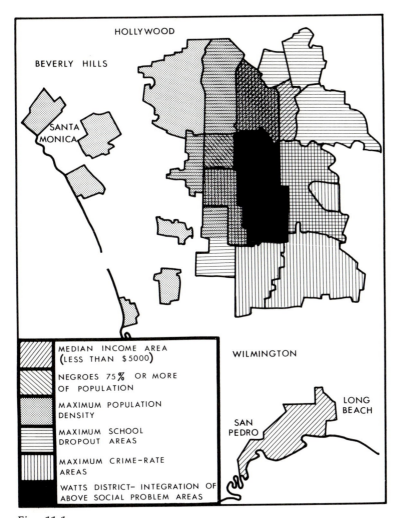

Fig. 11.1

The coincidence of social problems in Watts, Los Angeles. (Redrawn from Lessing, 1968. Map by Max Gschwind for *Fortune Magazine*. Source: Space General Corporation. Reprinted by permission.)

the religious ghetto

The original ghetto was inhabited by the Jews of medieval Italy. One of the major contemporary scenes of religious ghettoization, however, is in Northern Ireland, where Protestants and Catholics are strongly segregated residentially. A study of Belfast by Boal (1970) showed that religious groups tended to occupy spatially separated territories, with well-recognized boundaries, such

as the Shankill-Falls divide (Fig. 11.2). Analysis of activity systems, including residential relocations, premarriage addresses, school attendance,
neighboring and visiting patterns, newspaper readership, football team support, and other indicators demonstrated that Protestants and Catholics each
had a tightly knit social community with high internal levels of interaction.
There were hardly any linkages across the religious boundary, which could be
regarded as a religious precipice. It must be realized that on most other
socioeconomic counts the groups were very similar, with the same types of
working-class occupations and almost identical housing.

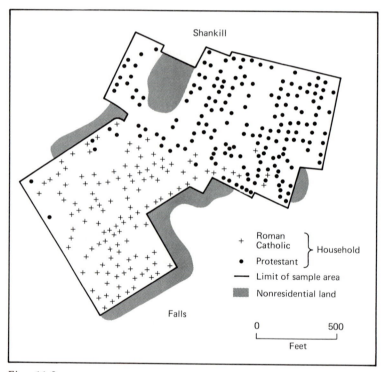

Fig. 11.2

Religious ghettoization at the Shankill-Falls Divide, West Belfast, Northern
Ireland. (Redrawn from F. W. Boal, "Social Space in the Belfast Urban Area,"
Irish Geographical Studies, 1970, by permission of the author.)

The religious ghettoization of Belfast shows no sign of breaking down.
Traditional working-class districts of rented housing remain highly segregated and new suburban developments for owner-occupiers are also reli-

giously homogeneous. Public housing, although originally integrated, rapidly becomes homogeneous through selective household relocations. "In the Belfast area, insofar as people have any residential choice, they exercise it by moving from less segregated to more segregated housing" (Boal, 1970, 391). Often choice is replaced by compulsion. The report of the Community Relations Commission, analyzing the results of the four years of violence 1969–72, noted that over 60,000 people had been forced to abandon their homes because of intimidation. "At least one in nine people in Belfast has been forced to leave home and move to an area of his or her religion" (*Daily Telegraph* 1 June 1973).

The result is propinquity without community, for the boundary lines between religious territories are frequently only the width of a residential street. Within their self-segregated home-base territories, the two religious groups pursue separate ways of life in terms of family organization, attitudes, activity systems, and voting behavior (Boal, 1971; Douglas, 1974). Interreligious contact is limited largely to conflict (Boal, 1972).

the racial ghetto

For many millions of North Americans, life in a racial ghetto is an everyday experience. In the United States much attention has been focused upon the rapidly expanding black ghettos of the urban North and West, and in particular upon the declining quality of life in such areas (Rose, 1969; Albaum, 1973). Ghettos need not be slums, if the latter are defined as areas of heavy deterioration of physical structures. Watts, a relatively pleasant and habitable Los Angeles area, has nothing like the squalor of Harlem. Yet both areas experienced major riots during the late 1960s. In the Watts riots 30,000 out of 200,000 black people rioted, leaving 34 dead, 1,032 injured, and almost 4,000 arrested, and causing up to $200 million in property damage (Cohen, 1970). A high proportion of the residents sympathized with the riots, and were hostile toward the largely white merchants of the area who were accused of overcharging, selling inferior goods, rudeness, and other discriminatory practices. Although the riots made whites more aware of black problems, they did not necessarily make the whites feel more sympathetic. As in Northern Ireland, the chief contact between the opposing groups is some form of conflict.

Again, strong territoriality not only in residential location but also in activity patterns is apparent (Deskins, 1970; Rose, 1970). Deskins' study of the residence-workplace linkages of blacks and whites in Detroit showed that between 1953 and 1965 racial activity systems tended toward greater segregation (Fig. 11.3). Although black ghetto residents may make frequent moves, they tend to remain within the ghetto (Fig. 11.4).

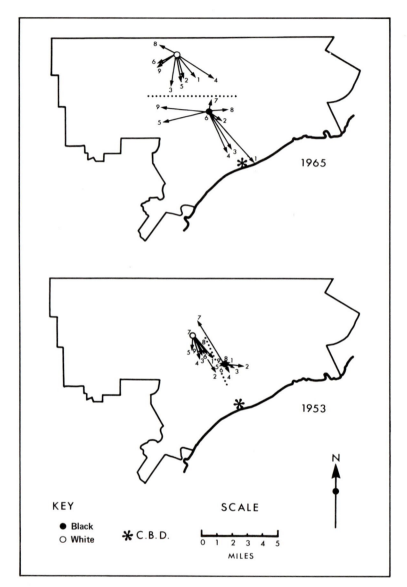

Fig. 11.3

Increasing racial segregation in Detroit. Residence-workplace vectors by occupational groups adjusted to mean centers of residence. (Redrawn from M. Albaum (ed.), *Geography and Contemporary Issues,* 1973, by permission of Donald R. Deskins, Jr. and John Wiley & Sons, Inc.)

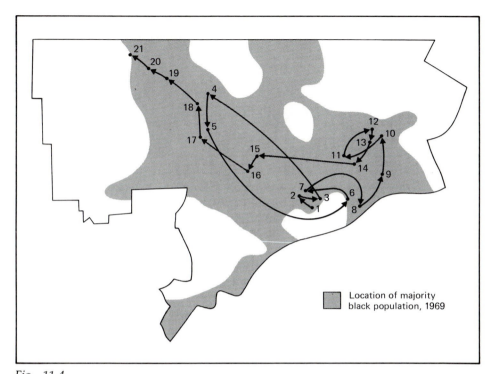

Fig. 11.4

The 21 residential relocations of Gwendolyn Warren in Detroit. (Redrawn by permission of the Detroit Geographical Expedition and Institute from Discussion Paper No. 3.)

Two quotations from ghetto children illustrate the special quality of ghetto life and both its positive and negative values:

> In Black neighborhoods it is much different with kids playing together than it is in White neighborhoods. The feeling is different. I went to school with white kids in elementary school but it was not the same. Every Black was sisters and brothers. We had something in common . . . (Warren, 1975)

> I wish they would stop killing people around My block and Rhonda's block. I keep dreaming that I will get hurt. But that is not true. I keep saying to my mother I don't want to go out. But my mother says it is sunny out. I said that is not what's wrong. I'm scared that someone will hurt me . . . (Joseph, 1969)

Recent black assertiveness will not increase interaction between blacks and whites (Brown, 1974). Indeed, despite the Erlichs' fear of world cultural homogenization (Erlich and Erlich, 1970), in residential location and activity pattern terms there remain major gulfs between racial and ethnic groups. And segregation is not simply black-white or white-other; there is ample evidence of strong segregation patterns between and among blacks, Puerto Ricans, Asians of various types, and various European groups (Taueber, 1965).

the poverty ghetto

Black ghettos are frequently areas of poverty. Poverty, however, is no respecter of races. A variety of both positive and negative views of poverty exist (Duhl, 1963b), and there is a growing literature on the spatial aspects of both rural and urban poverty (Albaum, 1973). Poor rural migrants to cities, constrained by both economic and social factors, overwhelmingly locate in the inner city. They remain in the inner city because of job constraints, social pressure, kinship ties, and lack of mobility (Davies and Fowler, 1972). Adams (1972) has linked the United States urban riots of the 1960s with problems of stimulation, stress, and personal space in the inner-city poverty areas (Chapters 3, 7).

There are many routes into poverty (Rein, 1967). Inadequate nutrition, housing, and income are not only attributes of poverty but also contribute to its perpetuation. Moreover, to be raised in poverty may condemn one, and one's children, to endless poverty. As in religious and racial solidarity, however, there may be a positive side to poverty. Oscar Lewis (1966), in work on slums in the United States, Puerto Rico, and Mexico, has found that many slum dwellers have a life-style which incorporates a ready-made set of solutions for poverty-related problems, and thus serves an important adaptive function. As this phenomenon has been observed in both rural and urban areas in several different countries, Lewis has termed it the *culture of poverty*. The negative side of the culture of poverty is overwhelming, however, and Lewis sees deprivation in one generation leading inexorably to deprivation in the next because of cultural impoverishment, indifference, fatalism, hopelessness, misunderstanding of childrens' educational needs, lack of self-respect, apathy, ignorance, and inadequate incomes. With variations, this view is supported by a number of sociologists (Gans, 1972).

Urban Renewal and Forced Relocation

One common characteristic of the ghettoized populations of the inner city is relative powerlessness. The people are helpless in the face of urban-planning decisions made by professional planners and politicians. The implications of this powerlessness have been nowhere more obvious than in the *urban renewal* process which swept through the North American and European inner city in the 1950s and 1960s.

Urban renewal is an integrated series of steps taken to maintain or upgrade the economic and social health of an urban area. First coined in the 1940s as an alternative to slum clearance, the term refers to a deliberate effort to change the urban environment through planned, large-scale adjustment of existing city areas to present and future requirements for urban living and working. Renewal may involve the *conservation* of older structures still in good condition, or the *rehabilitation* of substandard structures to meet a prescribed standard. Mostly commonly, however, it involves *redevelopment*, the elimination of existing structures and their replacement by other buildings. This process takes place most frequently in the large areas of physically deteriorated residential structures on the fringe of downtown. As the process is extremely costly, federal governments are strongly involved.

The aims of urban renewal are many. The most obvious aim is economic. Central-city blight, the loss of the well-off to the legally independent peripheral suburbs, the related loss of businesses and industries, and increasing social costs all serve to reduce the effective tax base of the central city. As the metropolis decentralizes, the central city becomes merely one — and usually the poorest and most dilapidated — of a series of clustered but legally separate entities. A major aim of urban renewal is therefore to bring back to the central city those who can support its costs; only with the effective reoccupance of the central city by the middle classes will there be a significant reconstruction of the city's tax base.

Related aims include the need to retain the city center as a cultural nexus. Independent suburbs with homogeneous populations cannot support the mix of cultural amenities which has traditionally been located downtown, the point of maximum accessibility for the population of the urban region. As American central cities have become largely the environment of the poor and black, urban renewal has also aimed to reintroduce racial and social mixing in the city center as a corollary of the campaign for integration in the suburbs. Finally, urban renewal embraces the concept that, as poor housing quality demoralizes its inhabitants, improved structures should introduce slum dwellers to a better quality of life.

All these are laudable aims. In practice, however, they have not received equal attention. Economic motives have proved most important in almost all renewal schemes. Attracting the middle classes back to the central city and reconstructing the tax base have generally involved the clearing of large areas of dilapidated housing and its replacement by either nonresidential uses or by medium- or high-rent apartment complexes. In either case the people who were moved to make way for renewal "are unlikely to enjoy any part of the brave new world erected over their former homes" (Marris, 1963, 118).

In the first 12 years of urban renewal following the U.S. Housing Act of 1949, urban renewal projects displaced about 85,000 families in nearly 200 American cities. In 1967 Frieden estimated that federally funded renewal and highway programs were about to displace up to 100,000 families and 15,000 businesses per year, mostly in urban areas. Because the chief effect of urban renewal has been to destroy low-rent housing, and because renewal has pulled down more houses than it has built, it has been strongly criticized (Jacobs, 1961; Wallace, 1968; Blumenfeld, 1969; Sayegh, 1972). Within individual cities, renewal planning has been fragmentary and uncoordinated, based on short-run economic goals, and lacking an overall conceptualization or strategy. The purchasing power of displaced families has actually been reduced, for virtually every analysis of family relocation has found that people pay higher rents or have higher overall costs after moving than they did before. Moreover, many small marginal businesses, such as the "momma and poppa" corner store, receive inadequate compensation for displacement, almost always face higher rents and costs in the new location, lose clientele, face heavier competition, and thus suffer reduced income or liquidation. Renewal agency surveys suggest that over one third of all relocated businesses are likely to fail. In sum, by attacking the physical expressions of poverty, notably substandard housing, rather than poverty itself, *The Federal Bulldozer* (Anderson, 1964) of urban renewal became a vicious tool dedicated to the perpetuation of poverty.

the pathology of forced relocation

The physical removal, often against their will, of large numbers of inner-city people has social and psychological as well as economic repercussions. To illustrate this, the case of the West End of Boston will be discussed in some detail. The renewal of the West End has become a *cause célèbre* in planning circles, has led to much rethinking by urban planners, and has probably been more intensively studied than any other renewal project.

In the 1950s about 10,000 people inhabited the West End's 48-acre site in the heart of Boston. Like the still extant North End nearby, the West End was inhabited largely by low-income immigrants, over 40 percent of whom were of Italian origin. As with similar inner-city areas, it was characterized by high densities, mixed land uses, aged tenements, many small shops and businesses, and a communal life lived as much in the street as indoors (Whyte, 1955). Gans, who spent much time in the area, recorded it as a socially tight multigenerational ethnic ghetto with strong internal linkages but little significant social contact with Boston as a whole. In short, the West End was inhabited by *Urban Villagers* (Gans, 1962a).

Boston's city fathers viewed the West End as a suitable site for urban renewal because of its location close to downtown, adjacent to the high-class area of Beacon Hill, and with a frontage on the Charles River. The chief motives for public renewal were a desire to replace the tenement-dominated skyline with a prestigious high-rent complex which would bring in much more municipal income and would hopefully induce a spiral of private renewal. The area was recommended for renewal in 1949, but did not receive federal approval until 1957. Soon afterwards demolition began, and within a decade the area had become the site of office blocks, government centers, luxury apartments, and extensions of the Massachusetts General Hospital.

Every West Ender who was renewed out of the area was guaranteed space in the luxury apartments built on the site. In financial terms, this was not a realistic alternative. Moreover, only about 15 percent of the displaced persons found replacement housing, including public housing, through the aid of renewal officials. Most dispersed to other areas of Boston with the same high density and mixed land use environment as the West End (Hartman, 1966). Such replacements of so-called slum housing by luxury apartment towers have been condemned as less slum clearance than slum shifting or slum relocation, and as "land grabs aided by government subsidies and the powerful privilege of eminent domain" (Higbee, 1960, 86). Little wonder that among blacks urban renewal is identified, bitterly, as "negro removal."

Forced relocation has identifiable effects. Several reports on the West End indicate that many of its inhabitants had strong attachments to the area and did not wish to leave. What the relocatees lost was a mutually supportive physical and social environment where the high density and mixed land uses facilitated interaction among friends and relatives. About 90 percent of the inhabitants identified themselves as West Enders (Ryan, 1963). West Enders perceived a sharp geographical and social boundary between their territorial home base and other parts of the city; a girl who married a non–West Ender and left the area was said to have "married outside." For male West Enders, the salient social relationships were the family-kinship group and the "hanging group" which hung around a local corner or bar. Both these networks were strongly based on propinquity.

Forced relocation from this environment proved disruptive and disturbing for many. The loss of close spatial links with friends and relatives and the loss of a feeling of enclosure and safety were very apparent. Hartman (1963) found that 76 percent of the West Enders had unreserved positive feelings about the area, and reported potential relocatees as saying:

> I love it. I was born and brought up here. I like the conveniences, the people, I feel safe . . . I'm going to miss it terribly.

and

> I loved it very much. It was home to me. I was very happy. Everyone was nice. All my relatives lived there.

Gans also reports the feelings of persons about to be relocated:

> I wish the world would end tonight . . . I'm going to be lost
> without the West End. Where the hell can I go?

and

> It isn't right to scatter the community to the four winds. It pulls
> the heart out of a guy to lose all his friends.

Fried (1963), in a study of the effects of relocation on women, found that among those who had previously reported liking living in the West End "very much," 73 percent showed evidence of extreme grief. Even 34 percent of those who were ambivalent or negative about the West End grieved severely for their lost home area. The grief syndrome included vomiting, intestinal disorders, crying spells, nausea, general sadness, and depression. This reaction is similar to the characteristics of grief and mourning for a dead person, but in this case is related to the loss of both spatial identity and group identity following forced residential relocation. Gans tells of West Enders returning both during and after the demolition to walk through the rubble-strewn streets of their former home.

Since the pioneering studies of Boston's West End, relocation pathologies have been identified in many parts of the world. Bourdieu (1964) has shown that of all the upheavals suffered by Algerians at the hands of the French, the resettlement of the rural population had the most profound and lasting consequences. Turnbull (1972) reports the horrifying changes wrought by the relocation of the Ik tribe in Uganda from a fertile valley to crowded locations in inhospitable terrain. Ik society collapsed; malicious competition, hostility, and treachery replaced kindness and cooperation. The disintegration and disorientation of Ik society in some ways parallels the social and psychological problems associated with Western urban industrial society (Chapter 7).

From the latter, Mrs. Hattie Carvery tells of the renewal of Africville, a black section of Halifax, Nova Scotia (Hartnett, 1970):

> They took our homes . . . the city moved us out of Africville in
> city garbage trucks . . . They put us right down in the slums, a
> lot of us . . . It was our settlement, our community. It was ev-
> erything to us . . . They offered us a wee little miserable bit of
> money for our homes and then we were held with the threat
> over our heads that if we didn't oblige the city they were going
> to bulldoze over us anyway . . . The white people shamed Af-
> ricville so much that . . . a good many of the young people . . .

don't want to own their own heritage . . . They made them ashamed. We weren't ashamed. We were proud.

Besides inducing relocation pathologies, renewal may not even be effective in the physical task of providing families with adequate homes. The city of Victoria, British Columbia, renewed the Rose-Blanshard area in the late 1960s, compelling 157 families to move out of their homes. The chief purpose was to remove an area of blighted housing, provide modern public housing, and improve the effectiveness of the road pattern. There were also significant changes in the lives of the displaced households. The chief effect was to spread the former Rose-Blanshard inhabitants through other blighted areas of Greater Victoria, for less than one quarter of the displaced households expressed a desire to return to the low-rent housing which had replaced their former homes. Of the relocatees sampled, 15 percent remained in poor-quality housing and 25 percent experienced a decrease in housing quality. "Equally as many of the Rose-Blanshard households were living in sub-standard dwellings after renewal as before . . . If the renewal program . . . meant to relieve the city of blighted . . . housing and, as a corollary, to provide housing for low-income families, then it was only marginally effective" (Robertson, 1973, 91).

Similar effects have been found after slum clearance and relocation in Europe, notably in Britain where vast central renewal schemes have moved millions of persons to suburban public housing estates. Nor is the phenomenon confined to nonsocialist nations. A study of four cities in Czechoslovakia found that 40-60 percent of the respondents were satisfied with what the planners regarded as blighted housing (Musil, 1972). When told that renewal was inevitable, only 17 percent wanted their new dwelling to be located outside the home area. Musil found that these renewal areas were characterized by a modified extended family system with a high spatial concentration of mutually related persons at all stages of the life cycle, and who were socially linked by mutual help and visiting. Between half and two thirds of all relatives lived within 15 minutes' walking distance of each other.

Public Housing

One solution to the problem of substandard housing has been to relocate families in specially built public-housing projects. The term *public housing* is in fact a misnomer, for most projects have income ceilings which permit their occupation by low-income tenants alone. The general lack of a sliding scale of rents based on family income ensures that most North American public-housing projects immediately reghettoize the poor.

public housing in Britain

Approximately 30 percent of the British population lives in some form of public housing. In consequence, the social stigma attached to the occupancy of such an environment is less evident than in North America. Much of the public-housing stock is in suburban duplexes, competing in quality with privately built developments.

Several surveys have concentrated on the effects of relocating working-class families from the inner city to new public-housing estates on the city periphery. In Oxford, Mogey (1955) compared two very similar groups, one of which occupied old, deteriorated housing and the other the newest housing project in the city. He suggested that the experience of physical relocation to new housing had profound effects on attitudes and life-styles. In particular:

1. The rigid division of labor common in the inner-city environment was replaced by closer family cooperation in tasks.

2. The extended family's dominant role in social life was much reduced, and a nuclear family pattern began to emerge.

3. Whereas social relationships in the inner city were strongly oriented toward kin, those relocated to the peripheral estate showed a strong preference for ties with nonrelated neighbors and friends.

4. Though the inner-city group had little aspiration for better housing, the housing estate population had clear aspirations for further improvement in housing quality. This was due in part to dissatisfaction with the design of the public housing.

Overall, Mogey suggested that the restricted home range of the inner-city dweller was expanded by relocation, and that the new environment was an important factor in changing the family from a "neighborhood-centered unit" to a "family-centered unit" (Mogey, 1956). In short, the working-class family loosened its kin obligations and moved attitudinally and socially toward middle-class suburban norms (Chapter 10).

Young and Willmott (1962) performed a similar study on residents of Bethnal Green, inner London, who had moved to a peripheral public housing estate called Greenleigh. The change was generally from two or three damp rooms in nineteenth-century row housing to a spacious modern home with all conveniences. One of the major justifications for the move given by adults was to provide a better atmosphere for raising children, an attitude common to most persons moving to suburban locations (Chapter 10). As in Oxford, the relocation to Greenleigh broke extended family and friendship ties. Homogeneous land uses restricted interactional opportunities; one pub per 400 people in Bethnal Green was replaced by one per 5,000 in Greenleigh.

Many former pursuits were abandoned, and television use rose far more rapidly than among those families remaining in Bethnal Green. As a Mr. Curtis so aptly stated: "You lose contact with parents and relatives once you move out here. You seem to center yourself more on the home. Everybody lives in a little world of their own."

The extent of the change was remarkable. The semidetached housing occupied in Greenleigh, with its private open space, promoted privacy where little had been before. Moreover, it was now impossible to make contact with parents on a regular basis (Table 11.1) because of the distances involved. A complete social system based on matrilocality was thus disrupted. Previously, more than two out of every three people had their parents living within two or three miles. Mum, the matriarch, presided over the family clan and gave help and support to all. Couples frequently lived in the same house, street, or locality as the wife's parents. Most activities, including jobs and recreation, were within walking distance.

TABLE 11.1

CHANGES IN WEEKLY CONTACTS AFTER RELOCATION

	Average Number of Contacts per Week with Own and Spouse's Parents and Siblings		
	Before Leaving Bethnal Green	Greenleigh 1953	Greenleigh 1955
Husbands	15.0	3.8	3.3
Wives	17.2	3.0	2.4

Source: Young and Willmott (1962)

In contrast, the Greenleigh resident's parents were now far away. He had no relatives to turn to in the immediate vicinity. He discovered a need to organize life more closely, to develop a time sense, and to be prepared to travel. Once just around the corner, his shops and workplace, friends and relatives were now far beyond walking distance. Cars and telephones became necessary in order to organize a more scattered home range into a manageable whole. Some families adjusted to these changes only with difficulty and many remained ambivalent. Both Bethnal Green and Greenleigh had positive attractions. The conflict was expressed by a woman who, on being asked if she would like to return from the suburbs to the inner city, replied:

> I'd say no. I'd say that for the children's sake. They do love it here, and it's so much better for them. But if it were for myself alone, I'd say yes.

Other students of the same relocation phenomenon have weighed the advantages and disadvantages of relocation and decided that what was gained by relocation hardly compensated for what was destroyed (Hole, 1959). That such suburban public housing environments cannot accommodate all low-income types is devastatingly illustrated in John Arden's play, *Live Like Pigs* (1961).

public housing in the United States

This negative view of relocation to public housing is more common in the American literature, despite the fact that only about one percent of North Americans live in public housing. One reason for this negative view is that public-housing projects in North America are rarely of the suburban type just described. Most frequently they consist of immense complexes of high-rise towers set in stark grounds without private open space.

A celebrated example of such a project is the Pruitt-Igoe complex in St. Louis. The inner city of St. Louis included extremely dilapidated slum areas which were replaced by the Pruitt-Igoe project in 1954. About 12,000 persons were relocated into 43 11-storey high-rise structures covering 57 acres. Initially integrated, the project rapidly became a black ghetto. Many of the black families were headed by women, many were unemployed and on welfare, many were ill-educated.

Rainwater's study *Behind Ghetto Walls: Black Family Life in a Federal Slum* (1970) includes verbatim, taped interviews with Pruitt-Igoe residents which enable the reader to grasp something of the atmosphere of the project. Details of daily life, community, marital roles and disruption, parental and childhood behavior, and black lower-class identity and culture indicate that the high-rise tower is not a suitable environment for this group. Indeed, Pruitt-Igoe rapidly deteriorated. Paint peeled, windows were smashed, electrical wiring was ripped out, trash was piled high, the elevators became the repositories for human waste. Street gangs roamed the open spaces, and rape, vandalism, and robbery were common. As these most readily took place in elevators and stairwells, families began gradually to abandon the upper storeys. Despite low rents, fear-induced abandonment increased until by the early 1970s all but 16 of the 43 high-rise structures were vacant. By 1972 the utter failure of the project was evident in the demolition of a number of its component structures.

Studies in Venezuela and Puerto Rico confirm the unsuitability of the high rise for poorly educated low-income groups with low environmental competence. Carlson (1959, 1960) found that the life-styles of rural migrants cleared from shanty towns could not be recreated in the high rise. As these persons had no other behavior models, they had no comprehension of how to live in the high rise. Strong leadership, education, community facilities, and

The failure of public housing: Pruitt-Igoe, St. Louis. Demolition began in April 1972 of several 11-story buildings wholly evacuated by their black occupants, who found them uninhabitable (Credit: UPI.)

apartment ownership were necessary to reduce the life-style disruption caused by relocation.

In Puerto Rico, public housing *(caseríos)*, built to a high standard of design, was provided for slum dwellers. The public-housing dwellers paid lower rents, were less crowded, controlled more space, were located in a much healthier area, and had access to a wider range of facilities than their slum counterparts. Yet 65 percent of the slum dwellers liked the slums, and 86 percent of the men and 71 percent of the women in the *caseríos* disliked their public housing project (Hollingshead and Rogler, 1963). Slum dwellers disliked the filth and mud of their neighborhood most, but *caserío* families disliked most the restrictions placed on them by the Public Housing Authority. Most notably, the housing authority did not recognize the extended-family system of the slums, renting only to nuclear families. Thus strong kinship ties were violated. The rules and regulations imposed by the management violated the norms of lower-class life in many ways. When asked about their ideal home, both slum and *caserío* dwellers indicated a private, walled, single-family house. This being unattainable, however, the overwhelming preference was for the freedom and informality of the slum. Indeed, Back (1962) describes the refusal, unexpected by the planners, of a majority of slum residents to be relocated into objectively superior housing provided by the Public Housing Authority.

Oscar Lewis' sensitive studies of Puerto Rican life in *La Vida* (1966) provide some personal details of the costs of relocation from slum to *caserío*. In the housing project the relocatees experienced lower rents, a bathroom, an electric stove, lots of closet space, shelves, and other amenities, and freedom from rats. On the other hand, they also experienced loneliness, the prying of unknown neighbors, the fear of traffic, higher food and utilities costs, harassment by the authorities, boredom, and lack of support from now physically distant relatives. There were many things that could not now be done in safety, such as selling lottery tickets, receiving stolen goods, borrowing money, or a little half-hearted prostitution. Perhaps the major difference was the impersonality of the *caserío*, the forced dependence upon faceless authorities and impersonal utilities corporations. This is summed up in one low-income relocatee's reaction to her new electric stove:

> The main advantage of the electric stove is that . . . I . . . have lunch ready in no time. In La Esmeralda I had to wait for the kerosene to light up well before I could even start to cook. And this stove doesn't smoke and leave soot all over the place either. Still, if the power fails again or is cut off because I don't pay my bill, the kids will just have to go hungry. I won't even be able to heat a cup of milk for them. In La Esmeralda, whenever I didn't have a quarter to buy a full gallon of gasoline, I got ten cents' worth. But who's going to sell you five or ten cents' worth of electricity?

the problem of design

One of the major problems besetting the high-rise public-housing complex is that of suitable architectural design. As discussed in Chapter 10, apartment blocks are sociofugal and provide few semiprivate spaces where interaction can occur. This may be an eminently suitable environment for middle-class persons and those not oriented toward familism. Slums, in contrast, are generally sociopetal, with constant use of the streets, sidewalks, and corners as semiprivate meeting grounds or territories.

Slum physical environments strongly support a spontaneous, highly interactive, street-oriented, communal life-style. House doors and windows open directly to the street, enabling constant surveillance of, and interaction with, passers-by. The many small stores increase the opportunity for contact between relatives and neighbors, who also frequent local pubs, bars, and other common facilities. People sit and chat in semipublic open spaces and the entry of strangers or suspicious characters is readily noticed. North American public housing provides none of these interactive environments.

Pruitt-Igoe's design is typical. It was praised by architects for the absence of wasted space between dwelling units. But it is in just such "wasted space" that neighboring relations develop in normal slums. Slum dwellers do not tend to neighbor within their homes. When asked their reactions to the project, many inhabitants expressed the now-familiar attitudinal dichotomy between in-home convenience and neighborhood dislike (Yancey, 1972). Pruitt-Igoe residents were pleased with the warmth and the fact that sufficient space permitted each child to have a room of his own. On the other hand, they expressed distress about their inability to control their children when the latter were outside the apartment (Chapter 10) and about their lack of friendships and neighboring activities. Similar questions asked of adjacent slum dwellers revealed an opposite response; while dissatisfied with his apartment, the typical slum dweller was very satisfied with his neighborhood. In Pruitt-Igoe, then, freedom from the slum's overcrowding and physical danger from cold, poor wiring and plumbing, and fires, was paid for by the loss of the informal social network of support so commonly found in the slum. In the words of one project dweller:

> I've got no friends here. There's none of this door-to-door coffee
> business of being friends here or anything like that. Down here
> if you are sick you just go to the hospital. There are no friends
> to help you.

The lower class relocatee thus experiences the trauma of a rapid transition from a strong, informal neighboring setting to an institutional setting which discourages personal relationships and for the warmth of neighborly help substitutes impersonal public welfare facilities (Chapter 4).

Lack of suitable space wherein to neighbor, however, is compounded by the inability of residents to informally control stairwells, elevators, and corridors. Unlike the tenement slum environment, the high rise provides no windows or semipublic spaces whereby residents may informally survey, and thus control, the public spaces from their private spaces. Consequently elevators and stairwells become the scenes of muggings, assault, and harassment; "If it weren't for the project police the teen-agers would take over" (Yancey, 1972, 131). In contrast, public housing in Baltimore has shown that an architectural design which provides common space and facilities leads to an increased amount of neighboring and mutual aid among persons moving from a slum into a housing project (Wilner *et al.*, 1962).

Planning and Design Implications

Life-styles are clearly of major importance in deciding an individual's satisfaction or ability to cope with a dwelling environment. Architectural design is of vital importance in hindering or facilitating life-style expression. Three general solutions to the problem of providing suitable accommodation for low-income persons presently living in seriously substandard and dangerous housing have been suggested.

life-style–congruent public housing

In cases where the slum is so badly deteriorated as to be beyond repair, public housing will probably be needed. If so, projects should be so designed that the informal social interactions of the slum can be recreated. A horizontal layout is therefore more appropriate than a high rise, with a minimum of elevators and stairwells closed to public scrutiny. Wide corridors with interior windows, so that residents can see into the corridor from their homes, would improve child surveillance and control. Private and semiprivate open spaces both inside and outside the building should be contrived to encourage social interaction and eye contact. Where high rises must be constructed, outside elevators could be used, and outdoor walkways, or "streets in the sky," provided for every storey. In Sheffield, England, an inner-city row-house atmosphere has been recreated in high-rise public housing by means of wide, continuous, outdoor balconies. This enables each tenant to have an outside door, permits neighboring and the surveillance of children, and acts as a normal street traversed by newspaper boy, milk delivery man, and mailman.

In high-rise design the concept of *defensible space* must be invoked (Newman, 1972). Data from New York suggest that the incidence of crime in public-housing projects relates directly to project size, the number of floors, and the difficulty of surveillance of nonprivate spaces. Newman suggests a series of improvements which would render such projects more defensible. In particular he is concerned with ensuring that all space appears to belong to someone, that the no-man's-lands of secluded stairwells and enclosed elevators should be avoided. Design should foster proprietory attitudes on the part of residents toward adjacent nonprivate space. Positioning of windows to enhance surveillance is important here; as Jacobs (1961) suggests, there must be eyes upon the street.

The adoption of strong territorial attitudes fostered by design is likely to act as a deterrent to potential criminals. This is apparent in the slum, where "deviant behavior . . . finds its location in the power vacua of socially claimed space" (Ley and Cybriwsky, 1974b). These authors found that abandoned cars were more likely to be vandalized when parked outside doorless areas, near institutional land uses, and against vacant houses or stores, all of which are territorially unclaimed areas. Two major problems in Newman's analysis of defensible space require further elucidation, however. First, he assumes that designed-in visual cues will be understood and adhered to by residents and strangers alike, and second, he assumes that residents and criminals are two separate populations. In reality, public-housing residents frequently victimize their own neighbors, and the same phenomenon has been found among suburban teenage gangs (Chapter 10).

Clearly, the "reformers' myth" that new homes for the poor are sufficient provision for their needs without consideration of life-style, is erroneous (Dennis, 1969). Even an interaction-facilitative design, however, will not promote confident neighboring unless public-housing management policies become less draconian. Because of their life-styles, and especially their extended family relationships, many public-housing tenants continually break the multitudinous rules governing tenancy in the project. Neighboring is frequently inhibited because people fear that to reveal themselves in any way may result in their being turned in to the authorities by jealous or overly zealous neighbors. Some of these problems could be overcome if whole slum communities were rehoused together in approximately the same configuration as before.

slum rehabilitation

There is ample evidence that high-density slum environments are the preferred dwelling environment for many. Much of the evidence from the West End of Boston, Puerto Rico, and elsewhere, as reported above, supports this contention. Fried and Gleicher (1961) found that most of the West End's inhabitants experienced a variety of satisfactions from living in the area, notably because of strong kinship and neighbor contacts. These satisfactions were intensely embedded in space; the home vicinity was perceived as an extension of the home, and to many respondents their neighborhood, if not the whole of the West End, *was* home. Social life occurred in an almost uninterrupted flow between apartment and street, a life-style totally inhibited by high-rise towers or suburban layouts. In short, the West Enders felt that they belonged, that the West End was part of their identity.

Work in Chicago, St. Louis, and other metropolitan areas among both white and black low-income groups suggests that though social and economic factors largely determine the life-styles of the poor, the latter have developed ways of coping with poverty, and thus of making it less oppressive. Local informal neighborhood relationships are a major coping mechanism (Wolfe *et al.*, 1968; Suttles, 1968). Neighborhood satisfaction is closely tied to the presence of informal networks of friends and relatives (Foote *et al.*, 1960; Gans, 1962a, b; Fried, 1963). In some cases these informal relationships may crystallize into institutions such as the block club. In black ghettos block clubs provide mutual support for members and also organize community projects, from cleaning up the streets and giving childrens' parties to organizing a community open house whereby outsiders could "pay a dollar to see a real slum" (Hall, 1969). Adverse design, in the form of existing public housing, renders the recreation of such interaction systems almost impossible.

Persons involved in these social networks rarely feel that their dwelling environment is a slum in need of urban renewal. If slums are defined as areas "physically, socially, or emotionally harmful to their residents or to the community at large" (Gans, 1959), then the areas which planners and the middle classes generally regard as slums may be less deserving of that title than many public housing projects. In Toronto a long-term slum resident explained to city planners that his neighborhood was not a slum and did not need renewal; "It's a good, solid, working man's area," he said (Lorimer and Philips, 1971). Drawing examples from several major American cities, Jacobs (1961) gives personal accounts of how socially cohesive neighborhoods fell into disorder after physical change imposed by planners under the guise of renewal. The emphasis in all these accounts is that slum life is as normal as middle-class life, and that high-density inner-city environments are socially valuable living environments and should be preserved by rehabilitation rather than destroyed by total redevelopment.

Despite the clear evidence that incongruity between life-style and environment may lead to social disruption, there has been some reaction against catering to the special life-styles of ethnic and low-income groups. In part this has developed as a response to the oversentimentalization of slum life by fashionable planners and antiplanners during the 1960s. There is considerable evidence for this point of view. Many slum residents, though liking their neighborhood, dislike their housing conditions. There is a general desire for single-family housing (Chapter 4). Some studies have demonstrated social and psychological improvement on the part of those relocated from slum to public housing (Wilner and Walkeley, 1963; Chapter 8). In some cases blacks have welcomed the renewal of their neighborhoods (Wolf and Lebeaux, 1966). The lauded extended family may be as much a burden as a blessing; a relocatee states (Lewis, 1966):

> It's not that I miss my family very much . . . relatives can be
> very bothersome. But you do need them in case you get sick be-
> cause then you can dump the children on them.

Finally, the heavy emphasis of recent social planning investigations on the life-styles of minorities has been viewed as unjustified "ethnic crap" (Michelson, 1970, 62). In a blistering attack on social planners Nowlan (1974) states: "The thinking man used to smoke Relocation-Integration; now he prefers Neighbourhood-Community, because it tastes good like a panacea should."

residential integration

Planners with the above views are more likely to regard ethnic and low-income life-styles as temporary stages in the long process of eventual assimilation into the majority culture. For them, environments which promote class and racial integration are preferred solutions. Hence public housing projects should be placed in middle-income neighborhoods.

Kriesberg, for example, found that socioeconomic status differences were not a major barrier to social interaction between project tenants and other neighborhood residents. He suggests that if project isolation could be overcome, low-income families would come into contact with middle-income families through churches, schools, other institutions, childrens' play, and personal friendship and acquaintance. Through such contact both groups would be made aware of each other, false stereotypes would be shattered, and low-income people would be provided with new models of behavior which might help them adapt more readily to their new environment. In sum, "locating public housing projects in a middle-income neighborhood might offer project tenants an opportunity to learn, develop, and express the life-style of middle-income families" (Kriesberg, 1969, 276).

This view clearly violates the tenets of the slum preservers. Moreover, it assumes that the project tenants are willing to reject their original life-style in favor of upward mobility and conformity to middle-class standards of behavior. In support of the latter point the work of Marris, and Young and Willmott, outlined earlier in this chapter, suggests that the move from slum to suburbia can result in significant and unintended changes in working-class life-styles with a tendency toward a nuclear family home-orientation. Middle-class movers to the suburbs, on the other hand, do not undergo significant changes in life-style that they had not intended.

One residential integration problem is whether planners have the moral right to destroy the physical underpinnings of minority life-styles and hasten the absorption of minority groups into the middle-class behavior mainstream. Another question is: Will it work? Little information exists on the recent experiments in class and life-style mixing. As reported in Chapter 10, the available results are not encouraging. Gans found that working-class people quickly became isolates in a middle-class community.

American central cities are rapidly becoming compartmentalized into extremes of high and low housing values as the middle classes leave for the suburbs (Davis, 1965). And in the suburbs strong opposition has been expressed both to the planned influx of low-income families and to the more general threat of open-housing legislation (Brunn and Hoffman, 1970; Wheeler, 1971). Indeed, one might argue that, as in age and class segregation, the continuing segregation of groups with radically different life-styles preserves urban variety and vitality and prevents the destruction of viable minority subcultures. Certainly, "highly segregated sectors are the most efficient form for the existing system of interaction" (Boal, 1970). What matters is that people should have a choice.

Summary

1. Theoretically the individual may choose from among a large number of life-styles, the most common of which are familism, consumerism, careerism, localism, and cosmopolitanism.
2. One of the major life-style dichotomies is between suburban and inner-city styles. Their very different forms of familism are supported by differing physical environments.
3. Life-style choice rarely exists for those involuntarily ghettoized because of race, poverty, religion, or other characteristics. Slums, however, contain persons who choose to live there despite, or because of, the possibly high incidence of pathologies.
4. Urban renewal has displaced large numbers of the ghettoized of the inner city. Forced relocation may induce dissatisfaction and pathologies such as the grief syndrome.
5. The move to public housing may generate new life-styles which are more readily facilitated by the physical environment. The move to North American high-rise public housing, however, frequently results in increased deviance after relocation.
6. The destruction of slum-supported kin and friendship ties, loss of a sense of place identity, harsh management policies, and architectural designs which discourage territorial control of open space, and encourage sociofugality and crime, are among factors responsible for tenant dissatisfaction with high-rise public housing.
7. Suggested solutions to this problem include public housing which supports the retention of slum life-styles, slum rehabilitation without relocation, and induced life-style change through residential integration.

Further Reading

FRIED, M. and P. GLEICHER (1961), "Some Sources of Residential Satisfaction in an Urban Slum," *Journal of the American Institute of Planners* 27: 305–15.

NEWMAN, O. (1972), *Defensible Space*. New York: Macmillan.

RAINWATER, L. (1970), *Behind Ghetto Walls: Black Family Life in a Federal Slum*. Chicago: Aldine.

SUTTLES, G. (1968), *The Social Order of the Slum*. Chicago: University of Chicago Press.

CHANGE AND DECAY

Planned and Unplanned Change in the Central City Neighborhoods of Philadelphia (1970s)

(Courtesy of Roman Cybriwsky)

North of the Central Business District (CBD) the black ghetto of North Philadelphia shows all the signs of inner city abandonment. The store-front church perhaps indicates the last hope of the often elderly inhabitants who remain in the area.

Unemployed blacks "hanging-out" on a corner in North Philadelphia. The bar and take-out restaurant indicate a favorite gang meeting place.

Further south, on the CBD fringe, expressway construction threatens Chinatown.

On the southern CBD fringe, in contrast, one of the worst slums in Philadelphia was renovated in the 1960s by high-income in-migrants who now occupy the historic houses and high-rent apartment blocks of Society Hill.

Similar private renewal by young professionals is occurring in nearby Queen Village, a white, working-class ethnic neighborhood. This process is known as private renewal or "gentrification."

Some of the previous inhabitants of "gentrified" areas now occupy public housing. This view of Queen Village contrasts high-rise public housing, largely black, with foreground older structures occupied by working-class whites.

PLANNING FOR PEOPLE

The Process of Urban Renewal in Victoria, B.C. from the Point of View of the Renewed (1969–72)

(Courtesy of Victoria Press)

Government ministers and the contractor dig the first sod of the Rose-Blanshard low rental housing scheme, 1969.

The original occupants move out. For their fate, see p. 291.

Certain families resist removal.

City officials armed with crowbars successfully evict the last holdout.

Demolition of the last house on the site.

The Rose-Blanshard area: the former blighted neighborhood and the present public-housing structures.

III

PLANNING

12

PLANNERS VERSUS THE PLANNED-FOR

The dominant situation in modern life is individuals living in a setting which was not built for them.*

Serge Boutourline

The effect of environment upon behavior was discussed in Chapters 6–11. It is now time to take the reverse position and analyze the effects of behavior upon environment. The behavior to be considered in detail is the creation of the built environment in which we live. If this environment can influence our behavior, as has been previously suggested, then the nature of its creators and the processes by which this creation occurs must command our interest.

Mismatch between Behavior and Environment

As noted in Chapter 1, when the built environment is altered by purposive behavior, the latter frequently involves elements of design and planning. By its very nature, however, planning is imperfect. Though we are all idealists, ideals are seldom realized. The needs of the users of a proposed environment are imperfectly known to the planners, who are thus compelled to act upon whatever data they have derived from experience and intuition. As will be discovered later in this chapter, political and economic forces often ensure that the original plan does not materialize. Thus there is frequently a lack of fit between the built environment and behaviors occurring within it.

---

*   Serge Boutourline (1970), "The Concept of Environmental Management," in H. M. Proshansky, W. H. Ittelson, and L. G. Rivlin (eds.), *Environmental Psychology: Man and his Physical Setting*. New York: Holt, Rinehart & Winston, pp. 496–501.

The careful reader will have noticed a growing emphasis upon planning during his progression through this book. In almost all chapters, cases of mismatch between desired behavior and the planned environment have been elucidated. Elderly female patients or airport occupants are unable to converse because planned chair arrangements have resulted in sociofugality (Chapter 3). Neighborhood units are often neither recognized nor used as such by their inhabitants (Chapter 4). Citizens' activities in and images of the urban environment frequently differ from those of the professional (Chapter 5). The design problems of high density environments are noted in Chapter 7, and Chapter 8 discusses the efforts of planners to promote feelings of neighborliness and community via the manipulation of functional distance. Chapters 10 and 11 recount the violation of preferred life-styles through the processes of life-level and life-cycle integration, slum clearance, urban renewal, forced relocation, and public housing construction. In Chapter 9 the dichotomy between the planners and the planned-for emerged in terms of environmental attitudes and preferences. It is now time to draw all these threads together.

This final section of the book therefore turns to a consideration of planning in general terms. Though brief references will be made to concepts discussed earlier, no detailed repetition of these is provided. Rather, the problems which briefly emerged in Chapter 9 are now given further consideration, namely: What are the beliefs, attitudes, and values of the planner? and How can the attitudes, values, and needs of the ordinary citizen be incorporated into the planning process?

In the discussion which follows, the processes of *planning* and *designing* are, for the sake of convenience, regarded as interchangeable terms. Indeed, in some cases the bureaucrats and politicians who approve the plans are included in the overall designation of *planner*. Although design (of structures) and planning (of complexes of structures) differ markedly, chiefly in terms of scale of operations, they frequently overlap. For example, the structure of a building's internal space should not be designed without a consideration of its relationship to the building as a whole, to the siting and regional context of the building and its neighbors, and to the behavior expected to occur therein. Further, both design and planning are ultimately concerned with the creation of environments within which people will pass much of their everyday lives.

A further assumption made in the following chapters is that good design will improve human welfare. This is not necessarily true, and there has been some recent criticism of the concept. The problem lies, however, in the nature of *good design* and *human welfare*. In general, if the design is sufficient to permit a choice of behaviors on the part of the user, and enhances rather than hinders the choice made, satisfaction on the part of the user may result. If this occurs without reducing the satisfactions of other users or potential users, then good design has indeed promoted human welfare. At a very obvious level, good design in elevators should include press buttons within easy reach of persons of below average height.

Planning, in essence, seeks to promote a better fit between behavioral needs and environmental props. It attempts to provide environments which help, rather than hinder, the individual in the performance of the thousands of actions that make up his everyday life. Planners may better perform this task if they are aware of any behavioral regularities which occur at the organism-environment interface. That this awareness is not yet as great as one might wish is illustrated by a study of the problems of childrens' play in high-rise apartments (White, 1953). From this emerged three major problems which typify modern planning:

1.   Many of the problems discussed were incapable of solution within the framework of existing planning policy;

2.   Most of the planners, architects, and officials had no living experience of the conditions for which they were legislating and planning;

3.   Yet there was little opportunity for the expression of consumer opinion or for cooperation between planner and consumer.

It is because of this atmosphere of ignorance and divisiveness, resulting in structures which do not fit their occupants' needs, that an attempt is now made to elucidate the nature of the planning process.

The Planning Process

Man is, in essence, a planning animal. An integration of the accumulated knowledge of the past with reasoned future outcomes based on expectations and needs results in a plan for achieving desired goals. Only temporarily, as, for example, in the case of a patient in an operating theater, is an individual reduced to a state of no past, no future, and no opportunity to modify his environment. Man as environment modifier, however, is not our concern here. He is essentially reacting to an environment already created by man acting as a large-scale transformer of environments.

Environmental transformers today are frequently professional designers and planners. The word planning, however, covers a multitude of activities, from the direction of national economies to the organization of future social facilities to meet the demands resulting from population shifts. In this book we are concerned with the planning and design of the built environment of urban settlements. In common with all types of planning, this process initially involves the formulation of goals. Once the goals have been decided upon, the planning process in both the British and American traditions has followed remarkably similar lines (Palmer, 1971; Grabow and Heskin, 1973; Lang and Burnette, 1974). An intelligence phase of survey and research is followed by an analysis of appropriate data and the formulation of one or several alternative plans based on this information (Fig. 12.1). A choice of the best alternative is then made and the plan is implemented. Traditionally, there has been little or no evaluation of the effect of the planned structure upon those who occupy it.

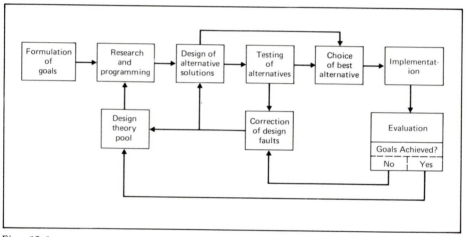

Fig. 12.1

A generalized model of the design process.

Those who plan and design structures which other people occupy clearly have the potential for enormous and lasting influence upon the lives of these occupants. Buildings are semipermanent; they rarely change significantly between completion and demolition. Street plans are almost absolutes; streets are the fossils of the city. The power of the planner over the behavior and well-being of others is clearly great, but its expression has changed significantly during the historical development of planning in the Western world (Fig. 12.2). Three major phases of this development may be distinguished.

autocratic planning

From the creation of the world by God in 4004 B.C. to the reconstruction of Paris in the nineteenth century the prevailing organizational feature of planning was autocracy. To be sure, the majority of the world's population lived

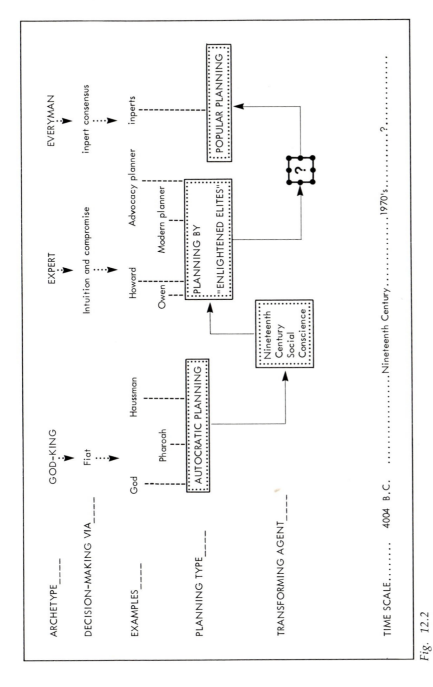

Fig. 12.2

A development model of the planning process. (Redrawn from *Environment and Behavior* 3, No. 2 (June 1971), by permission of Sage Publications, Inc.)

outside cities and continued to build in a traditional, unself-conscious way. But wherever cities were erected, the god-king, the priests, the emperor, or the baron decreed the major lineaments of urban form. There is no need to resurrect the formal layouts of ancient cities as examples; the rigid geometrical layouts of Greek and Roman cities were implanted by colonialists throughout the world until the present century. The checkerboard pattern of Salt Lake City reflects a religious order based on biblical geometry as interpreted by Joseph Smith.

Baron Haussmann, true to the autocratic tradition, transformed the structure of Paris in the mid-nineteenth century by constructing a network of broad boulevards which replaced the formerly chaotic tangle of medieval streets. Choay (1969) suggests that Haussmann's major aim was to impose a sense of unity upon the fragmented city. The legend persists, however, that Napoleon III's concern was to reduce rioting by replacing the narrow winding medieval streets by broad arteries along which police and army could assemble, maneuver, and charge. Wide boulevards were also essential for the ostentatious displays of power common to autocratic regimes.

The essence of autocratic planning is a concern with public edifices which reflect the goals of national or community leaders (Chapter 13). Compared with these, the planning of citizens' dwellings is of no significance (Pawley, 1971). According to Hitler (1943, 264), who was very concerned that the architecture of the Third Reich should reflect the glory of the German National State:

> What the ancient had before his eyes was less the humble
> houses of private owners than the magnificent edifices of the
> whole community. Compared to them the dwelling house sank
> to an insignificant object . . .

Goodman (1972) suggests that much modern American architecture is similarly dedicated to the glorification of the church, the state, and the business corporation through the medium of the public environment, while the improvement of citizens' housing remains at the level of lowest priority.

planning by enlightened elites

It was not until the mass urbanization of the nineteenth century that widespread public concern was voiced for the living conditions of the citizen. Individual factory owners, social investigators, and public health officials were among the many agitators for urban planning reform. Many of these groups were concerned to uplift the masses by imposing higher moral and social standards upon them. The result, in late nineteenth-century Europe and North America, was a series of regulations specifying minimum standards for street layouts, housing, and public facilities. Compromise was inevitable, however, for many entrepreneurs in the building business were powerful lobbyists. And inevitably, the minimum standards specified by law became the norm.

The other problem associated with the public regulation of private building was the rise of the design expert. The latter was, and is, a person with a strong grounding in the physical and aesthetic aspects of building design. Traditionally, however, he had very little knowledge of how the occupants of a particular building actually use it or feel about it. Thus the designed environment reflects the largely untested assumptions about human behavior held by the urban planner. The expert must, in general, use his experience and his intuition to discover what the public wants, what the public needs, and what is good for the public. Only recently have attempts been made to involve the public directly in the planning process (see Chapter 14). In general, the expert still remains at arm's length from his user-client. Thus, although he is planning with the good of the public in mind, unlike the autocratic planner, there is still likely to be significant mismatch between the built environment and the citizen's behavior within it.

popular planning

The present stage of planning by elite bodies such as trained experts, public officials, and a multitude of powerful interest groups will terminate when the public at large is able to initiate and supervise the carrying out of projects, rather than simply responding to a set of proposals handed down from on high. Such a situation, where the public becomes "they" and experts are replaced by *inperts,* may seem unrealistic at the present time. Yet there are growing demands by citizens for greater control of their environment, and certain squatting groups seem well along the road to self-help (see Chapter 14).

The Planner and the User

"Planners are not doctors; they do not deal with individuals" (Bolan, 1971). Indeed, the planner's *client* today is likely to be a specific but rather impersonal group which might be labeled *government* or *planning commission.* Modern architects also rarely work for individuals; their skills are largely used by public organizations and private corporations. In either case the *user-client,* he who actually inhabits the building, has little input into the decision-making which results in the formulation of the goals which are to be achieved by the design.

Sir Henry Wotton's delineation of design goals, promulgated in the early seventeenth century, is frequently cited by architects (Lipman, 1974):

> In Architecture as in all other Operative Arts, the end must direct the Operation. The end is to build well. Well building hath three Conditions, Commodite, Firmeness, and Delight.

Delight, an aesthetic experience, is a product of the designer as artist. It is achieved by personal giftedness and intuition. *Firmeness* is a product of the designer as engineer. It is achieved through technological skill. *Commodite* refers to the satisfactory occupation and use of the structure by the user-client. It might be achieved by insight, by experience, or by these combined with knowledge of behavioral norms derived from architectural and social science research.

Unfortunately, the goal of commodite has usually been eclipsed by the other two goals. Until World War I delight dominated the architectural world; the architect typically enjoyed the patronage of a wealthy client who demanded works of art (Kaye, 1960). Since World War I rapid changes in technological and managerial skills have emphasized firmeness, resulting in the severely functional boxes which grace the central cities of the modern world. Despite recent emphasis on social engineering, the user-client's commodite has rarely been given prime emphasis. Several recent analyses of the nature of planning suggest reasons for this, including the elitist self-image of the planner, erroneous planning and design assumptions and ideologies, the vast social distance between the designer and the designed-for, and the constraints imposed upon design by administrative systems and vocal middle and upper-class groups who tend to be identified exclusively as the public interest (Bolan, 1971; Tabb, 1971; Lipman, 1974).

Whatever the reason for the neglect of the user, it is clear that there is an almost absolute lack of contact between the designer and the user. Designers are educated and articulate; many user-clients are less educated and often inarticulate. This exacerbates the already immense social gap between them. The planners and the planned-for effectually speak different languages, and the designer is frequently more concerned with design awards granted by other specialists with similar tastes than with the needs and aesthetics of the public. The results of such exercises include Rudolph's Art Architecture Building at Yale which, though "great architecture," with a citation for good design, "made so many people so uncomfortable that some even tried to burn it down" (Sommer, 1974b, 130).

The social distance between planner and planned-for is further widened by administrative distance (Lipman, 1974). Plan sponsors are usually committees or large corporate bodies. The user-clients of a future structure are frequently unidentified until the design is complete, and thus have no opportunity to specify their needs. Politicians and elitist pressure groups, however, suffer no such drawback. Planners' designs are ultimately subject to the approval of politicians as well as the plan's sponsor. In many cities the political process is manipulated by *power elites* (Hunter, 1953; Mills, 1956), each consisting of influential upper-class persons who are able to achieve consensus and make their opinions felt among the elected decision makers. The latter are frequently persons strongly connected with real estate development, as has been graphically illustrated for Canadian cities by Lorimer (1972) and Hurst (1975).

Pressure groups, defined as collections of individuals who consciously band together, amalgamate their strength, form policies, and undertake action in pursuit of their goals, are frequently short-term organizations or are concerned with only a single issue (Zeigler, 1964). The power elite, however, exerts continuous pressure for its own ends through overlapping representation on school boards, planning commissions, and boards of university governors, through the direction of banks, construction firms, mortgage companies, and the media, and through membership of prominent clubs, charities, and other cultural and civic organizations. Working and middle class groups are effectively debarred from these influential bodies and rarely attain key positions of power. An examination of membership structures of such bodies frequently reveals a recurring list of names, a small group of people who are "the real planners" of the urban environment (Porter, 1965).

Individual designers are often acutely aware of the social, political, and economic constraints imposed upon them (Cohen, 1970). The elder Gumbril, in Huxley's *Antic Hay* (1948, 27), speaks of "no privacy . . . always this horrible jostling with clients and builders and contractors and people, before one can get anything done. It's really revolting." But Gumbril was concerned with the design of mansions for the rich. More poignantly, one of the designers of the Pruitt-Igoe public housing project in St. Louis (Chapter 11) laments his subjugation to the constraints which produced buildings which people left in droves (Goodman, 1972, 132):

> As an architect, if I had no economic or social limitations I'd solve all my problems with one-story buildings. Imagine how pleasant it would be to always work and plan in spaces overlooking lovely gardens filled with flowers.
>
> Yet, we know that within the framework of our present cities this is impossible to achieve. Why? Because we must recognize social and economic limitations and requirements. A solution without such recognition would be meaningless.

Yet these very limitations frequently result in the failure of the structure to accommodate the needs of its users. Sommer (1974b) speaks of *hard architec-*

ture in reference to structures designed largely to satisfy the needs of the sponsor for neatness, security, or janitorial efficiency but which, in satisfying these needs, have a repressive effect upon their occupants. A typical example of hard architecture is the American urban playground, designed primarily for ease of maintenance, but which appeared to an observer as "asphalt barracks yards behind wire mesh screen barriers . . . an administrator's heaven and a child's hell" (Allen, 1968). Caught in this web of economic, social, and political constraints, planners find themselves unable to respond to the needs of the users of the planned facility (Fig. 12.3).

Designers, moreover, are often hesitant to consider any involvement of the public in the design process. According to Rapoport (1970), designers have not only neglected the public but have also tried to eliminate any effects the user-client might have upon the design. When user participation is approved of, the users are frequently carefully selected from the same class

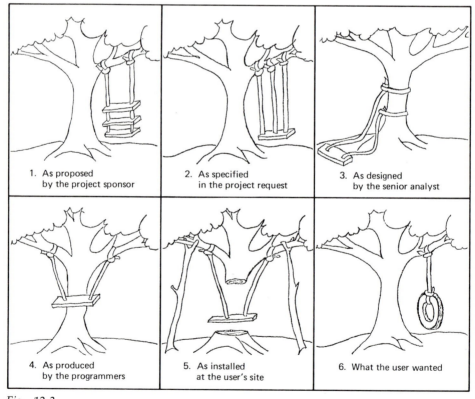

1. As proposed
   by the project sponsor

2. As specified
   in the project request

3. As designed
   by the senior analyst

4. As produced
   by the programmers

5. As installed
   at the user's site

6. What the user wanted

Fig. 12.3

A cynical view of the design process. (Source unknown.) Compare Fig. 12.1.

stratum as the designer. Broady's *Planning for People* (1968) belies its title in that the author seems to restrict user input to citizen organizations whose members include architects, surveyors, town planners, teachers, journalists, and other persons with degrees or professional qualifications. Broady also asserts that the average citizen is insensitive to all but the practical aspects of design and thus merits less consideration than middle-class and professional persons whose social altruism is sufficient to provide for the needs of the lower orders (Stacey, 1971). This is clearly a case of planning by enlightened elites (Fig. 12.2).

Planning Ideologies

The most restrictive constraints under which the planner must work are not those imposed by others but those imposed by himself. The designer's self-conception is of major importance here. Gumbril the elder regarded himself as a master builder, concerned only with cathedrals, town halls, universities, public libraries, office blocks, and magnificent country mansions. On occasion, however, he stooped to (Huxley, 1948, 29):

> designing model cottages for workmen . . . It's too much. In the old days these creatures built their own hovels, and very nice and suitable they were too. The architects busied themselves with architecture . . .

which, of course, did not include housing for the masses.

In a similar manner Graham Greene's antihero in *A Burnt-Out Case*, the architect Querry, was interested only in space, light, and proportion. "A great Catholic architect," he built restrained and ascetic modern churches which were heartily disliked by their congregations who preferred more traditional designs. But providing his user-clients with what they wanted was not Querry's goal. In his statement, "I wasn't concerned with the people who occupied my space — only with the space" (Greene, 1963, 46), Querry sums up the traditional outlook of the designer.

Derived from the experience of perceptive novelists, this view of the designer as an elitist with a narrow interest in personal goals or traditional solutions is supplemented by Sewell's (1971b) study of the attitudes and perceptions of engineers and public health inspectors. Though great reliance is placed upon such specialists to define problems and recommend solutions, their capacity for taking a holistic view of any problem-solution complex was seriously questioned by the study. Water pollution, for example, was perceived by engineers as an economic problem which could be solved by the application of the appropriate technology. Public health officials, however, saw it as a health problem which could be dealt with by the imposition of regulations regarding chemical composition. Most of the professionals interviewed were not only sceptical about public involvement in the issue, but also about the potential contributions of professionals from outside their own area of expertise.

One of the most hopeful recent directions taken by socially conscious professionals has been to question their own beliefs in a systematic manner. The call for an evaluation of the designer's belief system has been made repeatedly in recent years (Pahl, 1970; Rapoport, 1970; Goodman, 1972). Such an approach is clearly more amenable to analysis than modern design platitudes which frequently assert no more than "that either designers ought to understand *people,* or that people ought to understand *designers,* or both" (Studer and Stea, 1966). Craik (1972) suggests that it is proper that we should be seeking to evaluate the value orientations, social attitudes, environmental dispositions, and life history factors of environmental users. It is of equal importance, however, that we also elucidate the same personality characteristics of environmental designers and managers, in order to understand the assumptions they make and the goals they seek when engaging in environmental decision making.

As no considerable body of research has yet emerged on this area, any discussion of planners' ideologies must necessarily be subjective. Several design critics have attempted to define the basic ideology of planners and architects (Foley, 1960; Lipman, 1974; Pahl, 1970; Rapoport, 1970; Goodman, 1972; Mitchell, 1974). From these analyses several common ideological themes emerge.

the designer as form giver

It is a basic assumption of many designers that the designer provides the structural forms which solve the sponsor's needs. In a word, the designer decides the nature of the built environment. Some major designers have in fact been form givers; the concepts of Le Corbusier, Wright, and van der Rohe, for example, have been influential in the shaping of modern cities. Most designers, however, do not ultimately decide how the environment is to be shaped.

In producing a plan, whether of a single building or of a complete city, the designer is clearly subject to a wide range of external constraints. The significance of these constraints renders it impossible to consider the planner as solely responsible for the ultimate design. Cooper and Hackett (1968) found that the designer was merely one of a number of actors, all of whom had some influence on the final plan. The nondesigners included plan sponsors, lawyers, unions, building contractors, government bodies, and the like.

Pushkarev (1965) and others have stressed the influence of banks, insurance corporations, and mortgage companies. Mather (1972) has shown how the inflexibility of the more than 6,000 local building regulatory codes in the United States has prevented innovation, restricted the development of inexpensive, industrially produced housing, and rendered housing generally less responsive to human needs than is desired. Overwhelming all these constraints is the influence exerted by politics and the economics of profitability.

Finally, Ackerman (1969) suggests that architects traditionally adopt one of two positions when dealing with clients. These are the *pragmatic*, or give-'em-what-they-want school, and the *egoistic*, or give-'em-what-I-want school. The first provides the sponsor with his requirements, which may or may not be suitable for the eventual occupants of the building. The second type may become a form giver if his clients are sufficiently pliable. If so, the result is a building designed less for its inhabitants than as "an isolated work of art, an inhabitable sculpture." Clearly, even when the designer does become a form giver, the results may be unacceptable to all except his sponsor and himself.

the importance of the physical environment

Despite recent changes, including the input of social science and the development of professional planning schools, the traditions of the architect-planner and engineer-planner remain strong. An important part of this traditional belief system is the notion that physical structures and their organization should be the major preoccupation of planners. Even for many urban research workers, "the prototypical urban problem is a metropolitan (and usually a land-use) problem" (Popenoe, 1969). Some planners have seen their central function as simply the improvement of the quality of the physical environment (Foley, 1960).

More frequently, however, the emphasis on physical structures has involved a belief that design has a major influence on human behavior. Thus peoples' lives may be shaped and changed by means of appropriate design. The case for and against environmental determinism has been argued in Chapter 8. There is no conclusive evidence that the physical environment is a more influential behavior shaper, however, than the contextual or personal environments (Chapters 9–11).

Emphasis on the planner's crusade to improve the physical conditions of the planned-for has its roots in middle-class reactions to the squalid conditions of the poor in nineteenth-century cities. The British housing reformers of that era were convinced that improved housing would be an instrument for building character among the downtrodden. *Sewer socialism,* popular at the turn of the century in the United States, drew attention to the relationship between housing, overcrowding, and deviance. It is not a great step from these concerned beliefs, however, to a blind belief in the behavior-modification capacity of new housing. Explained in Chapter 11, this belief has had its concrete expression in recent American public housing policies with often disastrous consequences for the relocatees and a resulting shock to the belief system of the planners (Seligman, 1957, 106):

> Once upon a time we thought that if we could only get our problem families out of those dreadful slums, then papa would stop taking dope, mama would stop chasing around, and junior would stop carrying a knife. Well, we've got them in a nice new apartment with modern kitchens and a recreation center. And they're the same bunch of bastards they always were.

Such simple, one-factor, utopian solutions to urban problems ignore the realities of cultural and economic relationships. Yet, according to Palmer (1971), a belief in the overwhelming behavioral importance of physical design remains a basic tenet of planning thought.

Attachment to such a concept may lead to the extremes of social engineering, where the users of a structure are manipulated to fit a plan which the designer believes to be a vital step along the road toward the betterment of the human condition. Such concepts have become "an established tradition in the short history of modern architecture" (Lipman, 1974). The arrogance of the social engineers has been questioned by several critics, but it is not clear how many planners have indulged in the extremely naive concepts of architectural determinism attacked so vigorously by Broady (1968). That the number may be large is implied in Young and Willmott's (1962, 198) indictment of British slum clearance and public housing schemes:

> even when the town planners have set themselves to create communities anew as well as houses, they have still put their faith in buildings, sometimes speaking as though all that was necessary for neighbourliness was a neighbourhood unit, for community spirit a community center.

the community focus

As noted above, planners have paid much attention to the concept of community. One of the three strands of British planning ideology identified by Foley (1960) was a concern to provide the physical basis for a better urban community life. The same concern has been frequently voiced in North America, particularly in relation to the neighborhood unit concept (Chapter 4). In both areas the community focus has frequently included a strong anti-urban bias. An anthology of quotations from influential designers and critics (Musgrave, 1966) includes descriptions of the modern city as an:

> Incongruous mantrap of monstrous dimensions (Frank Lloyd Wright) . . . [an] irrelevant urban concentration (Prince) . . . a fibrous tumor (Wright) . . . a nightmare (Doxiadis) . . . a deplorable morass (Osborn) . . .

Anti-urban biases frequently involve a rural ideology, reflected in attempts to contain urban growth and in the planning of low-density suburban residential areas.

The role of the planner in the fostering of community life in planned residential areas has rarely been questioned. Community life is fostered, theoretically, through appropriate design (Chapter 8). Although there are almost as many definitions of community as there are planners and sociologists, a single general concept of community appears repeatedly in twentieth-century planning thought. This is the *Gemeinschaft* community, where social bonds are based upon close personal kinship and friendship ties, as opposed to the *Gesellschaft* community, where social relationships are impersonal, specialized, and contractual (Lipman, 1971; Goodey, 1974a). The *Gemeinschaft* community is typical of rural, agrarian settlements, and is found also among the unassimilated urban villagers of major cities (Chapter 11).

With its emphasis on small size, rootedness in place, common values, local activity patterns, and frequent social interaction with neighbors, the *Gemeinschaft* community is hardly typical of the modern urban resident in North America. Its popularity with planners is, in fact, a middle-class harking back to the virtues and values of an almost vanished rural way of life. Modern urban society is characterized by cultural pluralism and a diversity of lifestyles, many of which reject the concept of community. Common open space, for example, should theoretically promote community feeling on the lines of the old village green (Whyte, 1968). Yet people generally prefer tiny private lots to large public open spaces, and neighboring may even be encouraged thereby (Chapter 8).

Rosow (1961) asserts that community integration is not significantly greater in planned neighborhoods than in unplanned residential areas. Although Zehner (1971) found residents of planned neighborhoods to be more satisfied with their environment than those in less planned areas, there was no indication of any great difference in community feeling. Moreover, there has been a growing realization that Webber's "nonplace urban realm" (Chapter 4) is now the prevailing reality of modern cities. In consequence, *community* has recently lost its dominant position in planning ideology. This is reflected in an emphasis — in plans developed since the 1960s — on loosely gridded nonconcentric city forms, with a dispersal of activities and an emphasis on accessibility and freedom of choice rather than the close juxtaposition of home, work, and shopping (Willatts, 1971).

the search for order

Planning reports are replete with terms such as *order, balance, regularization,* and the like. This desire for order corresponds to Pahl's ideology of neatness and Foley's assertion that planners see themselves as judges who are concerned to reconcile competing land claims so as to produce a consistent, balanced, and orderly arrangement of land uses. Sommer, in *Tight Spaces,* believes that the inspiration for much modern architecture is the prison cell, product of an American fixation on security which is clearly fostered by the orderliness of hard architecture. Schools, housing projects, and commercial buildings in both North America and Europe are increasingly designed for security and custody, as well as ease of maintenance. The latter, as has already been discussed in Chapter 3 and elsewhere, is promoted by orderliness but in turn promotes dissatisfaction and even pathology on the part of the users.

Orderliness is an urban middle-class preoccupation. It is frequently distressing for a suburbanite to experience the apparent chaos of a family farm or the littered debris of an Indian reservation. Almost instinctively, we experience the impulse to tidy the area. "Wasted space," so valuable in the public housing project (Chapter 11), is to be eliminated on the grounds of neatness and economy. Balanced neighborhoods must be achieved, irrespective of the wishes of the various social and cultural groups with respect to residential integration (Weaver, 1963). This orderly mentality is in part responsible for the packing away of the deviant and dependent members of society in institutions (Rothman, 1971), whereas in the early nineteenth century community care provided an alternative which is only now being revived. Orderliness is also related to a tendency to define situations in terms of arbitrarily designated sets of criteria. Confronting a Boston planner with data on the low delinquency, infant mortality, disease, and death rates in the North End, Jacobs received the reply: "Why, that's the worst slum in the city. It has two hundred and seventy-five dwelling units to the net acre" (Jacobs, 1961, 10).

Perin (1974, 41) suggests that design professionals merely share in the ordinary human need to order the universe. Chaos, the unpredictable, and the unmanageable promote anxiety. Order, sequence, neatness, and regularity reduce anxiety. The question, of course, is: Anxiety on the part of whom, the planner or the occupant of the space? Thus Perin asserts:

We must continually ask the question, as we go about our business of creating order, *whose* chaos are we taming? *Whose* comfort about the unpredictable and the unmanageable are we decreasing?

elitism

Clearly, many of the ideologies, assumptions, and assertions noted above are bound up with an overall belief that the designer knows best. Architects are especially prone to statements such as Gideon's (1948) self-assumed goal of reinstating basic human values through design. Naturally, the human values which are to be reinstated are those of the architect. Elitism further manifests itself in the belief "that good design is self-evident, that the designers and the public agree about environmental quality, and that concepts such as neighborhood . . . and privacy are commonly shared" (Rapoport, 1970). Even a brief acquaintance with the contents of this book should serve to shatter any such belief system.

Nevertheless, ignoring the social and administrative distance between themselves and their user-clients, planners persist in attempting to specify human relationships through design to the point of community disruption. A planning report produced for the British government (Shankland, Cox, and Associates, 1966) explicitly desired to create "social happiness" and "harmonious relationships," based on the assumption that "social integration can be assisted by physical integration." Deliberate disruption as a policy is typified by the statement of a major British government planner that slums should be demolished and their inhabitants relocated "even though the people seem to be satisfied with their miserable environment and seem to enjoy an extrovert social life in their own locality" (Burns, 1963).

Elitist planners have been indicted as reactionary conservatives who support the established order (Palmer, 1971; Goodman, 1972). Many planning and architecture schools still attempt to train architects as form givers and tend to reinforce the traditional alliance of architecture with the power elite (Ackerman, 1969). When confronted with behavioral data regarding user-clients' concepts of space, as outlined throughout this book, a young architect cried (Mitchell, 1974, 18):

> Architecture is difficult enough having to learn about form,
> structure, and perspective, and how to deal with ignorant
> clients, and now you bring in all these other behavioral facts —
> it's just too much. I sometimes wish I had practised in medieval
> Florence and had to present my plans only to the Medici or the
> Roman Catholic Church.

Such an attitude supports the view of architecture as a "look at" experience rather than a "live in" one, and is reinforced by the general support given to experts by policy makers. Spiro T. Agnew, for example, stated: "You don't learn from people suffering from poverty, but from experts who have studied the problem" (*New York Times*, 17 October 1968).

Goodman's searing indictment of planning, significantly entitled *After the Planners* (1972), is only the latest of a series of calls for the redirection of planning toward the goals of the user-client. As early as 1945 Churchill was concerned about the unreality of the planner's cherished assumptions and conventional wisdom. In 1961 Jacobs asserted that (1961, 13):

> The pseudoscience of city planning and its companion, the art of city design, have not yet broken with the specious comfort of wishes, familiar superstitions, oversimplifications, and symbols, and have not yet embarked upon the adventure of probing the real world.

In 1972 Goodman's assertion that an overall design grows out of the need of design professionals to explain the design in simplistic terms to bureaucrats, neither of whom live in the environment designed for, was joined by Fromm's (1972) suggestion that planning presently serves the aims of production, technology, and corporate organization rather than the growth and development of human beings. As such, planners may not be visible symbols of oppression, as the military and the police may be; they are instead "the soft cops" (Goodman, 1972, 53).

Protest and Reaction

The fact that designers and the public have very different value systems is more apparent to the public than to the design profession (Rapoport, 1970). Throughout history, the major response to planned environments on the part of the planned-for has been adaptation. The 1960s, however, saw an upsurge of protest against planning by the enlightened elites (Fig. 12.2), which may be regarded as an initial thrust toward planning reform, if not popular planning.

Protest by the citizen has taken many forms. Rent strikes, riots, marches, boycotts, labor strikes, and civil disorder are the most apparent forms. Fanning (1975) traces the modern nonviolent citizen-action movement back to the preservationists of the nineteenth century. On a more personal level, John Betjeman typifies a variety of middle-class poets and novelists who, like the architecture critic Ada Louise Huxtable of the *New York Times*

(Cliff, 1971a), do battle to preserve landscapes and buildings of historic and aesthetic value. Betjeman's poetry vilifies those who destroy old structures and agrarian landscapes only to replace them with sterile, planned communities. In "The Town Clerk's Views" (1970) he mocks the planner's ideology of order and neatness:

> Hamlets which fail to pass the planner's test
> Will be demolished. We'll rebuild the rest
> To look like Welwyn mixed with Middle West.
> All fields we'll turn to sports grounds, lit at night
> From concrete standards with fluorescent light:
> And over all the land, instead of trees,
> Clean poles and wires will whisper in the breeze.

Betjeman, however, is clearly guilty of rural sentimentality.

More important than offended bourgeois aesthetics is the offense to the viable neighborhood afforded by major highway and urban renewal plans. Urban freeways are frequently routed through the neighborhoods of minority groups and the poor, who have little economic or political power to prevent the implementation of such plans. Community action by these groups, frequently supported by radical planners and other professionals, has had some success in recent years. Lupo *et al.* (1971) and Fellman and Brandt (1970, 1971), for example, detail the protests of Boston area residents against proposed freeways which could destroy their neighborhoods. Anti-urban renewal and antihighway efforts have recently had conspicuous success in Boston, San Francisco, New Orleans, New York, and Washington, D.C. (Goodman, 1972; Wolpert *et al.*, 1972).

Protest action, however, is essentially a response to perceived threat. It is usually generated in the hope of preserving existing structures, and is reactive rather than creative. It is, in effect, a demand that "they" take notice of "the little people" (Fellman and Brandt, 1971). Response by decision-makers has frequently taken the form of consultation with protest groups on a temporary basis. A more long-term approach has been a growing concern among planners and policy-makers to derive behavioral data from the public for use in the planning process.

This has generally taken the form of *evaluation studies* of various types. Numerous studies of satisfaction have been performed, especially with regard to student satisfaction with college residence halls (Hsia, 1967; Davis and Roizen, 1971; Cliff, 1971b). In *Design Awareness* (1971) Sommer presents "The New Evaluator Cookbook" which gives details of interviews, large- and small-scale surveys, expert ratings, observation techniques, self-surveys, and simulated environments which may be used to derive information from the public. *Predesign evaluation,* usually involving the collection of behavioral data as well as the elicitation of prospective user-clients' desires and requirements, is matched by *postdesign evaluation,* which seeks to measure the success of the design and gain some insight into its shortcomings so that future designs may be suitably modified. It is important also to evaluate the beliefs and objectives of the designers (Becker, 1971; Craik, 1972), and perhaps, to permit the designers to evaluate the evaluation of the evaluators (Eckbo, 1971).

Modern evaluation systems are indeed an advance on reactive protest. They tend, however, to treat the user-client as no more than a respondent. They are, therefore, essentially a passive means of involving the user-client in the design process. Encouragement of the active participation of the user-client is one of the most recent trends in planning thought. Parr (1971b) suggests that communities should make their own decisions regarding social and environmental change, while Rittel (1972) states that the planning process is essentially an argumentative one and thus the user can and should participate in all design decisions. The result of citizen protest, recent governmental interest in citizen participation, and planners' questioning of their own biases and procedures could well be some deprofessionalization of the planning process and a blurring of the distinction between planner and planned-for (Grant, 1972).

The modern planner is thus faced with three alternative models. (1) He may continue in the established tradition of planning *for* people with only token consultation (see Chapter 13). (2) He may follow the road of deprofessionalization and plan *with* people, a process involving strong collaboration between planner and user-client on an egalitarian basis (see Chapter 14). Or (3) he may withdraw almost totally from the planning process to facilitate the development of planning *by* people (see Chapter 14).

Further Reading

BROADY, M. (1968), *Planning for People.* London: National Council of Social Service.

LORIMER, J. (1972), *A Citizen's Guide to City Politics.* Toronto: James Lewis & Samuel.

SOMMER, R. (1974), *Tight Spaces: Hard Architecture and How to Humanize It.* Englewood Cliffs, N.J.: Prentice-Hall.

ZEISEL, J. (1975), *Sociology and Architectural Design.* New York: Russell Sage Foundation.

13

PLANNING FOR PEOPLE

He's a real Nowhere Man,
Sitting in his Nowhere Land,
Making all his Nowhere plans for Nobody.
He's as blind as he can be,
Just sees what he wants to see,
Nowhere Man can you see me at all?*

J. Lennon/P. McCartney
The Beatles

As envisaged by The Beatles, the planner's activity pattern is so removed from that of the citizen that the latter figures in the plan merely as a cipher. Both autocratic planners and traditional enlightened elites favor the continuation of a form of planning which severely restricts any input on the part of the user-client. This planning process is still largely the norm, and is carried on today by planners who feel that they already know what the public wants, what it needs and, above all, what is good for the public. Such a conceptualization of planning frequently culminates in a desire to provide a totally planned environment in which everything has its place and nothing is left to chance.

The Total Institution

Completely planned environments have been termed *total institutions.* Total institutions reflect a planning ideology which stresses the incapacity of the user-client to function effectively without paternalist guidance, and a perceived need to protect the community from external threat. The prototypical total institution is the asylum (Goffman, 1961), but the concept has also been applied to cases where complete communities have been created *in toto* by a single entrepreneur, corporation, or public agency. In relation to the planning of new towns and cities, Brooks (1971) distinguishes three major characteristics of the total institution.

1.   There is initially a sharp separation between the planner and the planned-for. The premise appears to be that the community is utterly incapable of planning for itself.

2.   The planning staff, together with their outside consultants, the majority of whom will never reside in the community, attempt to specify the goals of the community. The planners' values thus receive concrete expression in the townscape.

3.   There is also an attempt to establish barriers between residents and outsiders. This is most readily achieved by separating the town plan from its regional context and instituting separate fiscal arrangements.

Brooks suggests that these features are muted as new residents, with ties outside the community, bring in new goals and values, including a demand for participation in the planning process. However, the speed of this devolutionary process depends on several factors, including the degree of planner commitment and the nature of the inhabitants. Three types of total institutions, the company town, the new town, and utopia, will be considered in more detail in this chapter.

The Company Town

All the features of the total institution are present in the company town. Company towns are communities built, owned, and operated by a single entrepreneur or corporation (Porteous, 1970). Though commonly associated with primary industries, notably forestry and mining, there have been many instances of manufacturing towns built and operated wholly by a single company. One of the major characteristics of the company town, where the employer controls housing, stores, schools, and public facilities, as well as employment, is the opportunity it affords for the control of labor.

Labor has often been one of the least manipulable factors of industrial production. As an animate, sentient input, it has the most exacting demands in terms of storage. Physical plant may operate continuously, but social, psychological, and physiological constraints, frequently supported by labor legislation, limit the industrial operative's working day to between one-half and three-quarters of his waking day.

In urban-industrial societies man's minimum needs for rest, privacy, and territorial expression have ensured that the major proportion of the land area of cities is given over to housing. Such accommodation has been provided through a variety of strategies. Speculative builders have profited by supplying houses for sale or rent. In contrast, the worker has occasionally provided his own shelter. Developed largely in the twentieth century, a third strategy involves government intervention through developer support or the direct supply of public housing (Chapter 11).

An alternative solution to the problem of housing industrial workers is the provision of dwellings directly by the employer. Such housing is usually for rent only, and thus the worker is to some extent bound to his employer. A variety of motives lies behind the decision to construct company housing, which ranges from a few dwellings in a preexisting settlement to a complete town. Companies frequently provide a small number of luxury dwellings for the attraction and retention of key personnel. Entrepreneurs have on occasion acted philanthropically; by building houses they have successfully shielded their workers from rapacious landlords and speculative builders.

Where an entire company town is constructed, however, company housing has proved an effective means of worker control. If the industrialist is landlord as well as employer, his relationship with his employees extends beyond the plant and into the workers' homes. Employers may thus exert considerable influence over the social and political, as well as the economic life of the residents of company towns, sometimes with dire results, as in the case of Pullman, Illinois (Ely, 1885; Buder, 1967). Trade union organization may be prevented, religious bigotry fostered, and social class structures fossilized; dissenters and radicals may be dismissed from their jobs, and consequently from their homes, and thus from the company town itself. Such excesses, including a lurid history of strike suppression in the coal and copper towns of the American West, in Chile, and elsewhere, have been the basis for the notoriously poor public image of the company town (Hunt *et al.*, 1925). In view of its generally repressive nature, Tunnard concluded that the company town, though formerly common in the United States, is "utterly un-American in its tendencies" (1970, 168).

Company towns are most frequently associated with extractive industries. Because of the great weight loss involved in primary processing, the towns are typically resource located, though such settlements may also appear at the sites of other factors of production, such as water supplies and ports. Some company towns have been so closely resource located that the extension of operations has compelled their removal (Allen, 1966). Haphazard site planning may result in the poor living conditions frequently associated with location close to a noxious effluent source.

Physical planning in company towns has often been conspicuous by its absence; entrepreneurs are characteristically oriented toward production and profit, rather than the onerous task of housing their employees. Whether planning is apparently haphazard or extremely detailed, several common features are apparent:

1.   general dominance of the settlement by the physical expressions of economic enterprise, brought about by a close juxtaposition of town and plant, and by the physical orientation of the town toward buildings representing company institutions; and

2.   a gridiron or radial grid street layout which, coupled with the contemporaneous nature of buildings and architectural uniformity, produce a drab, monotonous townscape.

Cities developing without the doubtful benefits of one-industry control characteristically exhibit ethnic and socioeconomic class segregation patterns through the operation of complex social, economic, and political forces (Chapters 10, 11). In company towns, however, the company is able to indulge in deliberate residential zoning from the outset. The occupational hierarchy of the plant traditionally has been imposed upon the town in terms of residential segregation. Common elements include:

1.   deliberate ethnic and socioeconomic segregation in housing location;

2.   creation of a graded series of house quality styles which are allocated to employees not according to need (i.e., family size) but according to class; and

3.   creation of separate institutions for each class.

As each town is "the rational result of the decision of a board of directors," one would expect the physical and social planning of such settlements to be based upon rational company goals, whether implicit or explicit (Schlakman, 1935, 14). In their review of the philosophy behind the layout of Lowell, Massachusetts, the Goodmans concluded that "the architecture . . . everywhere proved the integration of the ideological and industrial plan" (Goodman and Goodman, 1947, 42). Insofar as the chief goal of the company is unhindered production, the town should be so arranged that the company is everywhere seen to be the dominant force in local economic life. Too often this goal can be achieved only by the exercise of complete company control over the siting of facilities, buying and selling, the residential location of individuals, the organization of social life, and the like. "The most important single feature of company housing is the autocratic control which employers wield over the inhabitants of their town" (Tunnard, 1970, 166).

The company towns of El Salvador, Potrerillos, and Chuquicamata, developed by the U.S.-based Anaconda Company in the Atacama desert of northern Chile, amply illustrate the social and physical planning characteristics outlined above. The extreme weight loss associated with the extraction, concentration, smelting, and refining of copper assured these settlements of minehead locations. Each town is physically dominated by copper-mining operations. The partially collapsed mountain of copper outside El Salvador, slowly being demolished from within by the block-caving method, is the outstanding feature of the local scene. At Chuquicamata, the open pit mine is not visible from the town, but the tailings dump, known locally as "the cake," towers above the settlement. The town of Potrerillos slopes upward to the smokestacks of the railhead smelter. Smelters operate continuously and thus are all too visible and audible during the hours of darkness. In no town is it possible to ignore the physical presence of the plant on which all inhabitants directly or indirectly depend, especially when sulfur fumes are blown over the townsites by contrary winds.

Potrerillos best exemplifies the physical layout of the traditional company town plan, with the close juxtaposition of townsite and plant and the concentration of company stores, offices, and company-supported institutions, such as churches, on high ground overlooking the dwellings (Fig. 13.1). In an attempt to reduce the atmosphere of company dominance, the minehead, concentrator, and townsite of El Salvador were sited about two miles apart. The traditional focus upon company store, church, and company offices remains within the townsite, however, and indeed is strengthened by the radial plan; all streets lead to the company store which, as elsewhere, becomes the social focus of the town (Fig. 13.2).

Each town has been organized upon a grid or radial pattern. Architectural monotony is prevalent, although the half-dozen styles of concrete-block housing in El Salvador have been rendered less uniform in appearance by pastel color washes. Potrerillos and Chuquicamata contain a large variety of housing styles, built at different periods and in several materials, but two types predominate. *Calaminas,* largely of corrugated iron, and adobes, built with bricks made primarily from mine tailings, are typically arranged in long single-story rows. The grid street system and the predominance of grey and green house colors produce an overall effect of drab conformity.

Major social divisions are part of company town life. Planned social zoning is apparent in the distinct American and Chilean sections, generally separated by undeveloped land, a *cordon sanitaire.* In Chuquicamata and El Salvador this land contains the company hospital, symbol of a mere community of pain between two groups which differ strongly in language, mores, education, life-style, and position in the occupational and social-class hierarchy. A policy of separation of the two groups has been strictly adhered to in almost all public situations, from schools and social clubs to movie-house

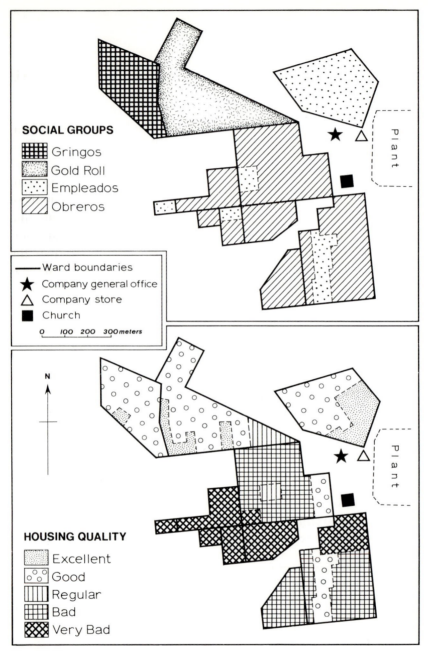

SOCIAL GROUPS

▦ Gringos
▒ Gold Roll
⋮⋮ Empleados
▧ Obreros

— Ward boundaries
★ Company general office
△ Company store
■ Church

0   100   200   300 meters

N

HOUSING QUALITY

░ Excellent
○ Good
▥ Regular
▦ Bad
▧ Very Bad

Fig. 13.1

Social groups and housing quality in Potrerillos, Chile, 1970. (Reproduced by permission from the *Annals* of the Association of American Geographers, 64, 1974.)

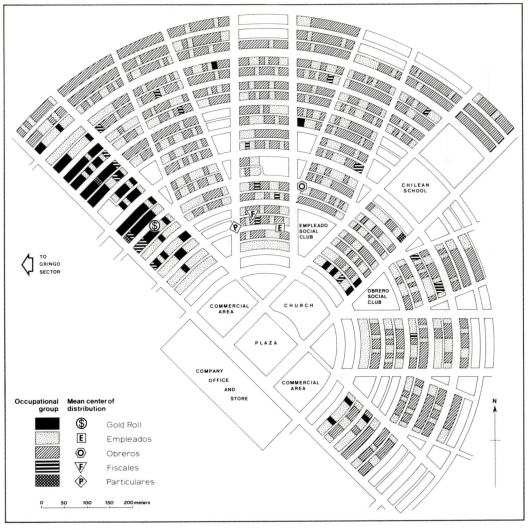

Occupational group	Mean center of distribution
Gold Roll	$
Empleados	E
Obreros	O
Fiscales	F
Particulares	P

0   50   100   150   200 meters

TO GRINGO SECTOR

CHILEAN SCHOOL

EMPLEADO SOCIAL CLUB

OBRERO SOCIAL CLUB

COMMERCIAL AREA

CHURCH

PLAZA

COMPANY OFFICE AND STORE

COMMERCIAL AREA

N

Fig. 13.2

Social groups in El Salvador, Chile, 1970. (Reproduced by permission from the *Annals* of the Association of American Geographers, 64, 1974.)

seating arrangements. The distinction between Chilean and alien, however, is only one of many social divisions in the Atacama copper towns. Extensive unstructured interviewing during 1970 revealed in all three towns the same ingroup-outgroup framework of distinct social groups, coalescing or dividing in accordance with the nature of the perceived outgroup (Fig. 13.3).

All persons concerned with copper mining felt united in terms of isolation from and economic contrast with the rest of Chile; the towns are physically isolated from the mainstream of Chilean life, and the high wages earned

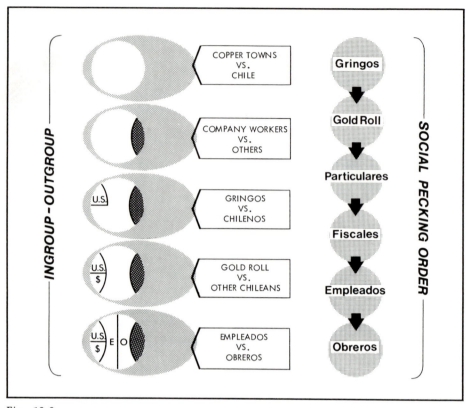

Fig. 13.3

Social divisions in Chilean company towns. (Reproduced by permission from
the *Annals* of the Association of American Geographers, 64, 1974.)

by copper workers have earned them the envy and distrust of their compa-
triots. Within each town, company personnel were distinguished from non-
company workers, who fall into two groups: *fiscales* are government employees, including police, post office workers, and teachers in the Chilean
schools; *particulares* comprise all other persons permitted by the company to
operate facilities, such as private stores, churches, and bus lines, within the
company estate. Company personnel were sharply divided between the
gringos, largely North American and West European technical, office, and
supervisory staff, and *chilenos.* Equally sharp divisions were apparent within
the *chileno* group; Chilean supervisory staff, known locally as the "gold roll,"

have traditionally been paid in U.S. dollars, which were readily exchanged upon the black market for several times their official value; the value of the Chilean *peso* is constantly diminishing. Chileans receiving wages in the national currency were further divided socially. Labor legislation in Chile has long distinguished between *empleados,* generally white-collar or skilled employees, and semiskilled or unskilled *obreros.* The former are paid monthly and receive substantial fringe benefits, whereas *obreros* are employed on a daily wage basis and their benefits are relatively low.

The relationship between socioeconomic class and housing quality was clear. *Gringos* invariably occupied more spacious, better appointed houses of superior construction; they frequently possessed the major luxuries of trees and a lawn. Because of its recent construction, the housing of El Salvador is of a uniformly high quality. The monotonous tracts of apparently identical housing in Chuquicamata and Potrerillos, however, include housing varying greatly in age and condition. Qualitative house-quality ranking by company welfare officials was used to relate house quality to social class, and in both cases there was a strong correlation between the two. Using objective statistical measures, it was also found that all social groups were strongly segregated from each other (Porteous, 1974).

Even El Salvador, built in the 1950s by a management somewhat chastened by the anticompany-town feelings of copper workers and Chileans at large (Porteous, 1973b), showed evidence of deliberate segregation. Although there was an attempt to intermix gold roll, *empleado,* and *obrero* housing, gold roll employees clearly occupied the sector closest to the *gringo* quarter (Fig. 13.2). Segregation analysis produced a clear indication of the social ordering of El Salvador, with a segregation gradient representing varying social distance between groups along the continuum *gringo*-gold roll-*empleado-obrero.* The mean centers of distribution of the residences of each subgroup in El Salvador affirm this social pecking order (Fig. 13.2).

Western concepts of company-town social planning, derived from nineteenth- and early twentieth-century North America, have been transferred bodily to Chile. In the Atacama company towns the reasons for planned segregation and the traditional town plan were made explicit in 1970 by certain officials who agreed that their company towns were originally designed to support the direct line of economic and social command which culminated in the *gringo* group. To foster this goal, company control had to be made explicit, and was expressed in the orientation of each town toward a nexus of company institutions, in the grid pattern and architectural uniformity which evoked a sense of corporate power and worker discipline, in the spatial expression of the social pecking order, and in the dependence of workers on company-provided or company-licensed facilities. Above all, a major spatial and social gap was maintained between the *gringos,* who were responsible for planning and house allocation, and the remainder of the population.

The New Town

The company town is an expedient solution to the problems of physical isolation or social control as perceived by the private entrepreneur. In sharp contrast, the new-town concept has at its roots a concern for the social welfare of the public, and is most frequently developed by public agencies, although privately built new towns were once common, and are once again being built, notably in North America. In the archetypal company town, planning was directed largely *against* the employee, whereas the essence of the new-town ideal is that the goal of planning is to promote the well-being of the user-client.

The squalor of nineteenth-century industrial cities encouraged certain philanthropic employers to attempt to free their workers from the noisome city by erecting *model communities* in a more pastoral setting. This movement brought into being a whole wave of new communities in Europe (Ashworth, 1954; Armytage, 1961; Bell, 1969). In Britain alone, an assortment of utopian idealists (for example, Owen), socially conscious industrialists (Wedgwood), Quakers (Cadbury, Richardson, Salt), and chocolate (Cadbury, Rowntree) and soap (Lever, Price) manufacturers were responsible (Darley, 1975). The towns they built span the century, from Owen's New Lanark (1816) to Cadbury's Bournville (1879) and Lever's Port Sunlight (1886). The idea was given physical expression independently throughout Europe and North America.

According to Pollard (1965), the majority of such model communities came into being through the dictates of simple economic necessity. This does not deny, however, the philanthropism of some nineteenth-century industrialists, even if their social concern was a subsidiary motive for town building. The model-communities movement had much influence on the development of modern concepts of government intervention in urban planning while the low-density arrangement of model communities and the builders' concern for the social implications of design laid the foundation for the *garden city* movement.

Garden cities, as envisaged by Ebenezer Howard (1898), were to be limited to a population of about 30,000 people, and were to contain sufficient employment opportunities to render them economically self-sufficient. In terms of physical planning (Fig. 13.4), they were to be "spaciously laid out to give light, air, and gracious living well away from the smoke and grime of the factories and surrounded by a greenbelt that would provide both farm produce for the population and opportunity for recreation" (Schaffer, 1970, 4). In a reaction to the problems of London, Letchworth Garden City (1903) and Welwyn Garden City (1920) were built beyond the metropolitan suburbs.

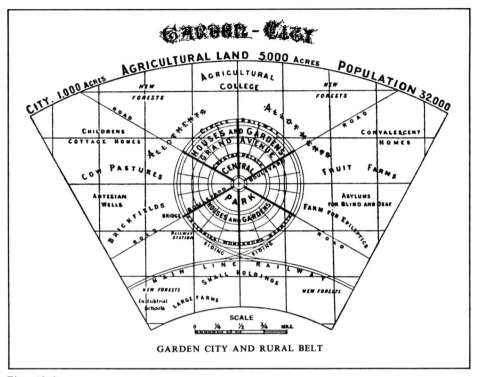

GARDEN CITY AND RURAL BELT

Fig. 13.4

Ebenezer Howard's Garden City concept. (Reproduced from *Garden Cities of Tomorrow* by permission of Faber and Faber Ltd., London, and The M.I.T. Press, Cambridge, Mass.)

Though these were not wholly successful, Howard's planning principles had an enormous influence on urban planning in Britain, Europe, and North America. His emphases on small overall size, a suburban-style physical layout, segregated land uses, healthfulness, an encircling greenbelt of nonurban land, and economic self-sufficiency have become watchwords of twentieth-century planning. Though some of these principles are admirable, Howard's means of achieving them was not. Despite his concern for the garden citizens, he was essentially an elitist. "He conceived of planning as essentially paternalistic, if not authoritarian . . . in each case the plan must anticipate all that is needed and be protected, after it is built, against any but the most minor subsequent changes" (Jacobs, 1961, 19). Unfortunately, this paternalism, as well as the other features of the garden city, was carried over into the *new-town* movement.

Garden-city principles formed the basis for the world's first legislated new-town policy, which was passed by the British parliament in 1946 (Osborn and Whittick, 1969). Since that time an ambitious program of new-town development has had a major impact on life and landscape in Britain. By 1950 14 new towns had been designated, and by 1967, 21 had been started. Though the earlier towns all had population targets below 100,000, modern new towns have target populations of up to 250,000. The combined target population of the British towns already designated is approximately three million people, 1.4 million being already in residence in 1970.

The garden-city and new-town concepts were enthusiastically adopted elsewhere, notably in Northern Europe (Sweden and Finland) and in North America. In the United States Radburn, New Jersey, became the first community planned to accommodate both automobile and citizen without clash or collision. Two major features of European new towns were not popular in North America, however. The decentralization of industry and population to self-contained communities beyond the metropolis has not been as apparent as in Europe. Most United States new towns operate as suburban commuter dormitories. Further, whereas European new towns are largely developed by public agencies, the creation of North American new towns, with the exception of the three greenbelt towns built during the administration of Franklin Roosevelt, has been left entirely to the private corporation. On this basis, over one hundred new communities are at present being developed in the United States (Weiss *et al.*, 1971). Elsewhere, Third World countries with strong British influence, such as Ghana and Malaya, have developed publicly built new towns. Since 1948 new towns have played a vital role in Israel's national development program (Spiegel, 1967).

New-town programs have a variety of economic and regional planning objectives, including curbing the diseconomic growth of major metropolitan areas, providing growth poles in stagnant regions, and preventing the loss of agricultural land through unplanned urban sprawl (Rodwin, 1956). As a major experiment in comprehensive planning they also have explicit social goals, including the provision of a healthy housing environment, self-sufficiency in shopping and employment, the fostering of social-class integration and a sense of community, and the encouragement of citizen participation in town organization.

The goal of a *healthful housing environment* was a reaction, like that of Ebenezer Howard, against the perceived squalor of the inner city. As discussed in Chapter 7, large cities were regarded as conducive to social, mental, and physical pathologies, whereas new towns, where residents would be closer to nature, would have a beneficent influence on both health and morals. This point of view is derived from early nineteenth-century conceptions of urban and rural life, as expressed in Disraeli's *Sybil* (1881) and first espoused by the entrepreneurs who founded model industrial villages.

Healthfulness was to be achieved by providing the former inhabitants of gardenless urban row housing with gardens front and back, treed streets, and ample open space. These features have indeed been major successes in terms of resident satisfaction. When asked what they liked about Cumbernauld, a Scottish new town, residents typically remarked upon the clean fresh air, the comfortable house, and the suitability of the environment for raising children (Zweig, 1970). Compared with residents in unplanned suburbs, American new-town residents proved more satisfied with their neighborhood environment, especially with regard to outdoor play space (Zehner, 1971). Low- and medium-density housing arrangements with ample open space became almost a fetish, however, and such designs were laid out in environmentally unsuitable areas. Generous open space, for example, is both useless and oppressive in the hot, dry Israeli desert climate (Brutzkus, 1964).

Although such layouts were generally satisfying to their residents, there is little evidence that the planners' goal of increased healthfulness — physical, mental, and moral — has been achieved. As noted in Chapter 8, such a new housing environment can lead to greater self-esteem, slightly fewer periods of illness, and marginally better school performance. These benefits, however, may be nullified by the financial problems of moving to a new area (Porteous, 1972), or by sociopsychological problems related to loss of place-related kinship and friendship webs (Chapter 11). Moreover, the concept of small-town life being in some way more wholesome than city life is not borne out by the studies of novelists, sociologists, and planners (Alonso, 1970). In short, the traditional image of the alienating city and the cohesive small town is a gross and misleading oversimplification.

In contrast to the planned segregation of company towns, planned *social integration* was a major goal of new towns, notably in Britain with its long history of class conflict. The original new-town planners congratulated themselves on having the courage to acknowledge the existence of social classes, and then attempted to legislate class differences out of existence (Petersen, 1966). Social balance was to be achieved within each town, and in many cases within each neighborhood, by a close mixture of housing types.

The consequences of this kind of neighborhood integration planning have been explored in Chapters 4, 10, and 11. It is sufficient to state here that such idealistic aims are rarely achieved in practice, and that a close mixture of people of very different life-styles "tends to lead to polite coolness or outright hostility between neighbors" (Darke and Darke, 1974, 38). By selective migration, moreover, housing areas in new towns eventually became class homogeneous. In a review of a large number of studies of planned class mixing Michelson (1970) concludes that the evidence points toward a distinct lack of success. Further, as was noted in Chapter 11, persons moved from the inner city to peripheral communities frequently change their life-style, most notably in reducing dependence upon kin and friendship ties and increasing emphasis on the nuclear family. As expressed by a British builder, "our customers choose freedom rather than neighbourliness" (Willis, 1969).

In concentrating upon social-class integration, other forms of social variability have been neglected. Racial minorities are notably absent from new towns. Age is another problem. The typical new town in Britain is inhabited by young families, with a marked lack of elderly persons and teenagers. This skewed age structure may, of course, normalize with time, but only if housing of the appropriate types is provided at the appropriate phase of development. Willmott (1967) has shown how unbalanced age-structures lead to housing shortages, lack of diversity in housing types resulting in visual monotony, an associated feeling of social monotony, and problems of social service provision.

Closely bound up with the concept of social balance is the concept of *community*. This in turn is associated with the idea that new towns should be self-contained. Residents should have not only their homes but also their jobs and major shopping areas within the town. Presumably, the intense overlap of activity patterns and shared problems and benefits should result in community feeling. The failure of this ideology (Chapter 12) has been suggested in Chapter 4 in relation to neighborhoods and elsewhere in this book in relation to the planned integration of social groups. Just as socially integrated neighborhoods rapidly take on a particular class coloration through selective relocation, so it has proved impossible in Britain to prevent commuting into new towns from other settlements and out of new towns to major metropolitan centers. In North America new-town commuting is the norm.

Further, there is little evidence that the strategic location of community and neighborhood facilities and the creation of neighborhood units has any significant influence on the development of neighborhood and community consciousness. Much research suggests the opposite (Chapter 4; Willmott, 1967). As noted earlier, "families may wish to use their opportunities to live a family-central rather than a community-central life" (C.H.A.C., 1967, 49). People are also generally unwilling to restrict themselves to a local and therefore small range of choices in shopping and entertainment.

Moreover, community development is frequently not adequately supported by the plan. New towns have been criticized by their residents on the grounds that the town center goes dead after six every evening, that it is a commercial center and not a social center, that low-density residential areas make a viable bus service impossible, and that communication between neighborhoods is lacking (Darke and Darke, 1974). Since the late 1950s, neighborhood units have been out of favor with British planners because of their lack of success, though Willmott (1967) feels that this reaction has been taken too far.

Closely related to community development is the goal of *citizen participation* in planning. Presumably a small community would foster this. Significant resident input into the new-town planning process has, however, been negligible. In Bramalea, a private enterprise new town outside Toronto, development was expedited by secret cooperation between financiers, developers, and local politicians. The result, an expensive, ugly collection of houses without efficient public transportation or civilized amenities, is "a monument to the developers' greed" (Stewart, 1970). Ironically, in his review of participation in the British new-town planning process, Willmott is concerned largely with the participation of sociologists rather than the people from whom they gather data.

The major problem here is that the existing new-town planning process is particularly unsuitable for public participation. Before a new town has any residents, several years of development planning are required. Rarely can specific groups of relocatees be identified before they are transferred to a new town. Alonso (1970) compares the new town to a spaceship, the flight of which is preprogrammed. After launching, travelers can make only small choices of their own. Alonso suggests that the tensions between developer and residents in a new town are frequently a product of the residents' struggle for increasing autonomy in the face of the developer's dedication to the smooth unfolding of the plan.

Preplanned communities suffer much trauma during the transfer of power from the planner to representatives of the residents. In this connection Columbia, Maryland, has been extensively studied. Built by developer James Rouse, Columbia in 1971 had 12,000 residents occupying several neighborhoods grouped around village centers. Rouse has been eulogized as a private enterprise new-town planner and publicly built new towns in Europe have been compared unfavorably with Columbia (Brekenfeld, 1971).

More critical analysis by a series of planners, however, suggests that despite Columbia's elaborate plans for eventual citizen participation, the town may be likened to a company town (Godschalk, 1973). Centralized developer control of all important planning decisions precluded significant public input into decision making. Brooks regards Columbia as a prime example of a total institution in that residents were merely the consumers of a packaged community; Rouse developed and controlled the planning of Columbia in the manner of the enlightened elites:

> The ideals of James Rouse combined the city beautiful tradition,
> a deeply religious communitarian ideology, and a firm faith in
> the free enterprise system (Brooks, 1971, 376).

Thus low-income housing was neglected because of a fear of overspill from the black ghettos of Baltimore and Washington, community has been forced upon the population, and the new town has not yet come to terms with the problems of the region into which it has been implanted (Brooks, 1974).

Utopia

Many of the concepts already discussed in this chapter have a flavor of utopianism. In contrast to *deductive* planning, which merely draws up blue-prints and assumes that economic development leads to social progress, and *inductive* planning, which attempts to coordinate public policies in a whole series of overlapping areas, *utopian* planning generally aims to create a "beautiful social harmony" with little relation to the real world of conflict and scarce resources (Petersen, 1966; Pahl, 1970, 127). Utopian planning has one immediate drawback; utopia (literally "no place") is, as Sir Thomas More (1516) suggested over four centuries ago, unattainable. Equally unattainable is *eutopia* (ideal place), though it would be preferable to avoid *dystopia* (bad place).

Various approaches to utopia, the meaning of which has become de-based to mean an ideal place, include the psychological, the philosophical, the socialist, the communitarian, and the religious (Manuel, 1966). Most have a future orientation. Very broadly, utopias may be divided into social and physical categories (Meyerson, 1961). Social utopias tend to be literary in form, generally ignore the physical environment, and concentrate upon so-cial, economic, and political issues (Johnson, 1968). Physical utopias tend to emphasize the importance of design. Both, however, have a similar goal, that of manipulating the inhabitants of their utopia into a state of harmony, happiness, and social and ecological equilibrium. Those opting for design utopias are often of the belief that physical design will automatically induce the desired behavior patterns.

Design utopias have been especially common in the nineteenth and twentieth centuries (Powell, 1971). In the present century many of their perpetrators have been influential architects operating in the master-builder tradition. As the grand design is normally the brainchild of a single person, designed utopias vary widely in form. This may be illustrated by the contrast between two utopias designed between the two World Wars.

Le Corbusier (1925) was beguiled by mass production and technological power, and their expression in airplanes and ships. His *Radiant City*, like these vehicles, was based on a functional purity of design. Totally constructed of standardized modules of reinforced concrete, the city was to be 95 percent open park, focusing upon a cluster of enormous towers in which all human functions would be carried on. Space, treated as if it were wholly undiffer-entiated, was ordered geometrically. The architect regarded the city as a machine, and defined a dwelling as a machine for living in. Moreover, the city machine was viewed aesthetically as an enormous freestanding sculpture. Almost no attention was given to the machine's three million inhabitants. Le Corbusier's ideas radically changed prevailing notions of design in favor of simplicity and clear statements of purpose enshrined in concrete, steel, and glass. His legacy is visible the world over in the shape of monotonous highrise slabs housing apartments and corporate offices.

Frank Lloyd Wright's vision was somewhat more humane. A rugged individualist with a strong belief in territoriality (Chapter 2) and rural values, Wright (1958) wished to provide every human being with a piece of ground with which he could identify himself. Unlike Le Corbusier, who used the automobile to centralize, Wright saw his *Broadacre City* as a decentralized automobile-based settlement with a minimum lot size of one acre. Furthermore, Wright concentrated his genius upon designing houses, the chief characteristic of which was a harmony between the built structure and its natural surroundings. In further contrast with Le Corbusier, Wright established the principle that the interior accommodation of human needs should take precedence over the exterior purity of architectural form (Twombley, 1974). But despite his more humane view and his stated willingness to allow urbanites time to adjust to his new order, Wright clearly saw himself as a messiah, hoping to redeem his fellow man through design, the spirit of which Twombley calls "a kind of therapeutic environmentalism."

This single-minded devotion to a single principle of design which will result in eternal human happiness is the distinguishing mark of architectural utopists. Few of them have followed the Wrightian trend. On the contrary, the tendency has almost always been toward the *megastructure,* an enormous self-contained building complex housing all human activities, of which Le Corbusier's Radiant City was but a prototype. To take a few examples only, Soleri (1969) envisions a future human state where all present urban problems have been solved and from which the profit motive has disappeared. The inhabitants of this utopia would be housed in *arcologies,* single three-dimensional structures several times the height of the Empire State Building and each housing one million people. An extension of this is the *Compact City* (Dantzig and Saaty, 1973) which heavily utilizes the vertical dimension and the elimination of day and night differences to create a compact, efficient megastructure. Buckminster Fuller (1967) is one of many architects who have suggested cities of one million people floating in the sea. Doxiadis (1968) looks forward to an *ecumenopolis,* a world city of superhuman dimensions.

Fortunately, perhaps, for those of us who might not fit the social and environmental mold prescribed by the post-Corbusier architectural utopists, utopias have seldom appeared on the earth in concrete form. The most thoroughgoing adaptation of Le Corbusier's urban design conceptions has been Brasilia, the new capital of Brazil set in the highland interior of that country. This city (Evenson, 1969, 108):

> comprises a cross-axial plan in which a sweeping motor freeway
> punctuates its intersection with a classically ordered government

axis by means of a multilevel transport center. Bordering the freeway are residential superblocks containing standardized apartment blocks set amid open space, while the business center near the hub is designed for unified high-rise building.

The planners of Brasilia have indeed obeyed Le Corbusier's injunction to bring sun, space, and greenery into the city. But the sun bakes the earth, the greenery languishes to brown, the open spaces are unused. One does not walk in Brasilia. The distances are too large, and the human spirit is dwarfed by endless horizontal space punctuated by enormous vertical blocks. Besides, the city was designed for the automobile, and pedestrians are at a discount. While the car-owning rich inhabit the central area, the poor painfully climb the steep red-earth freeway embankments to the bus station from whence buses carry them to the less planned satellite towns and squatters' shacks on the city fringe. If Brasilia was designed for people, only the well-to-do were considered; Brazil emphatically does not have a high level of automobile ownership.

But Brasilia was not primarily designed for people. It was built as an enormous sculpture, a symbolic statement to the effect that Brazil was abandoning its alien-dominated, coastal-oriented past and was forging a new identity through the conquest of its interior frontier. The architect, Lucio Costa, ignored appeals to build only after a careful study of the region had been made. Full of the arrogant certainty of the architectural utopist, he regarded the building of this total environment as "a deliberate act of possession, a gesture in the colonial tradition of the pioneers, of taming the wilderness" (Tuan, 1974, 171). The design of Brasilia is that of an airplane or a bird. In the words of Tuan: "Brasilia is a bird come down to earth, a new Jerusalem descending out of heaven from God." Few Brazilians seem to want to live there.

Le Corbusier, however, was perfectly capable of producing his own utopias. In 1951 the Punjab government gave him the opportunity to design Chandigarh, an entirely new government headquarters city "which would symbolize the essential functions of society as he understood it" (Khosla, 1971). As in Brasilia, the emphasis has again been placed on monumental government buildings between which no meaningful spatial relationship seems to exist (Jacobs, 1967). A rectilinear road pattern, the lack of relationship between housing and streets, the absence of scattered local community facilities, and wide avenues almost wholly empty of human life, bespeak a sense of rigidity and an overall drabness.

Whereas Brasilia is in plan like a bird, Le Corbusier laid out Chandigarh as a symbolic representation of the human body. A major lung of open space, the Leisure Valley, runs the whole length of Chandigarh. The vast open spaces provided, however, tend to remain unused because of climatic problems, the sheer walking distances involved, and the influence of high level bureaucrats which results in the expenditure of most park maintenance energy in high income sectors. Thus the well-to-do with lovely gardens also enjoy well-kept parks which they hardly need, whilst those of the less influential languish untended. Equally maldistributed is residential space. As in Brasilia, senior government officials, all with cars, live mostly within walking distance of their offices. Junior clerks and office cleaners, however, must suffer lengthy bus or bicycle journeys from the outskirts. Bureaucratic juggling has also ensured the location of most amenities within easy reach of the well-to-do. In terms of social interaction, surveys by Punjab University have shown that friendship and kinship ties do not coincide with the planned neighborhood sectors (Khosla, 1971).

The Master Planner

The essence of many forms of planning which fail to consult the user-client is embodied in the *master plan*. A master plan is a preconceived overall solution to a set of design problems. It is a blueprint which is meant to be followed come what may. Individuals must adapt. Too frequently, however, especially in utopian schemes, the master plan is based on unsound, idiosyncratic philosophical and social principles when formulated, and frequently fails to fulfil its promise when implemented. In both Brasilia and Chandigarh, for example, the master planners were renowned architects who succeeded in producing several remarkable individual buildings. In these cities, however, planning — which involves arranging relationships between many buildings and their users — degenerated into automobilism, open spacism, and monumentalism.

   Alexander (1966), in an examination of a large number of planned or actualized ideal cities including Chandigarh, a Solerian arcology, and many new towns, makes the point that all these plans are arranged in tree form, whereas a city is not a tree. By tree, he refers to a hierarchical arrangement of fragmented physical and social groupings in which individual units have no relationships with equals, only with items higher or lower in the hierarchy (Fig. 13.5). Such an authoritarian structure is eminently suitable for a military camp or a company town, where the chain of command from superior to inferior is symbolized in the physical plan. It is also suitable for a traditional society where friendship and kinship ties form closed units rooted in space, such as the neighborhood and village compound. In most modern cities, however, social relationships form a semilattice (Fig. 13.5) rather than a tree. We tend to live in a "nonplace urban realm" and our friends and relatives are scattered beyond the immediate vicinity of our homes (Chapter 4). Orderly minds, however, instinctively gravitate to the tree system with its absence of ambiguity, complexity, and overlap. In consequence, notes Alexander, the ideal cities we plan are doomed to failure because we are "trapped in a tree." If people succeed in living fulfilling lives in such environments it is in spite of the plan, rather than because of it.

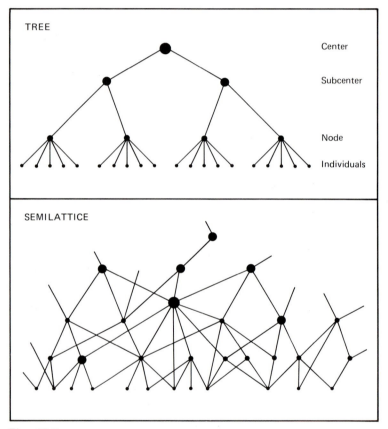

Fig. 13.5

Models of city structure and social relationships (after C. Alexander).

Orlans (1953), an early commentator on British new towns, agrees with Alexander that master planning, especially in its utopist form, founders because of its failure to consider what Tolstoy termed "the inexpressible complexity of everything that lives." Moreover, simple, generalized utopian plans are frequently based on a belief in the efficacy of technology in the solution of social as well as physical planning problems. The ideologies of

order, community, and design as a behavior determinant are related preoc-
cupations.

The master planner and his plan are, above all, inflexible. As Paul Simon
(1972) has sung:

> So long, Frank Lloyd Wright . . .
> Architects may come and
> Architects may go and
> Never change your point of view.*

Such inflexibility is especially disturbing in view of the master planner's
reliance on ideologies which provide no incentive for him to consult or
consider those who are to occupy his planned paradise. Those who oppose
The Plan are ignored or reprogrammed (Sommer, 1969), while "those who
impose it acquire special license from the splendor of the world they are
creating" (Petersen, 1966). Among modern social planners with such an *idée
fixe* one of the most extreme is Skinner (1971), who would modify our
behavior into socially valuable modes by means of a technology of behavior
which involves total control of the individual's environment. Skinner's
utopia, *Walden Two* (1948), was organized by a Board of Planners who exer-
cised totalitarian control over the community, ostensibly for the inhabitants'
own good. At this point design problems become irrelevant, for man can be
reshaped to fit whatever environment is created. The question then becomes
"not so much what sort of environment we want, but what sort of man we
want" (Sommer, 1969, 172).

Recent advances in technology and social engineering suggest that the
means for realizing eutopia are almost at hand. All we need is someone who
is right! In Skinner's utopia, as in Huxley's *Brave New World* (1955), everyone is
happy despite, or perhaps because of, the absence of the concept of freedom.
Yet the gut feeling of most individuals, one suspects, would be that any
manipulation of others, regardless of the goodness of the outcome, is a
violation of their essential humanity. At this stage of evolution, human beings
still require two basic freedoms, the right to be unhappy and the related right
to rebel.

The master planner who ignores these essential freedoms epitomizes
enlightened-elite planning, being chronically unaware that one man's dream
may be another's nightmare. Domes, sea cities, and megastructures emerge
from the fertile minds of the utopists, while citizens follow the superhighway
to a sprawling suburbia which is perhaps one step along the way to the
realization of Wright's Broadacre City. Such a wide conceptual separation of

---

*   "So Long, Frank Lloyd Wright." © 1969 Paul Simon. Used with permission.

the designer from the citizen is likely to result in ideological rigidification on the part of the planners, and infantilization on the part of the planned-for.

Further Reading

BROOKS, R. O. (1971), "Social Planning in Columbia," *Journal of the American Institute of Planners* 37: 373–79.

PORTEOUS, J. D. (1974), "Social Class in Atacama Company Towns," *Annals of the Association of American Geographers* 64: 409–17.

SCHAFFER, F. (1970), *The New Town Story*. London: Paladin Books.

ZEHNER, R. B. (1971), "Neighborhood and Community Satisfaction in New Towns and Less Planned Suburbs," *Journal of the American Institute of Planners* 37: 379–85.

14

PLANNING BY
AND WITH PEOPLE

Plan Man Can;
But no man, be he never so tyrannic or Panjandrian,
Neronian, Titonian, or vainly Ozymandian,
Arabian or Fabian, enchanted Kubla-Khanian,
Or Pan-Humanitarian, or Franc' Hispan-Falangian,
                    *Can Plan Man.**

                              Sir Frederic Osborn

The emperor Nero burned Rome with the intent of raising a more grandiose urban monument among its ashes. Enlightened elites have razed what they perceived to be unsatisfactory environments in order to provide inarticulate citizens with more suitable surroundings. Both autocracy and elitist paternalism are at a discount today. In the 1970s planners are increasingly displaying the symptoms of role confusion. The growth of citizen protest against the urban environment (Page, 1970), the rise of the public participation movement, the loss of credibility on the part of the expert (Meyerson, 1969), and increasing self-criticism have led many planners to question seriously their own values, assumptions, and goals. If planning *for* people is rejected, two paths are open. Planning may be accomplished *by* people, or the gap between the planners and the planned-for should be reduced so that planning *with* people becomes feasible. It should be noted that this chapter does not pretend to exhaustively cover all methods of planning by and with people which are presently in use. As throughout this book, the reader is encouraged to confirm, contradict, or modify its statements in the light of his or her own experience.

---

*   Sir Frederic Osborn (1959), *Can Man Plan? and Other Verses.* London: Harrap. Reprinted by permission.

Planning by People

Popular planning (Fig. 12.2) occurs when a group of nonprofessionals organize the planning and construction of large-scale urban building projects.
In contrast with the modern architect's concern with public buildings (Chapter 12), popular planners concentrate their energies almost wholly upon
housing environments. Citizen planning is hardly known in modern urban-
industrial states, where only a negligible proportion of the population is in
any way involved in its dwellings before their occupation. In complete contrast, environments planned by their inhabitants are a major element in the
residential areas of nonwestern cities. Moreover, whereas the individual in
Western society who builds his own house is concerned with his house alone,
in the Third World there is active cooperation in the planning of self-built
residential areas.

third-world squatters

Builders of what is frequently termed *uncontrolled urban growth* are generally
known as squatters. In South America, Asia, and Africa squatting is a response on the part of lower-income groups to their feeling of powerlessness
in the face of economic insecurity and the average person's inability to own or
control land. Contemporary urbanization in these areas is characterized by a
large and rapid flow of immigrants from rural areas to a few large cities in
each country. In contrast to conditions during the flood period of British and
North American urbanization, which occurred before World War I, the
modern migrant to a Third-World city is not likely to find either a permanent
job or a suitable dwelling for rent. Speculators and developers in the cheap
housing field do not exist on any scale in Third-World nations. Furthermore,
much land suitable for housing is held in large tracts by private owners or
government agencies. And much of this land is blatantly unused.

Urban squatting in the Third World therefore takes the form of the
conquest of unoccupied public or private land by the homeless or those living
in extremely overcrowded conditions in existing city slums. This land is
usually on the outskirts of major cities. Occupied in a body by a number of
squatters, the land is rapidly covered with a variety of makeshift shelters
constructed from reeds, cardboard cartons, oil drums, and any other available
material. With time, these ramshackle structures may be replaced by more
permanent buildings.

The sheer number of squatters in the Third World emphasizes the
failure of traditional economic and construction systems to provide basic
shelter for all. Squatter settlements, known variously as *barriadas* in Peru,
bidonvilles in North Africa, *geçekondu* in Turkey, and *bustees* in India, are

familiar to all who have ventured to the peripheries of major Third-World cities. Accurate figures are difficult to obtain, but estimates suggest that squatters make up between 20 and 50 percent of the populations of such cities as Manila (Philippines), Karachi (Pakistan), Istanbul (Turkey), Caracas (Venezuela), and Santiago (Chile), as well as numerous cities throughout Africa (Abrams, 1964). Squatters are also found in the remaining frontier regions of urban-industrial nations, as in cities close to Indian reservations in the American Southwest and around the larger settlements of the Canadian North (Lotz, 1965; Bucksar, 1970).

Among the policy makers of their respective countries squatters have a poor image. Squatting is usually illegal; the squatters have no rights to the land they occupy. Their settlements initially lack services, including piped water and sewerage. Coupled with high densities and overcrowding, these conditions constitute, in the eyes of public health officials, a fertile breeding ground for disease. Social welfare officials point to the high incidence of poverty, unemployment, disorientation, and alienation. Police officials find difficulty in imposing law and order, and taxation and planning officials bemoan the unplanned sterilization of land by persons too poor to pay taxes.

Such evaluations tend to regard the squatter as marginal to the mainstream of society. The huge squatter populations, however, are an inherent component of society in developing nations in that they form a vast pool of cheap labor on which manufacturing and service industries draw (McTaggart, 1971). The very abundance of this labor generally precludes any of the rights associated with labor in the Western world, such as job security, an efficient welfare system, unionization, and the right to decent housing.

Squatters, moreover, are frequently characterized as degraded misfits whose lives are nasty, brutish, and short. To be sure, slums of despair (Chapter 11) exist, their inhabitants eking out their existence from day to day in appalling conditions. More common, however, are the slums of hope, occupied by persons with valid aspirations who see squatting as their only hope for a decent dwelling in a society which can or will do nothing for them. Nor are squatting settlements wholly comprised of criminals and bloodthirsty revolutionaries, as many local newspapers would have us believe. Although the majority of squatters are of lower-income status, housing and land availability problems extend into the middle classes. It is not uncommon to find medical personnel, lawyers, teachers, policemen, and members of skilled trades building houses in squatter areas.

Negative stereotypes of squatters, however, have been supportive of one of the major techniques used to deal with them. This has simply involved an evacuation of the settlement by police, who then bulldoze down the painfully erected shacks and force the squatters to move on. The ineffectiveness of this slum-clearance approach has been apparent almost everywhere. The sheer number of squatters in any Third-World city makes police action a daunting task; there are about one million squatters in Calcutta, for example. In many countries squatters have become a potent political force which policymakers cannot afford to offend. Finally, the demolition of squatting areas is not even a temporary solution; as there is nowhere else to go, the squatters simply take over another area of unoccupied land.

There is nowhere else to go because traditional solutions to the housing problem do not work in underdeveloped countries. Attempts have been made to provide shelter in the form of conventional public-housing programs modeled on those operating in Europe and North America. The rents asked, however, albeit quite low, are often beyond the capacity of persons lacking permanent jobs. Such projects tend to cream off the higher-income levels among the squatters; as in North America (Chapter 11), urban renewal and public-housing schemes do not necessarily benefit those for whom they are ostensibly designed. Loans for conventional house building are also unavailable on a large scale, mainly because capital is scarce. Private housing development suffers from the same capital scarcity. All these schemes benefit the middle classes rather than the poor.

Where these schemes have been tried they have almost invariably failed to reduce the number of squatters by any significant proportion. Squatter settlement growth rates of over 12 percent per annum are common, twice the rate of world city growth as a whole, and five times the rate of world population increase (Turner, 1967). Squatters in Peru have done more city building in the last twenty years than was achieved during the previous four centuries. It has been estimated that at the present rate of squatter clearance and rehousing in conventional dwellings, the squatter settlements of Calcutta would take approximately one hundred years to clear (Van Huyck and Rosser, 1966). City development in the Third World is clearly out of control. The inescapable conclusion is that there is no alternative to the squatter settlement. Planners might therefore consider the positive aspects of self-built housing and attempt to incorporate it into the mainstream of urban development.

This realization has been slow to emerge. Although the social and administrative gap between planners and planned-for in the Western world is great (Chapter 12), in the Third World it is frequently an unbridgeable gulf. Speaking of a conflict between planners and people in Venezuela, an American anthropologist writes (Peattie, 1970, 87):

> the administrators are superior not only in power and position but also in social class to those whom they administer, and their feelings about the social class difference is such as to suggest notions of caste.

Planners, administrators, and engineers may therefore be unwilling even to meet with those they plan for. In Venezuela planners have only recently been allowed to include squatter settlements on their land-use maps (Johnson, 1971).

In recent years, however, there has been an increasing appreciation of the validity of the squatting process in the face of the abject failure of conventional housing programs. There are several positive aspects of squatting as it is now practised.

1. Self-built housing frees scarce capital for investment in other economic sectors. Construction generates very little other employment and does not earn overseas exchange. In contrast, investments which result in economic development increase employment security and thus encourage eventual investment in more conventional forms of housing.

2. Squatter housing requires no initial investment of labor or materials other than those provided by the squatter himself.

3. Squatter settlements are frequently built and maintained in a spirit of cooperation. Squatters have evolved highly sophisticated methods of communal land takeover, public facility provision, and self-policing (Andrews *et al.*, 1973). There is a considerable reservoir of initiative and organizational ability among squatters.

4. The extreme cheapness of squatter housing frees much of the small family income for food, essential material goods, and education.

5. Each family builds its dwelling at its own pace to suit its own needs. A rough shack of canes or flattened cardboard boxes may be transformed into a one- or two-story masonry dwelling over a period of more than ten years (Fig. 14.1). There is no mismatch between family and building as there would be if each family was provided with a standard government-built unit.

6. Finally, and perhaps most important of all, self-built housing provides the squatter with a concrete expression of his own initiative, effort, and achievement. In territoriality terms (Chapter 2) the squatter shack provides its owner with an identity.

The chief desire of the squatter is for acceptance, both legal and social. During the 1960s a number of countries, recognizing the inevitability of squatting, began to look upon it as a positive solution to current housing problems. Utilizing waste materials, providing their own labor, and with excellent organizational abilities, squatters require the minimum of direction in housing development. Their chief practical problems appear to be the acquisition of legal tenure to the land they occupy, and the installation of basic utilities and facilities such as sewerage, water supplies, and transportation to and from the city.

Calcutta has operated a *bustee* improvement program for some years. Public efforts consist largely of providing water, sewerage, storm drainage,

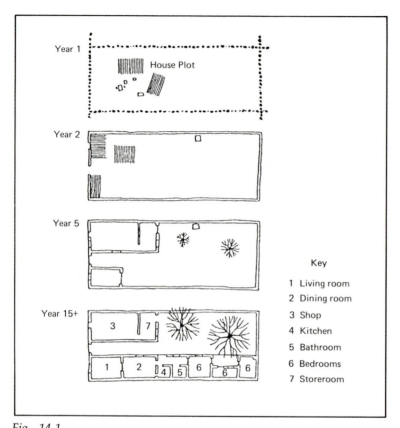

Fig. 14.1

Stages in squatter dwelling development, Peru. (Redrawn, by permission, from W. Mangin and J. Turner in *Progressive Architecture,* copyright 1968, Reinhold Publishing Corporation.)

street paving, and electricity connections. Several South American countries have set up informal agencies to help squatters plan their land invasions, secure legal tenure, and lay out efficient utility lines before house construction. The provision of basic housing shells (roof, columns, and a plumbing wall), as in Venezuela, is expensive and probably not necessary. A combination of these schemes has been adopted by the World Bank, which supports sites-and-services projects in several countries (Laquian, 1974).

squatting in the western world

There has been some speculation to the effect that self-help community development by the urban poor, as operated by Third-World squatters, could be a valid model for solving urban housing problems in Europe and North

America. This form of planning by people, with a minimum of government intervention, is certainly attractive because of its economic, social, and psychological advantages.

It is unlikely, however, that the squatter solution could be exported to the United States or countries with similar political and economic systems (Mangin and Turner, 1968). Several systematic differences between the urban-industrial world and the Third World make this point clear.

1.   Governments in the Third World are generally not strong enough to prevent the mass invasion of land by squatters. There is frequent acquiescence to squatting simply because so much land is government owned. More land is privately owned in urban-industrial nations, and governments are generally sufficiently powerful to prevent mass squatting.

2.   Squatters in the Third World tend to have the same social characteristics and cultural background as the vast bulk of the population. Lower-income groups make up the largest percentage of any Third-World society, and thus the goals of the squatter are readily apparent to the nonsquatter. In contrast, the urban poor in the United States are vastly outnumbered by the suburban middle class which differs markedly from them in life-style, attitudes, and racial composition.

3.   Further, the poor in urban-industrial nations are infantilized and controlled by welfare bureaucracies. They experience a feeling of overall powerlessness (Rein, 1967). Their Third-World counterparts, having no welfare system to turn to, are compelled to help themselves in collaboration with their fellows. The results of this autonomy include increased self-esteem, higher morale and self-confidence, and the collective achievement born of community creation.

4.   Finally, could the above problems be overcome, the would-be squatter in the Western world would find himself caught up in a maze of building codes and regulations which would effectively prevent the construction of the essence of the squatter's housing solution, a makeshift dwelling which is improved over the years according to the rhythm of the family's social and economic development. Though housing which was added to as children were born or married was once common in North America, the development of the nuclear family and of stringent building codes have all but ended this flexible mode of housing provision. Turner (1967) has shown how building and planning regulations, designed to improve modern housing standards, have exacerbated housing problems in the Third World. Middle-class administrators, with ideologies of neatness and completeness, exhibit rooted objections to the idea of permitting people to live in only partially completed environments.

Consequently, squatting in the Western world has not generally been creative in the sense that squatters have increased the housing stock. In contrast, squatting in North America and Europe usually involves the illegal occupation of abandoned or vacant buildings. Particularly in the United States, large numbers of houses in the inner city are being abandoned. The number of vacant buildings in Newark, New Jersey, totals approximately five percent of the total building stock (Sternlieb and Burchell, 1973). Other dwellings are condemned by the authorities as unfit for occupation. Although some cities, such as Baltimore, have instituted urban-homesteading programs, whereby vacant houses may be reoccupied at little or no cost, many officially vacant or condemned dwellings are taken over by squatters.

In New York squatters in condemned buildings demand the right to stay and point out that urban renewal will remove them from both their neighborhood and their nearby jobs (Jorgenson, 1971). In Greater London a variety of local, informal squatters' associations plan and carry out the occupation of buildings left vacant by order of various levels of government (Clare, 1973). In Boston low-income groups have occupied newly renovated apartment blocks, preventing the scheduled entry of higher-income tenants (Goodman, 1972). Legal strategies for community cooperation include the self-help service groups which are beginning to flourish in North American cities, most notably in the fields of education (community schools), transportation (car pools), and cooperative food buying (Ballabon, 1972). Some experiments in self-built housing have been attempted; students at the Davis campus of the University of California have achieved satisfaction, privacy, and a sense of community through the construction of their own housing (Corbett, 1973). The same trend is apparent among the inhabitants of the more successful communes.

Goodman regards these actions as *guerrilla architecture,* and admits that this will not solve housing or related social problems because it cannot be operationalized on the scale achieved by Third-World squatters. Guerrilla architecture, however, may be part of an overall strategy designed to demystify the planning profession, destroy the dependency relationship between planner and planned-for, and raise the consciousness of the user-client concerning both his rights and his needs.

Planning with People

Consciousness raising among both the citizen and the design profession is now ongoing in a wide variety of ways. The ultimate goal, an egalitarian inpert-expert relationship which might approximate to popular planning (Fig. 12.2), is far off. Several major planning trends, however, none of them without practical or philosophical faults, suggest that this goal has at least been identified as one worth aiming for.

planner activism

Since the early 1960s several government-directed attempts have been made to involve citizens in the planning process at the local level. The Model Cities program in the United States, the Neighborhood Improvement program in Canada, and the Community Development projects in Britain have been of this type (Carney and Taylor, 1974). Effective control, however, remains in the hands of government, and unfamiliarity with the bureaucratic system reduces both the capacity and the will of citizens to participate.

Systems which involve public consultation have also been instituted. However, when the public is considered in this manner its participation is generally limited to one of two forms (Fig. 14.2):

1. an attempt to adjust the public to a plan already formulated or in operation, a Procrustean process which leads to the realization of the planner's goal; or

2. a choice between a number of alternatives put forward by elite groups, resulting in a compromise goal.

The first strategy is illustrated by a recent study of urban transplantation in Chile (Porteous, 1972). A government-sponsored plan for the evacuation of about 18,000 persons from the isolated American-built mining towns of Sewell and Caletones to the provincial capital of Rancagua was put into operation between 1967 and 1971. The apparent goal was to integrate the miners, long accustomed to the restrictive, paternalist society of the company town (Porteous, 1970), into the mainstream of Chilean life. It was expected by the planners that company workers would be only too pleased to leave the rigors of Andean life at an altitude of 8,000 feet, where educational, recreational, and occupational opportunities were extremely limited and where paternalism resulted in the loss of individual initiative and therefore in the extreme dependence of the worker upon the company.

An attitudinal survey, however, revealed that over 15 percent of the population sampled were not willing to accept the transplant. Among other anxieties, they expressed concern about the time and cost of commuting from city to mine, the availability of education in Rancagua, and the higher cost of living and growth of family problems expected in the city (Table 14.1). One might hypothesize that class differences between staff and workers would account for some variation in response, but a Chi² statistical analysis showed no significant difference between the two groups in their attitudes to the problems involved in transplantation. It would seem that the difficulties of moving were anticipated equally by both classes of workers, the general unease about the outside world being a major unifying factor.

Regarding most of these anxieties as due to misinformation, the planners launched a massive information campaign throughout 1970. Transplan-

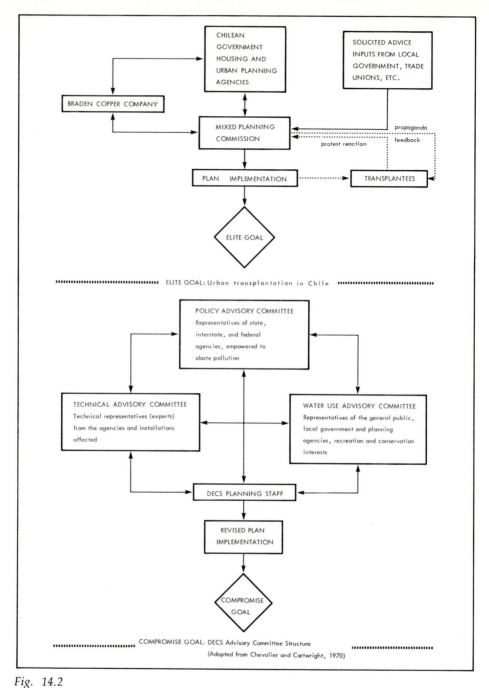

Fig. 14.2

Two forms of public participation in planning. (Reprinted from *Environment and Behavior* 3, No. 2 (June 1971), by permission of the publisher Sage Publications Inc.)

TABLE 14.1

EMPLOYEE ATTITUDES TO TRANSPLANTATION FROM
CALETONES TO RANCAGUA, CHILE, 1969–70

| | Respondents | | |
Problem Preventing Movement	Unskilled and Semiskilled	Skilled and Staff	Total
Not interested in public housing	30	9	39
Reasons pertaining to work (e.g., commuting)	26	7	33
Education	15	7	22
Cost of living	10	4	14
Movement possible under certain conditions (e.g., house size available)	11	3	14
Family problems	10	3	13
Hospitalization problems	6	2	8
No reason given for unwillingness to move	11	1	12
$n =$	119	36	155

Source: Porteous (1972)

tees were reassured by radio, television, films, and newspapers that the relocation, though not painless, would be beneficial in the long run. Social leaders were contacted and encouraged to speak positively about the relocation. This was particularly effective with women, who showed great concern about the education of their children. Meetings were set up where workers could ask questions and air their grievances. Through this token form of participation acquiescence was achieved and by 1974 the two towns were largely evacuated.

Where the public is given a choice between alternatives, public attitudes and opinions may receive more attention. The Delaware Estuary Comprehensive Study (DECS), as described by Chevalier and Cartwright (1970), included a system whereby channels were opened to facilitate the flow of proposals, reactions, and feedback among technical experts, power-wielding bodies, and public-interest groups. There was an attempt to incorporate the recommendations of all these groups into an information-recycling system which, after long debate, finally emerged with a suboptimal solution. Such a compromise solution, however, may in reality please no one. In the case of DECS, Alternative Plan III — according to the authors a "rational middle ground" — was considered the maximum permissible change by industry, as "reasonable" by local government and planning bodies, but only as "a step forward" by public-interest groups.

There are several problems relating to these consultative methods of public involvement. Identifying the public is an almost impossible problem. There is no guarantee that a public-interest group represents the public at large; indeed, the opposite is usually the case. Further, planners may welcome such consultative techniques as mere tokens of public involvement in a process where the planners retain ultimate control. Moreover, it is clear that many planners' view of the public is restricted to articulate middle-class groups. Burke, reviewing the means by which citizens may become involved in administration, favors those means which involve citizens who are representative of diverse groups, knowledgeable of issues, and influential in the community. This will achieve, in Burke's words, "a sense of participation and an opportunity for leadership" (1968, 293).

A similar preoccupation with elite groups among the public is exhibited by Broady (1968) and Masaldan (1965), both of whom have produced books incorporating the words *planning* and *people* into their titles. Indeed, Masaldan's aim is, like that of the Chilean planners discussed above, to secure public support for a plan already formulated. This is to be achieved through frequent discussion in professional circles and in newspapers! The failure to promote involvement by means of the media has been documented by Goodey (1974b). Somewhat more appropriate is *storefront planning,* where planning officials abandon their formal offices, occupy a vacant neighborhood store, and encourage passers-by to drop in and discuss plans that are likely to affect the neighborhood.

encounters

Planner activism frequently fails because of the involvement of only certain groups of citizens, because of problems of communication with less articulate groups, and because techniques such as consultation may be used as mere tokens of the participation needed to satisfy modern planning requirements. The problem of communication has been attacked in a number of ways. Encounter groups have been organized, whereby citizens confront designers in lengthy sessions which uncover both the assumptions of the expert and the needs of the inpert (Dempsey, 1972). Community development workshops, which employ many techniques besides confrontation, have facilitated communication between groups which otherwise would never make contact (Brill et al., 1970).

An important mode of encounter is simulation gaming, whereby players take roles in the development of a model city. Opportunities for self-realization occur when designers' roles are played by citizens and vice versa (Godschalk, 1970; Rose, 1972). Other games have been developed to acquaint both designer and citizen with the latters' often unrealized needs. The house design game, for example (Summers, 1972), involves the determination of family housing needs, the construction of a house based on those needs, and the simulation and evaluation of the operation of the house. At the neighborhood scale, Monopoly-like games have been used to determine what residents value most in their home area. Michelson (1966), for example, found that the personal utopias thus produced were not strongly individualistic. Indeed, a residential neighborhood of well-separated, single-family dwellings with a major shopping center nearby would serve the ideals of 30 percent of his sample. Such techniques, however, are limited by the public's unawareness of the full range of possibilities.

advocacy planning

The techniques already described are most likely to involve middle-class groups or those who already take an interest in planning. A large proportion of the population, however, is politically inactive or apathetic (Key, 1961; Milbrath, 1965), yet it is most likely this group that will be disturbed by major planning proposals such as highways and urban renewal (Chapters 11, 12). In an attempt to involve previously inarticulate lower income and minority groups in the planning process, and in particular to provide them with a means of expressing their interests, Davidoff (1965) suggested advocacy planning.

Advocacy planning essentially provides a communications link between politicians, planners, and citizens. Professional planners enter the political process by absorbing the values of the citizen group, and then using their technical abilities to argue for the interests of those who lack the expertise either to oppose existing plans or to propose their own. Through the expertise lent by the advocate such groups are provided with a voice which will be heard with respect in the councils of both planners and politicians. By this means user-clients are transformed into clients who retain their own expert. Advocacy planning became immediately popular in the mid-1960s, and it is suggested (Spiegel, 1968) that the process has reoriented planning from the designation of land for the placement of physical objects to a lively concern with human needs at the neighborhood level. Advocacy planning renders the planning process less remote, expands the options available to the client group, and promotes physical developments which are in accord with unique community life-styles. The founder of one of the first advocacy planning centers sums up the movement in his statement that though advocate planners are probably no more competent to plan than the average slum dweller, they are far better prepared to deal with the public agencies which are responsible for urban change and project funding.

Though an appealing concept, advocacy planning has received much criticism. The advocate, of course, is not always successful in achieving the aims of his client (Peattie, 1970). Frequently the advocate finds that his clients' main concern is to protest a highway project or an urban-renewal scheme (Skjei, 1972); action is thus limited merely to reaction and rarely involves creation. In some cases the values and technical interests of the advocate are more apparent in advocacy hearings than the needs of the clients who are supposedly represented by him (Peattie, 1968). Moreover, it is not always certain that the advocate can gain the trust of his clients, that he can detect accurately what they want, or that he can resist manipulating them into demanding what he thinks they need. Local groups are frequently myopic and often fail to realise that certain issues cannot be treated on a decentralized, local basis (Meyerson, 1969). Advocacy also proceeds on the false assumption that local communities are homogeneous groups with common needs. Finally, Goodman (1972, 236) opposes advocacy because it fails to promote effective citizen control of the processes which affect their lives, it leads to no radical alteration of overall policies, and it "induces people to accept the bureaucratic norms of present social institutions."

One solution to the above objections to the representation of groups by advocates would be for people to represent themselves. A number of authors (Babcock and Bosselman, 1968; Barwig *et al.*, 1972) have suggested neighborhood centers where citizen-generated planning ideas could be worked out and where decisions might be made about zoning, densities, housing, open space, and related issues by citizen boards. The problems involved in such a concept are legion; they include entrenched opposition to the evolution of a local tier of urban government in areas where the ward system is not used, fears of the control of such boards by unrepresentative groups, the difficulty of identifying neighborhoods and achieving consensus (Chapter 4), and the inevitable need for the technical expertise of the professional planner.

open-ended design

This approach is the one most closely related to the process of physical design. The concept of open-endedness or indeterminacy in design relates strongly to the general human preference for complexity and ambiguity (Chapter 9). It also relates to the satisfactions achieved through personal involvement in dwelling construction and community development, as found among Third-World squatters. It is a rejection of the totally designed environment as expressed in the total institution (Chapter 13). Design indeterminacy essentially involves the provision of basic structures and layouts by architects and planners, and the completion of these by the occupants. Basic provision may include almost total construction, with basement and attic rooms left unfinished and blank public walls provided for community artwork, or the erection of a simple housing shell which is substantially modified by the resident.

Open-ended design has been studied in several environments (Rapoport, 1970), and the concept appears to have merit at all three levels of territoriality (Chapter 2–5). Open-endedness facilitates personalization of space through personal involvement in environmental manipulation (Sommer, 1968b). The classic study of microscale neighboring by Festinger *et al.* (1950) discovered that social organization was enhanced in unfinished surroundings, which provided a focus for cooperation and interest. Sieverts (1969) suggests that open-endedness leads to increased involvement with the environment which in turn promotes imageability. Above all, indeterminacy promotes flexibility and choice. As yet, open-endedness has been most successful in housing and office environments, and has been partially responsible for the apparent success of the Chilean relocation described earlier in this chapter.

Participation or Control

Since the early 1960s the planning process has experienced a period of drastic change. Under pressure from organized protest groups (Chapter 12), and from members of the planning profession (Slayton and Dewey, 1953), decision makers have increasingly come to accept the possibility that citizens should take both passive (Chapter 12) and active roles in planning. Some theorists would go beyond citizen participation, however, to citizen control. Arnstein (1969) has formulated an eight-rung ladder of participation in which the height of the rung corresponds to the citizen's power to determine planning decisions (Fig. 14.3). The bottom two rungs describe types of nonparticipation which are designed to educate or cure the citizen, as in the Chilean relocation described above. The next three rungs are forms of tokenism which allow participants to air their concerns but provide no assurance of satisfaction. Only the upper rungs provide for citizen power.

In this formulation, participation becomes little more than the struggle of those without power to take over control from the power elite (Kasperson and Breitbart, 1974). There is no indication of the need of the citizen controllers for the designer's expertise. Recent experience with participation, moreover, has produced a number of valid criticisms of citizen involvement.

1.   Lack of political and technical prowess among community groups makes them easy prey for co-optation by politicians or bureaucracies (Ley, 1974). Co-optation involves the neutralization of opposition by including dissenters as participants without surrendering control over the decision-making process.

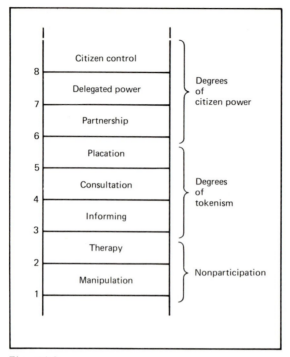

Fig. 14.3

Citizen participation. (Redrawn from S. Arnstein, "A Ladder of Citizen Participation," *Journal of the American Institute of Planners* 35, July 1969, by permission of the author and the *Journal.*)

2.   Community groups are frequently undisciplined in their pursuit of goals, and are frequently torn by internal dissension or conflict with potential allies, usually over issues of status.

3.   In participation situations one or more nonrepresentative, self-interest groups is often able to manipulate the decision process to serve its own ends (Reynolds, 1969; Simmie, 1971).

4.   Lack of expertise, inertia, and fear of the results of novel proposals impel citizens to oppose whatever is proposed (Wilson, 1963; Davies, 1966; Clavel, 1968; Lemon, 1974). The goals pursued by citizen participation thus tend always toward the preservation of the status quo.

5.   Interest groups veto each others' proposals because it is always easier to organize resistance than to reach agreement. Full participation is often a prescription for nondecision or may lead to wasteful delays in implementation (Hardwick and Hardwick, 1974). Meyerson (1969) suggests that the greater the amount of citizen participation, the less the likelihood that positive action will be taken.

6. As already suggested in this chapter, the myopia of local groups may prevent or irretrievably delay the formulation or implementation of city-wide or long-range plans.

7. It is likely that, given the existing sociopolitical system, nonparticipants will always form the bulk of the population. On these grounds radical planners suggest that participation is a diversion from the primary goal, that of changing existing institutions (Goodman, 1972).

On both pragmatic and ethical grounds, however, public participation is likely to be embraced increasingly by planners, politicians, and public, not least because it is now eminently fashionable in bureaucratic circles. In pragmatic terms, public participation requires consideration because pressures for it are likely to intensify. Further, through this process designers will become most vividly aware of the needs of those they design for. On ethical grounds, public participation recognizes the right of people to make some input into decisions which affect them. Participation, moreover, is said to have beneficial effects upon both individual and society (C.O.G.P., 1972), including the broadening of the intellect, the enhancement of self-esteem, the promotion of independence and initiative, improved sensitivity to the needs of others, greater political equality for the underprivileged, greater involvement in and responsibility for decisions on the part of the public, and the provision of a permanent and effective counterweight to the power of politician and bureaucrat.

It is unlikely, however, that full participatory democracy in planning will ever be achieved. Because of its unwieldiness, we are uncertain that it should even be regarded as a goal. In large populations, citizen control is likely to unbearably delay decision making. The goal should rather be to achieve varied forms of collaboration between expert and inpert based on mutual trust (Mitchell, 1974). The minimum requirement, however, is opportunity to participate and encouragement to do so. The latter could well be enhanced by effective design training for the public. Several planning workbooks have already been designed to help community residents decide what they want in their neighborhood and to prepare proposals for the implementation of such changes (Dixon, 1969). Workbooks designed to promote environmental sensitivity in children have also appeared (G.F.E.E., 1970) and a wide range of alternatives for environmental education are being explored (Swan, 1971).

Environmental education and consciousness raising among the public, however, need to be matched by similar procedures designed to enhance the awareness of planners and politicians. Thus while education for participation is a long-term strategy, short-term tactics such as advocacy planning, confrontation, and open-ended design will, despite their faults, be required in the interim. In particular, until the problems inherent in citizen participation have been resolved, passive citizen involvement in the form of pre- and post-design evaluation (Chapter 12) should continue to be a major input into the design process (Marans and Lansing, 1969).

It is impossible as yet to design any ultimate model for public participation in the planning process. Implementation mechanisms for citizen involvement are now evolving. Hopefully, they will stress not uniformity but flexibility and choice. An assessment of the state of the art in 1976 would likely reveal no general agreement on ways, means, or ends. What is significant is that new attitudes have emerged on the part of both planner and citizen.

It should no longer be possible for the planner to take the elitist view and boldly state: "The planner must understand people and anticipate their every need" (Schaffer, 1970, 70). Nor should the citizen continue to act as a Cheerful Robot (Mills, 1959), always willing to accept environmental change by delegating his responsibility to the expert with the phrase: "Of course, I'm not in a position to criticize" (Betjeman, 1971, 12). There is no need, however, for the citizen to become a controller or a technical expert. Rather, he should be able to articulate his own needs and to distinguish between the designer's technical advice and the designer's personal judgments. If these goals were achieved, together with a better understanding of the nature of human behavior in the urban environment, both inpert and expert might be able to collaborate in the realization of the most suitable designs for tomorrow's cities. As Alcaeus of Lesbos recognized nearly three thousand years ago:

> Not houses finely roofed nor the stones of walls well-builded;
> nay, nor canals and dockyards make a city, but men able to use
> their opportunity.

Those who fail to use their opportunity may continue to get the environments they deserve.

Further Reading

GOODMAN, R. (1972), *After the Planners.* New York: Simon & Schuster.

KASPERSON, R. E. and M. BREITBART (1974), *Participation, Decentralization, and Advocacy Planning.* Washington, D.C.: Association of American Geographers.

PEATTIE, L. (1970) *The View from the Barrio.* Ann Arbor: University of Michigan Press.

TURNER, J. C. (1967), "Barriers and Channels for Housing Development in Developing Countries," *Journal of the American Institute of Planners* 33: 167–81.

APPENDIX: SOURCES

Sources for the study of the interdisciplinary interface between behavior, environment, and design are widely scattered and often difficult to locate. Those readily available are categorized as follows:

A. **Critiques** Includes reviews of the nature of man-environment relations, environmental psychology, etc., extensive general research and literature reviews, and attempts to provide philosophical and structural underpinnings for the emerging discipline.

B. **Readers** Major collections of relevant articles and reports, often reprinted from journals, and usually strictly edited.

C. **Bibliographies** Structured compilations of articles, monographs, and reports, frequently with annotations.

D. **Journals** Periodicals which frequently contain articles relevant to the field.

E. **Conference proceedings** Collections of papers delivered at conferences, usually loosely edited.

F. **Organizations** Institutions which support research, hold conferences, disseminate information, and publish journals or proceedings.

G. **Information systems** Sources of information on publications, researchers, and data.

H. **Directories** Lists of scholars actively engaged in research in the area.

I. **Techniques** Sources which specialize in design-related behavioral research methodology.

Categories of Sources

A. Critiques

1. I. ALTMAN (1975), *The Environment and Social Behavior.* Monterey, Calif.: Brooks/Cole. Detailed analysis of privacy, personal space, territory, and crowding. Concentrates wholly on microspace, i.e., "the family, a pair of people, or other small social groups" (p. 2). Good review of human territoriality at this level.

2. D. CANTER (1975), *Psychology for Architects,* New York: Halsted Press. Short introduction to psychological concepts and techniques relevant for architectural design.

3. K. H. CRAIK (1970), "Environmental Psychology," *New Directions in Psychology,* Vol. 4, pp. 1–121. New York: Holt, Rinehart & Winston. Major initial attempt to review the field. Especially useful for exploration of the psychology-geography interface, and for discussion of research methodologies ranging from experimentation to aesthetic appreciation of environment. Good coverage of nonurban environment. Lacks coherent structure, however. Excellent preparatory reading.

4. C. M. DEASY. (1974), *Design for Human Affairs.* New York: Schenkman/Halsted Press. Attempt to show how architectural design and planning can be made more responsive to human needs through behavioral research.

5. E. T. HALL (1966), *The Hidden Dimension.* Garden City, N.Y.: Doubleday. A rather personal view of the importance of spatial relationships in human behavior.

6. C. MERCER (1975), *Living in Cities: Psychology and the Urban Environment.* London: Penguin Books. Brief overview of much of the urban MER area, but with a "specifically psychological perspective" (p. 9) rather than an interdisciplinary approach. Chapter 3 is a useful critique of prevailing trends in traditional psychology.

7. W. MICHELSON (1970), *Man and His Urban Environment: A Sociological Perspective.* Reading, Mass.: Addison-Wesley. Important attempt to summarize the literature, mainly from a sociological viewpoint, up to 1969. Good summary in the form of 24 generalizable findings of value to designers.

8. C. PERIN (1970), *With Man in Mind: An Interdisciplinary Prospectus for Environmental Design.* Cambridge, Mass.: M. I. T. Press. An argument for interdisciplinary research to bring behavioral science concepts into the forefront of environment design practice. The concept of "behavioral circuits" is put forward as a framework for bridging the gap between what we design and what we want.

9. J. D. PORTEOUS (1971), "Design With People: The Quality of the Urban Environment," *Environment and Behavior* 3: 155–78. Uses a micro-meso-macro space scalar model for organizing environmental behavior and contains section on People and Planning.

10. A. RAPOPORT (1970), "Observations Regarding Man-Environment Studies," *Man-Environment Systems* 1: P1(1–28). Good short introduction to field from the designer's point of view. Exceptionally condensed.

11. T. SAARINEN (1969), *Perception of Environment*. Washington, D.C.: Association of American Geographers Resource Paper 5. Geographer's viewpoint, where *perception* is a catch-all term for the behavior-environment interface. Organized on scalar lines, from personal space, through the city as a whole, to the country and the world.

12. R. SOMMER (1974), *Tight Spaces: Hard Architecture and How to Humanize It*. Englewood Cliffs, N.J.: Prentice-Hall. Designed environments, unresponsive to human needs, are shown to dehumanize their inhabitants. Solutions are proposed.

13. Y-F. TUAN (1972), "Environmental Psychology: A Review," *Geographical Review* 62: 245–56. Interesting, lengthy review of and commentary on Proshansky, H. M., W. H. Ittelson, and L. G. Rivlin (1970), *Environmental Psychology*.

14. Y-F. TUAN (1974), *Topophilia*. Englewood Cliffs, N.J.: Prentice-Hall. "A study of environmental perception, attitudes, and values" (subtitle). Cultural and philosophical approach to environmental appreciation, with a good understanding of psychology-geography interrelationships. Urban chapters, however, are weak.

15. J. F. WOHLWILL (1970), "The Emerging Discipline of Environmental Psychology," *American Psychologist* 25: 303–12. Review of sudden growth of interest by psychologists in environmental studies. Discussion of benefits of such an approach, and the problems involved in researching the area.

16. J. ZEISEL (1975), *Sociology and Architectural Design*. New York: Russell Sage Foundation, Social Science Frontiers 6. Concentrates primarily on developing strategies for improving design methodology through the incorporation of social science techniques and perspectives.

B. Readers

1. G. BELL and J. TYRWHITT (1972), *Human Identity in the Urban Environment*. London: Pelican Books. Forty-five reprints from *Ekistics* (itself mainly a journal of reprints). Sections 2–4 are most useful. A sixth section on urban Japan.

2. L. DUHL (1963), *The Urban Condition*. New York: Simon & Schuster. An early collection of 29 papers, many previously presented at the

American Orthopsychiatric Association Conference in 1962. Strong emphasis on urban renewal and public housing problems, and on social action.

3. P. W. ENGLISH and R. C. MAYFIELD (1972), *Man, Space, and Environment: Concepts in Contemporary Human Geography*. New York: Oxford University Press. Sections 1–3 most valuable for papers by Lowenthal, Tuan, and Gould.

4. W. R. EWALD (1967), *Environment for Man: The Next Fifty Years*. Bloomington: Indiana University Press. Chiefly useful for the papers by Alexander and Carr. Strong physical planning orientation.

5. H. J. GANS (1968), *People and Plans: Essays on Urban Problems and Solutions*. New York: Basic Books. Collection of Gans' own articles. Wide coverage of themes from determination of behavior by physical environment to urban renewal and suburban problems.

6. R. GUTMAN (1972), *People and Buildings*. New York: Basic Books. A very useful selection of 26 articles, tightly organized in five sections. One of the best readers in this area.

7. R. GUTMAN and D. POPENOE (1970), *Neighborhood, City and Metropolis: An Integrated Reader*. New York: Random House. Attempts to relate sociological theory to social action through the planning process. Only about one fifth of the 60 articles are environmentally relevant.

8. E. JONES (1975), *Readings in Social Geography*. London: Oxford University Press. Part Two (concepts of space) has six useful reprints. A few others (e.g., Gans) are also relevant.

9. R. W. KATES and J. F. WOHLWILL (1966), *Man's Response to the Physical Environment*. Vol. 22, No. 4 of *Journal of Social Issues*. The thirteen papers include some of the classics of the field, much reprinted elsewhere.

10. J. LANG, C. BURNETTE, W. MOLESKI, and D. VACHON (1974), *Designing for Human Behavior: Architecture and the Behavioral Sciences*. Stroudsburg, Pa.: Dowden, Hutchinson & Ross. Important summaries of architecturally relevant behavioral research, research methodologies, and major issues such as the relationship between designer and designed-for.

11. H. M. PROSHANSKY, W. H. ITTELSON, and L. G. RIVLIN (1970), *Environmental Psychology: Man and His Physical Setting*. New York: Holt, Rinehart & Winston. Monumental collection of 65 reprinted papers, held together by lengthy section introductions by the editors. Six sections, from theory and psychological processes to planning and methodology. Many classics of the field; some unusual inclusions. Strong institutional bias, notably toward hospital research.

12. J. H. SIMS and D. D. BAUMANN (1974), *Human Behavior and the Environment: Interactions between Man and his Physical World*. Chicago: Maaroufa Press. Eighteen articles, many dealing with the nonurban

environment. Seven are appropriate to the study of behavior in the built environment.

13. J. F. WOHLWILL and D. H. CARSON (1972), *Environment and the Social Sciences: Perspectives and Applications.* Washington, D.C.: American Psychological Association. Twenty-three papers include sections on crowding, institutions, residential areas, and decision making.

C. Bibliographies

1. G. BELL, E. RANDALL, and J. E. R. ROEDER (1973), *Urban Environments and Human Behavior: An Annotated Bibliography.* Stroudsburg, Pa.: Dowden, Hutchinson & Ross. Comprehensive bibliography compiled from summaries of relevant literature (to 1972) by 37 graduate design students. Because of the large number of contributors, annotations suffer from unevenness of quality. Many references are incomplete and there are numerous typographical and other errors. Nevertheless, a well-organized and very useful work, quite the best in the field.

2. J. D. HARRISON (1969), *An Annotated Bibliography on Environmental Perception with Emphasis on Urban Areas.* Monticello, Ill.: Council of Planning Librarians Exchange Bibliography 93. Somewhat derivative and only partially annotated.

3. M. HEYMAN (1964), "Space and Behavior: A Selected Bibliography," *Landscape* 13: 4–10. An early attempt, comprising 36 annotated selections.

4. J. A. JAKLE (1970), *The Spatial Dimensions of Social Organization: A Selected Bibliography for Urban Social Geography.* Monticello, Ill.: Council of Planning Librarians Exchange Bibliography 118. Strongly oriented toward geographical contributions of an urban nature. Not annotated.

5. R. MONTGOMERY (1969), *A General Booklist on Urban Design.* Monticello, Ill.: Council of Planning Librarians Exchange Bibliography 84. Short, clear annotations of urban design classics from Le Corbusier to Lynch.

6. D. E. MORRISON, K. E. HORNBACK, and W. K. WARNER (1974), *Environment: A Bibliography of Social Science and Related Literature.* Washington, D.C.: U.S. Environmental Protection Service. Nearly 5,000 items, mostly related to the nonurban environment, but with urban sections. Not annotated.

In addition, some of the readers cited in this bibliography contain bibliographies of varying length, the best being in Gutman (1972) and Lang *et al.* (1974).

Further bibliographies of topical interest have been published in the Exchange Bibliography series of the Council of Planning Librarians (Mrs. Mary Vance, Editor, P.O. Box 229, Monticello, Illinois 61856, U.S.A.).

This series is now approaching its one-thousandth bibliography. For example, recent topical bibliographies include the following personality-cult issues:

No. 676. *The New York School of Environmental Psychology* (Ittelson, Proshansky, *et al.*), 1974, by P. Bycroft.

No. 677. *Kenneth Craik's Environmental Psychology*, 1974, by T. Ottar.

No. 678. *Irving Altman's Environmental Psychology*, 1974, by R. Mathews.

No. 679. *David Canter's Architectural Psychology*, 1974, by N. Higginbottom.

D. Journals

1. Key periodicals which invariably include articles of relevance for the behavior-environment-design interface include:

   Design and Environment (R C Publications, 6500 Goldsboro Road, Washington, D.C. 20034, U.S.A.).

   Environment and Behavior (Sage Publications, 275 South Beverly Hills, Calif. 90212, U.S.A.).

   Journal of the American Institute of Planners (917 15th St. N.W., Washington, D.C. 20005, U.S.A.).

2. Other journals of major importance are:

   American Journal of Sociology (University of Chicago Press, 5750 Ellis Avenue, Chicago, Ill. 60037, U.S.A.).

   Ekistics (P.O. Box 571, Athens 136, Greece).

   Landscape (Box 7177, Landscape Station, Berkeley, Calif. 74707, U.S.A.).

   Man-Environment Systems (A.S.M.E.R., P. O. Box 57, Orangeburg, N.Y. 10962, U.S.A.).

   Town Planning Review (Liverpool University Press, 123 Grove St., Liverpool 7, England).

3. Journals directed mainly at the design professional but which have carried articles on design research include:

   Architectural Association (A.A.) *Quarterly* (U.K.-U.S.A.).

   Architectural Design (U.K.).

   Architectural Forum (U.S.A.).

   Architectural Psychology Newsletter (U.K.).

   Architecture Plus (U.S.A.).

   Built Environment (U.K.).

   Design Methods Group Newsletter (U.S.A.).

Environment and Planning (U.K.).

Forma (U.K.).

Journal of Architectural Research (U.K.-U.S.A.).

Journal of the Town Planning Institute (U.K.).

Progressive Architecture (U.S.A.).

Town and Country Planning (U.K.).

4. More than fifty other journals occasionally include relevant articles. For a list of these, see Bell *et al.* (1973) pp. 244–5. To this list should be added:

Annals of the Association of American Geographers (U.S.A.).

Area (U.K.).

Habitat (Canada).

Human Ecology (U.S.A.).

Human Factors (U.S.A.).

Journal of Social Issues (U.S.A.).

Milieu (U.S.A.).

Professional Geographer (U.S.A.).

Psychology Today (U.S.A.).

Scientific American (U.S.A.).

Sociometry (U.S.A.).

Trans-Action (U.S.A.).

E. Conference Proceedings

1. J. ARCHEA and C. EASTMAN (1970), *Proceedings of the Second Environmental Design Research Association Conference.* Pittsburgh: Carnegie Mellon University/EDRA 2.
2. W. D. BLISS (1975), *Proceedings, Symposium on Environmental Effects on Behavior.* Bozeman, Montana: Environmental Design Group of the Human Factors Society and Montana State University.
3. C. BURNETTE (1971), *Architecture for Human Behavior.* Philadelphia: American Institute of Architects.
4. D. CANTER (1970), *Architectural Psychology: Proceedings of the Conference held at Dalandhui, University of Strathclyde.* London: RIBA Publications.
5. B. HONIKMAN (1971), *Proceedings of the Architectural Psychology Conference at Kingston Polytechnic.* London: Kingston Polytechnic and RIBA Publications.
6. R. KULLER (1974), *Architectural Psychology: Proceedings of the Lund Conference.* Stroudsburg, Pennsylvania: Dowden, Hutchinson & Ross.

7. W. J. MITCHELL (1972), *Environmental Design: Research and Practice*. Los Angeles: University of California/EDRA 3–AR 8 (2 vols.).
8. W. F. E. PREISER (1973), *Environmental Design Research* (EDRA 4). Stroudsburg, Pennsylvania: Dowden, Hutchinson & Ross (2 vols.).
9. H. SANOFF and S. COHN (1970), *Proceedings of the First Environmental Design Research Association Conference*. Raleigh, N.C.: North Carolina State University/EDRA 1.
10. C. W. TAYLOR, R. BAILEY, and C. H. H. BRANCH (1967), *Second National Conference on Architectural Psychology*. Salt Lake City: University of Utah.

F. Organizations

1. American Institute of Architects (AIA)
   1735 New York Avenue NW
   Washington, D.C. 20006, U.S.A.

   Carries out research projects; publishes working papers; research clearing house; holds annual Architect-Researchers' Conference (1972, jointly with EDRA); publishes *Journal of Architectural Research* jointly with RIBA.

2. American Psychological Association (APA)
   1200 17 Street NW
   Washington, D.C. 20036, U.S.A.

   Recently established a Task Force on Environment and Behavior, with a newsletter of that name (W. White, editor).

3. American Sociological Association (ASA)
   1722 N Street NW
   Washington, D.C. 20336, U.S.A.

   Recently established an ad hoc committee on environmental sociology, with a liason with AIA. Annual meetings.

4. Association of American Geographers
   1710 16 St. NW
   Washington, D.C. 20009, U.S.A.

   Holds annual meetings with several relevant sessions; publishes *Annals of the Association of American Geographers*, Conference *Proceedings*, and *Professional Geographer* as well as an issue-oriented *Resource Paper* series.

5. Association for the Study of Man-Environment Relations (ASMER)
   P.O. Box 57
   Orangeburg, N.Y. 10962, U.S.A.

   Holds sessions at the annual meetings of the American Association for the Advancement of Science; compiles the *International Directory of*

Behavior and Design Research; publishes *Man-Environment Systems* (with Canadian and U.S. regional issues).

6. Environmental Design Research Association (EDRA)
P.O. Box 23129
L'Enfant Plaza Station
Washington, D.C. 20006, U.S.A.

Holds yearly conferences with comprehensive published proceedings.

7. Human Factors Society (Environmental Design Group)
P.O. Box 1369
Santa Monica, California 90406.

Held first conference, with published proceedings, in 1975.

8. Royal Institute of British Architects
66 Portland Place
London W1N 4AD, England.

Holds conferences; publishes *RIBA Journal;* coordinates research; publishes *Journal of Architectural Research* jointly with AIA.

G. Information Systems

For information retrieval systems, data banks, journal abstracts, research indexes, etc., see W. F. E. Preiser (1974), *Research on Architecture and Human Behavior.* Monticello, Ill.; Council of Planning Librarians Exchange Bibliography 673.

H. Directories

1. The first directory in the field, providing an interdisciplinary listing of about two hundred scholars, was: *1967 Directory of Behavior and Environmental Design* (Research & Design Institute, Providence, Rhode Island, U.S.A.).

2. The latest comprehensive directory is: *International Directory of Behavior and Design Research* (A.S.M.E.R., P.O. Box 57, Orangeburg, N.Y. 10962, U.S.A.).

I. Techniques

No single research paradigm exists for the study of human behavior in the urban setting. In the present state of the art a great variety of approaches is being used. Design researchers have themselves been engaged in behavioral research approaches as various as controlled experiments with laboratory rats and the self-reportage of subjective feelings toward buildings or spaces. Social scientists engaged in design-related research have brought with them a battery of traditional techniques, including experimentation, gaming, interviews, observation, and questionnaires. Recording structure varies from the phenomenological ("This is what I feel about . . . ") to tightly controlled experiments in artificial environments. Equipment ranges from pencil-and-paper or tape recorder, for the recording of impressions, to complex arrays of traveling cameras and hodometers which accurately record human movements in space. Moreover, approaches vary according to degree of manipulation of the subject, from minimal (observation) to maximal (experimentation).

A single source giving a complete overview of design-related behavioral research methods is not yet available. However, a number of sources present and discuss a significant array of techniques for the elicitation of behavioral data.

1. T. L. BURTON and G. E. CHERRY (1970), *Social Research Techniques for Planners.* London: George Allen and Unwin. Introduction to social surveys for planning purposes. Intensive review of questionnaire design, sampling techniques, and data analysis.

2. D. CANTER (1974), *Psychology for Architects.* London: Applied Science Publishers. Chapter 6 considers a number of techniques useful in architectural research.

3. K. H. CRAIK (1970), "Environmental Psychology," *New Directions in Psychology,* Vol. 4, pp. 1–121. New York: Holt, Rinehart & Winston. This lengthy review of the state of environmental psychology up to 1970 is interspersed with discussions and examples of varied methodologies (notably pp. 8–12, 21–41). On pp. 65–95 is presented a detailed research paradigm for research on the comprehension of environment, with discussion of environmental dimensions, observers, media of presentation of the environment, and response formats for data elicitation.

4. J. LANG, C. BURNETTE, W. MOLESKI, and D. VACHON, eds. (1974), *Designing for Human Behavior: Architecture and the Behavioral Sciences.* Stroudsburg, Pa.: Dowden, Hutchinson & Ross. Part Three contains nine papers on methodology, including observation; surveys, questionnaires, and interviews; unobtrusive measures; experimentation; and various building evaluation techniques.

5. W. MICHELSON, ed. (1975), *Behavioral Research Methods in Environmental Design.* New York: Halsted Press. Rather than an evaluation of a wide range of techniques by one or two authors, this work comprises several detailed discussions of specific approaches. These include pencil-and-paper tests, observation, time budget studies, and photographic recording techniques.

6. W. J. MITCHELL, ed. (1972), *Environmental Design: Research and Practice.* Los Angeles: University of California/EDRA 3–AR 8 (2 vols.). Like

other EDRA proceedings, these volumes contain many discussions of techniques in behavioral research.

7. G. T. MOORE, ed. (1970), *Emerging Methods in Environmental Design and Planning.* Cambridge, Mass.: M.I.T. Press. Proceedings of the first international conference of the Design Methods Group. Heavily structured toward the physical environment, theoretical issues, and engineering solutions.

8. H. M. PROSHANSKY, W. H. ITTELSON, and L. G. RIVLIN, eds. (1970), *Environmental Psychology: Man and His Physical Setting.* New York: Holt, Rinehart, & Winston. Although many of the 65 papers in this volume give full details of the techniques used, Part Six (Methods in Environmental Research) contains six papers chosen to illustrate divergent methods. Not all of them are specific discussions of techniques, however.

9. R. SOMMER (1972), *Design Awareness.* Corte Madera, Calif.: Rinehart Press. Contains the "New Evaluator Cookbook," a compendium of techniques for design evaluation.

10. E. J. WEBB, D. T. CAMPBELL, R. D. SCHWARTZ, and L. SECHREST (1966), *Unobtrusive Measures: Nonreactive Research in the Social Sciences.* Chicago: Rand McNally. A collage, often amusing, of techniques for the elicitation of behavioral data without interfering with or manipulating the subject. Techniques vary from the recording of noseprints on glass to sophisticated hidden hardware. Major emphasis is on archival records and observation, but some commentary on questionnaires and other reactive methods.

11. Other sources, notably *Man-Environment Systems*, frequently contain reviews of methods. *Design and Environment, Environment and Behavior*, the *Design Methods Group Newsletter*, and the British Conference proceedings edited by Canter (1970) and Honikman (1971) are also useful.

REFERENCES

ABBOT, E. A. (1884), *Flatland*. Republished (1952), New York: Dover.

ABERNATHY, W. D. (1968), "The Importance of Play," *Town and Country Planning* 36: 471–75.

ABRAMS, C. (1964), *Man's Struggle for Shelter in an Urbanizing World*. Cambridge, Mass.: M.I.T. Press.

ABRAMS, M. (1964), "Changing Needs of Different Age Groups," in British National Conference on Social Welfare, *Communities and Social Change*. London: National Council of Social Service.

ACKERMANN, J. S. (1969), "Listening to Architecture," *Harvard Educational Review* 39: 4–10.

ADAMS, J. S. (1969), "Directional Bias in Intra-Urban Migration," *Economic Geography* 45: 302–23.

———— (1972), "The Geography of Riots and Civil Disorders in the 1960s," in M. Albaum (ed.), *Geography and Contemporary Issues*, pp. 542–64. New York: Wiley.

AIELLO, J. R. (1972), "A Test of Equilibrium Theory: Visual Distance in Relation to Orientation, Distance, and Sex of Interactants," *Psychonomic Science* 27: 335–36.

———— and S. E. JONES (1971), "Field Study of the Proxemic Behavior of Younger Children in Three Subcultural Groups," *Journal of Personality and Social Psychology* 19: 351–56.

ALBAUM, M. (ed.) (1973), *Geography and Contemporary Issues*. New York: Wiley.

ALBERT, S. and J. M. DABBS (1970), "Physical Distance and Persuasion," *Journal of Personality and Social Psychology* 15: 265–70.

ALEXANDER, C. (1966), "A City is Not a Tree," *Architectural Forum* 112: 58–62.

ALLAND, A. (1972), *The Human Imperative*. New York: Columbia University Press.

ALLEE, W. C. (1938), *The Social Life of Animals*. New York: Norton.

ALLEN, J. B. (1966), *The Company Town in the American West*. Norman: Oklahoma University Press.

ALLEN, LADY (1968), *Planning for Play*. Cambridge, Mass.: M.I.T. Press.

ALLPORT, F. H. (1955), *Theories of Perception and the Concept of Structure.* New York: Wiley.

ALLPORT, G. W. (1935), "Attitudes," in C. Murchison (ed.), *Handbook of Social Psychology.* Worcester, Mass.: Clark University Press.

ALONSO, W. (1964), "The Historic and Structural Theories of Urban Form: Their Implications for Urban Renewal," *Land Economics* 40: 227–31.

———— (1970), "The Mirage of New Towns," *Public Interest* 19: 3–17.

ALTMAN, I. (1975), *The Environment and Social Behavior.* Monterey, Calif.: Brooks/Cole.

———— and W. W. HAYTHORN (1967), "The Ecology of Isolated Groups," *Behavioral Science* 12: 169–82.

ANDERSON, J. and M. TINDALL (1972), "The Concept of Home Range: New Data for the Study of Territorial Behavior," in W. J. Mitchell (ed.), *Environmental Design: Research and Practice.* Los Angeles: University of California/EDRA 3.

ANDERSON, M. (1964), *The Federal Bulldozer.* Cambridge, Mass.: M.I.T. Press.

ANDREWS, P., M. CHRISTIE, and R. MARTIN (1973), "Squatters and the Evolution of a Lifestyle," *Architectural Design* 43: 16–25.

APPLEYARD, D. (1969), "Why Buildings are Known: A Predictive Tool for Architects and Planners," *Environment and Behavior* 1: 131–56.

———— (1970), "Styles and Methods of Structuring a City," *Environment and Behavior* 2: 100–18.

———— and M. LINTELL (1972), "The Environmental Quality of City Streets: The Residents' Viewpoint," in W. J. Mitchell (ed.), *Environmental Design: Research and Practice.* Los Angeles: University of California/EDRA 3.

————, K. LYNCH, and J. MYER (1964), *The View From the Road.* Cambridge, Mass.: M.I.T. Press.

ARDEN, J. (1961), "Live Like Pigs," in T. Maschler (ed.), *New English Dramatists* 3, pp. 93–184. London: Penguin Books.

ARDREY, R. (1962), *African Genesis.* London: Collins.

———— (1966), *The Territorial Imperative.* New York: Atheneum.

———— (1970), *The Social Contract.* New York: Atheneum.

ARGYLE, M. and J. DEAN (1965), "Eye Contact, Distance, and Affiliation," *Sociometry* 28: 289–304.

————, M. LALLJEE, and M. COOK (1968), "Effects of Visibility on Interaction in a Dyad," *Human Relations* 21: 3–17.

ARISTOTLE (1932), *Politics.* Cambridge, Mass.: Harvard University Press.

ARMYTAGE, W. H. G. (1961), *Heavens Below.* London: Routledge.

ARNHEIM, R. (1965), *Art and Visual Perception.* Berkeley: University of California Press.

ARNSTEIN, S. (1969), "A Ladder of Citizen Participation," *Journal of the American Institute of Planners* 35: 216–24.

ASCH, S. E. (1952), *Social Psychology.* Englewood Cliffs, N.J.: Prentice-Hall.

ASHWORTH, W. (1954), *The Genesis of Modern British Town Planning.* London: Routledge.

ATHANASIOU, R. and G. A. YOSHIOKA (1973), "The Spatial Character of Friendship Formation," *Environment and Behavior* 5: 43–65.

BABCOCK, R. F. and F. P. BOSSELMAN (1968), "C.P.: A Suburban Suggestion for the Central City," *Land Use Controls* 2: 21–32.

BACHELARD, G. (1969), *The Poetics of Space.* Boston: Beacon Press.

BACK, K. W. (1962), *Slums, Projects, and People.* Durham, N.C.: Duke University Press.

BAILEY, A. (1972), "Noise is a Slow Agent of Death," in R. K. Yin (ed.), *The City in the Seventies,* pp. 144–49. Itaska, Ill.: F. E. Peacock.

BALLABON, M. B. (1972), "The Self-Service Group in the Urban Economy," *Journal of the American Institute of Planners* 38: 33–42.

BANGS, H. P. and S. MAHLER (1970), "Users of Local Parks," *Journal of the American Institute of Planners* 36: 330–34.

BARAN, P. and P. SWEEZEY (1966), *Monopoly Capitalism.* New York: Monthly Review Press.

BARDET, G. (1951), "Social Topography: An Analytical-Synthetic Understanding of the Urban Texture," *Town Planning Review* 22: 237–60.

BARKER, R. G. (1968), *Ecological Psychology.* Stanford, Calif.: Stanford University Press.

———— and L. S. BARKER (1961), "The Psychological Ecology of Old People in Midwest Kansas and Yoredale, Yorkshire," *Journal of Gerontology* 16: 144–49.

———— and P. V. GUMP (1964), *Big School, Small School.* Stanford, Calif.: Stanford University Press.

———— and H. F. WRIGHT (1951), *One Boy's Day.* New York: Harper.

———— and H. F. WRIGHT (1955), *The Midwest and Its Children.* Evanston, Ill.: Rowe, Peterson.

BARNETT, S. A. (1964), "Social Stress," *Viewpoints in Biology* 3: 170–218.

BARWIG, F., L. BRUTON, D. CORELIS, and J. P. PROTZEN (1972), "Precipitory Planning," in W. J. Mitchell (ed.), *Environmental Design: Research and Practice.* Los Angeles: University of California/EDRA 3.

BAUER, C. (1945), "Good Neighborhoods," *Annals of the American Academy of Political and Social Science* 242: 104–15.

———— (1952), *Social Questions in Housing and Town Planning.* London: University of London Press.

BAXTER, J. C. (1970), "Interpersonal Spacing in Natural Settings," *Sociometry* 33: 444–56.

BECHTEL, R. B. (1967), "Human Movement and Architecture," *Trans-Action* 4: 53–56.

BECKER, F. D. (1971), "Evaluating the Sacramento Mall," *Design and Environment* 2: 38.

———— and C. MAYO (1971), "Delineating Personal Distance and Territoriality," *Environment and Behavior* 3: 375–81.

BECKWITH, L. (1973), *About My Father's Business.* London: Arrow Books.

BELL, C. and R. BELL (1969), *City Fathers.* London: Barrie & Rockliff.

BELL, G. and J. TYRWHITT (eds.) (1972), *Human Identity in the Urban Environment.* London: Pelican Books.

————, E. RANDALL, and J. E. R. ROEDER (eds.) (1973), *Urban Environments and Human Behavior: An Annotated Bibliography.* Stroudsburg, Pa.: Dowden, Hutchinson & Ross.

BELL, W. (1965), "The City, the Suburb, and a Theory of Social Choice," in S. Greer, D. L. McElrath, D. W. Minar, and P. Orleans (eds.), *The New Urbanization,* pp. 132–68. New York: St. Martin's Press.

BENOIT, J. (1974), "Growing Old", reprinted in *Victoria Daily Times* 4 March 1975, from *Le Monde.*

BERGER, B. (1960), *Working Class Suburb.* Berkeley, Calif.: University of California Press.

BERLYNE, D. E. (1958), "The Influence of Complexity and Novelty in Visual Figures on Orienting Responses," *Journal of Experimental Psychology* 55: 289–96.

———— (1960), *Conflict, Arousal, and Curiosity.* New York: McGraw-Hill.

———— (1967), "Arousal and Reinforcement," in D. Levine (ed.), *Nebraska Symposium on Motivation.* Lincoln: University of Nebraska Press.

BERRY, B. (1965), "Internal Structure of the City," *Law and Contemporary Problems* 30: 111–19.

———— and F. E. HORTON (1970), *Geographic Perspectives on Urban Systems.* Englewood Cliffs, N.J.: Prentice-Hall.

BESHERS, J. (1962), *Urban Social Structure.* New York: Free Press.

BETJEMAN, J. (1970), *Collected Poems,* Enlarged Third Edition. London: Murray.

———— (1971), *Ghastly Good Taste.* New York: St. Martin's Press.

BICKMAN, L., A. TEGER, T. GABRIELE, C. McLAUGHLIN, M. BERGER, and E. SUNADAY (1973), "Dormitory Density and Helping Behavior," *Environment and Behavior* 5: 465–90.

BIDERMAN, A. D., M. LOURIA, and J. BACCHUS (1963), *Historical Incidents of Extreme Overcrowding.* Washington, D.C.: Bureau of Social Science Research.

BISHOP, R. L., G. L. PETERSON, and R. M. MICHAELS (1972), "Measurements of Childrens' Preferences for the Play Environment," in W. J. Mitchell (ed.), *Environmental Design: Research and Practice.* Los Angeles: University of California/EDRA 3.

BLAKE, R. C., R. B. WEDGE, and J. MOUTON (1956), "Housing Architecture and Social Interaction," *Sociometry* 19: 133–39.

BLASDEL, H. G. (1972), "Multidimensional Scaling for Architectural Environments," in W. J. Mitchell (ed.), *Environmental Design: Research and Practice.* Los Angeles: University of California/EDRA 3.

BLAUT, J. and D. STEA (1971), "Studies of Geographical Learning," *Annals of the Association of American Geographers* 61: 387–93.

BLUMENFELD, H. (1948), "Neighborhood Concept is Submitted to Questioning," in G. Bell, E. Randall, and J. E. R. Roeder (eds.) (1973), *Urban Environments and Human Behavior,* pp. 165–66. Stroudsburg, Pa.: Dowden, Hutchinson & Ross.

_____ (1969), "Housing and Urban Renewal Policies," lecture to Interdisciplinary Research Committee on Urban Problems, University of Victoria, 6 February 1969.

BLYTHE, R. (1970), *Akenfield: Portrait of an English Village.* New York: Delta Books.

BOAL, F. W. (1970), "Social Space in the Belfast Urban Area," in *Irish Geographical Studies*, pp. 373–93. Belfast: Queen's University Geography Department.

_____ (1971), "Territoriality and Class: A Study of Two Residential Areas in Belfast," *Irish Geography* 6: 229–48.

_____ (1972), "The Urban Residential Subcommunity: A Conflict Interpretation," *Area* 4: 164–68.

BOESCHENSTEIN, W. (1971), "Design of Socially Mixed Housing," *Journal of the American Institute of Planners* 37: 311–18.

BOGARDUS, E. (1926), "Social Distance in the City," in E. W. Burgess (ed.), *The Urban Community*, pp. 48–54. Chicago: University of Chicago Press.

BOLAN, R. S. (1971), "The Social Relations of the Planner," *Journal of the American Institute of Planners* 33: 386–96.

BOSSARD, J. H. S. and E. S. BOLL (1950), *Ritual in Family Living.* Philadelphia: University of Philadelphia Press.

BOTT, E. (1957), *Family and Social Network.* London: Tavistock.

BOULDING, K. E. (1956), *The Image.* Ann Arbor: University of Michigan Press.

BOURDIEU, P. (1964), *Le Deracinement.* Paris: Editions de Minuit.

BOWDEN, L. W. (1972), "How to Define Neighborhood," *Professional Geographer* 24: 227–28.

BOYD, D. W. (1965), "Selected Social Characteristics and Multi-Family Living Environment." Unpublished report, Environmental Research Foundation, Topeka, Kansas.

BREKENFELD, G. (1971), *Columbia and the New Cities.* New York: Ives Washburn.

BRENNAN, T. (1948), *Midland City.* London: Dobson.

BRERETON, J. L. (1971), cited in J. D. Porteous, "Of Mice and Men: A Review of *Behavior and Environment*," *Man-Environment Systems* 1, R11.

BRILL, R., E. CASTRO, and A. J. PENNINGTON (1970), "The Community Development Workshop," in H. Sanoff and S. Cohn (eds.), *EDRA 1 : Proceedings of the First Environmental Design Research Association Conference*, pp. 329–33. Raleigh, N.C.

BROADY, M. (1968), *Planning for People.* London: National Council of Social Service.

BRONFENBRENNER, U. (1974), "The Origins of Alienation," *Scientific American* 231: 53–61.

BROOKES, M. J. (1972), "Changes in Employee Attitudes and Work Practices in an Office Landscape," in W. J. Mitchell (ed.), *Environmental Design: Research and Practice.* Los Angeles: University of California/EDRA 3.

BROOKFIELD, H. C. (1973), "On One Geography and a Third World," *Transactions of the Institute of British Geographers* 58: 1–20.

BROOKS, R. O. (1971), "Social Planning in Columbia," *Journal of the American Institute of Planners* 37: 373–79.

———— (1974), *New Towns and Communal Values: A Case Study of Columbia, Maryland.* New York: Praeger.

BROWN, C. (1965), *Manchild in the Promised Land.* New York: New American Library.

BROWN, W. (1974), "Race and Culture: Urban Conflict and Reconciliation," in L. J. Evenden and F. F. Cunningham (eds.), *Cultural Discord in the Modern World*, pp. 189–94. Vancouver: B.C. Geographical Series 20.

BRUNETTI, F. A. (1972), "Noise, Distraction, and Privacy in Conventional and Open School Environments," in W. J. Mitchell (ed.), *Environmental Design: Research and Practice.* Los Angeles: University of California/EDRA 3.

BRUNN, S. D. and W. L. HOFFMAN (1970), "The Spatial Response of Negroes and Whites toward Open Housing: The Flint Referendum," *Annals of the Association of American Geographers* 60: 18–36.

BRUNSWICK, E. (1957), "Scope and Aspects of the Cognitive Problem," in H. Gruber, R. Jessor, and K. Hammond (eds.), *Cognition: The Colorado Symposium*, pp. 5–31. Cambridge, Mass.: Harvard University Press.

BRUTZKUS, E. (1964), *Physical Planning in Israel.* Jerusalem: Mifal Haschichpul.

BRUVOLD, W. H. (1973), "Belief and Behavior as Determinants of Environmental Attitudes," *Environment and Behavior* 5: 202–18.

BUCKSAR, R. G. (1970), "The Squatter on the Resource Frontier," *Arctic* 23: 201–204.

BUDER, S. (1967), *Pullman.* New York: Oxford University Press.

BULL, C. N. (1972), "Prediction of Future Daily Behaviors: An Empirical Measure of Leisure," *Journal of Leisure Research* 4: 119–28.

BUNTING, T. (1967), "Symbolic Urban Images: A Case Study of the New City Hall in Toronto." Unpublished M.A. thesis, University of Western Ontario.

BURGESS, J. A. (1974), "Stereotypes and Urban Images," *Area* 6: 167–71.

BURKE, E. M. (1968), "Citizen Participation Strategies," *Journal of the American Institute of Planners* 34: 290–1.

BURNEY, C. (1952), *Solitary Confinement.* New York: Coward-McCann.

BURNS, W. (1963), *New Towns for Old.* London: Leonard Hill.

BURTON, I. (1971), "The Social Role of Attitude and Perception Studies," in W. R. D. Sewell and I. Burton (eds.), *Perceptions and Attitudes in Resources Management*, pp. 1–6. Ottawa: Department of Energy, Mines, and Resources.

———— and R. W. KATES (1964), "The Perception of Natural Hazards in Resource Management," *Natural Resources Journal* 3: 412–41.

BURTON, T. L. (1971), "Identification of Recreation Types through Cluster Analysis," *Society and Leisure* 1: 47–64.

BUSSE, T. V., M. REE, M. GUTRIDE, T. ALEXANDER, and L. S. POWELL (1972), "Environmentally Enriched Classrooms and the Cognitive and Perceptual Development of Negro Preschool Children," *Journal of Educational Psychology* 63: 15–21.

BUTTIMER, A. (1969), "Social Space in Interdisciplinary Perspective," *Geographical Review* 59: 417–26.

CALHOUN, J. B. (1962), "Population Density and Social Pathology," *Scientific American* 206: 139–48.

————— (1966), "The Role of Space in Animal Sociology," *Journal of Social Issues* 22: 46–58.

————— (1973), "What Sort of Box?" *Man-Environment Systems* 3: 3–30.

CALLAN, H. (1970), *Ethology and Society: Towards an Anthropological View.* London: Oxford University Press.

CAMERON, W. B. (ed.) (1963), *Informal Sociology.* New York: Random House.

————— (1963), "Upward Skidding and the Automatic Value Shift," in W. B. Cameron (ed.), *Informal Sociology,* pp. 95–106. New York: Random House.

————— and R. H. WHEELER (1963), "Physical Setting and Intellectual Climate," in W. B. Cameron (ed.), *Informal Sociology,* pp. 56–66. New York: Random House.

CAMPBELL, D. T. (1963), "Social Attitudes and Other Acquired Behavioral Dispositions," in S. Koch (ed.), *Psychology: A Study of a Science* 6. New York: McGraw-Hill.

CANTER, D. (1969), "Attitudes and Perception in Architecture," *A A Quarterly* 1: 24–31.

————— and S. CANTER (1971), "Close Together in Tokyo," *Design and Environment* 2: 60–63.

CAPLOW, T. and R. FOREMAN (1950), "Neighborhood Interaction in a Homogeneous Community," *American Sociological Review* 15: 357–66.

CAPPON, D. (1970a), "You're Living in the Wrong House," *Financial Post Magazine* 64: 8–16.

————— (1970b), "Canadian Cities: Their Health, Malaise, and Problems," *Habitat* 13: 2–10.

————— (1971), "Mental Health in the High Rise," *Canadian Journal of Public Health* 62: 426–31.

CARLSON, E. (1959), "High Rise Management: Design Problems found in Caracas," *Journal of Housing* 16: 311–14.

————— (1960), "Evaluation of Housing Project and Programmes: A Case Report from Venezuela," *Town Planning Review* 31: 187–209.

CARNEY, J. G. and C. TAYLOR (1974), "Community Development Projects," *Area* 6: 226–31.

CARP, F. M. (1970), "Correlates of Mobility among Retired Persons," in J. Archea and C. Eastman (eds.), *Proceedings, Second Environmental Design Research Association Conference,* Pittsburgh.

————— (ed.) (1972), *Retirement.* New York: Behavioral Publications.

CARPENTER, C. R. (1942), "Societies of Monkeys and Apes," *Biological Symposia* 8: 177–204.

————— (1965), "The Howlers of Barro Colorado Island," in I. De Vore (ed.), *Primate Behavior,* pp. 250–91. New York: Holt, Rinehart & Winston.

CARPENTER, C. S., F. VARLEY, and R. FLAHERTY (1959), *Eskimo*. Toronto: University of Toronto Press.

CARR, E. (1942), *The Book of Small*. Toronto: Clark Irwin.

CARR, S. (1967), "The City of the Mind," in W. R. Ewald (ed.), *Environment for Man: The Next Fifty Years*, pp. 197–226. Bloomington: Indiana University Press.

———— and D. SCHISSLER (1969), "The City as a Trip: Perceptual Selection and Memory in the View from the Road," *Environment and Behavior* 1: 7–35.

CARTHY, J. D. (1956), *Animal Navigation: How Animals Find their Way About*. London: Allen.

———— (1965), *Animal Behavior*. London: Aldus.

CATHER, W. (1918), *My Ántonia*. Boston: Houghton Mifflin.

C. H. A. C. (Central Housing Advisory Committee) (1967) *The Needs of New Communities*. London: Ministry of Housing and Local Government.

CHAPIN, F. S. (1951), "Psychology of Housing," *Social Forces* 30: 11–15.

———— (1965), *Urban Land Use Planning*. Urbana: University of Illinois Press.

———— (1968), "Activity Systems and Urban Structure: A Working Schema," *Journal of the American Institute of Planners* 34: 11–18.

———— (1971), "Free Time Activity and Quality of Urban Life," *Journal of the American Institute of Planners* 33: 411–17.

———— and R. K. BRAIL (1969), "Human Activity Systems in the Metropolitan United States," *Environment and Behavior* 1: 107–30.

———— and H. HIGHTOWER (1965), "Household Activity Patterns and Land Use," *Journal of the American Institute of Planners* 31: 222–31.

CHAUDHURI, N. C. (1959), *A Passage to England*. London: Macmillan.

CHEVALIER, M. and T. J. CARTWRIGHT (1970), "An Institutional Perspective of Environmental Perception: The Delaware Estuary Comprehensive Study." Paper presented at Symposium on the Role of Perceptions and Attitudes in Decision-Making in Resource Management, Victoria, B.C.

CHICAGO AREA TRANSPORTATION STUDY (1959), *Final Report*. Chicago: CATS.

CHOAY, F. (1969), *The Modern City: Planning in the Nineteenth Century*. New York: Braziller.

CHOLDIN, H. M. and M. J. McGINTY (1972), "Bibliography: Population Density, Crowding, and Social Relations," *Man-Environment Systems* 3: 131–58.

CHRISTALLER, W. (1966), *Central Places in Southern Germany*. Englewood Cliffs, N.J.: Prentice-Hall.

CHRISTIAN, J. J. (1950), "The Adreno-Pituitary System and Population Cycles in Mammals," *Journal of Mammalogy* 31: 247–59.

————, V. FLYGER, and D. E. DAVIS (1960), "Factors in the Mass Mortality of a Herd of Sitka Deer," *Chesapeake Science* 1: 79–95.

CHURCHILL, H. S. (1948), "An Open Letter to Mr. Isaacs," *Journal of the American Institute of Planners* 14: 40–43.

CLARE, J. (1973), "Squatters with a Touch of the Forsytes," *The Observer,* 12 January 1973.

CLARK, K. B. (1967), "Explosion in the Ghetto," *Psychology Today* 1: 30–38, 62–64.

CLARK, S. D. (1966), *The Suburban Society.* Toronto: University of Toronto Press.

CLAVEL, P. (1968), "Planners and Citizen Boards: Some Applications of Social Theory to the Problem of Plan Implementation," *Journal of the American Institute of Planners* 34: 130–39.

CLEM, P., K. AHERN, N. DAILEY, M. GAY, and M. SCANTLEBURY (1974), "A Comparison of Interaction Patterns in an Open Space and a Fixed Plan School," *Man-Environment Systems* 4: 59–60.

CLIFF, U. (1971a), "New York's Better Self," *Design and Environment* 2: 50–51.

_____ (1971b), "Evaluating Dorms at Guelph University," *Design and Environment* 2: 32.

C. O. G. P. (Committee on Government Productivity) (1972), *Citizen Involvement.* Toronto: Government of Ontario.

COHEN, H. (1970), "The Changing Role of the Planner in the Decision-Making Process," in E. Erber (ed.), *Urban Planning in Transition.* New York: American Institute of Planners.

COHEN, N. (1970), *The Los Angeles Riots: A Socio-Psychological Study.* New York: Praeger.

COLLISON, P. (1960), "Occupation, Education, and Housing in an English City," *American Journal of Sociology* 65: 588–97.

COOPER, C. (1972), "The House as Symbol," *Design and Environment* 3: 30–37.

_____ (1974), "The House as Symbol of the Self," in J. Lang, C. Burnette, W. Moleski, and D. Vachon (eds.), *Designing for Human Behavior,* pp. 130–46. Stroudsburg, Pa.: Dowden, Hutchinson & Ross.

_____ and P. HACKETT (1968), *Analysis of the Design Process at Two Moderate Income Housing Developments.* Berkeley, Calif.: Center for Planning and Development Research Working Paper 80.

CORBETT, J. A. (1973), "Student-Built Housing as an Alternative to Dormitories," *Environment and Behavior* 5: 491–504.

COX, K. R. (1968), "Suburbia and Voting Behavior in the London Metropolitan Area," *Annals of the Association of American Geographers* 58: 14–27.

CRAIK, K. (1970), "Environmental Psychology," *New Directions in Psychology* 4: 1–121.

_____ (1972), "An Ecological Perspective on Environmental Decision-Making," *Human Ecology* 1: 69–80.

CRAUN, R. M. (1970), "Visual Determinants of Preference for Dwelling Environs," in H. Sanoff and S. Cohn (eds.), *Proceedings, First Environmental Design Research Conference,* pp. 75–85. Raleigh, N.C.

CULLEN, G. (1961), *Townscape.* London: Architectural Press.

CUMMINGS, E. and W. E. HENRY (1961), *Growing Old: The Process of Disengagement.* New York: Basic Books.

DAHIR, J. (1947), *The Neighborhood Unit Plan: Its Spread and Acceptance*. New York: Russell Sage Foundation.

———— (1948), "Neighborhood Planning is a Three-in-One Job," *Journal of Housing* 5: 270–72.

DANTZIG, G. B. and T. L. SAATY (1973), *Compact City*. San Francisco: W. H. Freeman.

DARKE, J. and R. DARKE (1974), "Planned Paradise," *Habitat* 17: 36–40.

DARLEY, G. (1975), *Villages of Vision*. London: Architectural Press.

DAVIDOFF, P. (1965), "Advocacy and Pluralism in Planning," *Journal of the American Institute of Planners* 31: 331–38.

DAVIE, M. R. and R. J. REEVES (1939), "Propinquity and Residence before Marriage," *American Journal of Sociology* 44.

DAVIES, J. C. (1966), *Neighborhood Groups and Urban Renewal*. New York: Columbia University Press.

DAVIES, S. and G. L. FOWLER (1972), "The Disadvantaged Urban Migrant in Indianapolis," *Economic Geography* 48: 153–67.

DAVIS, D. E. (1971), "Physiological Effects of Continued Crowding," in A. H. Esser (ed.), *Behavior and Environment*, pp. 133–47. New York: Plenum Press.

DAVIS, G. (1972), "Using Interviews of Present Office Workers in Planning New Offices," in W. J. Mitchell (ed.), *Environmental Design: Research and Practice*. Los Angeles: University of California/EDRA 3.

———— and R. ROIZEN (1971), "Architectural Determinants of Student Satisfaction in College Residence Halls," *Man-Environment Systems* 1: S43.

DAVIS, J. T. (1965), "Middle Class Housing in the Central City," *Economic Geography* 41: 238–51.

DAVIS, K. (1973), "Man's Adjustment to Cities," in K. Davis (ed.), *Cities: Their Origin, Growth, and Human Impact*, pp. 1–6. San Francisco: W. H. Freeman.

D. C. P. (1971), *The Visual Environment of Los Angeles*. Los Angeles: Department of City Planning.

DE BEAUVOIR, S. (1972), *Old Age*. New York: William Collins.

DE FLEUR, M. and F. R. WESTIE (1963), "Attitudes as a Scientific Concept," *Social Forces* 42: 17–31.

DE JONGE, D. (1962), "Images of Urban Areas: Their Structures and Psychological Foundations," *Journal of the American Institute of Planners* 28: 266–76.

———— (1967), "Applied Hodology," *Landscape* 17: 10–11.

DE LAUWE, P-H. C. (1960), *Famille et Habitation*. Paris: Centre National de la Recherche Scientifique.

———— (1965), *Des Hommes et Des Villes*. Paris: Payot.

DE LONG, A. (1970), "Dominance-Territorial Relations in a Small Group," *Environment and Behavior* 2: 170–91.

DE SAINT-EXUPÉRY, A. (1943), *The Little Prince*. New York: Harcourt, Brace & World.

DE VISE, P. (1973), *Misused and Misplaced Hospitals and Doctors*. Washington, D.C.: Association of American Geographers Resource Paper 22.

DEE, N. and J. C. LIEBMAN (1970), "A Statistical Study of Children at Urban Playgrounds," *Journal of Leisure Research* 2: 145–59.

DEEVEY, E. S. (1960), "The Hare and the Haruspex: A Cautionary Tale," *American Scientist* 48: 415–29.

DEMPSEY, D. (1972), "Man's Hidden Environment," *Playboy* (May): 108–10, 222–26.

DENNIS, N. (1969), "Mass Housing and the Reformers' Myth," *Planning Outlook* 6: 7–13.

DENNIS, W. (1966), *Group Values Through Childrens' Drawings*. New York: Wiley.

DENTLER, R. A. (1968), *American Community Problems*. New York: McGraw-Hill.

DESKINS, D. R. (1970), "Residence–Workplace Interaction Vectors for the Detroit Metropolitan Area: 1953 to 1965," in M. Albaum (ed.), *Geography and Contemporary Issues*, pp. 157–74. New York: Wiley.

DESOR, J. A. (1972), "Toward a Psychological Theory of Crowding," *Journal of Personality and Social Psychology* 21: 79–83.

DEWEY, R. (1950), "The Neighborhood, Urban Ecology, and City Planners," *American Sociological Review* 15: 502–507.

DIAISO, R., D. M. FREIDMAN, L. MITCHELL, and E. SCHWEITZER (1971), *Perception of the Housing Environment*. Pittsburgh: University of Pittsburgh Urban and Environmental Health Planning Paper 2.

DICKINSON, J. C., R. J. GRAY, and D. M. SMITH (1972), "The Quality of Life in Gainesville, Florida," *Southeastern Geographer* 12: 121–32.

DISRAELI, B. (1881), *Sybil*. London: Longmans Green.

DIXON, J. M. (1969), "Planning Workbook for the Community," *Architectural Forum* 131: 32–40.

DOSEY, M. A. and M. MEISELS (1969), "Personal Space and Self-Protection," *Journal of Personality and Social Psychology* 11: 93–97.

DOUGLAS, J. N. H. (1974), "Voting Behavior and Constitutional Reform in Northern Ireland," in L. J. Evenden and F. F. Cunningham (eds.), *Cultural Discord in the Modern World*, pp. 127–42. Vancouver: B.C. Geographical Series 20.

DOWNS, R. M. (1970), "The Cognitive Structure of an Urban Shopping Center," *Environment and Behavior* 2: 13–39.

———— and D. STEA (eds.) (1973), *Image and Environment: Cognitive Mapping and Spatial Behavior*. Chicago: Aldine.

DOXIADIS, C. (1968), *Ekistics*. London: Hutchinson.

DRESCHLER, R. J. (1960), "Affect Stimulating Effects of Colors," *Journal of Abnormal and Social Psychology* 61: 323–28.

DREVER, J. (1964), *A Dictionary of Psychology*. London: Penguin Books.

DREW, C. (1972), "Research on the Psychological Behavioral Effects of the Physical Environment," *Review of Education Research* 41: 447–65.

DROETTBOOM, T., R. J. McALLISTER, E. J. KAISER, and E. W. BUTLER (1971), "Urban Violence and Residential Mobility," *Journal of the American Institute of Planners* 37: 319–25.

DUBOS, R. (1965), *Man Adapting*. New Haven, Conn.: Yale University Press.

———— (1968), *So Human an Animal*. New York: Scribners.

DUFFY, F. (1969), "Role and Status in the Office," *A A Quarterly* 1: 4–13.

DUHL, L. (1963a), "The Changing Face of Mental Health," in L. Duhl (ed.), *The Urban Condition*. New York: Simon & Schuster.

———— (1963b), "Planning and Poverty," in L. J. Duhl (ed.), *The Urban Condition*. New York: Simon & Schuster.

DUNCAN, O. D. and B. DUNCAN (1957), "Residential Distribution and Occupational Stratification," in P. K. Hatt and A. J. Reiss (eds.), *Cities and Society*, pp. 183–96. New York: Free Press.

———— and A. J. REISS (1956), *Social Characteristics of Urban and Rural Communities, 1950*. New York: Wiley.

DUNHAM, H. W. (1965), *Community and Schizophrenia: An Epidemiological Analysis*. Detroit: Wayne State University Press.

DUOSKIN, S. (1970), "The Disabled's Encounter with the Environment," *Design and Environment* 1: 60–63.

DURKHEIM, E. (1951), *Suicide*. New York: Free Press.

DURLAK, J. T., B. E. BEARDSLEY, and J. S. MURRAY (1972), "Observation of User Activity Patterns in Open and Traditional Plan School Environments," in W. J. Mitchell (ed.), *Environmental Design: Research and Practice*. Los Angeles: University of California/EDRA 3.

EASTMAN, C. M. and J. HARPER (1971), "A Study of Proxemic Behavior: Toward a Predictive Model," *Environment and Behavior* 3: 418–37.

EATON, L. K. (1970), "The American Suburb: Dream and Nightmare," in R. G. Putnam, F. J. Taylor, and P. G. Kettle (eds.), *A Geography of Urban Places*, pp. 342–47. Toronto: Methuen.

ECKBO, G. (1971), "Evaluating the Evaluation," *Design and Environment* 2: 39–40.

EDWARDS, A. L. (1957), *Techniques of Attitude Scale Construction*. New York: Appleton-Century-Crofts.

EIBL-EIBESFELDT, I. (1970), *Ethology: The Biology of Behavior*. New York: Holt, Rinehart & Winston.

ELGIE, R. (1970), "Rural Immigration, Urban Ghettoization, and Their Consequences," *Antipode* 2: 35–54.

ELLENBERGER, H. (1971), "Behavior Under Involuntary Confinement," in A. H. Esser (ed.), *Behavior and Environment*, pp. 188–203. New York: Plenum Press.

ELTON, C. S. (1924), "Periodic Fluctuations in the Numbers of Animals," *Journal of Experimental Biology* 2: 119–63.

ELY, R. T. (1885), "Pullman: A Social Study," *Harper's Monthly* 70: 452–66.

ERIKSON, E. (1964), "Genital Modes and Spatial Modalities," in E. Erikson (ed.), *Childhood and Society*. New York: Norton.

ERLICH, P. R. and A. H. ERLICH (1970), *Population, Resources, Environment: Issues in Human Ecology*. San Francisco: W. H. Freeman.

ERRINGTON, P. (1956), "Factors Limiting Higher Vertebrate Populations," *Science* 124: 304–307.

ESSER, A. H. (1972), "A Biosocial Perspective on Crowding," in J. F. Wohlwill and D. H. Carson (eds.), *Environment and the Social Sciences*, pp. 15–58. Washington, D.C.: American Psychological Association.

_____ (1973), "Structures of Man-Environment Relations," in W. F. E. Preiser (ed.), *Environmental Design Research*. Stroudsburg, Pa.: Dowden, Hutchinson & Ross.

_____ (1974), "Environment and Mental Health," *Science, Medicine, and Man* 1: 181–93.

_____, A. S. CHAMBERLAIN, E. D. CHAPPLE, and N. S. KLINE (1965), "Territoriality of Patients on a Research Ward," *Recent Advances in Biological Psychiatry* 7: 36–44.

EVANS, G. W. and W. EICHELMAN (1974), "An Examination of the Information Overload Mechanism of Personal Space," *Man-Environment Systems* 4: 61.

_____ and R. B. HOWARD (1973), "Personal Space," *Psychological Bulletin* 80: 334–44.

EVENSON, N. (1969), *Le Corbusier: The Machine and the Grand Design*. New York: Braziller.

EVERITT, J. and M. CADWALLADER (1972), "The Home Area Concept in Urban Analysis," in W. J. Mitchell (ed.), *Environmental Design: Research and Practice*. Los Angeles: University of California/EDRA 3.

EYLES, J. D. (1968), *The Inhabitants' Images of Highgate Village*. London: L.S.E. Geography Discussion Papers 15.

FALUDI, E. G. (1963), "The Case for the High Rise," *Ontario Housing* 9: 11–15.

FANNING, D. M. (1967), "Families in Flats," *British Medical Journal* 18: 382–86.

FANNING, O. (1975), *Man and His Environment: Citizen Action*. New York: Harper & Row.

FARIS, R. E. L. and H. W. DUNHAM (1939), *Mental Disorders in Urban Areas*. Chicago: University of Chicago Press.

FARR, L. E. (1967), "Medical Consequences of Environmental Noises," *Journal of the American Medical Association* 202: 171–74.

FEBVRE, L. (1925), *A Geographical Introduction to History*. London: Routledge & Kegan Paul.

FELDMAN, A. S. and C. TILLY (1960), "The Interaction of Social and Physical Space," *American Sociological Review* 25: 877–84.

FELLMAN, G. and B. BRANDT (1970), "A Neighborhood a Highway Would Destroy," *Environment and Behavior* 2: 281–301.

_____ (1971), "Working-Class Protest Against an Urban Highway," *Environment and Behavior* 3: 61–79.

FENDRICK, J. M. (1967), "A Study of the Associations Among Verbal Attitudes, Commitment, and Overt Behavior in Different Experimental Settings," *Social Forces* 45: 347–55.

FESTINGER, L. (1951), "Architecture and Group Membership," *Journal of Social Issues* 7: 152–63.

————, S. SCHACHTER, and K. BACK (1950), *Social Pressures in Informal Groups*. New York: Harper.

FIREY, W. (1945), "Sentiment and Symbolism as Ecological Variables," *American Sociological Review* 10: 140–48.

FISHBEIN, M. (1967), *Readings in Attitude Theory and Measurement*. New York: Wiley.

FISHMAN, J. (1956), "An Examination of the Process and Function of Social Stereotyping," *Journal of Social Psychology* 43: 27–64.

FISKE, D. W. and S. R. MADDI (1961), *Functions of Varied Experience*. Homewood, Ill.: Dorsey Press.

FITCH, J. M. (1965), "Experiential Bases for Aesthetic Decision," *Annals of the New York Academy of Sciences* 128: 706–14.

FOLEY, D. L. (1960), "British Town Planning: One Ideology or Three?" *British Journal of Sociology* 11: 211–31.

FOOTE, N. N., J. ABU-LUGHOD, M. M. FOLEY, and L. WINNI (1960), *Housing Choices and Housing Constraints*. New York: McGraw-Hill.

FORSHAW, J. H. and P. ABERCROMBIE (1943), *County of London Plan*. London: Macmillan.

FORWARD, C. N. (1973), "The Immortality of a Fashionable Residential District," in C. N. Forward (ed.), *Residential and Neighbourhood Studies in Victoria*, pp. 1–39. Victoria, B.C.: Western Geographical Series 5.

FRAME, J. (1961), *Faces in the Water*. New York: Braziller.

FRANKENBERG, R. (1965), *Communities in Britain: Social Life in Town and Country*. London: Pelican Books.

FREEDMAN, J. (1971), "The Crowd — Maybe Not So Madding After All," *Psychology Today* 5: 58–61.

————, S. KLEVANSKY, and P. ERLICH (1971), "The Effect of Crowding on Human Task Performance," *Journal of Applied Social Psychology* 1: 7–25.

FRIED, M. (1963), "Grieving for a Lost Home," in L. J. Duhl (ed.), *The Urban Condition*, pp. 151–71. New York: Simon & Schuster.

———— and P. GLEICHER (1961), "Some Sources of Residential Satisfaction in an Urban Slum," *Journal of the American Institute of Planners* 27: 305–15.

FRIEDEN, B. J. (1967), "Environmental Planning and the Elimination of Poverty," *Journal of the American Institute of Planners* 33: 164–66.

FROMM, E. (1972), "Humanistic Planning," *Journal of the American Institute of Planners* 38: 67–71.

FRY, A. M. and F. N. WILLIS (1971), "Invasion of Personal Space as a Function of the Age of the Invader," *Psychological Record* 21: 385–89.

FULLER, B. (1967), "Man with a Chronofile," *Saturday Review* (April): 14–18.

GAD, G. (1973), "Crowding and Pathologies: Some Critical Remarks," *Canadian Geographer* 17: 373–90.

GALLE, O. R., W. R. GOVE, and J. M. McPHERSON (1972), "Population Density and Pathology: What Are the Relations for Man?" *Science* 176: 23–30.

GANS, H. J. (1959), "The Human Implications of Current Redevelopment and Relocation Planning," *Journal of the American Institute of Planners* 25: 15–25.

———— (1961a), "The Balanced Community: Homogeneity or Heterogeneity in Residential Areas," *Journal of the American Institute of Planners* 27: 176–84.

———— (1961b), "Planning and Social Life: Friendship and Neighbor Relations in Suburban Communities," *Journal of the American Institute of Planners* 27: 134–40.

———— (1962a), *The Urban Villagers*. New York: Free Press.

———— (1962b), "Urbanism and Suburbanism as Ways of Life," in A. M. Rose (ed.), *Human Behavior and Social Processes*, pp. 625–48. Boston: Houghton Mifflin.

———— (1963), "Effects of the Move from City to Suburb," in L. J. Duhl (ed.), *The Urban Condition*, pp. 184–98. New York: Simon & Schuster.

———— (1967), *The Levittowners*. New York: Pantheon Books.

———— (1972), *People and Plans*. London: Pelican Books.

GEIGER, H. K. (1968), *The Family in Soviet Russia*. Cambridge, Mass.: Harvard University Press.

GERST, M. S. and H. SWEETWOOD (1973), "Correlates of Dormitory Social Climate," *Environment and Behavior* 5: 440–64.

GETIS, A. and B. BOOTS (1971), "Spatial Behavior: Rats and Man," *Professional Geographer* 23: 11–14.

G. F. E. E. (Group for Environmental Education, Inc.) (1970), *Our Man-Made Environment* 7. Cambridge, Mass.: M.I.T. Press.

GIBSON, E. M. (1973), "Lotus Eaters, Loggers, and the Vancouver Landscape," in L. J. Evenden and F. F. Cunningham (eds.), *Cultural Discord in The Modern World*, pp. 57–74. Vancouver: B.C. Geographical Series 20.

GIBSON, J. J. (1958), "Visually Controlled Locomotion and Visual Orientation in Animals," *British Journal of Psychology* 49: 182–94.

———— (1966), *The Senses Considered as Perceptual Systems*. Boston: Houghton Mifflin.

GIDEON, S. (1948), *Mechanization Takes Command*. New York: Oxford University Press.

GIGGS, J. A. (1973), "The Distribution of Schizophrenics in Nottingham," *Transactions of the Institute of British Geographers* 59: 55–76.

GILBERT, A. (1972), "Observations about Recent Correctional Architecture," in *New Environments for the Incarcerated*, pp. 7–14. Washington, D.C.: U.S. Law Enforcement Assistance Administration.

GLACKEN, C. J. (1967), *Traces on the Rhodian Shore: Nature and Culture in Western Thought from Ancient Times to the End of the Eighteenth Century*. Berkeley: University of California Press.

GLASER, D. (1964), *The Effectiveness of a Prison and Parole System.* Indianapolis: Bobbs-Merrill.

GLASS, R. (ed.) (1948), *The Social Background of a Plan: A Study of Middlesborough.* London: Routledge & Kegan Paul.

GLEASON, J. J. (1972), "Imaginative Modes of Perceiving the City: The Architectural Metaphor in Twentieth Century American Literature," in W. J. Mitchell (ed.), *Environmental Design: Research and Practice.* Los Angeles: University of California/EDRA 3.

GODSCHALK, D. (1970), "Negotiate: An Experimental Planning Game," in H. Sanoff and S. Cohn (eds.), *Proceedings, First Environmental Design Research Association Conference,* pp. 345–49. Raleigh, N.C.

———— (1973), "New Communities or Company Towns: Analysis of Resident Participation in New Towns," in H. S. Perloff and N. C. Sandberg (eds.), *New Towns: Why and for Whom?* New York: Praeger.

GOFFMAN, E. (1961), *Asylums.* Garden City, N.Y.: Anchor Books.

———— (1963), *Behavior in Public Places.* New York: Free Press.

———— (1972), *Relations in Public: Microstudies of the Public Order.* London: Penguin Books.

GOLDBERG, T. (1969), "The Automobile: A Social Institution for Adolescents," *Environment and Behavior* 1: 157–85.

GOLDSTEIN, S. and K. B. MAYER (1961), *Metropolitanization and Population Change in Rhode Island.* Providence, R.I.: Rhode Island Development Council Planning Division.

GOLLEDGE, R. G., L. A. BROWN, and F. WILLIAMSON (1972), "Behavioral Approaches to Geography," *Australian Geographer* 12: 59–79.

GOODCHILD, B. (1974), "Class Differences in Environmental Perception," *Urban Studies* 11: 157–69.

GOODEY, B. (1974a), "The Sense of Place in British Planning," *Man-Environment Systems* 4: 195–202.

———— (1974b), *Images of Place.* Birmingham, England: University of Birmingham Center for Urban and Regional Studies Occasional Paper 30.

GOODMAN, L. A. and W. H. KRUSKAL (1954), "Measures of Association for Cross-Classifications," *Journal of the American Statistical Society* 49: 732–64.

GOODMAN, P. and P. GOODMAN (1947), *Communitas.* New York: Random House.

GOODMAN, R. (1972), *After the Planners.* London: Pelican Books.

GOODWIN, J. (1964), "What is a Slum?" *The Independent* 17: 4.

GORDON, M. (1964), *Sick Cities.* New York: Macmillan.

GOTTLIEB, D. (1957), "The Neighborhood Tavern and the Cocktail Lounge," *American Journal of Sociology* 62: 559–62.

GOTTMAN, J. (1970), "Urban Centrality and the Inter-weaving of Quaternary Activities," *Ekistics* 29: 322–31.

GOULD, H. A. (1960), "The Micro-Demography of Marriage in a North Indian Area," *Southwest Journal of Anthropology* 14: 476–91.

GOULD, P. R. (1966), *On Mental Maps*. Ann Arbor: Michigan Inter-University Community of Mathematical Geographers.

———— (1967), "Structuring Information on Spacio-Temporal Preferences," *Journal of Regional Science* 7: 259–74.

———— and R. R. WHITE (1968), "The Mental Maps of British School Leavers," *Regional Studies* 2: 161–82.

GOWANS, A. (1964), *Images of American Living*. New York: Lippincott.

GRABOW, S. and A. HESKIN (1973), "Foundations of a Radical Concept of Planning," *Journal of the American Institute of Planners* 36.

GRANT, D. P. (1972), "Systematic Methods in Environmental Design," *Man-Environment Systems* 2: 335–44.

GREENE, G. (1963), *A Burnt-Out Case*. London: Penguin Books.

GREGOIRE, M. (1971), "The Child in the High Rise," *Ekistics* 31: 331–33.

GRIFFITT, W. and R. VEITCH (1971), "Hot and Crowded: Influences of Population Density and Temperature on Interpersonal Affective Behavior," *Journal of Personality and Social Psychology* 17: 92–98.

GUARDO, C. J. (1969), "Personal Space in Children," *Child Development* 40: 143–51.

GUHL, A. M. (1965), "Sociobiology and Man," *Bulletin of the Atomic Scientists* 21: 22–24.

GUILION, S. (1971), "Crowding Makes Nasty People," reprinted in *Victoria Daily Times* 9 July 1971, from *The German Tribune*.

GULICK, J. (1963), "Images of the Arab City," *Journal of the American Institute of Planners* 29: 179–97.

GULLIVER, F. P. (1908), "Orientation of Maps," *Journal of Geography* 7: 55–58.

GUMP, P. V. (1971), "Milieu, Environment, and Behavior," *Design and Environment* 8: 48–50, 60.

GUTMAN, R. (1963), "Population Mobility in the American Middle Class," in L. J. Duhl (ed.), *The Urban Condition*, pp. 172–83. New York: Simon & Schuster.

———— (1966), "Site Planning and Social Behavior," *Journal of Social Issues* 22: 103–15.

HALKETT, I. (1975), "The Urban Residential Lot as Activity Space." Unpublished Ph. D. thesis, Australian National University.

HALL, E. T. (1959), *The Silent Language*. Garden City, N.Y.: Doubleday.

———— (1966), *The Hidden Dimension*. Garden City, N.Y.: Doubleday.

———— (1969), "The Facility of Communication in a Cultural Environment," in J. D. Porteous and C. W. Porteous (eds.), *A Report on the Symposium: The Use of Space by Animals and Men*. Cambridge, Mass.: M.I.T. Department of City and Regional Planning.

———— (1971), "Proxemics and Design," *Design and Environment* 2: 24–5, 58.

———— (1974), "Meeting Man's Needs in Artificial Environments," in J. Lang, C. Burnette, W. Moleski, and D. Vachon (eds.), *Designing for Human Behavior*, pp. 210–20. Stroudsburg, Pa.: Dowden, Hutchinson & Ross.

———— and G. WEKERLE (1972), "High Rise Living: Can One Design Serve Both Young and Old?" *Ekistics* 33: 186–91.

HANDLIN, D. P. (1972), "The Detached House in the Age of the Object and Beyond," in W. J. Mitchell (ed.), *Environmental Design: Research and Practice.* Los Angeles: University of California/EDRA 3.

HARDIN, G. (1968), "The Tragedy of the Commons," *Science* 162: 1243–48.

HARDWICK, W. G. (1974), *Vancouver.* Don Mills, Ontario: Collier-Macmillan.

———— and D. F. HARDWICK (1974), "Civic Government: Corporate, Consultative, or Participatory?" in D. Ley (ed.), *Community Participation and the Spatial Order of the City,* pp. 89–96. Vancouver: B.C. Geographical Series 19.

HARRIS, F. R. and J. V. LINDSAY (1972), *The State of the Cities.* New York: Praeger.

HARTMAN, C. (1963), "Social Values and Housing Orientations," *Journal of Social Issues* 19: 113–31.

———— (1966), "The Housing of Relocated Families," in J. Q. Wilson (ed.), *Urban Renewal: The Record and the Controversy,* pp. 293–335. Cambridge, Mass.: M.I.T. Press.

HARTNETT, J. J., K. G. BAILEY, and F. W. GIBSON (1970), "Personal Space as Influenced by Sex and Type of Movement," *Journal of Psychology* 76: 139–44.

HARTNETT, K. O. (1970), *Encounter on Urban Environment.* Ottawa: Canadian Broadcasting Corporation.

HARVEY, D. (1969), "Conceptual and Measurement Problems in the Cognitive-Behavioral Approach to Location Theory," in K. R. Cox and R. G. Golledge (eds.), *Behavioral Problems in Geography,* pp. 35–68. Evanston, Ill.: Northwestern Studies in Geography 17.

HASSAN, Y. (1965), "The Movement System as an Organizer of Visual Form." Unpublished Ph.D. thesis, M.I.T.

HEARN, G. (1957), "Leadership and the Spatial Factor in Small Groups," *Journal of Abnormal and Social Psychology* 104: 269–72.

HEBB, D. O. (1955), "Drives and the C.N.S.," *Psychological Review* 62: 243–54.

HEILWEIL, M. (1973), "The Influence of Dormitory Architecture on Resident Behavior," *Environment and Behavior* 5: 377–412.

HENDRICKS, F. and M. MACNAIR (1970), "Concepts of Environmental Quality Standards Based on Life Styles," *Ekistics* 30: 139–44.

HERMAN, M. W. (1964), *Comparative Studies of Identification Areas in Philadelphia.* City of Philadelphia Community Renewal Program, Technical Report No. 9.

HERON, W. (1957), "The Pathology of Boredom," *Scientific American* 196: 52–56.

HERSHBERGER, R. G. (1972), "Toward a Set of Semantic Scales to Measure the Meaning of Architectural Environments," in W. J. Mitchell (ed.), *Environmental Design: Research and Practice.* Los Angeles: University of California/EDRA 3.

HIGASA, T. (1960), "A Study of the Planning Unit and the Organization of Facilities of the Residential Unit," *Ekistics* 10: 232–34.

HIGBEE, E. (1960), *The Squeeze: Cities Without Space.* New York: Morrow.

HINSHAW, M. and K. ALLOTT (1972), "Environmental Preferences of Future Housing Consumers," *Journal of the American Institute of Planners* 38: 102–107.

HITLER, A. (1943), *Mein Kampf*. Boston: Houghton Mifflin.

HOGGART, R. (1957), *The Uses of Literacy*. London: Chatto & Windus.

HOLE, V. (1959), "Social Effects of Planned Rehousing," *Town Planning Review* 30: 161–73.

HOLLINGSHEAD, A. B. and F. C. REDLICH (1958), *Social Class and Mental Illness*. New York: Wiley.

HOLLINGSHEAD, A. B. and L. H. ROGLER (1963), "Attitudes toward Slums and Public Housing in Puerto Rico," in L. J. Duhl (ed.), *The Urban Condition*, pp. 229–45. New York: Simon & Schuster.

HOLSTI, O. (1969), *Content Analysis for the Social Sciences and Humanities*. Reading, Mass.: Addison-Wesley.

HONIKMAN, B. (1972), "An Investigation of the Relationship Between Construing of the Environment and Its Physical Form," in W. J. Mitchell (ed.), *Environmental Design: Research and Practice*. Los Angeles: University of California/EDRA 3.

HOROWITZ , M. J., D. F. DUFF, and L. O. STRATTON (1970), "Personal Space and the Body Buffer Zone," in H. M. Proshansky, W. H. Ittelson, and L. G. Rivlin (eds.), *Environmental Psychology*, pp. 214–20. New York: Holt, Rinehart & Winston.

HORTON, F. E. and D. R. REYNOLDS (1971), "Effects of the Urban Spatial Structure on Individual Behavior," *Economic Geography* 47: 36–48.

HOWARD, E. (1898), *Tomorrow: A Peaceful Path to Reform*. London: Sonnenschein.

HOWARD, E. (1920), *Territory in Bird Life*. New York: Dutton.

HOWARD, R. B., F. G. MLYNARSKI, and C. G. SAUER (1972), "A Comparative Analysis of Affective Responses to Real and Represented Environments," in W. J. Mitchell (ed.), *Environmental Design: Research and Practice*. Los Angeles: University of California/EDRA 3.

HOWE, G. M. (1963), *A National Atlas of Disease Mortality in the United Kingdom*. London: Nelson.

HOYT, H. (1939), *The Structure and Growth of Residential Neighborhoods in American Cities*. Washington, D.C.: Federal Housing Administration.

HSIA, V. (1967), *Residence Hall Environment*. Architectural Psychology Program: University of Utah.

HULL, C. L. (1943), *Principles of Behavior*. New York: Appleton-Century-Crofts.

HUNT, E. S., F. G. TRYON, and J. H. WILLITS (1925), *What the Coal Commission Found*. Baltimore: Williams & Wilkins.

HUNTER, F. (1953), *Community Power Structure*. New York: Doubleday.

HUNTINGTON, E. (1945), *Mainsprings of Civilization*. New York: Wiley.

HURST, M. E. E. (ed.) (1975), *I Came to the City*. Boston: Houghton Mifflin.

HUTT, C. and M. VAIZEY (1966), "Differential Effects of Group Density on Social Behavior," *Nature* 209: 1371–72.

HUXLEY, A. (1948), *Antic Hay*. London: Penguin Books.

———— (1955), *Brave New World*. London: Penguin Books.

INEICHEN, B. (1972), "Home Ownership and Manual Workers' Life Styles," *Sociological Review* 20: 391–412.

ISAACS, R. (1948a), "The Neighborhood Theory," *Journal of the American Institute of Planners* 14: 38–40.

———— (1948b), "Are Urban Neighborhoods Possible?" *Journal of Housing* 5: 177–80.

ITTELSON, W. H. (1960), "Some Factors Influencing the Design and Function of Psychiatric Facilities." Unpublished manuscript, Brooklyn College Psychology Department.

————, H. M. PROSHANSKY, and L. G. RIVLIN (1970a), "The Environmental Psychology of the Psychiatric Ward," in H. M. Proshansky, W. H. Ittelson, and L. G. Rivlin (eds.), *Environmental Psychology*, pp. 419–39. New York: Holt, Rinehart & Winston.

———— (1970b), "Bedroom Size and Social Interaction of the Psychiatric Ward," *Environment and Behavior* 2: 255–70.

IZUMI, K. (1965), "Psychosocial Phenomena and Building Design," *Building Research* 2: 9–11.

JACKSON, J. B. (1956), "Other-Directed Houses," *Landscape* 6: 29–35.

———— (1957), "The Stranger's Path," *Landscape* 7: 11–15.

JACOBS, A. B. (1967), "Observations on Chandigarh," *Journal of the American Institute of Planners* 33: 18–26.

JACOBS, J. (1961), *The Death and Life of Great American Cities*. New York: Vintage Books.

JANISOVA, H. (1971), "Leisure Time of City Residents in the Light of Urban Living Conditions and Environment," *Society and Leisure* 1: 121–44.

JOHNS, E. (1965), *British Townscapes*. London: Arnold.

JOHNSON, J. W. (1968), *Utopian Literature: A Selection*. New York: Random House.

JOHNSTON, R. J. (1971), "Squatter Settlements in South American Cities," *Perspective* 8: 1–7.

———— (1972), "Activity Spaces and Residential Preferences: Some Tests of the Hypothesis of Sectoral Mental Maps," *Economic Geography* 48: 199–211.

JONASSEN, C. T. (1949), "Cultural Variables in the Ecology of an Ethnic Group," *American Sociological Review* 14: 32–41.

JONES, K. (1975), "The Mobility of the Elderly: A Study of a Suburban Silver Threads Centre." Unpublished M.A. thesis, University of Victoria, B.C.

JONES, M. M. (1972), "Urban Path Choosing Behavior," in W. J. Mitchell (ed.), *Environmental Design: Research and Practice*. Los Angeles: University of California/ EDRA 3.

JONES, S. E. (1971), "A Comparative Proxemics Analysis of Interaction in Selected Subcultures of New York City," *Journal of Social Psychology* 84: 35–44.

JORGENSON, L. (1971), "New York's Squatters: Vanguard of Community Control?" *City* 5: 35–39.

JOSEPH, S. M. (ed.) (1969), *The Me Nobody Knows: Childrens' Voices from the Ghetto*. New York: Avon Books.

JOURARD, S. M. and R. FRIEDMAN (1970), "Experimenter-Subject Distance and Self-Disclosure," *Journal of Personality and Social Psychology* 15: 278–82.

JUNG, C. (1969), *Memories, Dreams and Reflections*. London: Collins.

KANE, J. N. and G. L. ALEXANDER (1965), *Nicknames of Cities and States of the United States*. New York: Scarecrow Press.

KAPLAN, S. (1973), "Cognitive Maps in Perception and Thought," in R. M. Downs and D. Stea (eds.), *Image and Environment*, pp. 63–78. Chicago: Aldine.

KASMAR, J. (1970), "Development of a Usable Lexicon of Environmental Descriptors," *Environment and Behavior* 2: 153–70.

KASPERSON, R. E. and M. BREITBART (1974), *Participation, Decentralization, and Advocacy Planning*. Washington, D.C.: Association of American Geographers Resource Paper 25.

KATES, R. W. and J. F. WOHLWILL (1966), "Man's Response to the Physical Environment," *Journal of Social Issues* 22: 15–28.

KAUFMAN, M. T. (1970), "Frustrations of the Metropolis Breed Rudeness and Insensitivity," reprinted in *Victoria Daily Times* 17 March 1970, from *New York Times*.

KAYE, B. (1960), *The Development of the Architectural Profession in Britain: A Sociological Study*. London: Allen & Unwin.

KEELEY, K. (1962), "Prenatal Influence on Behavior of Offspring of Crowded Mice," *Science* 135: 44–45.

KELLER, S. (1966), "Social Class in Physical Planning," *International Social Science Journal* 18: 494–512.

———— (1968), *The Urban Neighborhood: A Sociological Perspective*. New York: Random House.

KELLY, J. G. (1972), "Coping and Adapting to the High School Environment," in W. J. Mitchell (ed.), *Environmental Design: Research and Practice*. Los Angeles: University of California/EDRA 3.

KENT, D. P., R. KASTENBAUM, and S. SHERWOOD (eds.) (1972), *Research Planning and Action for the Elderly: The Power and Potential of Social Science*. New York: Behavioral Publications.

KERR, M. (1958), *The People of Ship Street*. New York: Humanities Press.

KETCHAM, B. (1971), "City of Victoria Offenders: A Survey of Suicides, Attempted Suicides, Juvenile Delinquency and Domestic Quarrels." Unpublished paper, University of Victoria Geography Department.

KEY, V. O. (1961), *Public Opinion and American Democracy*. New York: Knopf.

KHOSLA, R. (1971), "Chandigarh: Dream and Reality," *Geographical Magazine* 43: 678–83.

KIRA, A. (1966), *The Bathroom: Criteria for Design*. Ithaca, N.Y.: Center for Housing and Environmental Studies, Cornell University.

KIRK, W. (1951), "Historical Geography and the Concept of the Behavioral Environment," in G. Kuriyan (ed.), *Indian Geographical Journal: Silver Jubilee Edition*, pp. 152–60. Madras: Indian Geographical Society.

———— (1963), "Problems of Geography," *Geography* 47: 357–71.

KLAUSNER, S. Z. (1971), *On Man in His Environment*. San Francisco: Jossey-Bass.

KLECK, R. (1969), "Physical Stigma and Task Oriented Interactions," *Human Relations* 22: 53–60.

KLEIN, H-J. (1967), "The Delimitation of the Town Centre in the Image of its Citizens," in University of Amsterdam, Sociographical Department (eds.), *Urban Core and Inner City*, pp. 286–306. Leiden: Brill.

KLEIN, M. W. (1966), "Factors Related to Juvenile Gang Membership Patterns," *Sociology and Social Research* 51: 49–62.

KLOPFER, P. H. (1969), *Habitats and Territories: A Study of the Use of Space by Animals*. New York: Basic Books.

———— and J. P. HAILMAN (1967), *An Introduction to Animal Behavior*. Englewood Cliffs, N.J.: Prentice-Hall.

KLUCKHOHN, F. R. and F. L. STRODTBECK (1961), *Variations in Value Orientations*. Evanston, Ill.: Row, Peterson.

KOESTLER, A. (1968), "Rebellion in a Vacuum," in B. Crick and W. A. Robson (eds.), *Protest and Discontent*, pp. 14–24. London: Penguin Books.

KOFFKA, K. (1935), *Principles of Gestalt Psychology*. London: Kegan Paul.

KOROSCIL, P. M. (1971), "The Behavioural Environmental Approach," *Area* 3: 96–99.

KRECH, D., R. S. CRUTCHFIELD, and E. L. BALLACHEY (1962), *The Individual in Society*. New York: McGraw-Hill.

KRECH, D., M. R. ROSENZWEIG, and E. L. BENNETT (1960), "Effects of Environmental Complexity and Training on Brain Complexity," *Journal of Comparative and Physiological Psychology* 53: 509–19.

———— (1962), "Relation Between Brain Chemistry and Problem-solving among Rats Raised in Enriched and Impoverished Environments," *Journal of Comparative and Physiological Psychology* 55: 801–807.

KRIESBERG, L. (1969), "Neighborhood Setting and the Isolation of Public Housing Tenants," in P. Meadows and E. H. Mizruchi (eds.), *Urbanism, Urbanization, and Change*, pp. 276–91. Reading, Mass.: Addison-Wesley.

KUETHE, J. L. (1962a), "Social Schemas," *Journal of Abnormal and Social Psychology* 64: 31–38.

———— (1962b), "Social Schemas and Reconstruction of Social Object Displays from Memory," *Journal of Abnormal and Social Psychology* 65: 71–74.

KUPER, L. (ed.) (1953), *Living in Towns*. London: Cresset Press.

KUTNER, B., C. WILKINS, and P. R. YARROW (1952), "Verbal Attitudes and Overt Behavior Involving Racial Prejudice," *Journal of Abnormal and Social Psychology* 47: 649–52.

LADD, F. C. (1970), "Black Youths View their Environment: Neighborhood Maps," *Environment and Behavior* 2: 74–99.

———— (1972), "Black Youths View Their Environments," *Journal of the American Institute of Planners* 38: 108–15.

LAI, C-Y. (1974), "Human Crowding in Hong Kong," in M. C. R. Edgell and B. H. Farrell (eds.), *Themes on Pacific Lands*, pp. 141–80. Victoria, B.C.: Western Geographical Series 10.

LAMANNA, R. A. (1964), "Value Consensus among Urban Residents," *Journal of the American Institute of Planners* 36: 317–23.

LANG, J. and C. BURNETTE (1974), "A Model of the Designing Process," in J. Lang, C. Burnette, W. Moleski, and D. Vachon (eds.), *Designing for Human Behavior*, pp. 43–51. Stroudsburg, Pa.: Dowden, Hutchinson & Ross.

————, W. MOLESKI, and D. VACHON (eds.) (1974), *Designing for Human Behavior*. Stroudsburg, Pa.: Dowden, Hutchinson & Ross.

LANGNER, T. S. and S. T. MICHAEL (1963), *Life Stress and Mental Health*. New York: Free Press.

LANSING, J. B. and L. KISH (1957), "Family Life Cycle as an Independent Variable," *American Sociological Review* 22: 512–19.

LA PIERE, R. T. (1934), "Attitudes versus Action," *Social Forces* 13: 230–37.

LAO TSE (1958), *The Wisdom of Lao Tse*. London: Michael Joseph.

LAQUIAN, A. A. (1974), "Slums of Hope . . . Slums of Despair," *Cooperation Canada* September/October, 3–11.

LASSEN, C. C. (1969), "Interaction Distance and the Initial Psychiatric Interview." Unpublished Ph.D. thesis, Yale University.

LAWTON, M. P. (1970a), "Ecology and Aging," in L. A. Pastalan and D. H. Carson (eds.), *Spatial Behavior of Older People*. Ann Arbor: University of Michigan.

———— (1970b), "Assessment Integration and Environments for Older People," *The Gerontologist* 10.

———— (1972), "Some Beginnings of an Ecological Psychology of Old Age," in J. F. Wohlwill and D. H. Carson (eds.), *Environment and the Social Sciences*, pp. 114–22. Washington, D.C.: American Psychological Association.

———— (1974), "The Human Being and the Institutional Building," in J. Lang, C. Burnette, W. Moleski, and D. Vachon (eds.), *Designing for Human Behavior*, pp. 60–71. Stroudsburg, Pa.: Dowden, Hutchinson & Ross.

LE CORBUSIER (1929), *The City of Tomorrow and Its Planning*. London: Architectural Press.

LE PLAY, F. (1855), *Les Ouvriers Européens*. Tours: Mame.

LECOMPTE, W. F. (1972), "Behavior Settings," in W. J. Mitchell (ed.), *Environmental Design: Research and Practice*. Los Angeles: University of California/EDRA 3.

———— (1974), "Behavior Settings as Data-Generating Units for Environmental Planner and Architect," in J. Lang, C. Burnette, W. Moleski, and D. Vachon (eds.), *Designing for Human Behavior*, pp. 183–93. Stroudsburg, Pa.: Dowden, Hutchinson & Ross.

LEDERER, W. J. and E. BURDICK (1958), *The Ugly American*. New York: Norton.

LEE, D. H. K. (1966), "The Role of Attitude in Response to Environmental Stress," *Journal of Social Issues* 22: 83–91.

LEE, T. (1962), "Brennan's Law of Shopping Behavior," *Psychology Reports* 11: 662.

———— (1968), "The Urban Neighborhood as a Socio-Spatial Schema," *Human Relations* 21: 241–68.

———— (1970), "Perceived Distance as a Function of Direction in the City," *Environment and Behavior* 2: 40–51.

LEIBMAN, M. (1970), "The Effect of Sex and Race Norms on Personal Space," *Environment and Behavior* 2: 208–46.

LEMON, J. T. (1974), "Toronto: Is it a Model for Urban Life and Citizen Participation?" in D. Ley (ed), *Community Participation and the Spatial Order of the City*, pp. 41–58. Vancouver: B.C. Geographical Series 19.

LESSING, L. (1968), "Systems Engineering Invades the City," *Fortune* 77: 154–57.

LEUBA, C. (1955), "Toward Some Integration of Learning Theories: The Concept of Optimal Stimulation," *Psychological Reports* 1: 27–33.

LEWIN, K. (1936), *Principles of Topological Psychology*. New York: McGraw-Hill.

———— (1951), "Field Theory and Learning," in D. Cartwright (ed.), *Field Theory in Social Science: Selected Theoretical Papers* by Kurt Lewin, pp. 60–86. New York: Harper & Row.

LEWIS, C. S. (1970), *The Chronicles of Narnia*. New York: Collier.

LEWIS, O. (1959), *Five Families*. New York: Basic Books.

———— (1966), *La Vida*. New York: Random House.

LEWIS, P. F. (1975), "Common Houses, Cultural Spoor," *Landscape* 19: 1–22.

LEY, D. (1974), "Problems of Co-optation and Idolatry in the Community Group," in D. Ley (ed.), *Community Participation and the Spatial Order of the City*, pp. 75–88. Vancouver: B.C. Geographical Series 19.

———— and R. CYBRIWSKY (1974a), "Urban Graffiti as Territorial Markers," *Annals of the Association of American Geographers* 64: 491–505.

———— (1974b), "The Spatial Ecology of Stripped Cars," *Environment and Behavior* 6: 53–68.

LEYHAUSEN, P. (1965a), "The Communal Organization of Solitary Mammals," *Symposium of the Zoological Society of London* 14: 249–63.

———— (1965b), "The Sane Community — A Density Problem," *Discovery* 26: 27–33.

———— (1968), "Dominance and Territoriality as Complements in Mammalian Social Structure." Paper read at American Association of Anthropological Sociology Symposium, Dallas.

LIEBERSON, S. (1963), *Ethnic Patterns in American Cities*. Glencoe, Ill.: Free Press.

LILLY, J. C. (1956), "Mental Effects of Reduction of Ordinary Levels of Physical Stimulation on Intact, Healthy Persons," *Psychiatric Research Reports* 5: 1–9.

LINDHEIM, R. (1966), "Factors Which Determine Hospital Design," *American Journal of Public Health* 56: 1668–75.

LING, A. (1967), *Runcorn New Town: Master Plan*. Runcorn, Cheshire: Runcorn Development Corporation.

LINN, K. (1968), "Neighborhood Commons," in G. Bell, E. Randall, and J. E. R. Roeder (eds.) (1973), *Urban Environments and Human Behavior*, p. 182. Stroudsburg, Pa.: Dowden, Hutchinson & Ross.

LIPMAN, A. (1971), "Professional Ideology: 'Community' and 'Total'," *Architectural Research and Teaching* 1: 39–49.

———— (1974), "The Architectural Belief System and Social Behavior," in J. Lang, C. Burnette, W. Moleski, and D. Vachon (eds.), *Designing for Human Behavior*, pp. 23–30. Stroudsburg, Pa.: Dowden, Hutchinson & Ross.

LIPSET, S. M. and R. BENDIX (1959), *Social Mobility in Industrial Society*. Berkeley: University of California Press.

LITTLE, K. B. (1968), "Cultural Variations in Social Schemata," *Journal of Personality and Social Psychology* 10: 1–7.

LOCK, M. (1948), *The Hartlepools: A Survey and a Plan*. London: Dobson.

LOO, C. M. (1972), "Effects of Spatial Density on Social Behavior of Children," *Man-Environment Systems* 2: 351–52.

LORENZ, K. Z. (1952), *King Solomon's Ring*. New York: Crowell.

———— (1966), *On Aggression*. New York: Harcourt, Brace & World.

LORIMER, J. (1972), *A Citizen's Guide to City Politics*. Toronto: James Lewis & Samuel.

———— and M. PHILLIPS (1971), *Working People*. Toronto: James Lewis & Samuel.

LORING, W. C. (1956), "Housing and Social Disorganization," *Social Problems* 3: 160–68.

LOTZ, J. (1965), "The Squatters of Whitehorse," *Arctic* 18: 173–88.

LOWENTHAL, D. (1961), "Geography, Experience, and Imagination: Towards a Geographical Epistemology," *Annals of the Association of American Geographers* 51: 241–60.

———— (1962), "Not Every Prospect Pleases," *Landscape* 12: 19–23.

———— (1964), "Images of Nature in America," *Columbia University Forum* 7: 34–40.

———— (1968), "The American Scene," *Geographical Review* 58: 61–88.

———— and H. C. PRINCE (1964), "The English Landscape," *Geographical Review* 54: 309–46.

———— (1965), "English Landscape Tastes," *Geographical Review* 55: 186–222.

LOWENTHAL, D. and M. RIEL (1972), *Milieu and Observer Differences in Environmental Associations*. Washington, D.C.: American Geographical Society Publications on Environmental Perception 7.

LOWREY, R. A. (1970), "Distance Concepts of Urban Residents," *Environment and Behavior* 2: 52–73.

LUPO, A., F. COLCORD, and E. P. FOWLER (1971), *Rites of Way*. Boston: Little, Brown.

LYMAN, S. M. and M. B. SCOTT (1967), "Territoriality: A Neglected Sociological Dimension," *Social Problems* 15: 236–49.

LYNCH, K. (1960), *The Image of the City*. Cambridge, Mass.: M.I.T. Press.

———— (1972), *What Time is This Place?* Cambridge, Mass: M.I.T. Press.

———— and M. RIVKIN (1959), "A Walk Around the Block," *Landscape* 8: 24–34.

MACMURRY, T. (1971), "Aspects of Time and the Study of Activity Patterns," *Town Planning Review* 42: 195–209.

MANGIN, W. and J. C. TURNER (1968), "The Barriada Movement," *Progressive Architecture* 49: 154–62.

MANN, P. H. (1958), "The Socially Balanced Neighborhood Unit," *Town Planning Review* 29: 91–98.

———— (1963), "The Internal Hierarchy of Sub-Areas in Urban Settlements," *Ekistics* 15: 34–38.

———— (1965), *An Approach to Urban Sociology.* London: Routledge & Kegan Paul.

MANNING, P. (1965), *Office Design: A Study of Environment.* Liverpool: The Pilkington Research Unit.

MANUEL, F. E. (1966), *Utopias and Utopian Thought.* Boston: Houghton Mifflin.

MARANS, R. W. and J. B. LANSING (1969), "Evaluation of Neighborhood Quality," *Journal of the American Institute of Planners* 35: 195–99.

MARCUSE, P. (1969), "Black Housing: A New Approach for Planners," in G. Bell, E. Randall, and J. E. R. Roeder (eds.) (1973), *Urban Environments and Human Behavior,* p. 174. Stroudsburg, Pa.: Dowden, Hutchinson & Ross.

MARGOLIS, J. (1961), "Rebellion or Delinquency?" *The Nation* 193: 31–32, 40.

MARK, L. S. (1972), "Modeling Through Toy Play: A Methodology for Eliciting Topographical Representations in Children," in W. J. Mitchell (ed.) *Environmental Design: Research and Practice.* Los Angeles: University of California/EDRA 3.

MARQUEZ, G. GARCIA (1970), *One Hundred Years of Solitude.* New York: Harper & Row.

MARRIS, P. (1963), "A Report on Urban Renewal in the United States," in L. J. Duhl (ed.), *The Urban Condition,* pp. 113–34. New York: Simon & Schuster.

MARSDEN, H. M. (1972), "Crowding and Animal Behavior," in J. F. Wohlwill and D. H. Carson (eds.), *Environment and the Social Sciences,* pp. 5–14. Washington, D.C.: American Psychological Association.

MARSH, G. P. (1864), *Man and Nature.* (1967 edition edited by D. Lowenthal) Cambridge, Mass.: Belknap Press.

MARTIN, A. E. (1967), "Environment, Housing and Health," *Urban Studies* 4: 1–21.

MARTINEAU, T. R. (1972), "The Urban Activity Model," in W. J. Mitchell (ed.), *Environmental Design: Research and Practice.* Los Angeles: University of California/EDRA 3.

MARX, L. (1964), *The Machine in the Garden.* New York: Oxford University Press.

MASALDAN, P. N. (1965), *Planning and the People.* New York: Asia Publishing House.

MASLOW, A. (1954), *Motivation and Personality.* New York: Harper & Row.

MASS OBSERVATION (1943), *The Pub and the People.* London: Gollancz.

MATHER, W. G. (1972), "Attempts to Introduce Human Requirements into Building Requirements," *Man-Environment Systems* 2: 117–24.

MAW, R. (1971), "Construction of a Leisure Model," *Ekistics* 31: 230–38.

MAXWELL, G. (1969), *Ring of Bright Water*. London: Pan Books.

MAYFIELD, R. C. (1972), "The Spatial Structure of a Selected Interpersonal Contact: A Regional Comparison of Marriage Distances in India," in P. W. English and R. C. Mayfield (eds.), *Man, Space, and Environment*, pp. 385–401. New York: Oxford University Press.

McCLENAHAN, B. A. (1945), *The Changing Urban Neighborhood*. Los Angeles: University of Southern California.

McHARG, I. (1969), *Design With Nature*. Garden City, N.Y.: Natural History Press.

McKAY, H. (1949), "The Neighborhood and Child Conduct," *Annals of the American Academy of Political and Social Science* 261: 32–41.

McKECHNIE, G. (1970), "Measuring Environmental Dispositions with the Environmental Response Inventory," in J. Archea and C. Eastman (eds.), *Proceedings, Second Environmental Design Research Association Conference*, Pittsburgh.

McKENZIE, R. D. (1926), "The Scope of Human Ecology," *Journal of Applied Sociology* 10: 316–23.

McLUHAN, M. (1964), *Understanding Media*. New York: McGraw-Hill.

McNEIL, E. B. (1970), *The Psychoses*. Englewood Cliffs, N.J.: Prentice-Hall.

McTAGGART, W. D. (1971), "Squatters' Rights," *Professional Geographer* 23: 355–59.

MEAD, M. (1966), "Neighborhoods and Human Needs," *Ekistics* 21: 124–26.

MEIER, R. L. (1959), "Human Time Allocation: A Basis for Social Accounts," *Journal of the American Institute of Planners* 25: 27–33.

———— (1962), *A Communications Theory of Urban Growth*. Cambridge, Mass.: M.I.T. Press.

———— (1968), "The Metropolis as a Transaction-Maximizing System," *Daedalus* 97: 1292–1313.

MEISELS, M. and F. M. CANTER (1970), "Personal Space and Personality Characteristics: A Non-confirmation," *Psychological Reports* 27: 287–90.

MEISELS, M. and C. J. GUARDO (1969), "Development of Personal Space Schematas," *Child Development* 40: 1167–78.

MERCER, D. (1971), "Discretionary Travel Behavior and the Urban Mental Map," *Australian Geographical Studies* 9: 133–43.

MERTON, R. K. (1948), "The Social Psychology of Housing," in W. Dennis (ed.), *Current Trends in Social Psychology*, pp. 163–217. Pittsburgh: University of Pittsburgh Press.

———— (1949), "Patterns of Influence," in P. Lazarsfeld and F. N. Stanton (eds.), *Communications Research 1948–49*, pp. 180–219. New York: Harper.

———— (1957), "Patterns of Influence: Local and Cosmopolitan Influentials," in R. K. Merton (ed.), *Social Theory and Social Structure*, pp. 387–420. New York: Free Press.

MESSER, M. (1966), "The Effects of Age Grouping on Organizational and Normative Systems of the Elderly," in *Proceedings, Seventh International Congress of Gerontology*, pp. 253–58. Vienna: Wiener Medizinischen Akademie.

MEYER, J. (1951), "The Stranger and the City," *American Journal of Sociology* 56: 476–83.

MEYERSON, M. (1961), "Utopian Traditions and the Planning of Cities," in L. Rodwin (ed.), *The Future Metropolis*. New York: Braziller.

————— (1969), "Ethical Issues Involved in Changing the Physical Environment," in *The Ethics of Change*, pp. 31–42. Toronto: Canadian Broadcasting Corporation.

MICHELSON, W. (1966), "An Empirical Analysis of Urban Environmental Preferences," *Journal of the American Institute of Planners* 32: 355–60.

————— (1967), "Potential Candidates for the Designer's Paradise," *Social Forces* 46: 190–96.

————— (1968), "Most People Don't Want What Architects Want," *Trans-Action* 5: 37–43.

————— (1970), *Man and His Urban Environment: A Sociological Approach*. Reading, Mass.: Addison-Wesley.

————— (1975), cited in C. Oberdorff, "What Really Goes on in the Suburbs," *Quest* 4: 54–62.

MILBRATH, L. W. (1965), *Political Participation*. Chicago: Rand McNally.

MILGRAM, S. (1970), "The Experience of Living in Cities," *Science* 167: 1461–68.

—————, J. GREENWALD, S. KESSLER, W. McKENNA, and J. WATERS (1972), "A Psychological Map of New York City," *American Scientist* 60: 194–200.

MILLER, J. E. (1961), "Residential Density: Relating People to Space rather than to Ground Area," *Journal of the American Institute of Planners* 27: 77–78.

MILLS, C. W. (1956), *The Power Elite*. New York: Oxford University Press.

————— (1959), *The Sociological Imagination*. New York: Oxford University Press.

MITCHELL, H. E. (1974), "Professional and Client: An Emerging Collaborative Relationship," in J. Lang, C. Burnette, W. Moleski, and D. Vachon (eds.), *Designing for Human Behavior*, pp. 15–22. Stroudsburg, Pa.: Dowden, Hutchinson & Ross.

MITCHELL, R. (1971), "Some Social Implications of High Density Housing," *American Sociological Review* 36: 18–29.

MITCHELL, R. and C. RAPKIN (1954), *Urban Traffic: A Function of Land Use*. New York: Columbia University Press.

MOGEY, J. M. (1955), "Changes in Family Life Experienced by English Workers Moving from Slums to Housing Estates," *Marriage and Family Living* 27: 123–32.

————— (1956), *Family and Neighborhood*. London: Oxford University Press.

MOLLER, C. B. (1968), *Architectural Environment and Our Mental Health*. New York: Horizon Press.

MONTAGU, M. F. A. (ed.) (1968), *Man and Aggression*. New York: Oxford University Press.

MONTGOMERY, R. (1966), "Comment on 'Fear and the House-as-Haven in the Lower Class'," *Journal of the American Institute of Planners* 32: 31–37.

MOORE, G. T. (1974), "Developmental Variations Between and Within Individuals in the Cognitive Representation of Large-scale Spatial Environments," *Man-Environment Systems* 4: 55–57.

MORRILL, R. L. and F. R. PITTS (1967), "Marriage, Migration, and the Mean Information Field: A Study in Uniqueness and Generality," *Annals of the Association of American Geographers* 57: 401–402.

MORRIS, D. (1968), *The Naked Ape*. New York: McGraw-Hill.

————— (1969), *The Human Zoo*. New York: McGraw-Hill.

MOYER, K. E. (ed.) (1971), *The Physiology of Hostility*. Chicago: Markham.

MUMFORD, L. (1948), "Britain and Her Planning Schemes," B.B.C. radio talk cited in N. Pearson (1962), "Planning a Social Unit," *Plan Canada* 3: 78–86.

————— (1954), "The Neighbourhood and the Neighbourhood Unit," *Town Planning Review* 24: 256–70.

MUNSINGER, H. and W. KESSEN (1964), "Uncertainty, Structure, and Preference," *Psychological Monographs: General and Applied* 78: 1–24.

MURDIE, R. A. (1969), *Factorial Ecology of Metropolitan Toronto 1951–61*. Chicago: University of Chicago Geography Department Research Papers 116.

MURPHY, P. E. (1973), "Apartment Location: The Balance Between Developer and Community," in C. N. Forward (ed.), *Residential and Neighbourhood Studies in Victoria*, pp. 149–177. Victoria, B.C.: Western Geographical Series 5.

————— and R. G. GOLLEDGE (1972), *Comments on the Use of Attitude as a Variable in Urban Geography*. Columbus: Ohio State Geography Discussion Paper 25.

MURPHY, R. E. (1966), *The American City*. New York: McGraw-Hill.

MUSGRAVE, N. (1966), "The City: An Anthology of Quotations," *Journal of the Royal Institute of British Architects* 73: 472–75.

MUSIL, J. (1972), "Sociology of Urban Redevelopment Areas: A Study from Czechoslovakia," in G. Bell and J. Tyrwhitt (eds.), *Human Identity in the Urban Environment*, pp. 298–303. London: Pelican Books.

MUTH, R. (1969), *Cities and Housing*. Chicago: University of Chicago Press.

MYERHOFF, H. L. and B. G. MYERHOFF (1964), "Field Observations of Middle Class Gangs," *Social Forces* 42: 328–36.

MYERS, K., C. S. HALE, R. MYKYTOWYCZ, and R. L. HUGHES (1971), "The Effects of Varying Density and Space on Sociality and Health in Animals," in A. H. Esser (ed.), *Behavior and Environment*, pp. 148–87. New York: Plenum Press.

MYRDAL, G. (1944), *The American Dilemma*. New York: Harper.

NAIRN, I. (1965), *The American Landscape*. New York: Random House.

NEWMAN, O. (1972), *Defensible Space*. New York: Macmillan.

NICE, M. M. (1941), "The Role of Territory in Bird Life," *American Midland Naturalist* 26: 441–87.

NORCLIFFE, G. B. (1974), "Territorial Influences in Urban Political Space: A Study of Perception in Kitchener-Waterloo," *Canadian Geographer* 18: 311–29.

NOWLAN, A. (1974), "A Crock of Jargon," *Books in Canada* 3: 31.

ORLANS, H. (1952), *Stevenage: A Sociological Study of a New Town*. London: Routledge and Kegan Paul.

————— (1953), *Utopia Ltd*. New Haven: Yale University Press.

ORLEANS, P. (1973), "Differential Cognition of Urban Residents: Effects of Social Scale on Mapping," in R. M. Downs and D. Stea (eds.), *Image and Environment*, pp. 115–30. Chicago: Aldine.

———— and S. SCHMIDT (1972), "Mapping the City: Environmental Cognition of Urban Residents," in W. J. Mitchell (ed.), *Environmental Design: Research and Practice*. Los Angeles: University of California/EDRA 3.

OSBORN, F. J. and A. WHITTICK (1969), *The New Towns: The Answer to Megalopolis*, 2nd ed. London: Leonard Hill.

OSGOOD, C. E., G. J. SUCI, and P. M. TANNENBAUM (1957), *The Measurement of Meaning*. Urbana, Ill.: University of Illinois Press.

OSMOND, H. (1957), "Function as the Basis of Psychiatric Ward Design," *Mental Hospitals* 8: 23–30.

PACKARD, V. (1972), *A Nation of Strangers*. New York: McKay.

PAGE, J. (1970), "A Protest at Urban Environment," in B. Crick and W. A. Robson (eds.), *Protest and Discontent*, pp. 98–109. London: Penguin Books.

PAHL, R. (1970), *Patterns of Urban Life*. London: Longmans, Green.

PALMER, J. A. D. (1971), "Introduction to the British Edition," in R. Goodman (1972), *After the Planners*, pp. 9–50. London: Pelican Books.

PAPPAS, P. (1967), "Time Allocation Study in Eighteen Athens Communities," *Ekistics* 140: 110–27.

PARK, R. E., E. BURGESS, and R. D. McKENZIE (eds.) (1925), *The City*. Chicago: University of Chicago Press.

PARR, A. E. (1965), "In Search of Theory," *Arts and Architecture* 82: 14–16.

———— (1971a), "Heating, Lighting, Plumbing, and Human Relations," *Landscape* 19: 28–29.

———— (1971b), "The Design of Cities," *A A Quarterly* 3: 22–26.

———— (1973), "Architecture, Art, and Pollution," *A A Quarterly* 5.

PARSONS, T. (1966), *Societies*. Englewood Cliffs, N.J.: Prentice-Hall.

PASTALAN, L. A. and D. CARSON (eds.) (1970), *Spatial Behavior of Older People*. Ann Arbor: University of Michigan Press.

PAWLEY, M. (1971), *Architecture Versus Housing*. London: Studio Vista.

PEARSON, N. (1962), "Planning a Social Unit," *Plan Canada* 3: 78–86.

PEATTIE, L. R. (1968), "Reflections on Advocacy Planning," *Journal of the American Institute of Planners* 34: 80–88.

———— (1970), *The View from the Barrio*. Ann Arbor: University of Michigan Press.

PEDERSON, D. M. (1973), "Developmental Trends in Personal Space," *Journal of Psychology* 83: 3–9.

PELLEGRINI, R. J. and J. EMPEY (1970), "Interpersonal Spatial Orientation in Dyads," *Journal of Psychology* 76: 67–70.

PERIN, C. (1970), *With Man in Mind: An Interdisciplinary Prospectus for Environmental Design*. Cambridge, Mass.: M.I.T. Press.

_____ (1974), "The Social Order of Environmental Design," in J. Lang, C. Burnette, W. Moleski, and D. Vachon (eds.), *Designing for Human Behavior*, pp. 31–42. Stroudsburg, Pa.: Dowden, Hutchinson & Ross.

PERRY, C. (1929), "The Neighborhood Unit," *Regional Plan of New York and its Environs* 7: 22–140.

_____ (1939), *Housing for the Machine Age*. New York: Russell Sage Foundation.

PETERSEN, W. (1966), "On Some Meanings of 'Planning'," *Journal of the American Institute of Planners* 32: 130–42.

PETERSON, E. T. (ed.) (1946), *Cities are Abnormal*. Norman, Okla.: University of Oklahoma Press.

PETERSON, G. L. (1967), "A Model of Preference," *Journal of Regional Science* 7: 19–32.

PFEIFFER, T. (1971), "Some References to the Study of Ethology," *Man–Environment Systems* 1: B4.

PIAGET, J. (1963), *The Child's Conception of the World*. Patterson, N.J.: Littlefield, Adams.

_____ and B. INHELDER (1948), *The Child's Conception of Space*. New York: Norton.

_____, and A. SZEMINSKA (1964), *The Child's Conception of Geometry*. New York: Harper.

PICK, F. (1941), *Britain Must Rebuild: A Pattern for Planning*. London: Routledge and Kegan Paul.

PLANT, J. S. (1930), "Some Psychiatric Effects of Crowded Living Conditions," *American Journal of Psychiatry* 9: 849–60.

POKORNY, A. D., F. DAVIS, and W. HALBERSON (1963), "Suicide, Suicide Attempts, and Weather," *American Journal of Psychiatry* 120: 371–88.

POLANYI, M. (1963), *The Study of Man*. Chicago: University of Chicago Press.

POLLARD, S. (1965), *The Genesis of Modern Management*. London: Arnold.

POLLOCK, L. S. (1972), "Relating Urban Design to the Motorist," in W. J. Mitchell (ed.), *Environmental Design: Research and Practice*. Los Angeles: University of California/EDRA 3.

POLLOWY, A-M. and M. BEZMAN (1972), "Design-Oriented Approach to Development Needs," in W. J. Mitchell (ed.), *Environmental Design: Research and Practice*. Los Angeles: University of California/EDRA 3.

PONTIUS, A. (1967), "A Neuro-Psychiatric Hypothesis about Territorial Behavior," *Perceptual and Motor Skills* 24: 1232–34.

POORKAJ, H. (1972), "Social-Psychological Factors and Successful Aging," *Sociology and Social Research* 56: 289–300.

POPENOE, D. (1969), "On the Meaning of 'Urban' in Urban Studies," in P. Meadows and E. H. Mizruchi (eds.), *Urbanism, Urbanization, and Change*, pp. 64–75. Reading, Mass.: Addison-Wesley.

PORTEOUS, C. W. (1968), "An Exploratory Examination of the Factors Involved in Friendship Formation in Male Student Halls of Residence of Differing Architectural Design." Unpublished B.A. Honors thesis, University of Hull, England.

_____ (1972), "Learning as a Function of Molar Environmental Complexity." Unpublished M.A. thesis, University of Victoria, B.C.

PORTEOUS, J. D. (1970), "The Nature of the Company Town," *Transactions of the Institute of British Geographers* 51: 127–42.

_____ (1971), "Design with People: The Quality of the Urban Environment," *Environment and Behavior* 3: 155–78.

_____ (1972), "Urban Transplantation in Chile," *Geographical Review* 62: 455–78.

_____ (1973a), "The Burnside Teenage Gang: Territoriality, Social Space, and Community Planning," in C. N. Forward (ed.), *Residential and Neighbourhood Studies in Victoria*, pp. 130–48. Victoria, B.C.: Western Geographical Series 5.

_____ (1973b), "The Company State: A Chilean Case Study," *Canadian Geographer* 17: 113–26.

_____ (1974), "Social Class in Atacama Company Towns," *Annals of the Association of American Geographers* 64: 409–17.

_____ (1975), "A Preliminary Landscape Analysis of Middle-Earth During its Third Age," *Landscape* 19: 33–38.

PORTER, J. (1965), *The Vertical Mosaic*. Toronto: University of Toronto Press.

POWELL, J. M. (1971), "Utopia, Millenium, and the Co-operative Ideal: A Behavioural Matrix in the Settlement Process," *Australian Geographer* 11: 606–18.

PREISER, W. F. E. (1972), "Behavior of Nursery School Children under Different Spatial Densities," *Man-Environment Systems* 2: 247–50.

_____ (1972), "The Use of Ethological Methods in Environmental Analysis," in W. J. Mitchell (ed.), *Environmental Design: Research and Practice*. Los Angeles: University of California/EDRA 3.

PRIEST, R. F. and J. SAWYER (1967), "Proximity and Peership: Bases of Balance in Interpersonal Attraction," *American Journal of Sociology* 72: 633–49.

PRINCE, H. C. (1971), "Real, Imagined, and Abstract Worlds of the Past," in C. Board *et al.* (eds.), *Progress in Geography* 3. London: Arnold.

PROSHANSKY, H. M. (1946), "A Projective Method for the Study of Attitudes," *Journal of Abnormal and Social Psychology* 38: 393–5.

_____ (1974), "Environmental Psychology and the Design Professions," in J. Lang, C. Burnette, W. Moleski, and D. Vachon (eds.), *Designing for Human Behavior*, pp. 72–80. Stroudsburg, Pa.: Dowden, Hutchinson & Ross.

_____, W. H. ITTELSON, and L. G. RIVLIN (1970), *Environmental Psychology: Man and His Physical Setting*. New York: Holt, Rinehart & Winston.

PUSHKAREV, B. (1965), "Scale and Design in a New Environment," in L. B. Holland (ed.), *Who Designs America?* Garden City, N.Y.: Doubleday.

RAINWATER, L. (1966), "Fear and the House as Haven in the Lower Class," *Journal of the American Institute of Planners* 32: 23–31.

_____ (1970), *Behind Ghetto Walls: Black Family Life in a Federal Slum*. Chicago: Aldine.

RAND, G. (1972), "Childrens' Images of Houses," in W. J. Mitchell (ed.), *Environmental Design: Research and Practice*. Los Angeles: University of California/EDRA 3.

RAPOPORT, A. (1969), *House Form and Culture*. Englewood Cliffs, N.J.: Prentice-Hall.

———— (1970), "Observations Regarding Man-Environment Studies," *Man-Environment Systems* 1: P1–28.

———— and R. E. KANTOR (1967), "Complexity and Ambiguity in Environmental Design," *Journal of the American Institute of Planners* 33: 210–21.

RATZEL, F. (1882, 1891), *Anthropogeographie*. Stuttgart.

RAWLS, J. R., R. E. TREGO, C. N. McGAFFEY, and D. J. RAWLS (1972), "Personal Space as a Predictor of Performance under Close Working Conditions," *Journal of Social Psychology* 86: 261–67.

RECKLESS, W. C. (1934), *Vice in Chicago*. Chicago: University of Chicago Press.

REIN, M. (1967), "Social Science and the Elimination of Poverty," *Journal of the American Institute of Planners* 33: 146–63.

RELPH, E. C. (1970), "An Inquiry into the Relations between Phenomenology and Geography," *Canadian Geographer* 14: 193–201.

REX, J. A. and R. MOORE (1967), *Race, Community, and Conflict*. London: Oxford University Press.

REYNOLDS, J. P. (1969), "Public Participation in Planning," *Town Planning Review* 40: 131–48.

RHODES, W. C. (1972), "An Overview: Toward a Synthesis of Models of Disturbance," in W. C. Rhodes and M. L. Tracy (eds.), *A Study of Child Variance*, pp. 541–600. Ann Arbor: University of Michigan Press.

RICCI, K. (1972), "Using the Building as a Therapeutic Tool in Youth Treatment," in *New Environments for the Incarcerated*, pp. 22–32. Washington, D.C.: U.S. Law Enforcement Assistance Administration.

RICHARDS, C. E. (1964), "City Taverns," *Human Organization* 22: 260–68.

RICHARDSON, E. (1967), *The Environment of Learning*. New York: Weybright & Talley.

RICHTER, D. (ed.) (1957), *Schizophrenia: Somatic Aspects*. New York: Pergamon.

RIEMER, S. (1950), "Hidden Dimensions of Neighborhood Planning," *Land Economics* 26: 197–201.

———— (1951), "Villagers in Metropolis," *British Journal of Sociology* 2: 31–43.

RIESMAN, D. (1958), "The Suburban Sadness," in W. M. Dobriner (ed.), *The Suburban Community*, pp. 375–408. New York: Putnam.

———— (1970), *The Lonely Crowd*. New Haven, Conn.: Yale University Press.

RITTEL, H. (1972), cited in D. P. Grant, "Systematic Methods in Environmental Design," *Man-Environment Systems* 2: 335–44.

RITTER, P. (1964), *Planning for Man and Motor*. New York: Macmillan.

ROBERTSON, R. W. (1973), "Anatomy of a Renewal Scheme," in C. N. Forward (ed.), *Residential and Neighbourhood Studies in Victoria*, pp. 40–100. Victoria, B.C.: Western Geographical Series 5.

ROBINSON, G. S. (1972), "Man's Physical and Juridical Relationships in Space," *Man-Environment Systems* 2: 21–36.

ROBINSON, S. (1970), "Directional Bias in Intra-Urban Migration." Unpublished B.A. Honors thesis, Monash University, Australia.

ROCK, I. and C. S. HARRIS (1967), "Vision and Touch," *Scientific American* 216: 96–104.

ROCKMAN, A. (1967), "Civic Buildings as Expressive Symbols." Unpublished M.A. thesis, University of Toronto.

RODWIN, L. (1956), *The British New Towns Policy.* Cambridge, Mass.: Harvard University Press.

ROIZEN, R. (1969), *Office Layout and the Behavior of Office Workers.* San Francisco: Environment Analysis Group.

ROKEACH, M. (1967), "Attitude Change and Behavior Change," *Public Opinion Quarterly* 30: 529–50.

———— (1970), "Long-Range Experimental Modification of Values, Attitudes, and Behavior." Paper presented at Symposium on Human Behavior and Its Control, American Association for the Advancement of Science, Chicago.

ROOS, P. D. (1968), "Jurisdiction: An Ecological Concept," *Human Relations* 21: 75–84.

ROSE, A. (1965), "Aging and Social Integration among the Lower Classes of Rome," *Journal of Gerontology* 20: 250–53.

ROSE, H. M. (1969), *Social Processes in the City: Race and Urban Residential Choice.* Washington D.C.: Association of American Geographers Resource Paper 6.

———— (1970), "The Development of an Urban Subsystem: The Case of the Negro Ghetto," *Annals of the Association of American Geographers* 60: 1–17.

ROSE, S. W. (1972), "RESIDE: A Gaming Method for Improving Environmental Interaction," in W. J. Mitchell (ed.), *Environmental Design: Research and Practice.* Los Angeles: University of California/EDRA 3.

ROSENBERG, G. (1968), "High Population Densities in Relation to Social Behavior," *Ekistics* 25: 425–27.

———— (1969), "The Landscape of Youth," *Ekistics* 28: 210–12.

———— (1970), *The Worker Grows Old.* San Francisco: Jossey-Bass.

ROSENZWEIG, M. R. (1966), "Environmental Complexity, Cerebral Change, and Behavior," *American Psychologist* 21: 321–32.

ROSOW, I. (1961), "The Social Effects of the Physical Environment," *Journal of the American Institute of Planners* 27: 127–33.

———— (1967), *Social Integration of the Aged.* New York: Free Press.

———— (1970), "Old People: Their Friends and Neighbors," *American Behavioral Scientist* 14: 59–69.

ROSS, H. L. (1961), "Reasons for Moves to and from a Central City Area," *Social Forces* 40: 261–63.

———— (1962), "The Local Community: A Survey Approach," *American Sociological Review* 27: 75–84.

ROSSI, P. H. (1955), *Why Families Move*. Glencoe, Ill.: Free Press.

ROTHMAN, D. J. (1971), *The Discovery of the Asylum*. Boston: Little, Brown.

ROUCEK, J. S. (1958), *Juvenile Delinquency*. New York: Philosophical Library.

ROZELLE, R. M. and J. C. BAZER (1972), "Meaning and Value in Conceptualizing the City," *Journal of the American Institute of Planners* 38: 116–22.

RUYS, T. (1971), "Windowless Offices," *Man-Environment Systems* 1: S49.

RYAN, E. (1963), "Personal Identity in an Urban Slum," in L. J. Duhl (ed.), *The Urban Condition*, pp. 135–50. New York: Simon & Schuster.

SAANICH, District of (1972), *Apartment Study*. Saanich, B.C.: Planning Department.

SAARINEN, T. F. (1969), *Perception of Environment*. Washington, D.C.: Association of American Geographers Research Paper 5.

———— (1971), "Research Approaches and Questionnaire Design," in W. R. D. Sewell and I. Burton (eds.), *Perceptions and Attitudes in Resources Management*, pp. 13–25. Ottawa: Department of Energy, Mines, and Resources.

SALINGER, J. D. (1951), *The Catcher in the Rye*. London: Hamilton.

SANDBURG, C. (1950), *Complete Poems of Carl Sandburg*. New York: Harcourt Brace and World.

SANOFF, H. and M. SAWHNEY (1972), "Residential Livability: A Study of User Attitudes toward Their Residential Environment," in W. J. Mitchell (ed.), *Environmental Design: Research and Practice*. Los Angeles: University of California/EDRA 3.

SANUA, V. D. (1969), "Immigration, Migration, and Mental Illness," in E. B. Brody, (ed.), *Behavior in New Environments*, pp. 291–352. Beverly Hills, Calif.: Sage.

SAUER, L. and D. MARSHALL (1972), "An Architectural Survey of How Six Families Used Space in their Existing Houses," in W. J. Mitchell (ed.), *Environmental Design: Research and Practice*. Los Angeles: University of California/EDRA 3.

SAYEGH, K. S. (ed.) (1972), *Canadian Housing: A Reader*. Waterloo, Ontario: University of Waterloo Faculty of Environmental Studies.

SCHAFFER, F. (1970), *The New Town Story*. London: Paladin Books.

SCHIFF, M. R. (1971), "The Definition of Perceptions and Attitudes," in W. R. D. Sewell and I. Burton (eds.), *Perceptions and Attitudes in Resources Management*, pp. 7–12. Ottawa: Department of Energy, Mines, and Resources.

SCHLAKMAN, V. (1935), *The Economic History of a Factory Town: A Study of Chicopee, Massachusetts*. Northampton, Mass.: Smith College Studies in History 20.

SCHMITT, R. C. (1957), "Density, Delinquency, and Crime in Honolulu," *Sociology and Social Research* 41: 274–76.

———— (1963), "Implications of Density in Hong Kong," *Journal of the American Institute of Planners* 29: 210–17.

———— (1966), "Density, Health, and Social Disorganization," *Journal of the American Institute of Planners* 32: 38–40.

SCHORR, A. L. (1963), *Slums and Social Insecurity*. Washington, D.C.: U.S. Department of Health, Education, and Welfare.

SEATON, R. W. and J. B. COLLINS (1972), "Validity and Reliability of Ratings of Simulated Buildings," in W. J. Mitchell (ed.), *Environmental Design: Research and Practice*. Los Angeles: University of California/EDRA 3.

SEELEY, J. R. (1959), "The Slum: Its Nature, Use, and Users," *Journal of the American Institute of Planners* 25: 7–14.

SEGAL, W. (1948), *Home and Environment*. London: Leonard Hill.

SEGALL, M. H., D. T. CAMPBELL, and M. J. HERSKOVITS (1966), *The Influence of Culture on Visual Perception*. Indianapolis: Bobbs-Merrill.

SELIGMAN, D. (1957), "The Enduring Slums," in Editors of Fortune, *The Exploding Metropolis*, pp. 92–114. Garden City, N.Y.: Anchor Books.

SELYE, H. (1956), *The Stress of Life*. New York: McGraw-Hill.

SEMPLE, E. C. (1911), *Influences of Geographical Environment*. New York: Holt.

SEWELL, W. R. D. (1971a), "Integrating Public Views in Planning and Policy Making," in W. R. D. Sewell and I. Burton (eds.), *Perceptions and Attitudes in Resources Management*, pp. 125–31. Ottawa: Department of Energy, Mines, and Resources.

———— (1971b), "Environmental Perceptions and Attitudes of Engineers and Public Health Officials," *Environment and Behavior* 3: 23–59.

SHANKLAND, COX, AND ASSOCIATES (1966), *Expansion of Ipswich*. London: H.M.S.O.

SHAW, C. R. and H. D. McKAY (1942), *Juvenile Delinquency and Urban Areas*. Chicago: University of Chicago Press.

SHEVKY, E. and W. BELL (1955), *Social Area Analysis*. Stanford, Calif.: Stanford University Press.

SIEVERTS, T. (1969), "Spontaneous Architecture," *A A Quarterly* 1: 36–43.

SIMAK, C. (1952), *City*. New York: Ace Books.

SIMMEL, G. (1957), "The Metropolis and Mental Life," in P. K. Hatt and A. J. Reiss (eds.), *Cities and Society*, pp. 635–46. New York: Free Press.

SIMMIE, J. M. (1971), "Public Participation: A Case Study from Oxfordshire," *Journal of The Town Planning Institute* 57: 161–62.

SIMMONS, J. (1968), "Changing Residence in the City: A Review of Intra-Urban Mobility," *Geographical Review* 58: 622–51.

SIMON, H. A. (1957), *Models of Man*. New York: Wiley.

SIMON, P. (1972), *The Songs of Paul Simon*. New York: Knopf.

SINTON, D. (1960), "Attitudes, A Source of the Housing Problem," in G. Bell, E. Randall, and J. E. R. Roeder (eds.), (1973), *Urban Environments and Human Behavior*, p. 218. Stroudsburg, Pa.: Dowden, Hutchinson & Ross.

SJOBERG, G. (1960), *The Pre-Industrial City*. New York: Free Press.

SKINNER, B. F. (1948), *Walden Two*. New York: Macmillan.

———— (1971), *Beyond Freedom and Dignity*. New York: Knopf.

SKJEI, S. S. (1972), "Urban Systems Advocacy," *Journal of the American Institute of Planners* 38: 11–24.

SLAYTON, W. L. and R. DEWEY (1953), "Urban Redevelopment and the Urbanite," in C. Woodbury (ed.), *The Future of Cities and Urban Redevelopment*. Chicago: University of Chicago Press.

SLOAN, S. A. (1972), "Translating Psycho-Social Criteria into Design Determinants," in W. J. Mitchell (ed.), *Environmental Design: Research and Practice*. Los Angeles: University of California/EDRA 3.

SMITH, D. M. (1973), *The Geography of Social Well-Being in the United States*. New York: McGraw-Hill.

SMITH, P. J. and J. G. HAYTER (1974), "The Function of Inner-city High Rise Apartments in Relation to Family Life Cycle and Residential Mobility." Paper presented at International Geographical Union New Zealand Regional Conference.

SMITH, R. A. (1970), "Crowding in the City: The Japanese Solution," *Landscape* 18: 3–10.

SMITH, W. S. (1966), *Transportation and Parking for Tomorrow's Cities*. New York: Automobile Manufacturers' Association.

SOEN, D. (1970), "Neighborly Relations and Ethnic Problems in Israel," *Ekistics* 177: 133–8.

SOLERI, P. (1969), *Arcology: The City in the Image of Man*. Cambridge, Mass.: M.I.T. Press.

SOLOMON, P., P. E. KUBZANSKY, P. H. LEIDERMAN, J. H. MENDELSON, R. TRUMBULL, and D. WEXLER (1961), *Sensory Deprivation*. Cambridge, Mass.: Harvard University Press.

SOLZHENITSYN, A. (1973), *The Gulag Archipelago*. New York: Harper & Row.

SOMMER, R. (1959), "Studies in Personal Space," *Sociometry* 22: 247–60.

———— (1961), "Leadership and Group Geography," *Sociometry* 24: 99–110.

———— (1965), "The Isolated Drinker in the Edmonton Beverage Room," *Quarterly Journal of Studies in Alcohol* 26: 95–110.

———— (1966), "The Ecology of Privacy," *Library Quarterly* 36: 234–48.

———— (1967), "Small Group Ecology," *Psychological Bulletin* 67: 145–52.

———— (1968a), "Intimacy Ratings in Five Countries," *International Journal of Psychology* 3: 109–14.

———— (1968b), "Hawthorne Dogma," *Psychological Bulletin* 70: 592–95.

———— (1969), *Personal Space: The Behavioral Basis of Design*. Englewood Cliffs, N.J.: Prentice-Hall.

———— (1970), "The Ecology of Study Areas," *Environment and Behavior* 2: 271–80.

———— (1971), *Design Awareness*. Corte Madera, Calif.: Rinehart.

———— (1972), "The Social Psychology of the Cell Environment," in *New Environments for the Incarcerated*, pp. 15–21. Washington, D.C.: U.S. Law Enforcement Assistance Administration.

———— (1974a), "Looking Back at Personal Space," in J. Lang, C. Burnette, W. Moleski, and D. Vachon (eds.), *Designing for Human Behavior*, pp. 202–209. Stroudsburg, Pa.: Dowden, Hutchinson & Ross.

————— (1974b), *Tight Spaces: Hard Architecture and How to Humanize It.* Englewood Cliffs, N.J.: Prentice-Hall.

————— and F. D. BECKER (1971), "Room Density and User Satisfaction," *Environment and Behavior* 3: 412–17.

SONNENFELD, J. (1966), "Variable Values in Space Landscape: An Inquiry into the Nature of Environmental Necessity," *Journal of Social Issues* 22: 71–82.

————— (1967), "Environmental Perception and Adaptation Level in the Arctic," in D. Lowenthal (ed.), *Environmental Perception and Behavior,* pp. 43–59. Chicago: University of Chicago Geography Research Paper 109.

————— (1972), "Geography, Perception, and the Behavioral Environment," in P. W. English and R. C. Mayfield (eds.), *Man, Space, and Environment,* pp. 244–51. New York: Oxford University Press.

SOROKIN, P. and C. BERGER (1939), *Time-Budgets of Human Behavior.* Cambridge, Mass.: Harvard University Press.

SOUDER, J. J., W. E. CLARK, J. I. ELKIND, and M. B. BROWN (1964), *Planning for Hospitals.* Chicago: American Hospital Association.

SOUTHWORTH, M. (1969), "The Sonic Environment of Cities," *Environment and Behavior* 1: 49–70.

SPIEGEL, E. (1967), *New Towns in Israel.* New York: Spiegel.

SPIEGEL, H. B. C. (1968), *Neighborhood Power and Control: Implications for Urban Planning.* New York: Columbia University Institute of Urban Environment.

SPROUT, H. and M. SPROUT (1956), *Man-Milieu Relationship Hypotheses in the Context of International Politics.* Princeton, N.J.: Center of International Studies.

————— (1957), "Environmental Factors in the Study of International Politics," *Journal of Conflict Resolution* 1: 309–28.

SPYKMAN, N. J. (1925), *The Sociology of Georg Simmel.* Chicago: University of Chicago Press.

SROLE, L. (1972), "Urbanization and Mental Health: Some Reformulations," *American Scientist* 60: 576–83.

—————, T. S. LANGNER, S. T. MICHAEL, M. K. OPLER, and T. A. C. RENNIE (1962), *Mental Health in the Metropolis: The Midtown Manhattan Study.* New York: McGraw-Hill.

STACEY, B. G. (1971), "Planning for People or People for Planning," *Man-Environment Systems* 1: R8.

STARR, R. (1967), *Urban Choices: The City and Its Critics.* London: Penguin Books.

STEA, D. (1965), "Space, Territoriality, and Human Movements," *Landscape* 15: 13–16.

————— (1969), "The Measurement of Mental Maps: An Experimental Model for Studying Conceptual Spaces," in K. R. Cox and R. G. Golledge (eds.), *Behavioral Problems in Geography,* pp. 228–53. Evanston, Ill.: Northwestern University Studies in Geography 17.

————— (1973), "Rats, Men, and Spatial Behavior, All Revisited," *Professional Geographer* 25: 106–12.

_____ (1974), "Architecture in the Head: Cognitive Mapping," in J. Lang, C. Burnette, W. Moleski, and D. Vachon (eds.), *Designing for Human Behavior*, pp. 157–68. Stroudsburg, Pa.: Dowden, Hutchinson & Ross.

_____ and R. M. DOWNS (1970), "From the Outside Looking In at the Inside Looking Out," *Environment and Behavior* 2: 3–12.

STEA, D. and D. WOOD (1974), *A Cognitive Atlas: The Psychological Geography of Four Mexican Cities*. Mexico, D. F.: Instituto Nacional de Bellas Artes, Cuadernos de Arquitectura.

STEIN, C. (1951), *Towards New Towns for America*. New York: Reinhold.

STEIN, M. R. (1960), *The Eclipse of Community*. Princeton: Princeton University Press.

STEINITZ, C. (1968), "Meaning and the Congruence of Urban Form and Activity," *Journal of the American Institute of Planners* 24: 233–48.

STEINZOR, B. (1950), "The Spatial Factor in Face-to-Face Discussion Groups," *Journal of Abnormal and Social Psychology* 45: 552–55.

STERNLIEB, G. and R. W. BURCHELL (1973), *Residential Abandonment*. New Brunswick, N.J.: Rutgers University Center for Urban Policy Research.

STEWART, W. (1970), "The Wrong Way to Solve the Housing Crisis," *Maclean's* (February): 23–27.

STILITZ, I. B. (1969), "The Role of Static Pedestrian Groups in Crowded Spaces," *Ergonomics* 12: 821–39.

STOKES, C. J. (1962), "A Theory of Slums," *Land Economics* 38: 187–97.

STOKOLS, D. (1972), "A Social-Psychological Model of Human Crowding Phenomena," *Journal of the American Institute of Planners* 38: 72–83.

STRAUSS, A. (1961), *Images of the American City*. Glencoe, Ill.: Free Press.

STREIB, G. F. (1970), "Old Age and the Family," *American Behavioral Scientist* 14: 25–39.

STRODTBECK, F. L. and L. H. HOOK (1961), "The Social Dimensions of a Twelve Man Jury Table," *Sociometry* 24: 397–415.

STUDER, R. G. (1969), "The Dynamics of Behavior-Contingent Physical Systems," in G. Broadbent and A. Ward (eds.), *Portsmouth College of Technology Symposium on Design Methods*. London: Lund Humphries.

_____ and D. STEA (1966), "Architectural Programming and Human Behavior," *Journal of Social Issues* 22: 127–36.

SUMMERS, L. (1972), "The House Design Game," in W. J. Mitchell (ed.), *Environmental Design: Research and Practice*. Los Angeles: University of California/EDRA 3.

SUTTLES, G. (1968), *The Social Order of the Slum*. Chicago: University of Chicago Press.

SWAN, J. A. (1971), "Environmental Education," *Environment and Behavior* 3: 223–29.

SYKES, G. (1958), *The Society of Captives*. Princeton, N.J.: Princeton University Press.

SZALAI, A. (1966), "Trends in Comparative Time Budget Research," *American Behavioral Scientist* 10: 1–31.

TABB, W. K. (1971), "Alternative Futures and Distributional Planning," *Journal of the American Institute of Planners* 38: 25–32.

TATHAM, G. (1951), "Environmentalism and Possibilism," in G. Taylor (ed.), *Geography in the Twentieth Century*, pp. 128–62. New York: Philosophical Library.

TAUEBER, K. E. (1965), "Residential Segregation," *Scientific American* 213: 2–9.

TAYLOR, G. (ed.) (1951), *Geography in the Twentieth Century*. New York: Philosophical Library.

TEAFF, J. D., M. P. LAWTON, and D. A. CARLSON (1973), "Impact of Age Integration of Public Housing Projects Upon Elderly Tenant Well-Being," *The Gerontologist* 13.

TERKEL, S. (1967), *Division Street: America*. New York: Discus Books.

THEIL, P. (1964a), "Processional Architecture," *Ekistics* 17: 410–13.

————— (1964b), "The Tourist and the Habitué." Unpublished working paper, College of Architecture and Urban Planning, University of Washington.

THOMAS, W. (ed.) (1956), *Man's Role in Shaping the Face of the Earth*. Chicago: University of Chicago Press.

THOMPSON, F. (1954), *Lark Rise to Candleford*. London: Oxford University Press.

THOMPSON, K. (1975), "Suicide and the Ambient Environment," *Landscape* 19: 45–47.

THOMPSON, W. R. and W. HERON (1954), "The Effects of Restricting Early Experience on the Problem-solving Capacity of Dogs," *Canadian Journal of Psychology* 8: 17–31.

THRASHER, F. M. (1927), *The Gang*. Chicago: University of Chicago Press.

THURSTONE, L. L. (1928), "Attitudes Can be Measured," *American Journal of Sociology* 33: 529–54.

TILLEY, C. (1961), "Occupational Rank and Grade of Residence in a Metropolis," *American Journal of Sociology* 67: 323–30.

TINBERGEN, N. (1953), *The Study of Instinct*. London: Oxford University Press.

TOFFLER, A. (1970), *Future Shock*. New York: Random House.

TOLKIEN, J. R. R. (1965), *The Lord of the Rings*. New York: Ballantine Books.

TOLMAN, E. C. (1932), *Purposive Behavior in Animals and Men*. New York: Century.

————— (1948), "Cognitive Maps in Rats and Men," *Psychological Review* 55: 189–208.

TOMEH, A. K. (1964), "Informal Group Participation and Residential Patterns," *American Journal of Sociology* 70: 28–35.

————— (1969), "Empirical Considerations on the Problem of Social Integration," *Sociological Inquiry* 39: 65–76.

TRABASSO, T. (1968), "Pay Attention," *Psychology Today* 2: 30–36.

TRITES, D. K., F. D. GALBRAITH, M. STURDAVANT, and J. F. LECKWART (1970), "Influence of Nursing-Unit Design on the Activities and Subjective Feelings of Nursing Personnel," *Environment and Behavior* 2: 303–34.

TROWBRIDGE, C. C. (1913), "Fundamental Methods of Orientation and Imaginary Maps," *Science* 38: 888–97.

TRYON, R. C. (1955), *Identification of Social Areas by Cluster Analysis*. Berkeley: University of California Press.

————— (1958), "Cumulative Communality Cluster Analysis," *Educational and Psychological Measurement* 18: 3–36.

————— (1967), "Predicting Group Differences in Cluster Analysis: The Social Area Problem," *Multivariate Behavioral Research* 2: 453–75.

TUAN, Y-F. (1968), "Discrepancies Between Environmental Attitudes and Behavior," *Canadian Geographer* 12: 176-91.

————— (1972), "Environmental Psychology: A Review," *Geographical Review* 62: 245–56.

————— (1974), *Topophilia*. Englewood Cliffs, N.J.: Prentice-Hall.

TUNNARD, C. (1970), *The City of Man*. New York: Scribner's.

TURNBULL, C. M. (1972), *The Mountain People*. New York: Simon & Schuster.

TURNER, J. C. (1967), "Barriers and Channels for Housing Development in Developing Countries," *Journal of the American Institute of Planners* 33: 167–81.

TWOMBLEY, R. C. (1974), *Frank Lloyd Wright*. New York: Harper & Row.

TYRWHITT, J. (1949), "The Size and Spacing of Urban Communities," *Journal of the American Institute of Planners* 15: 10–15.

U.S.O.E.O. (1966), *Maps of Major Concentrations of Poverty in Standard Metropolitan Statistical Areas of 250,000 or More Population*. Washington, D.C.: U.S. Office of Economic Opportunity.

VALINS, S. and A. BAUM (1973), "Residential Group Size, Social Interaction, and Crowding," *Environment and Behavior* 5: 421–39.

VAN HUYCK, A. P. and K. C. ROSSER (1966), "An Environmental Approach to Low-Income Housing," *International Development Review* 8: 15–18.

VANCE, J. E. (1967), "Housing the Worker," *Economic Geography* 43: 95–127.

VARMING, M. (1971), "The Planning of Motorroads in the Landscape," *Ekistics* 31: 247–50.

VASH, C. L. (1972), "Discrimination by Design: Mobility Barriers," in W. J. Mitchell (ed.), *Environmental Design: Research and Practice*. Los Angeles: University of California/EDRA 3.

VENTURI, R. (1966), *Complexity and Contradiction in Architecture*. New York: Museum of Modern Art.

VERNON, J. and J. HOFFMAN (1956), "Effect of Sensory Deprivation on Learning Rate in Human Beings," *Science* 123: 1074–75.

VERNON, J. and T. E. McGILL (1957), "The Effect of Sensory Deprivation upon Rote Learning," *American Journal of Psychology* 70: 637–39.

VERNON, R. (1962), *The Myth and Reality of Our Urban Problems*. Cambridge, Mass.: Joint Center for Urban Studies of Harvard and M.I.T.

VICTOR, J. and I. ROCK (1964), "Vision and Touch: Experimentally Created Conflict between the Two Senses," *Science* 143: 594–96.

VON FRISCH, K. (1974), *Animal Architecture*. New York: Harcourt Brace Jovanovich.

WALINSKY, A. (1964), "Keeping the Poor in their Place," *New Republic* 151: 15–19.

WALLACE, D. A. (1968), "The Conceptualizing of Urban Renewal," *University of Toronto Law Journal* 18: 248–58.

WARNER, L., M. MEEKER, and K. EELLS (1957), *Social Class in America.* Gloucester, Mass.: Peter Smith.

WARREN, G. (1975), "No Rats on Bewick," in M. E. E. Hurst (ed.), *I Came to the City*, pp. 31–39. Boston: Houghton Mifflin.

WATSON, A. (1966), "Social Status and Population Regulation in the Red Grouse," *Proceedings of the Royal Society Population Study Group* 2: 22–30.

WATSON, O. M. (1970), *Proxemic Behavior: A Cross-cultural Study.* The Hague: Mouton.

———— and T. GRAVES (1966), "Quantitative Research in Proxemic Behavior," *American Anthropologist* 68: 971–85.

WATTEL, H. L. (1958), "Levittown: A Suburban Community," in W. M. Dobriner (ed.), *The Suburban Community*, pp. 287–313. New York: Putnam.

WEAVER, R. C. (1963), "Major Factors in Urban Planning," in L. J. Duhl (ed.), *The Urban Condition*, pp. 97–112. New York: Simon & Schuster.

WEBB, E. J., D. T. CAMPBELL, R. D. SCHWARTZ, and L. SECHREST (1966). *Unobtrusive Measures.* New York: Rand McNally.

WEBB, E. J. and J. R. SALANCIK (1970), "Supplementing the Self Report in Attitude Research," in G. F. Summers (ed.), *Attitude Measurement*, pp. 317–27. Chicago: Rand McNally.

WEBBER, M. M. (1963), "Order in Diversity: Community without Propinquity," in L. Wingo (ed.), *Cities and Space*, pp. 23–54. Baltimore: Johns Hopkins Press.

———— (1964a), "The Urban Place and the Nonplace Urban Realm," in M. M. Webber (ed.), *Explorations into Urban Structure*, pp. 79–153. Philadelphia: University of Pennsylvania Press.

———— (1964b), "Culture, Territoriality, and the Elastic Mile," *Papers and Proceedings of the Regional Science Association* 13: 59–69.

WEISS, S. F., E. J. KAISER, and R. J. BURBY (1971), *New Community Development.* Chapel Hill, N.C.: University of North Carolina Center for Urban and Regional Studies.

WEISSBERG, N.C. (1964), "Commentary on de Fleur and Westie," *Social Forces* 43: 422–25.

WELLMAN, B. (1972), "High Rise, Low Rise, Community Ties," *Rapport* 1.

WELLS, B. (1965), "The Psycho-Social Influence of Building Environment," *Building Science* 1: 153–65.

———— (1967), "Individual Differences in Environmental Response," *Arena* 82: 167–71.

WENNER, L. B. (1964), "The Degree to Which Colors are Associated with Mood Tones," *Journal of Applied Psychology* 38: 432–35.

WERSHOW, H. (1969), "Aging in the Israeli Kibbutz," *The Gerontologist* 9: 300–304.

WERTHMAN, C. (1968), "The Social Meaning of the Physical Environment." Unpublished Ph.D. thesis, University of California at Berkeley.

WEST, J. (1945), *Plainville, U.S.A.* New York: Columbia University Press.

WHEELER, J. O. (1968), "Residential Location by Occupational Status," *Urban Studies* 5: 24–32.

_____ (1971), "Social Interaction and Urban Space," *Journal of Geography* 70: 200–203.

WHITE, G. F. (1966), "Formation and Role of Public Attitudes," in H. Jarrett (ed.), *Environmental Quality in a Growing Economy*, pp. 105–27. Baltimore: Johns Hopkins.

WHITE, L. E. (1953), "The Outdoor Play of Children Living in Flats," in L. Kuper (ed.), *Living in Towns*, pp. 235–58. London: Cresset Press.

WHITE, M. and L. WHITE (1962), *The Intellectual Versus The City*. Cambridge, Mass.: Harvard University Press.

WHITE, R. W. (1959), "Motivation Considered: The Concept of Competence," *Psychological Review* 66: 297–333.

WHORF, B. L. (1956), *Language, Thought and Reality*. Cambridge, Mass.: M.I.T. Press.

WHYTE, W. H. (1954), "The Web of Word of Mouth," *Fortune* 50: 140–43, 204–12.

_____ (1955), *Street Corner Society*. Chicago: University of Chicago Press.

_____ (1956), *The Organization Man*. Garden City, N.Y.: Doubleday.

_____ (1968), *The Last Landscape*. New York: Doubleday.

WICKER, A. W. (1972a), "Undermanning Theory and Research," cited in D. Stokols, "The Relation Between Micro and Macro Crowding Phenomena," *Man-Environment Relations* 3: 139–49.

_____ (1972b), "Mediating Behavior-Environment Congruence," *Behavioral Science* 17: 265–78.

WIENER, N. (1964), *The Human Use of Human Beings*. Boston: Houghton Mifflin.

WILLATTS, E. C. (1971), "Planning and Geography in the Last Three Decades," *Geographical Journal* 137: 311–38.

WILLEMS, E. P. (1973), "Behavior-Environment Systems: An Ecological Approach," *Man-Environment Systems* 3: 79–110.

WILLIS, F. N. (1966), "Initial Speaking Distance as a Function of the Speakers' Relationship," *Psychonomic Science* 5: 221–22.

WILLIS, M. (1969), "Sociological Aspects of Urban Structure," *Town Planning Review* 39: 296–306.

WILLITTS, F. K., R. C. BEALER, and D. M. CRIDER (1973), "Levelling of Attitudes in Mass Society: Rurality and Traditional Morality in America," *Rural Sociology* 38: 36–46.

WILLMOTT, P. (1962), "Housing Density and Town Design in a New Town: A Pilot Study at Stevenage," *Town Planning Review* 33: 115–27.

_____ (1967), "Social Research and New Communities," *Journal of the American Institute of Planners* 33: 387–98.

WILNER, D. and R. P. and WALKELEY, (1963), "Effects of Housing on Health and Performance," in L. Duhl (ed.), *The Urban Condition*, pp. 215–28. New York: Simon & Schuster.

WILNER, D., R. P. WALKELEY, T. PINKERTON, and M. TAYBACK (1962), *The Housing Environment and Family Life*. Baltimore, Md.: Johns Hopkins Press.

WILSON, A. P. (1968), "Social Behavior of Free-ranging Rhesus Monkeys with an Emphasis on Aggression." Unpublished Ph.D. thesis, University of California.

WILSON, J. Q. (1963), "Planning and Politics: Citizen Participation in Urban Renewal," *Journal of the American Institute of Planners* 29: 242–49.

WILSON, R. L. (1962), "Livability of the City: Attitudes and Urban Development," in F. S. Chapin and S. Weiss (eds.), *Urban Growth Dynamics*, pp. 359–99. New York: Wiley.

WINNICK, C. and H. HOLT (1961), "Seating Position as Non-verbal Communication in Group Analysis," *Psychiatry* 24: 171–82.

WINSBOROUGH, H. (1965), "The Social Consequences of High Population Density," *Law and Contemporary Problems* 30: 120–26.

WIRTH, L. (1938), "Urbanism as a Way of Life," *American Journal of Sociology* 44: 1–24.

WOHLWILL, J. F. (1966), "The Physical Environment: A Problem for a Psychology of Stimulation," *Journal of Social Issues* 22: 29–38.

WOLF, E. P. and C. N. LEBEAUX (1966), "Class and Race in the Changing City," in L. F. Schnore (ed.), *Social Science and the City*, pp. 99–129. New York: Praeger.

WOLFE, A., B. LEX, and W. YANCEY (1968), *The Soulard Area: Adaptations by Urban White Families to Poverty.* St. Louis, Mo.: Washington University Social Science Institute.

WOLFF, M. and V. HIRSCH (1970), "Some Pedestrian Observations," *Time Magazine* 11 May.

WOLFGANG, M. E. (1968), "Urban Crime," in J. Q. Wilson (ed.) *The Metropolitan Enigma*, pp. 270–311. Cambridge, Mass.: Harvard University Press.

WOLPERT, J. (1965), "Behavioral Aspects of the Decision to Migrate," *Papers and Proceedings of the Regional Science Association* 15: 159–69.

———— (1966), "Migration as an Adjustment to Environmental Stress," *Journal of Social Issues* 22: 92–102.

————, A. MUMPHREY, and J. SELEY (1972), *Metropolitan Neighborhoods: Participation and Conflict Over Change.* Washington, D.C.: Association of American Geographers Resource Paper 16.

WOOLS, R. M. (1969), "The Assessment of Room Friendliness," in D. V. Canter (ed.), *Proceedings of the Dalandhui Architectural Psychology Conference*, pp. 48–55. London: RIBA Publications.

WRIGHT, F. L. (1958), *The Living City.* New York: Horizon Press.

WYNNE-EDWARDS, V. C. (1962), *Animal Dispersion in Relation to Social Behaviour.* London: Oliver & Boyd.

YABLONSKY, L. (1962), *The Violent Gang.* New York: Macmillan.

———— (1964), "The Classification of Gangs," in R. S. Cavan (ed.), *Readings in Juvenile Delinquency.* New York: Lippincott.

YANCEY, W. L. (1971), "Architecture, Interaction, and Social Control," *Environment and Behavior* 3: 3–21.

_____ (1972), "Architecture, Interaction, and Social Control: The Case of a Large-Scale Housing Project," in J. F. Wohlwill and D. H. Carson (eds.), *Environment and the Social Sciences*, pp. 126–36. Washington, D.C.: American Psychological Association.

YEATES, M. H. and B. J. GARNER (1971), *The North American City*. New York: Harper & Row.

YOSHIOKA, G. A. and R. ATHANASIOU (1971), "The Effect of Site Plan on Social Status Variables on Distance to Friends' Homes," cited in R. Athanasiou and G. A. Yoshioka (1973), "The Spatial Character of Friendship Formation," *Environment and Behavior* 5: 43–65.

YOUNG, M. and P. WILLMOTT (1962), *Family and Kinship in East London*. London: Pelican Books.

ZAJONC, R. B. (1965), "Social Facilitation," *Science* 49: 269–74.

ZANNARAS, G. (1969), *An Empirical Analysis of Urban Neighborhood Perception*. Unpublished M.A. thesis, Ohio State University.

ZEHNER, R. B. (1971), "Neighborhood and Community Satisfaction in New Towns and Less Planned Suburbs," *Journal of the American Institute of Planners* 37: 379–85.

ZEIGLER, H. (1964), *Interest Groups in American Society*. Englewood Cliffs, N.J.: Prentice-Hall.

ZEISEL, J. (1974), "Fundamental Values in Planning with the Nonpaying Client," in J. Lang, C. Burnette, W. Moleski, and D. Vachon (eds.), *Designing for Human Behavior*, pp. 293–301. Stroudsburg, Pa.: Dowden, Hutchinson & Ross.

ZIMBARDO, P. G. (1969), "The Human Choice: Individuation, Reason, and Order vs. Deindividuation, Impulse, and Chaos," in W. J. Arnold and D. Levine (eds.), *Nebraska Symposium on Motivation: 1969*, pp. 237–307. Lincoln: University of Nebraska Press.

ZIPF, G. K. (1949), *Human Behavior and the Principle of Least Effort*. New York: Hafner.

ZLUTNIK, S. and I. ALTMAN (1972), "Crowding and Human Behavior," in J. F. Wohlwill and D. H. Carson (eds.), *Environment and the Social Sciences*, pp. 44–58. Washington, D.C.: American Psychological Association.

ZORBAUGH, H. W. (1929), *The Gold Coast and the Slum*. Chicago: University of Chicago Press.

ZUCKERMAN, M., H. PERSKY, L. MILLER, and B. LEVIN (1969), "Contrasting Effects of Understimulation and Overstimulation," in *Proceedings of the American Psychological Association 77th Annual Convention*, pp. 319–320. Washington: A.P.A.

ZWEIG, F. (1962), cited in S. Alderson, *Britain in the Sixties: Housing*, p. 58. London: Penguin Books.

_____ (1970), *The Cumbernauld Study*. London: Urban Research Bureau, Wates Ltd.

INDEX

INDEX